EXAMINING HOLISTIC MEDICINE

EXAMINING HOLISTIC MEDICINE

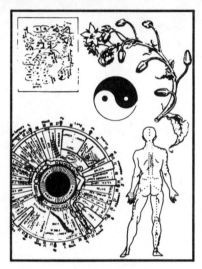

edited by
Douglas Stalker
and
Clark Glymour

PROMETHEUS BOOKS
Buffalo, New York

Published 1989 by Prometheus Books
700 East Amherst Street, Buffalo, New York 14215

Library of Congress Catalog Card Number: 85-63039

ISBN 0-87975-303-X (Cloth)
ISBN 0-87975-553-9 (Paper)

Printed in the United States of America

Dedicated to the memory of
Leonard K. Stalker, M.D., M.S.

Acknowledgments

We would like to thank Dr. Edward Friedlander for preparing most of the glossary entries. We would also like to thank the following for their advice and assistance: Herman Baker, Stephen Barrett, John Bruer (of the Macy Foundation), Edward Blanchard, Allen Buchanan, Lawrence Cohen, Leon Ellenbogen, Adolf Grünbaum, Hunter Heath, Thomas Jukes, Alison Kost, Myra Levine, Walter Mertz, Steven Mitchell, Edmond Murphy, Martin Orne, Noël Relyea, Richard Rivlin, Wallace Sampson, Kenneth Schaffner, Alvin Segelman, Robert Spitzer, Albert Strunkard, Arthur Taub, Bernard Tursky, Leonard White, Irvin Yalom, and James Harvey Young.

Contents

PART IV: EXAMINING HOLISTIC PRACTICES

Introduction

Why Examine Holistic Medicine?

The holistic movement encompasses a great many exotic therapies and alternative medical procedures: acupuncture, therapeutic touching, cancer therapy through visualization, Rolfing, flower remedies, reflexology, homeopathy, herbal medications, chiropractic, aroma therapy, chelation therapy, colonics, macrobiotic diets, hair analysis, iridology, psychic diagnosis, and polarity therapy, among others. Each of these procedures is described and endorsed in one book or another on holistic medicine. These therapies and treatments rarely pretend to compete with one another, although they may have next to nothing in common. They sometimes present themselves as alternatives to medical science, and sometimes as supplements to it. Holistic therapies come with a rhetoric about scientific method, the powers of mind over body, the responsibility of the individual, the insights of modern physics, and other philosophical topics. This collection of essays seeks to examine both the philosophical rhetoric of holistic medicine and the specific practices that holistic therapists use. The authors include distinguished scholars in the fields of philosophy, medicine, nursing, pharmacy, anatomy, optometry, medical psychology, and biomedical history. The reader will be able to judge for himself what informed, rational people think of the facts behind holistic medicine and its philosophy.

With so much real work to be done in the world, why bother to examine holistic medicine? Put simply, the social ramifications of the holistic movement render it a topic warranting serious professional and public scrutiny. Decisions about whether to take holistic medicine seriously, to support it or to oppose it, are decisions that reach far beyond those who are looking for treatment. These decisions also concern medical and nursing educators; licensing boards; those who construct licensing examinations; politicians, legislators, and jurists who must decide what legal role to give holistic medical practices; federal funding agencies; individual medical doctors and nurses; as well as insurance companies and those who pay their premiums. Each of these groups will be influenced, to one degree or another, by decisions about whether holistic medicine is legitimate,

9

or at least whether some forms of it are. With medicine and its substitutes so thoroughly linked with social policy, structure, and economics, how we assess holistic medicine will certainly have effects on the whole social fabric, so much so that our attitudes toward it should be of fundamental importance.

Holistic medicine is not any particular kind of therapy, or any particular therapeutic philosophy. It is a *social movement* that ties together an odd jumble of people: a Berkeley physicist, a "naturopathic healer" in rural Maine, a Pittsburgh chiropractor, a Harvard University professor of medicine, a former research psychiatrist at the National Institute of Mental Health, and thousands of other practitioners, sympathizers, and advocates. The shared aims that tie so many diverse people together are to institutionalize holistic medical practices, and, furthermore, to loosen the demands of evidence that we, as a society, impose on those who claim to cure or prevent disease. The first aim requires the second. As the essays in this volume show, only by abandoning the usual criteria of scientific evidence, and even the usual demands of rational thinking, can the claims of holistic medicants be established and made legitimate.

How significant is the holistic medical movement? After all, marginal, unorthodox, or "crank" medical doctrines have always been with us. H. L. Mencken welcomed the likes of Mary Baker Eddy because she and others of the same sort provided an opportunity for the Yahoos to exercise their right to be foolish and so get just what they deserved in the way of medical treatment. Nowadays, social commentators are rarely so detached as Mencken was, and few of us are so indifferent to the fates of others, even of Yahoos. The essays in this book make it apparent that the science of holistic medicine is bogus; that the philosophical views championed by the movement are incoherent, uninformed, and unintelligent; and that most holistic therapies are crank in the usual sense of that word: they lack any sound scientific basis. No doubt Mencken would be amused at all of this; he would see the holistic movement as yet another chance for free citizens to seek cures wherever they fancy them to be found. Should we have some other, more sober, attitude toward the holistic medical movement?

Perhaps we should, for several reasons. In the first place, holist advocacy blends a plausible request for preventive medicine and a reasonable concern for behavioral, environmental, and social causes of illness, with all sorts of crank therapies and diagnostics. Well-intentioned people may fail to realize that in endorsing these pleas in the name of holism, they also give comfort to the darker side of holistic medicine. Thus Edward Kennedy and George McGovern wrote forewords to two different compendia of holistic cures. Presumably they did so in the thought that preventive medicine is a good thing and that care for the social and environmental causes of illness is also good. Yet most of the therapies and diagnostics they implicitly endorsed are without any scientific basis, and several of them have been proven to be impotent. The philosophies of the books that Kennedy and McGovern endorse caricature or disparage scientific, rational testing of medical procedures, and the reasoning they exhibit is typically inadequate, even woefully so.

In the second place, the holistic movement is surprisingly well-organized and influential. There is an American Holistic Medical Association, an American Holistic Nursing Association, a Canadian Holistic Medical Association, and a British Holistic Medical Association. The conferences of the American Holistic Medical Association are recognized by the American Medical Association for continuing medical education credits. (Lest it be thought that such associations must be innocent of crankery, the 1984 meetings of the AHMA featured lectures on Spiritual Attunement, Electromagnetic Man, Free Radical Pathology, as well as Transpersonal Use of Imagery, and Shamanism). The American associations have representations and meetings throughout the country, as well as journals and newsletters to promote their work. There is also a Coalition of Holistic Health Organizations, located in Washington, D.C. The coalition is essentially a lobbying organization for crank medicine. Its membership includes thirty organizations, from the American Holistic Medical Association to the Connecticut Council for Massage Therapy and the Institute of Therapeutic Touch, and even something called the National Colon Hygiene Association. The coalition has lobbied against Claude Pepper's bill to make it a crime to sell medical treatments, drugs, or devices that are known to be unsafe or ineffective, or of unproven safety and efficacy. The holists have succeeded in obtaining the endorsements of major political figures, as we have already noted, and have obtained grant support from agencies such as the National Institute of Mental Health. The NIMH underwrote *Health for the Whole Person,* and the Office of Health Information and Health Promotion helped finance *New Directions in Healing* and *The Healing Partnership.* The first book is a popular compendium of holistic therapies and tenets. The second is a directory of holistic practitioners or sympathizers, containing everyone from serious medical scientists with social science connections to those with medical degrees who are willing to offer crank therapies to their patients. The directory also contains a glossary of "holistic" terminology. No therapy or diagnostic procedure is disavowed, no matter how much evidence there is against it. The editors have a wonderful talent for understatement. If a therapy is noted as "not yet proven," or the like, it means that the evidence against its efficacy is overwhelming. The third book is a collection of four essays, two of which elaborate standard holistic themes. We, at least, wonder about the institutional structure that funds such things. Holists have even appeared at major medical schools, including Harvard, the University of California at Los Angeles, Yale, and Georgetown. The greatest influence of the holists seems, however, to be in nursing. In her essay, Susan Williams documents this influence and describes some of its effects.

A third reason for taking the holistic movement seriously is that it has a successful model: chiropractic. Chiroprators are now licensed in all states, Congress has included chiropractic in Medicare, and the American Medical Association has revised its code of ethics by abandoning the principle that excluded professional association with chiropractors and others who use unscientific therapies. Chiropractors have achieved all this in the face of overwhelming evidence that their theories of healing and disease are dramatically false, and in the absence of any good evidence that chiropractic therapy has any specific benign effects. Without good research or good arguments, the chiropractors nevertheless have won the day through lawsuits (generally antitrust suits) and lobbying. In consequence, all of us are forced to support chiropractors through our tax payments, and some of us must endure their role in the legal system as "expert" witnesses on spinal injuries. The holistic movement might do even better, for it starts with an advantage over chiropractic, an advantage that may make it easier for holists to institutionalize their practices without the benefit of scientific argument. Their principal advantage is that they, unlike the chiropractors, are already entwined with the medical establishment. Barefoot healers come along with medical doctors and nurses who have abandoned all but the trappings of science, and many times that as well.

The present volume is divided into four parts. The first includes essays covering the background of holistic medicine and the controversy surrounding it. These essays will serve to acquaint readers with the holistic movement and its tenets, and to dispel some erroneous impressions about what holistic medicine is, where it came from, and whether it has any influence within the medical profession. In our essay "Engineers, Cranks, Physicians, Magicians" we argue that the leading holistic aims and tenets do not constitute a distinct conception of medicine for they amount to nothing more than banalities of orthodox medicine, truisms devoid of medical content, exaggerations devoid of relevance to the practice of medicine, or patent falsehoods. The holistic movement does contain, however, a reactionary impetus that is in direct opposition to the conception of medicine as scientific, and this leads holists to disparage not just scientific conclusions regarding their practices but also scientific reasoning itself. With this in mind, the medical historian James Whorton explores the real precursors of current holists, who repeatedly claim to be the medical heirs of the South African philosopher and statesman Jan Smuts, and to be applying the views he presented in his 1926 book *Holism and Evolution*. Professor Whorton demonstrates that today's holists are actually doctrinal heirs of nineteenth-century alternative medicine practitioners who attacked the medical establishment of their day and urged people to seek cures from the likes of homeopathy, hydropathy, and naturopathy.

In order to realize how much influence present-day holists can have on a medical profession, one need only study their success within the profession of nursing. Susan Williams, a professor of nursing, details how the language and beliefs of holists have found a place in nursing education, research, and practice by pointing to its presence in curricula, textbooks, seminars, journals, and professional organizations. Moreover, she explains how nursing has been easily converted to holism through a shared view about the role of nursing in health care, a concern with distinguishing nursing from medicine, and a failure to teach nurses how to critically evaluate medical literature.

Holists often discuss philosophical topics in order to promote their views as an alternative to those of orthodox medicine. The second part of *Examining Holistic Medicine* seeks to counter this tactic by including essays that take a sober look at these discussions and their alleged implications for medical research and practice. Austen Clark, an expert on the philosophy of mind, provides a sustained analysis of the charge that orthodox medicine fails to understand the role of the mind in disease and cure, because its concepts and methods employed cannot deal with psychosomatic phenomena and psychological causation. He argues, to the contrary, that the concept of psychosomatic disease is consistent with orthodox physiology and that psychosomatic effects can be incorporated into precise theories and submitted to rigorous tests along standard lines, while the holistic interpretation of psychosomatic disease involves an occult view of mind-body interaction that is at odds with both current physical science and the methods of science in general. In our essay entitled "Quantum Medicine" we consider the frequent claim that quantum physics and its philosophy show that traditional medical therapy and research are fundamentally in error, while holistic medicine and its therapies are on the right track because they alone are consistent with the new physics. Holists elaborate on this claim by discussing three principal themes from quantum physics concerning consciousness, reductionism, and causality. We show, however, that these elaborations amount to nothing more than a vague statement of some half-truth about quantum physics, which is then wildly exaggerated in an effort to justify a patent absurdity about biomedical research.

Promoters of holistic medicine are less than clear about their fundamental concept, that of holism, and they often make pronouncements about holism being at odds with reductionism and mechanism. Robert Brandon tries to clarify this concept and the disputes surrounding it within the philosophy of biology. He surveys the history of disputes over holism in the 1920s and 1930s between leading figures such as J. S. Haldane and Lancelot Hogben, and draws lessons from these disputes that apply to modern holistic versions. One lesson, for example, is that mechanism should neither be equated with reductionism nor regarded as incompatible with interconnections among one's objects of study. Professor Brandon goes on to show how current philosophy of biology can both adopt a mechanistic point of view and a moderate, empirically-based holism.

Holists are preoccupied with the role of the individual in health care, a view that has formed the basis for an ethical claim as one of their basic tenets. Put simply, this claim holds individuals personally responsible for their health. However, holists have not provided an elucidation of their concept of personal responsibility and its implications. Professor Daniel Wikler's essay analyzes this concept, as the holists have interpreted it, in an effort to disclose its multiple ambiguity. He examines the difficulties inherent in these interpretations, and how the holists have failed to support their position with convincing arguments. He concludes that their ethical claim must be viewed as more rhetorical and hortatory than clear and cogent.

The essays in Part Three deal with the methods holists use in trying to support their various medical practices. The philosophers Daisie and Michael Radner draw upon their recent research on pseudoscience in which they characterize nine marks of a pseudoscience in terms of styles of arguing or methods of reasoning that are based on misconceptions concerning what science is and how it proceeds. If a discipline exhibits even one of these marks, this suffices to show that something pseudoscientific is occurring. In their contribution entitled "Holistic Methodology and Pseudoscience," the Radners discuss the ways in which holists typically defend alternative medical practices such as acupuncture, homeopathy, herbal remedies, chelation therapy, and psychic healing. They find that these defenses often involve four marks of a pseudoscience: viz., anachronistic thinking, argument from spurious similarity, the Grab-Bag approach to evidence, and the refusal to correct in the light of criticism. The methodological section concludes with an essay by Dr. Thomas Chalmers, head of the Clinical Trial Unit at Mount Sinai Medical Center, in which he assesses the scientific quality of the *Journal of Holistic Medicine,* the official journal of the American Holistic Medical Association. In reviewing forty-seven articles in four volumes, Dr. Chalmers finds only nine trials of therapies, and of these only two are randomized control trials. While the holists have claimed that their journal publishes empirical studies on a par with those in regular medical journals, Dr. Chalmers reports that the trials are few and generally not well done. The studies suffer from such errors as a lack of adequate control with regard to measurements and separation of investigative agents. He concludes that the *Journal of Holistic Medicine* is far below the standard of scientific quality found in orthodox medical journals.

Holistic practitioners endorse many alternative forms of therapy and diagnosis as being of medical value. Part Four of provides essays that critically discuss some of the procedures that are favored by holistic practitioners and typically promoted in their writings. For example, iridology is like a number of holistic practices in that it diagnoses the whole body by observing a special part of the anatomy, the iris of the eye. Russell Worrall, a professor of optometry, discusses the obscure origins of this practice and its main claims: e.g., that iridology is plausible from an evolutionary point of view; that there is a functional iris-body connection serving to convey impressions from all over the body to the iris; that iridology can account for the way in which the central nervous system is functionally split; and that the diagnostic procedure cannot be tested in a neutral, scientific fashion. He points out that iridologists have not published one well-documented study with positive results, while two controlled studies have thoroughly negative results. Dr. Worrall concludes that iridology is a pseudoscience having no clinical value, yet not a harmless one insofar as it yields false-negative diagnoses.

Petr Skrabanek, a professor of medicine who has studied acupuncture extensively, covers its history in both the Orient and Europe, its much publicized uses for anesthesia in China during the 1950s, and its warrant from research studies in humans. He also discusses variants such as homuncular acupuncture, the endorphin explanation of how acupuncture is supposed to work, and the strategy acupuncturists adopt to promote their views. While admitting that some patients have a better response to acupuncture than a conventional placebo, Professor Skrabanek attributes this to its novelty and its trappings. He concludes that when acupuncture is discussed in terms of placebo, distraction, suggestion, hypnosis, and the natural history of disorders, it will lose all mystique and be relegated to a place among other counter-irritants.

The discussion of holistic diagnosis and therapy continues with an analysis of chiropractic medicine. Professor Edmund Crelin, an internationally known expert on anatomy, recounts his efforts to educate the unwary public about chiropractic. He explains how, as a volunteer for the Federal Drug Administration Bureau of Medical Devices, he tested chiropractic devices alleged to diagnose and treat spinal disorders, and how he found them to be worthless and at times even dangerous. He tells of testifying about gross inaccuracies in spinal charts used by chiropractors, and, most importantly, of a repeatable test he made of chiropractic's basic tenet, viz., that vertebral subluxations exist. The results of this test were published in 1973 and were completely negative. To this day no one has repeated the test and published contrary findings. In light of these and other considerations, Professor Crelin views chiropractic as an unscientific cult that has been effectively promoted by political rather than scientific means.

Dr. Oliver Wendell Holmes criticizes homeopathy, a system of medicine that dates from the early nineteenth century. His criticisms are presented in lectures given in 1842, which were subsequently published under the title "Homeopathy and Its Kindred Delusions." Holmes argues against the three cardinal doctrines of homeopathy: that diseases are cured by substances capable of producing symptoms similar to those of the disease under treatment, that medicinal substances are effective in minute doses, and that the psora or "itch" is the fundamental cause of at least seven-eighths of all chronic diseases. He proceeds to show that homeopathy was not supported in his day by evidence from the public, homeopathic practitioners, or independent physicians who conducted trials—a situation that has not changed.

Professor Edward Erwin, who has written extensively on the alleged benefits of psychotherapy, discusses some of the better known holistic psychotherapies and the clinical theories underlying them. In addition, he addresses the question of which therapies work for specific groups of clients and particular types of problems. After looking at the experimental, clinical, and theoretical arguments in support of Reichian therapy, bioenergetics, the Alexander technique, Rolfing, and dream therapy, Professor Erwin concludes that there is no solid evidence showing any of these therapies to be more effective than a credible placebo in relieving clinical problems or in producing therapeutic benefits.

The Simonton approach to cancer treatment is an example of the holistic insistence on the therapeutic power of one's mind. This treatment has patients use mental imagery techniques to visualize their strong white cells attacking their weak cancer cells. Dr. Edward Friedlander fully and carefully discusses the

Simonton approach, noting, among other things, that the Simontons' published statistics on remissions and survival periods do not support curative claims, and that while additional data has been promised, none has been forthcoming. Dr. Friedlander also shows that their case histories are poor evidence, and that the entire approach is based on a theory that is no longer widely accepted—the immune surveillance theory—yet the Simontons do not report testing the immune systems of their patients. Those physicians who recommend the Simontons' books are urged to warn their patients that there is no reason to believe the imagery approach can effect a cure, or that cancer is the result of faulty beliefs and attitudes.

Within the nursing profession there are now workshops, books, and courses on therapeutic touch, a form of therapy similar to the laying-on-of-hands and connected with paranormal phenomena. Philip and Mary Jo Clark critically review the research studies on therapeutic touch in order to determine whether there is any scientific basis for teaching and practicing this modality. They find that many studies have been poorly conducted and involve errors in subject selection, control for extraneous variables, use of statistical tests, and the like. In those studies that have been well-designed, they find the results to be only transient, of no statistical significance, or in need of independent replication. They conclude that, at present, there is no more than very weak support for therapeutic touch and that the current practice seems empirically no more than a placebo.

Holists frequently advocate nutrition therapies, especially those involving megadoses of vitamins such as vitamin C (ascorbic acid) for the prevention and cure of everything from the common cold to cancer. Dr. Edward Creagan and Dr. Charles Moertel, both of the Mayo Clinic, have conducted and published in the New England Journal of Medicine two prospective, double-blind randomized trials of vitamin C in high doses for patients with advanced cancer. Both studies are reprinted here, along with correspondence that resulted from their initial publication. On the basis of these studies, Drs. Creagan and Moertel conclude that high doses of vitamin C are not effective against advanced malignant disease whether or not the patient has previously undergone chemotherapy. They also discuss, and their studies illustrate, how tests of proposed cancer treatments can be properly designed and conducted.

Many holists turn not only to nutritional regimens and supplements but to herbal remedies as well, believing these plant remedies to be the natural and superior way to cure a variety of ailments. However, they typically display more enthusiasm for the prospective benefits than knowledge of the real facts regarding these substances. Scientific evidence concerning both the benefits and the hazards of herbs is conspicuously avoided. Professor Varro Tyler, a leading expert in the science of deriving medicines from natural sources, surveys both the general and specific hazards of many herbal medications. He points to general hazards involved in relying on herbal lore as well as the hazards involved in self-identification and self-collection of herbs; he documents the scientific evidence that certain herbs may produce cancer, allergic reactions, hormone-like effects, fetal malformations, respiratory problems, bowel catharsis, abortions, irritation of tissues, and various other toxic effects. Professor Tyler's comprehensive survey reveals that many herbal remedies have the same kinds of disadvantages as conventional drugs, and that laypeople who are ignorant of the technical findings about herbs cannot intelligently turn to them for medical purposes.

In contrast to the majority of holistic therapies, biofeedback is regarded within the scientific community as a respectable form of therapy. Due to this status, holists have presented it as one form of therapy that is not only supported by solid evidence but also in line with many of their basic tenets. Larry Young, an expert on clinical uses of biofeedback, describes the ways in which holists have promoted and elaborated biofeedback in an unscientific manner by failing to indicate clearly and consistently what the term means, by failing to specify adequately the purposes for which biofeedback is used, and by distorting and oversimplifying the psychophysiological principles underlying its operation and application. In consequence, he views the holists as impeding the education of health care professionals about the appropriate uses and limitations of biofeedback.

Examining Holistic Medicine concludes with a glossary of technical terms, most of whose entries were prepared by Dr. Edward Friedlander, and a select bibliography for those who would like to read further. The bibliography includes books and articles that promote holism, those that critically analzye it, and material addressing relevant topics.

The goals of the American Holistic Medical Association are bald enough. They want patients to ask their doctors "Are you a holistic physician?" and presumably to take their business elsewhere if the answer is negative. Their proselytizing fervor is equally plain: if each year every member of the AHMA would bring in another member, says a past president of that association, then in ten years every medical doctor in the United States would be among the holists. What kinds of institutions, practices, and science of medicine would this bring us? We think they would be utterly daffy. H. L. Mencken thought that a lot of American society was the same way, and that the best response was to laugh at it. Perhaps he was right. Were he available, we would have asked him to contribute a foreword to this rather somber collection. Since he is not, readers will have to judge for themselves whether or not holism is a laughing matter.

Part I

Background and Controversy

Clark Glymour, Ph.D. and Douglas Stalker, Ph.D.

Engineers, Cranks, Physicians, Magicians

Medicine in industrialized nations is scientific medicine. The claim tacitly made by American or European physicians, and tacitly relied on by their patients, is that their palliatives and procedures have been shown by science to be effective. Although the physician's medical practice is not itself science, it is based on science and on training that is supposed to teach physicians to apply scientific knowledge to people in a rational way.

The practice of medicine in the United States and in other industrialized nations is a form of consultant engineering. The subjects are people rather than bridges, but in many respects the professions of medicine and engineering are alike. We expect skilled engineers to be able to learn from experience and to get better at building bridges, because we believe that their training has subjected them to a rational discipline that has made them good learners about such matters. Sometimes, of course, we are disappointed. It is entirely the same with physicians, who must apply both explicit scientific principles and also a great deal of tacit knowledge to the treatment of their patients. Medical training is supposed to make physicians good at applying scientific knowledge to sickness, and it is also supposed to make medical doctors good at acquiring through practice an abundance of tacit knowledge useful to their craft.

There is no reason, either historically or logically, to conceive of the science used by physician engineers as necessarily physical science. Engineers need not care in principle whether the generalizations on which they rely are psychological, physical, or psychophysical; what they care about is that the generalizations be applicable and that their reliability be scientifically demonstrated. A great deal of what physicians learn consists of biologic and biochemical generalizations, broadly construed, but they also learn a substantial body of psychophysical generalizations which can be regarded as bridging the crevasse between mind and body. For example, generalizations concerning the effects of drugs, cor-

Reprinted by permission of the *New England Journal of Medicine* 308 (1983):960-964.

relating the location of pain with other physical symptoms of disease, and positing the causal factors in dizziness and senility connect the mental with the physical and are thus useful for medical engineering. If physicians learn relatively fewer generalizations that are entirely psychological or social in nature or that posit psychological mechanisms for physical effects, the reason is not that such generalizations are alien to the "medical model" but that relatively few of them are applicable and scientifically warranted.

There are alternative conceptions of the physician. Some of them play a dominant part in the understanding of medicine in other societies, and some serve to qualify the conception of the physician as engineer even in our own society. One such conception is that physicians are consolers. Another is that they are magicians who exercise occult powers to bring about healing. As magicians, they possess magical powers either because of the occult knowledge they possess or simply because of who they are—for example, because they stand in some special relation to gods or demons. Again, the physician may be understood to be someone who applies a reliable body of knowledge that is not warranted by science or by magic but is simply known and, so far as the community is concerned, always has been known. The warrant behind this conception of the healer is tradition and "common knowledge."

These distinctions are more logical than sociological, and a society may combine several of them in the roles it assigns to healers. A medicine man can combine traditional therapies with magical claims, and both with a bit of consolation. A physician engineer can act as consoler; nothing in either logic or social psychology forbids it. But certain combinations are impossible or extraordinarily unlikely. A physician engineer cannot honestly claim powers of magic or occult knowledge. The principles governing scientific reasoning and belief are negative as well as positive, and they imply that occult doctrines are not worthy of belief. Moreover, physician engineers have no immunity to moral or ethical constraints. On the contrary, they are by training and by culture enmeshed in a tradition of rational thought about the obligations and responsibilities of their profession.

Is there another, holistic, conception of medicine distinct from those described above? Certainly, many people seem to think so. In 1978 a group of medical and osteopathic physicians formed the American Holistic Medicine Association, which now publishes a journal and whose meetings have been recognized for educational purposes by the American Medical Association. Popular bookstores are filled with works on "holistic medicine," many edited by medical doctors and some recommended by such poltical eminences as Edward Kennedy and George McGovern. The same shelves boast best-selling books on holistic medicine authored by professors at distinguished medical schools and, in at least one case, by a physician administrator at the National Institutes of Health. The therapies described and recommended in a typical book of this genre include biofeedback, hypnosis, psychic healing, chiropractic, tai chi, iridology, homeopathy, acupuncture, clairvoyant diagnosis, human auras, and

Rolfing. One of the larger books of this kind was even subsidized by the National Institute of Mental Health.

What ties together the diverse practices described in such books as *Health for the Whole Person, Ways of Health,* and *The Holistic Health Handbook?* In part, a banal rhetoric about the physician as consoler; holistic dentists, for example, promise to take account of the spiritual factors affecting their patients' teeth. In part, familiar and rather useless admonitions about not overlooking the abundance of circumstances that may contribute to one condition or another. Such banalities are often true and no doubt sometimes ignored, with disastrous consequences, but they scarcely amount to a distinctive conception of medicine. Holist therapies can be divided into those that are adaptations of traditional medical practices in other societies—Chinese, Navaho, and so forth—and those that were invented, so to speak, the week before last by some relatively successful crank.

Insofar as it extends beyond banality, the holistic medical movement constitues both a deliberate attempt to substitute a magical for an engineering conception of the physician and an attack on scientific understanding and reasoning. Although the holistic movement does not contain a conception of medicine distinct from those we have discussed, it does contain a reactionary impetus to return the practice of medicine to the practice of magic and to replace logic and method with occultism and obfuscation.

Several conceptions of "holism" have been developed in the writings of holistic practitioners and their advocates. Most of them are vacuous; they are banalities of orthodox medicine, or they have no medical content and no applicability to any possible practice of medicine; they merely sound nice. Some are patently false. A much-repeated and trivial thesis, and moreover one that is said to characterize the sense in which holistic medicine is "holistic," amounts to no more than this: mental and physical properties are interdependent. Mental states affect physical states and physical states affect mental states. No one doubts it. To make such a claim seem somehow profound, holistic writers invariably conjoin it with a discussion of Cartesian dualism, insinuating that modern medicine follows Descartes in postulating an impassable chasm between the mind and the body. Modern medicine does no such thing, and could not even if it wanted to, since Descartes held no such view.

Another doctrine said to be holistic is that one's state of health is affected by everything. Whatever this means, it has nothing to do with any possible practice of medicine, for no one can attend to everything. If physicians cannot distinguish relevant from irrelevant factors, important from unimportant causes, then they can do nothing. A variant of this doctrine is not vacuous but merely vapid: "Fundamental to holistic medicine is the recognition that each state of health and disease requires a consideration of all contributing factors: psychological, psychosocial, environmental, and spiritual" (1). This is not a new revelation about medicine. Insofar as such multiple factors are known and believed to be important, they are routinely addressed in conventional medical practice. Patients who suffer from coronary heart disease may be treated with betablockers and antiplatelet drugs, and they may also be advised to change their work, their diet, their smoking habits, their exercise habits, and their living conditions.

A stronger thesis, also presented by the writer quoted above, is that "all states of health and all disorders are considered to be psychosomatic," which is to say that psychological conditions are major causal factors in every illness and in all morbidity (2). So understood, the claim does not present an alternative conception of medicine, only a patent falsehood. Psychological states are not in any ordinary sense causal factors in Down's syndrome, cholera, nephritis, or a host of other disorders. Of course, psychological states may affect how an affliction is endured, even if they do not cause the affliction, but that is a different matter. Even if we believed (albeit mistakenly) that psychological conditions were an important causal factor in every disorder, this imagined fact would not itself require a change in the conception of the physician as engineer. It would require that scientists try to identify such factors so that physician engineers might apply the additional knowledge.

These rhetorical flourishes fail to constitute a distinct conception of the physician's role, of medical knowledge, or even of nature. However, an extraordinary vision of the functioning of the body and mind that runs through much of the holistic literature is utterly different from the scientific viewpoint. The holistic claim is this: The entire body (and psyche) can be treated or diagnosed through the treatment or observation of a special part of the anatomy. However much this notion of holism may be at odds with the themes that seem to run through the holistic doctrines, it characterizes many of the treatments described in the literature on holistic medicine. Chiropractors, iridologists, reflexologists, tongue diagnosers, zone therapists, and many others all claim to treat or diagnose the whole from some anatomical part. Of course, they differ about which part, but that does not seem to bother either them or the editors of holistic books. Almost invariably, this rhetoric claims that manipulating a part of the body somehow restores an inarticulated "balance" or "harmony" to the whole (3).

At the base of the litany that each person must be treated as unique, that every part of the body is interdependent on every other part, and that body and mind are inseparable is the claim that holistic practitioners are absolved from demonstrating causal relations between their treatments and alleged therapeutic gains. They are under no obligation, they believe, to reconcile their claims about therapy with what is known about the causal pathways of the body. Their emphasis on the power of the mind is part theme and part tactic: the mind is supposed to be able to exert its power on parts of the body without regard to the laws of nature. The holistic practitioner sees the body in much the same way that magicians of old viewed the universe. The body becomes the last bastion of magic.

A magical view of the mind and body is antithetical to the scientific viewpoint, however much holistic therapists may parade what they take to be the trappings of science. Consequently, they make every effort to disparage rational assessments of their practices. A magical view of nature and mind and a mystical conception of knowledge are opposed not just to scientific conclusions but to scientific reasoning. Beyond disparaging the sort of rational assessment of their wares made by, say the Consumers Union, holistic advocates attack reason itself.

Sobel, a doctor of medicine, charges that "Competition and ethnocentrism have often prevailed over any real concern with the relative value or efficacy of different therapies," and that "There are substantial barriers to a serious and dispassionate evaluation of unorthodox medicine, not the least of which are posed by economic and political forces. . . " (4). These statements are doubtless true, but so what? Are there no objective, dispassionate evaluations of various holistic practices? What is wrong with the careful, reasoned evaluations of therapies, such as chiropractic, that are offered by the Consumers Union (5)? Although Sobel does not say so, the reader is left with the impression that because it is obvious that some evaluators are prejudiced by irrelevant factors, all negative assessments are unfounded. This is argument by innuendo. Having no tenable thesis of any interest, the holistic advocate states a claim that is a perfect banality and hopes the reader will draw a sweeping conclusion that is completely unwarranted. It is a tactic used throughout the literature on holistic medicine.

We are repeatedly told that holistic medicine has not really been investigated, that funds ought to be made available for conducting tests of holistic practices, and that meanwhile we should keep our minds open about holistic techniques. Although it might be interesting to know more about the physiological pathways that are correlated with such processes as the placebo effect, this has nothing to do with taking seriously the claims advanced by iridologists or zone therapists or even chiropractors. The claim to diagnose by examining the eye or to cure by massaging the foot is completely bogus; we know more than enough about the workings of the body to be reasonably certain that geometric features of the iris, for instance, do not provide the specific information about disorders that iridologists claim they do. And if a test is really necessary here, it can be and has been run cheaply: iridologists have been shown to fail as diagnosticians (6). Chiropractors and zone therapists could readily devise rigorous tests of their therapies if they wished to, but they don't. Of course, it is conceivable that the beliefs of scientific medicine are in error about one or another of these matters, but that is no reason for using public funds to investigate holistic claims. One cannot justify spending other people's money simply because one can imagine something to be true. The mere fact that holistic medicine is widespread and enduring is no reason to take its claims seriously; superstition, self-deception, stupidity, and fraud are ubiquitous and always have been.

It is unlikely that the lack of evidence concerning the specific curative powers of holistic therapies is the result of a conspiracy of disinterest. There are enormous rewards, financial and otherwise, for scientific demonstrations that new and inexpensive therapeutic procedures are effective. Holistic practitioners know these rewards full well. If they have been unable to produce sound scientific evidence of the efficacy of their therapies, we are not being closed-minded in concluding that the therapies probably have no specific effects of the kinds advertised. Certainly we should leave our minds open, but not, in the words of an eminent philosopher, the late Alan Ross Anderson, so open that our brains fall out.

The most fundamental attack made by advocates of holistic medicine is on reason itself: since science will not warrant holistic medicine, they imply that we should abandon science and the claims of reason. One common line of argument is derived from a radical misunderstanding of the contemporary philosophy of science. Some years ago, Thomas Kuhn claimed that scientific work in any particular field is normally governed by a "paradigm"—that is, by some concrete piece of work done in the past that is used as a model for subsequent scientific work. Newton's celestial mechanics provided a paradigm, as did Dalton's chemistry, Darwin's biology, and Einstein's electrodynamics. A paradigm contains fairly strict rules for determining what counts as solving a scientific problem, although these rules are seldom formulated explicitly. Over time, anomalous cases are collected that should conform to the paradigm but resist solution. As the number of such anomalies increases and they continue to resist the best efforts to resolve them, some scientists will inevitably begin to lose faith in the adequacy of the paradigm. This crisis of faith leads to attempts to replace the paradigm with a different conception—that is, it leads to revolutionary theories. If one or another of these theories can be applied successfully to the anomalous cases that have shaken belief in the extant paradigm, the new theory may become a competing paradigm, with its own advocates, problems, and standards. Because of this process, it often happens that a scientific subject contains two or more competing scientific paradigms, each with its own advocates. Since the advocates of competing paradigms do not fully share standards of explanation, procedures for interpreting data, or beliefs about how the world works, they tend not to understand one another fully.

Holistic advocates repeatedly cite Kuhn and claim that holistic medicine is an alternative paradigm with its own standards, one that cannot be understood or assessed by the practitioners of orthodox medicine (1, 4, 7-9). If the claim were valid, holistic practice would have to constitute a scientific tradition, albeit one in competition with the tradition of orthodox medicine. However, holistic medicine is not a scientific tradition. It has no paradigmatic work, no recognized set of problems, and no shared standards for what constitutes a solution to those problems; it also lacks the critical exchange among its practitioners that is characteristic of the sciences. Cranks have been common throughout the history of science, as Kuhn, a distinguished historian of science, knew well. The work of cranks does not constitute a scientific revolution, and no cranks appear among Kuhn's many examples.

Advocates of holistic medicine also attack reason on the basis of cultural relativism. Sobel claims that one person's physics is another's pseudoscience—in short, that evaluations of medical practices and claims are relative to culture (4). And of course that is correct. They are relative in the sense that they are different. In that sense they are also relative to education, beliefs, and many other things. But the fact that different cultures engender different beliefs does not mean that we should suspend our judgment about such beliefs and become, as it were, acultural. And recognizing that subcultures in our society differ in their beliefs about medicine and other matters does not in the least mean that a reasonable person should give these many conflicting claims equal credence.

Porkert recommends letting our brains fall out. Chinese medicine, he claims, "reposes upon the inductive and synthetic mode of cognition," whereas Western medicine has a "causal and analytic orientation" (10). Furthermore, observation of experimental results is incommensurable: "Thus . . . two physicians, the first observing in the pattern of the inductive and synthetic mode, the second oriented by causal analysis, will never succeed in making their positive data converge completely—not in spite of, but precisely because of, their high scientific standards" (10). An example of Western standards of measurement is the centimeter-gram-second system of physics; the Chinese standards are yin and yang, wood, fire, earth, metal, and water; and according to Porkert, one is as good as the other at producing knowledge. One can say, specifically and in boring detail, why it is false to state that honest observers cannot reach agreement on their descriptions of experimental outcomes—if not always on their implications. One can enumerate the functions served by systems of measurement and sound experimental designs that cannot be served by notions of wood, earth, metal, fire, and water. In giving the tedious details of such matters, one must use knowledge and reason in a way that is not delimited by geography or nationality. Porkert and his ilk do not want us to use either our reason or our knowledge in assessing the claims of "alternative" therapies and the methods used to support them.

If holistic-health advocates were content with encouraging sensible preventive medicine or with criticizing the economic organization of American medicine, we might be enthusiastic, but they are not. If the movement were without influence on American life, we would be indifferent, but it is not. Holistic medicine is a pablum of common sense and nonsense offered by cranks and quacks and failed pedants who share an attachment to magic and an animosity toward reason. Too many people seem willing to swallow the rhetoric—even too many medical doctors—and the results will not be benign. At times, physicians may find themselves in sympathy with the holistic movement, because some fragment of the rhetoric rings true, because of certain practices and attitudes they encounter in their daily work with colleagues and patients, or because of dissatisfaction with the economic and social organization of medicine. One hopes they will speak bluntly, but it does no good to join forces with cranks and quacks, magicians and madmen.

REFERENCES

1. Pelletier, K. R., *Holistic Medicine: From Stress to Optimum Health* (New York: Dell, 1979), 13.

2. Pelletier, K. R., *Mind as Healer, Mind as Slayer: A Holistic Approach to Preventing Stress Disorders* (New York: Dell, 1977), 318.

3. Sampson, W. I., "Wolves in Sheep's Clothing," in S. Barrett (ed.), *The Health Robbers: How to Protect Your Money and Your Life* (Philadelphia: George F. Stickley, 1980), 283–84.

4. Sobel, D. S., (ed.), *Ways of Health: Holistic Approaches to Ancient and Contemporary Medicine* (New York: Harcourt Brace Jovanovich, 1979), 224–26.

5. Editors of *Consumer Reports, Health Quackery: Consumers Union's Report on False Health Claims, Worthless Remedies and Unproved Therapies* (New York: Holt, Rinehart and Winston, 1980), 156–200.

6. Simon, A.; Worthen, D. M.; and Mitas II, J. A., "An Evaluation of Iridology," *Journal of the American Medical Association* 242 (1979):1385–89.

7. Carlson R. J., (ed.), *The Frontiers of Science and Medicine* (Chicago: Henry Regnery, 1975), 19–44.

8. Gordon, J. S., "The Paradigm of Holistic Medicine," in Hastings, A. C.; Fadiman, J.; and Gordon, J. S., (eds.), *Health for the Whole Person: The Complete Guide to Holistic Medicine* (New York: Bantam, 1980), 3–35.

9. Oyle, I., *The New American Medicine Show* (Santa Cruz, Calif.: Unity Press, 1979), 64–74.

10. Porkert, M., "Chinese Medicine: A Traditional Healing Science," in D. S. Sobel, (ed.), *Ways of Health,* 152–53.

James C. Whorton, Ph.D.

The First Holistic Revolution: Alternative Medicine in the Nineteenth Century

The onslaught of holistic programs of therapy has been so sudden and overwhelming, and backed by such clamorous exercises in the rhetoric of revolution, a person could hardly be blamed for deciding a New Age of Healing is indeed at hand and rushing off to join the crusade. Fortunately, history provides its usual sedative against fanaticism, revealing that behind the ideological smugness and claims to liberating originality, holistic medicine is actually new only as a term, not as a philosophy. It used to be called Hippocratic medicine, and by any name has been part of orthodox medical thought since its beginnings. The essential principles of holism are, after all, not terribly profound, being discovered rather quickly by any thoughtful, observant person who dedicates himself to helping the sick. The conscientious application of those precepts in the rush of daily practice is a separate matter, of course, made ever more difficult as medicine has become increasingly technical, mechanistic, specialized, and preoccupied with local pathology. In reaction to this "allopathic" medicine, various alternative approaches to healing have arisen, seeing and presenting themselves with holisticer-than-thou rectitude as the restorers of the healing art to Hippocratic purity. Familiar as that all sounds, however, the split between conventional and alternative systems of medicine began more than a century and a half ago, with rebels who, though unaware they were holistic (the word would not be seriously applied to medicine until the 1970s), attacked the medical establishment on all the same grounds and appealed to the same popular dissatisfactions and hopes as the descendants who now wear "holistic" as a badge.

Today's holistic practitioners, no matter how distinctive or bizarre their individual healing theories and methods, share a core doctrine of tenets derived from the central rule of treating the whole patient.[1] These include reverence for the healing power of nature (*vis medicatrix naturae*); the conviction that by virtue of working in cooperation with the *vis medicatrix* and producing no side effects, holistic methods constitute "natural" healing; a determination to de-mystify medicine and rouse the patient to assume greater responsibility for his own recovery and maintenance of health; emphasis on prevention of sickness and promotion of "wellness" by adherence to a healthful lifestyle; and an insistence that alternative therapies have been discovered and validated by clinical experience yet are rejected by allopathic practitioners because the methods cannot be readily explained by accepted theory. Though ever applicable, these tenets become especially compelling during periods of heightened public discontent with conventional care and distrust of physicians' skills and motives.

> At no period have the means for the acquirement or diffusion of medical knowledge been more various and multiplied, than the present—by the increased number of medical schools, the lectures of the learned professors, the formation of medical societies, the writings of able authors, the abundance of periodical publications, and the thousand facilities afforded by new discoveries and inventions; and yet, strange to say, the esteem and respect in which the medical profession is held by the better informed members of society and the public at large, was never at a lower ebb than at this time.[2]

So modern a ring has this lament. It was nonetheless published in 1851, when, as now, the clearest sign of an ebbtide in public confidence was the proliferation during the previous two decades of alternative or "irregular" systems of medical treatment. The rise of irregular medicine was, at one level, a practical, commonsense, revolt against the excessively heroic therapies favored by regular physicians. Iatrogenic illness became epidemic during the early 1800s, as bleeding (by incision, cupping, and/or leeching), purging (with calomel, a toxic mercury compound), blistering (with Spanish fly), and comparable thera-peutic assaults were prescribed with increasing frequency.[3] The irregulars, though, went beyond censuring practices, arguing dangerous treatments were only symptoms of an underlying problem, an erroneous philosophy. To them, it was a question of epistemology: does one arrive at therapeutic procedures by deduction from dubious theories, or should one operate without theoretical preconceptions and accept what clinical experience shows to be effective? With-out exception, nineteenth-century alternative practitioners denounced orthodox physicians as rationalists, by which was meant they were guided by logic, theory, and tradition; and with the same breath, irregulars congratulated themselves for being hardheaded empiricists whose insights had come from practical experi-ences with patients.

They did truly mean well, but the empiricism of the irregulars was only a counterfeit of the genuine article. In the first place, discovery was commonly assumed on the basis of inadequate data. More than once, a single observation or experience was glorified through *post hoc* reasoning into a revelation of nature's panacea. True empiricism discovers by repeated, critically evaluated experiences, not by "Eureka" intuitions. Secondly, alternative healers were guilty of the same crime for which they so persistently indicted medical doctors: they became rationalists. Time and again those foes of empty theory felt uncomfortable on their bare empirical foundations until they could surround themselves with an explanatory superstructure, no matter how ramshackle. Theirs in fact were the most top-heavy theoretical constructs of all. Their only genuine distinction from orthodox rationalism was that instead of deducing therapy from theory, they deduced theory from therapy. Not at all atypical was Carl Baunscheidt, a German businessman whose rheumatic hand was bitten by several gnats one afternoon in 1848. When the rheumatic ache subsided immediately after the gnats' attack, Baunscheidt decided he had discovered nature's method of cure and set about designing his *Lebenswecker,* or "Great Resuscitator," a sort of mechanical gnat used to puncture patients' skin with two-inch-long needles to allow the body to expel pathogenetic matter through the artificial openings.[4]

Natural (indeed, gnatural) as his therapy was, Baunscheidtism was still a relatively minor form of alternative medicine. The most popular was one that truly relied entirely on nature, homeopathy. A so much more refined mode of healing that dominated the realm of alternative medicine through the entire second half of the nineteenth century, homeopathy attracted clients primarily because it was holistic in virtually every present-day connotation of the term. It was, to begin, the gentlest medicine conceivable. Its discoverer, Samuel Hahnemann, was a German M.D. of the late 1700s who abandoned conventional practice after a few years of experience persuaded him he was nothing more than "the murderer and the tormentor of my brethren."[5] The experience that allowed him to become a savior instead occurred in 1790, when a dose of cinchona, the quinine-containing remedy for malaria, produced in him odd sensations similar to the symptoms of malaria. The very drug that relieved a particular disease in a sick man, in other words, had induced the same disease, or at least a close facsimile, in a healthy man. In the more general terms at which Hahnemann soon arrived, every disease must and can be cured by the specific drug that creates a similar set of symptoms: like cures like, *similia similibus curantur.*[6]

The "law of similia" dictated that all potential drug substances be tested on healthy volunteers to determine the symptom complexes associated with each. These drug "provings," as they were to be hallowed, were presumed to be made valid by using only healthy subjects as volunteers and requiring them to refrain from all other medications, alcohol, coffee, spicy food, heavy labor, and debauchery for the course of the experiment. All contaminating influences eliminated, Hahnemann felt confident that any abnormalities experienced by his volunteers must be drug induced. "A materia medica of this nature," he maintained, "shall be free from all conjecture, fiction, or gratuitous assertion [read rationalism]—it shall contain nothing but the pure language of nature, the results of a careful and faithful research."[7]

Hahnemann seems to have somehow overlooked the fact that people regularly experience "symptoms," unusual physical and emotional sensations, whether taking drugs or other stimulants, or not—especially if they have been forewarned that the experimental pills they have been given might, nay probably will, cause symptoms and that the symptoms might be mild and take several days or weeks to manifest themselves. Thus prepared by suggestion, Hahnemann's provers were inclined to regard the morning backache formerly charged to poor sleeping posture as a consequence of drugs, and to blame bad dreams on medicines rather than on too many meatballs. Hahnemann got all the headaches and drowsiness and pimples he asked for, and much more. As provings by the master and his followers accumulated, homeopathic handbooks of materia medica grew thick with near interminable symptom lists. In Hahnemann's own guide, for example, *chamomilla* (as chamomile a long-standing folk remedy for children's complaints) filled thirteen pages with its effects. These included

> Vertigo, especially when talking. . . . Dull, aching pain in the head, when sitting or reflecting. . . . Single, long stitches in the ear, especially when stooping, accompanied with inclination to find fault, and getting angry about trifles. . . . Grumbling and creeping in the upper teeth. . . . Violent desire for coffee. . . . Flatulent colic. . . . Itching pain at the anus. . . . erection in the morning. . . . Out of humor and headstrong even unto quarreling, at the appearance of the menses. . . . Burning pain in the hand, afternoon. . . . Great aversion to the wind. . . . Quarrelsome, vexatious dreams. . . . heat and redness of the right cheek. . . . Ill humor after a meal. . . . Stitches, irradiating from the abdomen into the chest, with constant thirst without heat, before midnight.[8]

Such a list, and its innumerable analogues, begged for derision. By the homeopaths' reckoning, a regular doctor joked, chamomile was "a fit agent for inquisitorial torture, instead of being the innocent thing which all nurses and old women think it to be."[9]

Homeopaths felt as much reverence for those lists as regulars did contempt. They were in fact what made the system holistic, for each drug's properties included psychological and emotional effects as well as physical ones; ill humor could be treated in conjunction with flatulent colic, and the whole patient—mind, spirit, and body—thus restored at once. The complexity and precision of each remedy's action, moreover, allowed the homeopathic practitioner to prescribe treatment that so exactly duplicated the complaints of each patient as to be tailor-made for his ensemble of pains. For Hahnemann, every man was his own disease, and each man could expect individualized therapy that addressed all of his specific needs, instead of the assembly-line, everyone-the-same treatments of orthodox M.D.s. The latter routinely bled and purged whether the patient's grumbling was in the upper teeth or lower, and his erections in the morning or evening.

Selection of the one and only remedy appropriate for each patient was time-consuming, requiring the doctor to take a thorough, fully itemized case history, and then to carefully comb the volumes of drug symptoms to find the perfect mate for the disease. The homeopath's willingness to take such time for an ordinary fee was one demonstration of his selfless devotion to his patients.

Still more impressive was the time taken to prepare each remedy once it had been identified. Hahnemann's clinical experiences in the late 1790s and early 1800s led him to the conclusion that smaller-than-usual doses gave much better results, until he approached the logical terminus of that line of thought, that no medicine gives the best result. He stopped imperceptibly short of that point, determining empirically that medicines were most effective when prepared by a special procedure of dilution to an infinitesimal level of concentration. Actually, several methods of dilution were found suitable; all more or less imitated the basic method of mixing one grain of drug with ninety-nine grains of lactose (milk sugar), somehow the one inert solid substance on the planet, and therefore the only acceptable diluent. The two compounds would be finely ground by mortar and pestle and intimately mixed to give a medicine to the first dilution, then one grain of that mixture (containing one one-hundredth of a grain of drug) mixed and ground with a second ninety-nine grains of lactose to reach the stage of the second dilution. A grain of that mixture (now harboring a mere one ten-thousandth of a grain of drug) would be blended with another ninety-nine grains of milk sugar, and the process repeated, not *ad infinitum,* but only to the thirtieth dilution. At that point a grain of the at last fully activated preparation would theoretically contain $1/10^{60}$ grain of the active drug. In reality, as could be calculated by the second half of the 1800s, a random grain was extremely unlikely to contain even a single molecule of the drug.[10]

Molecules, however, did not matter. As Hahnemann pondered this at first marvelous yet empirically established principle of potentiation by dilution, he came to see that the therapeutic power of a drug lay not in its matter, but in a force or energy or spiritual power residing within the matter. If one accepted that the human body was activated and regulated, given life and health, by an immaterial vital force or principle, and if disease represented a disruption of functioning of the vital force, then medicines could cure only by restoring that force. And if the vital force were spiritual rather than material, a drug could interact with the force only at the spiritual level. Drugs acted "dynamically" rather than atomically, and Hahnemann's dilutions of grandeur were necessary to strip away the material shell imprisoning every drug's spiritual essence. Once freed, that essence created an artificial, medicinal disease that expelled the weaker natural disease from the body. When medication was then discontinued, the medicinal disease declined and was itself overcome by the *vis medicatrix.*[11]

Homeopathy was a totally different therapeutic philosophy from that employed by traditional practitioners. They treated illness with drugs having no similarity or other set relation to the disease, practiced what should only be called allopathy," medicine "other than the disease." Hahnemann's introduction of "allopathy," however, was as much a strategic ploy as a linguistic invention. It implied that regular medicine was just another "pathy," no better and perhaps worse than competitors, and so encouraged medical consumers to shop around. Regulars, once they became aware of the term, were infuriated, and continued to fume into the twentieth century. As late as 1902 a popular guide for the young doctor entering the profession warned him to

> remember that the term "Allopath" is a false nickname not chosen by regular physicians at all, but cunningly coined, and put in wicked use against us, in his venomous crusade against Regular Medicine by its enemy, Hahnemann, . . . and ever since applied to us by our enemies with all the insinuations and derisive use the term affords. "Allopathy" applied to regular medicine is both untrue and offensive and is no more accepted by us than the term "Heretics" is accepted by Protestants, . . . or "Niggers" by the Blacks.[12]

Homeopathy also played to the sympathies of nineteenth-century laymen troubled by the already advanced tendency of allopathic theorists to reduce all life processes to molecular interactions; its exaltation of "dynamic" action is echoed today by holists' praise for spirit and energy as forces of healing. In America, public support was promoted further by a more direct strategy, the encouraging of people to take responsibility for their own treatments. The leader's role was here played by Constantine Hering, an M.D. who converted to homeopathy while still a young man in his native Germany, then came to Philadelphia in the 1830s and organized the area's handful of homeopaths into a budding profession. In *The Homeopathist, or Domestic Physician,* published in 1835, Hering offered two volumes of instruction to the layman on the selection of appropriate remedies for his everyday complaints. The books were accompanied by a "domestic kit" of forty broad-spectrum homeopathic remedies, each identified by number rather than by a mystifying Latin name. When sick, the sufferer had only to carefully list all his symptoms, find a corresponding symptom complex in Hering's catalogue, then swallow the numbered preparation recommended. As in professional texts, however, symptom complexes were defined with such hair-splitting detail that the search for one's match could occupy the better part of most illnesses. A headache, after all, was not simply a headache, any one to be cured the same as any other. A homeopathic headache was a protean malady, now assuming one multifaceted guise, now another, and each had to be vanquished by its own specific remedy. Number four was the weapon of choice against a headache characterized by

> pressing pain above the nose, mitigated by bending forward; pressing from within outwardly, shooting, throbbing; tearing in the forehead, as if a nail were driven through the head, piercing boring deep into the brain, with nausea, darkness before the eyes, aversion to light, pale countenance, much colorless urine; the pains cease for a time, upon a change of position, yet often returning after meals, at night after lying down, in the morning after getting up; the patient being very much affrighted, inconstant, or taciturn and dejected.

Number eight could also be used against a headache that worsened after rising in the morning, but only if it had as well jerking, pricking, stitches in the temples, particularly when the pain is only on one side of the head; accompanied with frequent giddiness, inclination to vomit, heaviness in the head, the eyes becoming beclouded, and unable to bear the light, rustling in the ears, or stinging, throbbing, and tearing in them; pale doleful countenance, no appetite, nor thirst; shivering, anxious, sometimes bleeding at the nose, palpitation of the heart.

When the head pain felt "as if the brains were shattered, crushed, burst," number one was the answer; when the face was "red and bloated," number three should be taken; if accompanied by a loathing of coffee, number thirteen; and when afflicting "stubborn, unruly children, fond of dainties," number seventeen.[13]

Domestic guides and kits from other manufacturers followed in profusion, some outselling the original. Frederick Humphreys boasted that sales of his set were in excess of twelve million by 1890, which even if the figure was inflated, demonstrates a remarkable level of public interest in homeopathy.[14] That interest was stimulated in the face of relentless opposition from the medical establishment. The American Medical Association included a clause in its original code of ethics meant specifically to squash homeopathy by forbidding consultations with unscientific practitioners.[15] Individual physicians, meanwhile, heaped ridicule on homeopaths as fast as they could shovel, making antihomeopathic satire perhaps the most popular genre of medical literature of the mid 1800s. But though their rebukes of the law of similia and the practice of dilution had wit as well as substance, they failed to slow the growth of the upstart sect. In the end, it was orthodox medicine that learned a lesson, having to admit that the usual recovery of patients under the homeopathic regimen of "placeboism etherealized"[16] was embarrassing proof that the aggressive and heroic measures of standard therapy were unnecessary. As one assault on homeopathic practitioners put it, they would be just as successful "were the similars left out and atoms of taffy or sawdust . . . substituted, to give their patients room to exercise their faith, and *nature* time and opportunity to do the work."[17] A New York physician, Dan King, enlarged on that theme:

> Perhaps Hahnemann did not live wholly in vain. . . . Through the use of his empty and inert means, we have been enabled to see what the innate powers of the animal organization can accomplish without medical interference. We have been taught to rely more upon these, and less upon art, and have seen the wonderful influence which the mind has over the bodily functions. . . . Henceforth the physician will look more carefully to the recuperative energies of nature and from the darkness and confusion which Hahnemann spread around, a clearer light may shine upon the path of medical practice. Henceforth the physician will lay a gentler hand upon his patient, and pursue a more expectant course. The public may not require physicians less, but will demand less of them in the way of positive medication.[18]

By the 1870s the positive medication of the heroic mid-century was on the wane, and homeopathy's example of trust in nature deserved much of the credit.

The homeopaths had hardly done it alone, though. Alternative healers of other persuasions had also demonstrated the power of the *vis medicatrix,* and not only to subdue disease, but to overcome treatment as well. For no other therapy could be so easy as Hahnemann's sugar pills, and some, most particularly Samuel Thomson's, could be so very much more rigorous as to rival allopathy's assault on the vital powers. Thomson, naturally, perceived his healing regimen to be a gentle enough adjuvant to the body's innate restorative force, since it was wholly derived from attentive study and self-experimentation in the laboratory of nature. As a boy in the 1770s and 1780s he had roamed the woods and fields around his New Hampshire cabin. There, nearly too curious for his own good, he had sampled every leaf, berry, and bark in his path, gradually becoming an expert in pharmaceutical botany.[19]

He at first used his knowledge for less than noble ends, frequently offering his most surprising discovery, lobelia—a potent emetic—to other boys "merely by way of sport, to see them vomit."[20] By the time he attained majority, though, unhappy experiences with allopathic doctors had moved him to try the medicinal value of his botanicals, and during the 1790s he steadily made the transition from farmer to itinerant healer and rebel against medical orthodoxy. First he determined an effective therapeutic program by experience, then he fabricated a theoretical rationale to support it. It was precisely the sort of theory to be expected from a practical-minded graduate of the school of hard knocks. The botanicals he had found to have curative virtue included several hot and spicy items, as well as his beloved lobelia: clearly disease must be a manifestation of the loss of heat from the body, and cure required nothing more than the reestablishment of heat. In the only slightly more complicated terms that represented the limits of Thomson's scientific sophistication, the maintenance of health and life demanded that an adequate supply of heat be generated by the burning of fuel (food) in the stomach, the body's fireplace. Like an ordinary fireplace, it burned inefficiently if fed too much or improper fuel, and became clogged with the ash and slag of inhibited digestion. Heat was then produced in too small a quantity, and not effectively distributed to the rest of the body. The rule of heat would begin yielding to the power of cold, the power of inertness or death, which by some unexplained mechanism manufactured "canker" and putrefaction throughout the body. Death would ultimately ensue unless the routed forces of heat were reinforced. That was why his "Emetic Herb" was a veritable panacea. Like a chimney sweep it scraped the human fireplace clean and equipped it to burn undampened. That was why he had found plants such as cayenne, red pepper, black pepper, and ginger to be beneficial in all illness. Hot, spicy drugs added their heat directly to the body, sustaining motion and life until digestion returned to full power. Peppers promoted sweating as well, which served to dislodge and eliminate those impure products of canker and putrefaction. The same was accomplished by "injections," or enemas, which scoured the intestines, and by steam baths, which added heat to the body at the same time they flushed it clean with perspiration. All those disparate therapies found by trial and error were linked together by their opposition to cold and its morbific progeny.[21]

It seems implicit in Thomson's writings that the heat, the source of life, is the *vis medicatrix*. Latin was beyond his abilities, but he said the same in English by repeatedly stressing that he sought only to assist nature to remove disease. He also hoped to strengthen nature to prevent disease, recommending proper living habits, especially diet, to save the heat from ever being seriously challenged by cold. As a man of the people, he had a hearty appetite for clichés, and the one about "an ounce of prevention" was a lifelong favorite.[22]

Those who ignored that advice—i.e., fell ill, and ended up as Thomson's patients—were likely to revise the proverb to "an ounce of prevention is better than a pound of lobelia." They fared no better than Thomson's unsuspecting childhood friends; if anything, they were more ill-treated, subjected to a thorough course of dosing that only began with the emetic. Consider the cure endured by a Marylander named Knappe in 1837. To start each day he took a half-hour steam bath:

> When the sweat rolls off as thick as your finger the body is washed with cold water and the patient is straightway put to bed with hot bricks to bring back his heat. Then a powerful vomitive is administered, composed of bayberry, of cayenne and lobelia, which suffer naught impure to remain in the stomach, and all these herbs are mixed in brandy, after which warm water is drunk until there has ensued the most extraordinary vomiting. Next the patient rises and takes a second bath, then takes again to his bed for an hour, surrounded with hot bricks. At the end of this time he takes two injections of penny royal, cayenne pepper, and lobelia, and the treatment is over for day.

"This horse-cure," Knappe hastened to add, "has given me strength and color." Nevertheless, he confessed, after his eleventh treatment he was "so sick that for three hours I gave no sign of life. . . . I am still spitting up matter and blood, but the pains are over and I feel a great deal improved. . . . My doctor is certain of my cure. Time shall tell us the rest."[23]

Time, unfortunately, tells nothing more of the courageous Mr. Knappe. There are no records to document his survival or destruction at the Thomsonian infirmary. His willingness to endure the therapy, however, cannot be explained by its mildness. Patients did not opt for botanical treatment because it was so much gentler than the heroic type. Thomson's success in attracting patients, an impressive degree of success, has to be accounted for by something other than the pleasures of emesis and cayenne enemas.

Fundamental to his popularity was Thomson's personal style. As direct and unpolished as his therapy, he rose to prominence in tandem with that democratic fervor that climaxed in the 1830s era of "Jacksonian democracy." An exuberant celebration of the virtues of the common people, Jacksonianism despised economic and intellectual elitism, and by those standards Thomson had impeccable credentials. A man who had survived enough hardship and disappointment to earn enshrinement in a country music ballad had he lived in a later century, he never bothered to retouch his portrait to cover a sizeable wart on his nose, and warts and all is how he presented himself to his public. Even his admirers vied to see who could make the greatest bumpkin of him, typical praise allowing that he was an "illiterate," a "mere plow-boy [who] spent his life among the clods of the valley, and [was] himself but little superior to the dust he walked on."[24] But as every Jacksonian knew, it was among the clods that true wisdom was to be found, not in the sterile pursuit of "book-larnin'." "Glory to the God of Nature," Thomson declared, "President of this college" in which he had matriculated.[25] Elsewhere, in reference to *medical* colleges, he insisted that "the learned have added nothing to the healing art; but they have done much in taking the knowledge of the simple remedies from the people."[26] A major part of his medical mission, therefore, was the demystification of the technical jargon used by physicians to enslave the unschooled, and in Thomson's writings diseases were identified by colloquial names that folks could understand: scalt head, salt rheum, itch, rattles, numbpalsy, and the relax.

The ultimate goal for this Old Hickory of medicine was full medical democracy, the granting of therapeutic autonomy to the common man. His first step down that path was taken in 1813, when Thomson persuaded the federal patent office to issue a patent on his system of medicine. As renewed twice subsequently, it gave him the exclusive right to practice—or to sell to others the right to practice—his special course of therapy. The second provision was the critical one for the future of Thomsonianism. The founder used it to construct a pyramidal health care system with himself at the apex and the American public—the common folk among them at least—providing the base. In between were the liaisons or Thomsonian "agents," who purchased from Thomson the right to sell to individual families the opportunity to dose themselves with lobelia. While an agent might also open an infirmary and doctor patients, he was first and foremost a peddler of "Family Right Certificates," licenses for families to use the botanicals in the privacy and convenience of their own homes. Each certificate cost twenty dollars; the agent kept ten dollars from the sale, Thomson got the rest.[27]

Twenty dollars was no trivial expenditure for a working man of the nineteenth century, even if the lobelia system was, as a Virginia agent gushed, "next to the Christian religion the greatest boon that has ever been granted by indulgent Heaven to the sons and daughters of affliction."[28] Yet, in 1839 Thomson calculated that he had sold one hundred thousand of his licenses, and that about three million Americans had adopted his system (apparently more than a few people were taking his medicines without paying for the right). The national population in that year was just approaching seventeen million, so if Thomson's figures were correct, nearly twenty percent of the country had given up on allopathic medicines in favor of botanicals. There is every reason to suspect Thomson of stretching his figures (when did any advertiser ever do otherwise?), except that other, independent estimates also indicate high levels of popular support. In 1835, the governor of Mississippi asserted that half the citizens of his state were Thomsonian, and soon after the regular physicians of Ohio (the third most populous state in the country) admitted that probably one-third of the public there preferred Thomsonian remedies.[29] The lobelia and steam regimen was evidently more popular in the South and Midwest than the Northeast. Nevertheless, if fully a third of Ohio went botanical, the overall national average might well have approached Thomson's guess. Even half that figure, or nine or ten percent, would have been a showing any chiropractor might envy today.

Part of the Thomsonian battle to give people complete responsibility for their own health was an attack on the institution of medical licensing. Today's holists regularly recommend the elimination of licensing restrictions, which interfere with the practice of alternative medicine and abridge the public's freedom of choice. Thus far they have captured few legislators' ears, yet in the 1830s and 1840s Thomsonian sympathizers laid siege to state houses until the licensing laws in nearly every state in the country had been repealed. Throughout that struggle, the enemy was reviled with the same phrase so popular today—"medical monopoly." Thomson also unleashed his fury against a second type of monopoly. Connected with the holistic movement today is a concern to demedicalize pregnancy and labor, to treat childbirth more as a natural process than as a potential disease requiring close medical monitoring and pharmacological and surgical interventions. The holistic way to give birth is to do it at home rather than in the hospital, with the assistance of a lay midwife rather than the supervision of an obstetrician. Thomson happened to mature during precisely the period that midwifery, the method of centuries, was beginning to be supplanted by obstetrics, and he, too, was angered by the change. The natural process of birth, he believed, was inhibited by the attendance of a male physican at this intimate function, and then disrupted totally by obstetricians too ready to resort to forceps, "the instruments of death"[30] that crushed fetal heads and lacerated mothers' reproductive organs. Thomson did not quite advise a complete demedicalization of pregnancy, however, for in his view the old method of relying on nature could be botanically assisted. Lobelia he reckoned to be as good for babies as adults, a "large tea-spoonful of brown emetic" being among his recommendations for "Treatment in the hour of Travail." With that kind of aid, "your children will be born naturally, as fruit falls from the tree, when ripe, of itself."[31]

Thomsonian ideology had still other components—romanticism and nationalism were especially pronounced. Self-care was its dominant theme, though, and while its every-man-his-own-physician pitch might seem the ultimate expression of patient-heal-thyself-holism, there was one other system that in its way was just as insistent on making patients fully responsible for their own well-being. Hydropathy was the creation of Austria's answer to Samuel Thomson, one Vincent Priessnitz. Although he was born thirty years after Thomson, in 1799, Priessnitz was also a farmer whose woodland wanderings made him privy to nature's curative secrets. In his case, the secret was water, cold applications of which were found by self-experimentation to heal injuries and ailments alike. Beginning as a traveling healer in the early 1820s, Priessnitz's skills matured so rapidly that by 1826 he could open the Hydropathic Institution of Gräfenberg in his home village. There his reputation quickly rose to international heights as complaints of every description yielded to his program of cold water baths and fresh air hikes. Within a decade, the annual pilgrimage of patients to Gräfenberg numbered in the hundreds, and they came from every nation of Europe and North America. They came, furthermore, despite the prospect of being roused from bed every morning at four, made to sweat for an hour, then to soak in a tub of water just collected from a mountain stream, then to divide the rest of the day between head-baths, sitz-baths, foot and other baths, drinking as much water as they could hold, and walking as many miles on Gräfenberg's mountain trails as they could manage. And there was also the douche bag, the regimen's most formidable component, a shower of stream water of several inches diameter falling from a height of ten to twenty feet. Novices were occasionally knocked flat by the douche, and sometimes injured—a patient who attended an English hydropathic institute one winter in the 1840s was stabbed by an icicle in his shower.[32]

Stab wounds healed themselves, of course, as did most of the other ailments treated at Gräfenberg. Because it was necessary to travel to Priessnitz's rural hospital, urgent, life-threatening conditions were virtually excluded. As a rule, hydropathic patients were victims of relatively mild or chronic complaints, many of which were self-limited, and some of which had undoubtedly been aggravated by the pressures and anxieties of hurried urban lives. "Stress" existed in the nineteenth century and stressed patients surely responded favorably to the early-to-bed-and-early-to-rise, regulated, and hygienic life-schedule imposed upon them at Gräfenberg. As a weary English nobleman discovered during his stay, "At the Water-Cure the whole life is one remedy."[33] Priessnitz's interpretation was that the cure was effected as swallowed water dissolved disease toxins internally, exercise-accelerated circulation carried toxins to the skin and lungs, and baths, sweating, and pure air washed morbid particles away.

The way it worked was less important than the fact that it did. Hydropathy spread westward in a steady flow, being introduced in the United States in 1843, at the height of public reaction against orthodox medical heroics. Thus, among its early successes were many patients who had suffered iatrogenic damage from allopaths. A Mississippi lady had been nearly "butchered by Pill givers," and a New York gentleman "blistered and cupped almost to death" before both were saved by hydropaths. J. J. P. of Philadelphia first let allopaths have "their own way with me, and cups and calomel . . . did their usual work," then cured himself in the Catskills' streams. N. N. had not only been "bled twenty times over" by regular doctors, but "Thomsonians had drugged and steamed her," too; only under hydropathy did she improve. Hydropathy could even cure inadvertently. A Baptist preacher long tortured by rheumatism was suddenly and permanently relieved after performing a series of baptisms in an icy river.[34]

Being a wonder-working alternative was only the first of hydropathy's claims as a forerunner of holism. Water, it was reiterated endlessly, was not just any alternative; it was a special substance, the chief component of the human body and of human blood, an indispensable nutrient, a "genial restorer and soft asuager."[35] It nourished the earth, the microcosm, too, its rains and rivers being the life's blood of all creation. Water possessed a powerful romantic attraction, an intrinsic association with life and beauty that hydropaths tapped again and again:

> What is there in nature so beautiful as water? In the form of genial spring showers, that fertilize and render fructiferous the earth—in the opening of flowerbuds—in glistening dew-drops—in sparkling fountains—in rivulets—in spring streams—in cascades—and in the delicate tear-drop that moistens the cheek of woman, how beautiful is this agent, every where so abundant—pure, simple water![36]

The "Cold Water Song" that became a kind of hydropathic anthem gave lyrical summation to water's full spender:

> All hail to pure cold water,
> That bright, rich gem from Heaven; . . .
> For life, and health, and gladness,
> It spreads the wide earth o'er.[37]

It was, in brief, the most natural of healing substances; it alone could penetrate all body tissues without harm, acting as a vehicle and solvent "to remove obstructions, wash away impurities, supply healthful nutriment, regulate temperature, relax intensive and intensify torpid action."[38] And even then it merely assisted the body to restore itself, for, according to Russell Trall, one of hydropathy's commanding figures, "All healing power is inherent in the living system."[39]

That being the case, Trall realized, other natural agents might stimulate the *vis medicatrix* nearly as effectively as water. Exercise and fresh air had been part of the system since its inception, and as he found massage, electricity, and other measures to be of value, Trall came to regard "hydropathy" as an unsatisfactory name. "Hygeio-Therapy" was a far better description, he believed, for a system that "adopts all the remedial appliances in existence, with the single exception of poisons," and—its central element—"restores the sick to health by the means which preserve health in well persons."[40] Hygeio-Therapy thus simply meant hygiene as therapy, curing by cleanliness, diet, exercise, air, and the other means people commonly employed to keep well. In Trall's (as in the contemporary holist's) view, health and disease were not opposite poles, but regions of a spectrum of life; no matter where one stood on that spectrum, the same measures, hygienic living, would carry him toward the health end, even into regions well beyond the ordinary understanding of health as mere absence of disease. Though he lacked the term, Trall understood "wellness" as well as any of its champions today.

His hygeio-therapeutic philosophy was the offspring of the union of hydro-pathy with a slightly earlier American health crusade, the Grahamite popular health reform movement. Sylvester Graham was a Presbyterian preacher turned temperance lecturer who, in the early 1830s, began to appreciate that alcohol can be as bad for the body as for the soul, and, broadening his perspective, he saw many other habits of life as physically self-destructive as drinking. Through books and lectures he soon formulated a "Science of Human Life" whose basic law was that all illness could be prevented by proper personal hygiene. Specific rules applying to diet, dress, sex, cleanliness, and other matters followed. They followed, however, not from scientific observation, but from Graham's pious logic, which rested on two unquestioned premises: the puritanical conviction that all pleasurable sensation was Satanic temptation in disguise, and the certainty that immoral behavior had to be unphysiological and unhealthful. An efficient God would not have designed things any other way. In practical transla-tion, that meant any activity appearing to be stimulating, to emotions as well as physical organs, was potentially pathological. Graham's was the antithesis of the later Playboy philosophy: if it feels good, don't do it! Those who did it, who drank whiskey, chewed tobacco, or enjoyed sex outside of marriage, were con-demned to suffer a stimulation-induced inflammation in the immediatly affected organ, an inflammation that could pass through the nervous system to all other parts of the body and show up as disease anywhere. Masturbatory insanity was the exemplification of this process.[41]

Grahamism also included much good common sense. On its index of pro-hibitions were gluttony, inactivity, neglect of bathing, tightly-laced corsets, and neckties. And although it originally denied the need for any kind of therapy, irregular or allopathic, it was a natural ally for the curative scheme of hydro-pathy. Graham trusted in the body's power to restore itself when put on the right regimen, worshipped water as the only nonstimulating beverage, and ad-vised daily cold water baths for cleanliness. Except for details of content and emphasis, that was Priessnitzian ideology. Drug-hating Grahamites could accept hydropaths because water was not a medicine, it was a natural substance, a physiological essential. Hydropaths attuned to therapy could still appreciate the Grahamites' preventive orientation—it utilized the same bathing and exercise for *preserving* body purity as they used to *achieve* body purity. The two sides quickly and happily merged, and by the 1850s the best presentations of health reform teachings were to be found in hydropathic journals, and in the water cures themselves.

The metamorphosis of hydropathy into hygeio-therapy actually meant that heavier demands were made of American patients. Because of the heightened importance of exercise, for example, invalids were not only expected to walk, they had to rejoice in their returning strength by riding horses, sailing and rowing boats, splitting and sawing logs, and/or digging in the garden. Some institutions prided themselves on the calisthenic paces patients were put through each morning. Trall's advertisement for his Hygeian Home touted the "extensive

Gymnasium Hall, with abundant apparatus and music," and he also provided, in a riverside grove, a platform for the enjoyment of "dancing gymnastics."[42] A typical workout—the program enforced by Nathan Bedortha at New Lebanon Springs, New York—began with easy warmups (deep breathing and arm rotations), progressed through more vigorous exertions (hopping, clapping hands over head, bending all directions from the waist), and culminated in the dynamic laughing exercise:

> This usually closes the course. After going through with the variety that has been presented, it will be readily imagined that the blood is circulating freely, and that there is a general glow through the system. This exercise is a propos for the last. It is designed to expel from the lungs all the vitiated gases that may be lodged in the air cells. The whole class stands in position, right hand raised, lungs filled, word is given. The right hand is brought down with the explosive action of the lungs—ha! Both hands then raised and brought down with a double explosion ha! ha! Both hands again raised and brought down with a triple explosion ha! ha! ha!

By the completion of ha! ha! ha! ha!, "the company are generally in a mood to prolong the exercise, and there are explosions in quick succession till the hall rings with the deep, loud and hearty laugh."[43] A reminder is in order ere the strenuousness of those sessions be laughed away. Not only were these patients rather than athletes; it was also the case that organized exercise was then a novel activity whose limits were under timid exploration—"aerobic" had not even been applied to bacteria yet.

By the tenets of the day, hydropathic patients were still less capable of heavy exertion because of their enervating diet. Nonhydropaths accepted without thinking that full strength and energy required generous portions of meat with each meal. Water-cure doctors felt compelled to examine that question more closely, though, and certainly more carefully than Priessnitz had. (He let his Gräfenberg patients eat everything, and lots of it.) The cornerstone of Grahamism, the very *sine qua non* of health, had been pure vegetable diet. Not all hydropaths required total abstinence from meat. They did, however, share Graham's belief that meat was stimulating, and regarded ordinary quantities of it as a inimical to recovery. Many—and Trall most notably—became confirmed vegetarians themselves, and at some institutions coerced patients into joining them. Trall allowed weak-willed patients small quantities of animal food, all the while educating them in proper diet and trying to lure them into his "Provision Depot" where Graham crackers, grits, hominy, oatmeal, and other pure farinaceous products were for sale.[44]

Trall was, in addition, an officer of the American Vegetarian Society from its founding in 1850, and his 1861 book entitled *The Scientific Basis of Vegtarianism* was the most concise presentation of the early arguments that a fleshless diet is more nutritious and digestible, less stimulating and fever-producing, and best adapted to human teeth and alimentary organs. It was also the most passionate—the storm clouds of civil war were already darkening the sky, yet

Trall could protest that the issue of North versus South was as nothing next to "hog versus hominy" and "chicken versus whortleberries." It would not be the election of Lincoln or Douglass, but the selection of corn and berries over ham and drumsticks that would remold "spears of blood and carnage into prunning [sic] hooks for the new Garden of Eden."[45] Other stimulating indulgences would also have to be curtailed before the new age could come to pass. Alcohol and tobacco provoked Trall's wrath too, as did excessive sexual activity. But while condemning too great a quantity, he offered candid advice on improving the quality of what sex one had left, including precautions to ease the fear of unwanted pregnancy. The primitive diaphragm was one contraceptive recommendation, but his preferred method was what would someday be called rhythm. Unfortunately, Trall (and most other doctors who ventured guesses at the female sexual cycle) did not catch the rhythm quite right. Mistaking menstruation as evidence of the approaching end of the fertile period, he advised that, "if intercourse is abstained from until ten or twelve days after the cessation of the menstrual flow, pregnancy will not occur."[46]

As consolation for surprise pregnancies, followers of hydropathy received more humane obstetrical care. Trall's opinion of allopathic obstetrics was only slightly higher than Thomson's had been. The demedicalization of labor and childbirth was a primary goal of hydropathic reform too. If any physical condition was natural and not to be treated as a disease, Trall argued, it was pregnancy. Yet "pregnant females . . . are bled, paregoric'd, magnesia'd, stimulated, mineralized, and poisoned, just as though they were going through a regular course of fever." He left forceps, anesthesia, and ergot (used to hasten labor) out of that list, but gave them their share of contempt elsewhere. All in all, he decided, "it is time, high time, that pregnant women . . . were rescued from the hands of these Philistines of the apothecary shop."[47] Water treatment was the rescue— hydropathic literature was crammed with midwifery advice, and with testimonials of women safely delivered by water. Mrs. O. C. W. was one of many who made the error of calling in an allopath during her first confinement: "all the 'regular' results followed. A broken breast, sore nipples, O horror! and the like, kept me confined to my bed nearly two months." At the commencement of her next labor, though, she took a sitz bath and a cold water enema, and was able to get up and eat a breakfast of Graham bread and water the morning after delivery. Within days she had returned to her usual level of activity.[48] Cases like hers only proved, by Trall's reckoning, that parturition should be safe and painless. Under the hygeio-therapeutic system it would be, but as long as women wore corsets they would distort their pelvic organs, and as long as they ate flesh their pelvic tissues would be less flexible and their fetuses' skulls would be harder. As with all other medical conditions, pregnancy was manageable by self-help.[49]

Hygeio-therapy was inherently a program of self treatment, being comprised of precisely those life activities over which the individual had control. Even the baths, needed to restore health to the negligent and disobedient, could be easily understood and—most of them—administered at home. The *Water-Cure Journal* ran regular articles on domestic self-care, and Trall's more than two dozen books were all written with an eye toward helping people help themselves. *The Mother's Hygienic Hand-Book* was a clear and informative guide to pregnancy, parturition, and child-care on hydropathic principles; and *Water-Cure for the Million* was just the work of domestic democratic medicine its name implied. Even the hefty two-volume *Hydropathic Encyclopedia* was addressed to popular readers as well as fellow practitioners. Other works took up diet and drink, while *The Illustrated Family Gymnasium* gave comprehensive instructions on home exercises—calisthenics, gymnastics, "kinesipathy"—from the easiest limb stretches to the most strenuous and acrobatic feats on the horizontal bar. Careful explanations of techniques of swimming, rowing, and horseback riding were included. There was even a section on vocal gymnastics for aspiring orators.

With a six-foot shelf of the works of Trall (including *The New Hydropathic Cook-Book,* whose recipes would freeze the heart of a *bon vivant*), one was set to weather all of life's storms. Sadly, though, many preferred braving the storms to taking refuge in a hydropathic shelter where physical exertion and meatless living would be demanded of them. As the asceticism of hygeiotherapy became more apparent, public interest declined and the system came to be more caricatured than admired. Typical of the jesting at hydropathy's expense was the report of the sick duck in London's St. James Park who cured himself hydropathically. Wobbling into the lake, the drake first took a foot bath, then floated into a sitz bath, plunged his head beneath the water for a head bath, and finally threw his head back and flapped his wings as if to shout "Priessnitz forever," but instead only said "Quack! Quack! Quack!"[50]

Although hydropathy nearly disappeared after Trall's death in 1877, it enjoyed a revival in the 1890s as the "water cure" of the German priest Sebastian Kneipp. In America Kneippism soon expanded to embrace other natural therapies, and in 1900 was rechristened naturopathy, though it differed in no important way from Trall's hygeiotherapy. The introduction of naturopathy reminds that while there were still more nineteenth-century alternative systems (magnetic healing, eclecticism, chrono-thermalism, and others), each with a unique theory and practice, all were linked by their reverence for nature and their reliance on natural recovery. Priessnitz and other irregulars may have deserved the "quack, quack, quack" japery of allopaths. At the same time, however, their repeated demonstrations of the strength and resiliency of the human body have tempered scientific medicine's urge to treat every ailment aggressively. A turn-of-the-century physician named I. N. Love perceived this as a civilizing, even Christianizing influence:

We needed the Emersons, Channings, Beechers, Theodore Parkers and Henry Drummonds in theology as pioneers to teach us that the greatest thing in the world is love, and to eliminate hellfire and brimstone from our philosophy; so too we needed Hahnemann and his satellites to instruct us along the lines of gentleness and moderation in medication, and demonstrate to us that our methods in Therapy were too heroic, had too much hell and damnation in them.[51]

The most succinct—and best—summary of the legacy of Hahnemann and his satellites, today's holistic practitioners included, was given by a contemporary of Dr. Love, Finley Peter Dunne's quintessential Irish folk philosopher, Mr. Dooley. Capping a barroom discussion of the relative merits of Christian Science and allopathic medicine, Mr. Dooley proposed "that if th' Christyan Scientists had some science an' th' doctors more Christianity, it wudden't make anny diff'rence which ye called in—if ye had a good nurse."[52]

NOTES

1. There are a number of sympathetic surveys of holistic methods and philosophies; especially useful is Berkeley Holstic Health Center, *The Holistic Health Handbook* (Berkeley: And/Or Press, 1978).

2. Senex, "The Past and Present State of the Medical Profession," *Boston Medical and Surgical Journal* 44 (1851):338.

3. For discussions of orthodox therapy in the early nineteenth century, see Alex Berman, "The Heroic Approach in 19th Century Therapeutics," *Bulletin of the American Society of Hospital Pharmacists* 11 (1954):321–27; and William Rothstein, *American Physicians in the Nineteenth Century: From Sects to Science* (Baltimore: Johns Hopkins University Press, 1972), 41–55.

4. Carl Baunscheidt, *Baunscheidtismus, or the New Curing Method* (Buffalo: J. Firmenich, 1862), [first American edition, from the sixth German edition].

5. Thomas Bradford, *The Life and Letters of Dr. Samuel Hahnemann* (Philadelphia: Boericke and Tafel, 1895), 25. For general histories of homeopathy, see Martin Kaufman, *Homeopathy in America: The Rise and Fall of a Medical Heresy* (Baltimore: Johns Hopkins University Press, 1971), and Harris Coulter, *Divided Legacy: The Conflict Between Homeopathy and the American Medical Association* (Richmond, Calif.: North Atlantic Books, 1982).

6. The full doctrine of homeopathy was presented by Hahnemann in his *Organon of Homeopathic Medicine* (Allentown, Pa.: Academical Bookstore, 1836), [first American edition, from the fourth German edition].

7. Ibid., 151.

8. Samuel Hahnemann, *Materia Medica Pura* (New York: W. Radde, 1846), vol. 2, 7–20.

9. Worthington Hooker, *Homeopathy: An Examination of Its Doctrines and Evidences* (New York: Charles Scribner, 1851), 132.

10. Hahnemann's article introducing the idea of potentiation by dilution is reprinted in English in R. E. Dudgeon (ed.), *The Lesser Writings of Samuel Hahnemann* (New York: W. Radde, 1852), 385–89.

11. Hahnemann, *Organon* (n. 6), 153.

12. D. W. Cathell and William Cathell, *Book on the Physician Himself* (Philadelphia: Davis, 1902), 300–301.

13. Constantine Hering, *The Homeopathist, or Domestic Physician* (Allentown, Pa.: Academical Bookstore, 1835), vol. 2, 9–15. For biographical information on Hering, see Calvin Kneer, *Life of Hering* (Philadelphia: Magee Press, 1940).

14. Ronald Numbers, "Do-It-Yourself the Sectarian Way," in Guenter, Risse, Ronald Numbers, and Judith Leavitt, eds. *Medicine Without Doctors* (New York: Science History Publications, 1977), 61.

15. Kaufman (n. 5), 48–62; Coulter (n. 5), 179–219.

16. P. W. Leland, "Empiricism and Its Causes," *Boston Medical and Surgical Journal* 47 (1852):292.

17. D. W. Cathell, *The Physician Himself and What He Should Add to His Scientific Acquirements* (Baltimore: Cushings and Bailey, 1882), 152.

18. Dan King, *Quackery Unmasked* (New York: S. S. and W. Wood, 1858), 132-33.

19. Samuel Thomson, *Narrative of the Life, etc. of Samuel Thomson* (Boston: Adams, 1835).

20. Ibid., 16.

21. Samuel Thomson, *New Guide to Health; or Botanic Family Physician,* (Boston: Adams, 1835), 8-78.

22. Ibid., 154-60.

23. Frank Halstead, "A First-hand Account of a Treatment by Thomsonian Medicine in the 1830s," *Bulletin of the History of Medicine,* 10 (1941):681-83.

24. Samuel Robinson, *A Course of Lectures on Medical Botany* (Boston: J. Howe, 1834), 10.

25. Thomson, *New Guide* (n. 21), 163.

26. Ibid, 151.

27. For more thorough treatment of the Thomsonian system of marketing, see Alex Berman, "The Thomsonian Movement and its Relation to American Pharmacy and Medicine," *Bulletin of the History of Medicine,* 25 (1951):405-28, 519-38; Joseph Kett, *The Formation of the American Medical Profession* (New Haven, Conn.: Yale University Press, 1968), 100-31; Rothstein, (n. 3), 125-151; and James Harvey Young, *The Toadstool Millionaires* (Princeton, N.J.: Princeton University Press, 1961), 44-57.

28. Quoted in James Breeden, "Thomsonianism in Virginia," *Virginia Magazine of History and Biography,* 82 (1974):160.

29. Young (n. 27), 54-55.

30. Thomson, *New Guide* (n. 21), 135.

31. Ibid., 134, 139, 145.

32. Lawrence Wright, *Clean and Decent* (New York: Viking Press, 1960), 159. For general coverage of hydropathy, see Richard Metcalfe, *Life of Vincent Priessnitz* (Richmond Hill, England: Metcalfe, 1898), and Harry Weiss and Howard Kemble, *The Great American Water-Cure Craze* (Trenton, N.J.: Past Times Press, 1967).

33. Edward Bulwer-Lytton, "Bulwer on Water-Cure," *Water Cure Journal,* 1 (1845):12.

34. John Duffy, (ed.), *Rudolph Matas History of Medicine in Louisiana* (Baton Rouge: Louisiana State University Press, 1962), volume 2, 39; "A Water Patient," *The Water-Cure in America* (New York: Fowlers and Wells, 1852), 33, 45, 103, 220-21.

35. Bulwer-Lytton (n. 33), 14.

36. Joel Shew, "Water," *Water-Cure Journal* 3 (1847):97.

37. Mrs. A. C. Judson, "Cold Water Song," *Water Cure Journal,* 2 (1846):111.

38. Russell Trall, *The Hydropathic Encyclopedia* (New York: Fowlers and Wells, 1854), vol. 2, 7.

39. Russell Trall, *Hand-Book of Hygienic Practice* (New York: Miller and Wood, 1864), 3.

40. Ibid., 4.

41. James Whorton, *Crusaders for Fitness: The History of American Health Reformers* (Princeton: N.J.: Princeton University Press, 1982), 13-131.

42. Weiss and Kemble (n. 32), 84-85.

43. Nathan Bedortha, *Practical Medication, or the Invalid's Guide* (Albany, N.Y.: Munsell and Rowland, 1860), 48.

44. Weiss and Kemble (n. 32), 82.

45. Russell Trall, *The Scientific Basis of Vegetarianism* (Philadelpha: Fowlers and Wells, 1861), 2, 16.

46. Russell Trall, *Sexual Physiology* (New York: M. L. Holbrook, 1881), 206.

47. Russell Trall, "Allopathic Midwifery," *Water Cure Journal,* 9 (1850):121; ibid., *Hydropathic Encyclopedia* (n. 38), vol. 2, 393.

48. "A Water Patient" (n. 34), 343.
49. Russell Trall, *Hydropathic Encyclopedia* (n. 38), vol. 2, 392.
50. Weiss and Kemble (n. 32), 48.
51. I. N. Love, " 'The Sarcasm of Love' and Hahnemann," *Medical Mirror* 14 (1903):54.
52. Finley Peter Dunne, *Mr. Dooley's Opinions* (New York: R. H. Russell, 1901), 9.

Susan M. Williams, R.N.

Holistic Nursing

Nursing has always prided itself on the belief that, as a profession, it cares for the "whole" patient. In contrast, other disciplines, notably medicine, are viewed as focusing on the patient's disease. These concepts are clearly reflected in a significant proportion of nursing theory, literature, and education. It is therefore not surprising that the holistic movement, which proclaims its concern for the whole person, has enjoyed widespread success and support from within the ranks of contemporary nursing.

Acceptance of holistic nursing by the profession is evident from the extensive inclusion of holism in the curricula of schools of nursing, from frequent references in the nursing literature, and from the increasing use of holistic jargon by nurses of all persuasions. Further evidence of this acceptance is supplied by the ever-increasing number of "holistic" seminars, workshops, and courses offered to nurses across the country. These programs deal with a wide range of subjects, including wellness lifestyles, acupuncture, visualization, massage, therapeutic touch, and biofeedback.

The American Holistic Nurses Association has an active membership and publishes a journal. Numerous textbooks for nurses are written from a holistic perspective and some are entirely devoted to the subject. Nursing schools in particular embrace the concepts of holism by incorporating them into curricula and by teaching such holistic techniques as therapeutic touch and visualization.

It is difficult to encompass the scope of holistic nursing, for there are many and diverse proponents. Thus the nature of holistic nursing as enunciated by its adherents ranges from what any reasonable person would regard as the commonsense practices of good nursing care, to unorthodox and unproven treatments that are the practice of quackery. Distinguishing between these extremes and understanding what holistic nursing is (as seen by nurses) requires first that one understand the nature of nursing itself.

DEFINITION OF NURSING

Nursing is a profession so diverse, yet so basic, that it has defied precise definition. Florence Nightingale gave what is perhaps the simplest and best description when she noted that nursing should "put the patient in the best condition for nature to act upon him."[1] She was concerned with man's relation to his environment and with the idiosyncracies of patients, cautioning readers to consider psychological as well as physical needs of the ill. It was clear from her writings that Nightingale believed the environment of the patient to be central to nursing. She also believed that the primary focus for nursing actions was to alter this environment in order to place the patient in the best condition for the reparative processes of nature to occur.

An alternative description of nursing has been offered by Virginia Henderson, one of nursing's eminent and respected educators and authors: "The unique function of the nurse is to assist the individual, sick or well, in the performance of those activities contributing to health or its recovery (or to peaceful death) that he would perform unaided if he had the necessary strength, will, or knowledge. And to do this in such a way as to help him gain independence as rapidly as possible."[2] Most recently, the American Nurses Association has formally adopted an official definition of nursing, which reads, in part, "nursing is the diagnosis and treatment of human responses to actual or potential health problems."[3]

Kelly, in citing a litany of definitions of nursing through its history, sums them up by observing that the central thread indicates that nursing deals with the health of the whole human being in interaction with his environment—that is, a holistic, humanistic focus.[4] The nursing process (nursing jargon for the basic steps in problem solving) is also increasingly being described in holistic terms.[5] Good nursing care is characteristically said to mean providing for patients' needs, whether they be physical, emotional, spiritual, or whatever. Total patient care along with TLC (tender loving care) was, and still is, the goal for nurses, although there are those who would argue convincingly that total care is both theoretically and practically impossible.[6]

As well as definitions, models and theories have been developed by nursing scholars to guide practice. These were developed in an attempt to clarify and establish the uniqueness of nursing as a science, and they incorporate many of the principles expressed by holism. Several pull tenets from the same "paradigms" as does holistic medicine and liberally quote from the works of Taoists and Confucians, holists, and reductionists, behaviorists and humanists, and incorporate Eastern and Western perspectives on health.

Examples of nursing theories that fit a holistic model include those of Rogers, Orem, and Roy. Roy's adaptation model sees the person as a biopsychosocial being who functions as a totality.[7] Roy theorizes a health-illness continuum stretching from peak wellness to death. Nursing is seen as assessing one's mode of adaptation along this continuum. Orem proposes a model of self-care with the nurse fulfilling client deficiencies.[8] Roger's theory of the unitary man states that man moves through time and space toward a state of well-being. She believes man is an energy field coexisting with nature. The universe is described as an open system in which generic man and the environment coalesce as energy force fields.[9]

These definitions and theories of nursing, all developed by nurses, are distinguished by their common concern for the health of patients, not merely with providing care for the sick or injured. Promoting health and well-being, nurturing those who are well in addition to the sick, accounting for the interaction of the individual and his environment, and assisting the patient toward "wellness" (whatever that may mean) have been emphasized from the beginning of nursing as a profession.

DEFINITION OF HOLISTIC NURSING

Since nursing's traditional definitions and theories have always been broad and general, what specifically differentiates "holistic nursing" from nursing in general? A look at definitions found in the nursing literature reveals that more is involved than mere attention to emotional, environmental, and physical needs. Commonly, holistic nursing is said to be involved with "mind-body-spirit interrelations," but definitions are so broad that the holistic approach is basically whatever one wants it to be. Consider this definition: ". . . holistic nursing . . . (is) the conscious application of the life processes of self-responsibility, caring, human development, stress, life-styling, communication, problem-solving, teaching/learning, and leadership and change in the intrapersonal, interpersonal and community systems through preventive, nurturative, and generative nursing."[10] One can hardly do better than that. The definition of holistic nursing supplied by the American Holistic Nurses Association (AHNA), the professional society for holistic nurses, is somewhat briefer. It states simply that holistic nursing is "the renewing and enhancing of the art of nurturing and caring for the whole person."[11]

What does all this mean? It shows that the language and beliefs of the holists find a familiar place within nursing definitions, conceptual frameworks, and theories. Recurring general themes emerge and may be summarized as follows:[12]

- Health is more than mere absence of disease; it implies unity of body-mind-spirit.
- Humans are open systems and interact with other systems.
- One's health is affected by one's attitudes and beliefs.
- Maximal health requires some reallocations of one's resources (or energies).
- Health and illness can be represented by a continuum.

- The proper focus of healing comes from within the individual himself.

- Illness may be viewed as not necessarily something to be cured but as an opportunity for growth and learning.

INFLUENCE OF HOLISTS IN NURSING

How successful have the holists been in incorporating the concepts and modalities of holistic care into nursing literature, education, practice, and research? The evidence is impressive. Many textbooks for nurses are written with some reference to commonly accepted holistic concepts. For example, a widely read general textbook for nursing students contains material on a holistic approach to illness, systems theories, stress theories, relaxation techniques, biofeedback, and autogenic training.[13] A major book for critical care nurses contains a chapter on the holistic approach to caring for the critically ill, the author stating that the alternative to holistic care is dehumanizing and fragmented care.[14] It is important to note, however, that for the most part, holistic care as perceived by these books means attention to psychological as well as physical needs, and does not imply support for unorthodox medical practices.

Some textbooks incorporate holism throughout the standard clinical material. In one, written for intensive care nurses,[15] the authors suggest switching from the biomedical model of practice to the "power unleashed by the concepts identified in the mind-body-spirit interrelationships."[16] This book also includes a case study that is said to illustrate an alternative approach to nursing care. A twenty-one-year-old man with acute myelogenous leukemia is described as being helped by a nurse through the use of imagery and meditation. The patient eventually dies and the author is careful to avoid drawing any unwarranted conclusions regarding his medical treatments, but the reader is clearly left with the impression that the use of alternative therapies made a significant contribution to his care.[17]

Several nursing books are devoted entirely to holistic nursing.[18] Common to these texts is a denunciation of what are seen as the deficiencies of the biomedical model of health care, a review of the Eastern concepts of healing as an alternative, a belief that nursing is the ideal profession to incorporate holism within its practice, and a discussion of various holistic therapies. As an example, in one text, multiple techniques are suggested as ideas for referral by nurses.[19] Included among them are Rolfing, polarity, psychic healing, iridology, and chiropractic practices.

In addition to numerous books, nurses also have a journal devoted to holistic nursing: the *Journal of Holistic Nursing,* published by the AHNA. Formed in 1981 by Charlotte McGuire, former assistant vice-president and director of patient services for American Medicare Incorporated (AMI), this group operates within the structure of the American Holistic Medical Association. The AHNA states that its purpose is to serve as an advocate of wellness and to promote the education of nurses in the concepts and practice of health for the whole person.[20] The organization publishes a resource directory of holistic centers and nursing practitioners as well as a newsletter for members. The newsletter, entitled *Beginnings,* prints classified advertisements for various holistic services and products. Typical is an advertisement from Herbal Tracers Ltd., in which AHNA members were offered herbal crystyallization analysis tests for $20 a slide.[21] Herbal Tracers would then donate $2.50 to the AHNA for each slide sent in.

Other "holistic" organizations for nurses include the East/West Academy of Healing Arts, founded by a nurse-acupuncturist. This organization sponsors courses on such subjects as acupuncture, therapeutic touch, nutrition, herbology, iridology, and psychic healing. The Council of Nurse Healers, founded in 1977, is a support group that claims to be dedicated to mobilizing patients' reparative powers through the transfer of energy within the nurse-client interaction.

INFLUENCE OF HOLISTS IN NURSING EDUCATION

Even a cursory look at catalogs and program descriptions from university schools of nursing, both undergraduate and graduate, will reveal the widespread adoption of holistic conceptual models, philosophies, and courses. As with holistic medicine, justification for the beliefs presented is made by frequent reference to Chinese medicine and the yin-yang, to the shifting paradigms of Thomas S. Kuhn, to Werner Heisenberg's uncertainty principle, to stress theories of Hans Selye, and to the concepts of high-level wellness and the wellness-illness continuum. Adoption of these philosophies and beliefs is regarded by many educators as indisputable proof of progressive programs and of nursing as a science.

Specific programs vary but the language has a familiar ring. One school of nursing will offer what it calls a clinically-oriented, holistic baccalaureate nursing degree,[22] and many departments of nursing will say their courses are holistically oriented. Medical-surgical, maternal-child, and community health tertiary care nursing courses are described as supporting nursing interventions that help clients achieve "successful adaptation to . . . high level wellness."[23] Certainly the content of some of these courses may entail little more than an overview of well-accepted health practices, but many also include instruction in the delivery of unproven alternative therapies. For example, a university undergraduate course called "Determinants of Wellness" includes discussion of therapeutic touch, guided imagery, yoga, herbal medicine, and acupuncture.[24]

Holism has become one of the most frequently offered subjects for continuing education seminars and workshops for nurses. In less than one year, I received mailings advertising acupuncture workshops by the Center for Chinese Medicine in Monterey Park, California (approved for credit by boards of nursing of three states and the American Association of Nurse-Anesthetists); an intensive training session in therapeutic imagery by Marquette University; therapeutic touch through the University of Virginia; and numerous opportunities to attend workshops on healing touch presented by the Gotach Center for health, directed by Nicola M. Taurasco, M.D., and approved by seven state boards of nursing. Dr. Taurasco advertises that these seminars on touch are a way for nurses to heal headaches, sinus troubles, abdominal or back discomforts, or to increase the patient's range of motion.

Even a well respected and technologically oriented professional nursing organization has offered seminars on holistic health covering such subjects as the "scientific" basis for holism, the benefits of holistic medicine as compared to those of allopathic, and the use of therapeutic touch and imagery in critical care.[25] Nurses in Manchester, England, attended a holistic workshop in 1984 presented by the school of nursing, which taught, among other topics, Shiatsu massage, aromatherapy, and Kirlean photography.[26] Of course, it should not be inferred from this that these various organizations endorse such holistic practices, yet they consider them important enough to include in programs so that interested nurses may learn about them.

INFLUENCE OF HOLISTS IN NURSING PRACTICE

Evidence for the incorporation of specific holistic nursing practices into actual nursing care is hard to find, since no systematic studies on the subject have been reported. A very real problem is determining what particular nursing actions are holistic. This problem arises from the very nebulous and broad definitions discussed earlier. Specific practices that are said to fall under the umbrella of holistic nursing vary from the simple and commonsense approach of looking after emotional needs to practices that are clearly questionable—such as iridology—with all manner of methods in between. A partial list gathered from textbooks and literature written by nurses for nurses lists all of the following as being holistic practices that nurses are encouraged to become familiar with: tai chi, homeopathy, acupuncture, acupressure, clairvoyant diagnosis, human auras, Rolfing, applied kinesiology, bioenergetic analysis, therapeutic touch, iridology, polarity, psychic reading and psychic healing, therapeutic massage, reflexology, color therapy, visualization, biofeedback, hypnosis, the Alexander technique, aikido, Feldenkrais method, Lomi body work, and dance therapy.

Works dealing with various holistic practices are characteristically presented as summaries of information about the techniques and suggestions for their use rather than scientific treatises. Reports often consist of superficial case discussions, or general discussion of how holistic nursing will help with a particular problem.[27] Unproven therapies are presented as alternatives to established medical practices and treated with equal preference to proven ones. There is a notable absence of qualifying statements for the use of these practices. In fact, they are made to appear universally efficacious. Nurses are even reassured that if they use holistic techniques and fail to achieve the desired results (certainly a possibility), it is probably because they don't understand or practice the philosophy behind them.[28]

A few examples will serve to characterize the literature. Cafoncelli reports the case of a woman who had breast cancer because of a persistent state of consciousness, and every cell also had the image of that cancer in it. She continues that the client must have a clear image of her own Godself and change her consciousness to purify the light she passes through her body.[29] I'm not sure that even Cafoncelli knows what that means, but it is impressive.

In the *Journal of Holistic Nursing,* an author presents a patient who received help with the Gerson diet (which the author refers to as a lesser-known oncological modality) from public health nurses.[30] She describes how the nurses helped the patient with detoxification enemas, administration of supplements, and toxin elimination. It is interesting that the author did not express concern for the use of this unorthodox treatment, but she was concerned that the nurses caring for the patient did not have relevant information available to them.[31] In order to help with this problem in the future, the author outlines a nursing care plan,[32] which she says will also apply to patients using laetrile and the Kelley Ecology or nonspecific metabolic therapy (which actor Steve McQueen used).

Other reports in the nursing literature are equally as enlightening. One author describes the Simonton imagery methods as "potent therapy for cancer" that have been "highly successful."[33] Nurses are reported to be best suited for practicing imagery because of their repeated long-term contact with patients and because of their ability to build a trusting relationship.[34] Shiatsu massage is said to be a complementary medical practice that should be incorporated into the daily bed bath.[35] Biofeedback will control hypertension thereby eliminating the need for drugs.[36] Lovejoy, in what is otherwise an acceptable review of biofeedback research, cannot resist closing by stating that biofeedback is a holistic concept that easily falls under Roger's theory of human-environmental reciprocity, helicy, and synchrony.[37] Ryman's article on aromatherapy supports the use of essential oils of plants, barks, roots, and flowers to alleviate such ailments as arthritis, colds, flu, sinusitis, pre- and post-menopausal tension, wound healing, scars, acne, stretch marks, and even wrinkles. Body organs selectively take up the oils by absorption through the skin. The reader may demonstrate this to himself by rubbing garlic on the feet and observing the smell hours later on the breath.[38]

Another widely used holistic nursing technique is therapeutic touch, which may be popular with nurses because it was developed by a nurse and because touching is a traditionally accepted part of nursing care. The practice is taught in many schools of nursing across the country. One source states that there were thirty-three university nursing departments teaching it in a formal course in 1979.[39] Undoubtedly the number has increased since then. A masters program in therapeutic touch has been offered for several years by New York University for the purpose of educating practitioners and for the development of underlying theories.

Therapeutic touch is defined as a healing combination of touch and meditation, and as an act of interpersonal energy transfer for the purpose of healing.[40] It derives from, but is different from, the laying on of hands, requiring no declaration of faith from the patient to be effective. Apparently the healer must believe, however. Conceptually, the healing process is thought to come from a healer whose health has given him access to an overabundance of "prana," which he channels as an energy flow to the healee.[41]

Results attributed to therapeutic touch are indeed impressive if one can believe the nursing literature. Findings include decreased pain and tension, detection of tumors, identification of stress, enhanced sharing and support of couples during delivery, and relaxation and anxiety reduction[42]; more rapid healing of wounds, decreased edema[43]; correlation with self-actualization; and effects on the metabolic, endocrine, and muscular systems.[44] Krieger reported that therapeutic touch also significantly increased hemoglobin levels of subjects, "prana" being intrinsic in the oxygen molecule.[45] These studies have been repeatedly criticized by scientists, not only for questionable use of the hemoglobin as the dependent variable, but also for faults in research methodology, which make the conclusions suspect.[46]

Indeed, a recent review of the literature offers little empirical support for the practice of therapeutic touch.[47] One obvious difficulty is that the "healing field" cannot be demonstrated, defined, or controlled. Characteristically, the holists are prepared to offer an excuse for the lack of evidence, stating that "physiological signs of healing are not a necessary component of the healing episode."[48] How tidy. Results of the few well-designed, double-blind studies that have been done have been transient, of no statistical significance, in need of replication, and have not adequately addressed the very real issue of the placebo effect.[49]

Regardless of the results of past studies, therapeutic touch is enthusiastically promoted by its supporters. I attended a lecture given by a nurse graduate faculty member, author, and researcher, who used an interesting method to demonstrate how therapeutic touch "works."[50] The audience was asked to bring their hands close together, without touching, and then to move them back away from each other. "What did you experience?" she wanted to know. The audience reacted with testimonials mentioning "heat, tingling," and a "pulling away feeling." "Would you describe it like a magnet pulling?" she asked. "Yes," responded eager members of the audience. "Is it bouncy?" "Yes" they replied, becoming more excited by the minute. She happily said that she had performed this "experiment" repeatedly on groups and she was always amazed at the similar results, which "demonstrate the energy available in our healing hands." Apparently this nurse researcher saw no conflict between the results obtained through her unscientific use of the power of suggestion with a noncontrolled sample and those one might obtain through careful study employing scientific methods.

INFLUENCE OF HOLISTS IN NURSING RESEARCH

This lack of rigid adherence to scientific methods for generating data is not uncommon in a large number of published reports dealing with holistic nursing practices. Although research conducted by nurses may be of the highest caliber, too often it is characterized by small convenience samples obtained through nonprobability methods and is of a single-shot, noncumulative variety. The theoretical perspective is more often psychological or psychosocial, not physiological in nature.[51]

Some researchers point to the difficulty of incorporating concepts dealing with holistic beings into traditional research designs as an explanation for the lack of quality research. Clearly, scientific methods would seem to be "reductionist" in character, and thus the antithesis of holism. Holism dictates that no phenomena may be reduced to discrete entities for analysis since the smallest part is inherently tied to and influenced by the larger. The accepted methods of science, in contrast, require objective observation of reality, narrowly defined into phenomena and precisely examined, tested, and interpreted.[52] The rigor of scientific method need not be an obstacle for the holistic researcher, however, since the economy of reductionism allows for simple studies based on holistic correlates.[53]

Studies that meet the criteria of science must be in greater evidence than they are now if those who advocate holistic practices in nursing wish to be taken seriously. The preponderance of superficial reports from poorly designed studies with no double-blind controlled methods, inexact measurements, inadequate baseline data, an absence of follow-up, and subjective findings simply do not lend credibility to holistic nursing claims. This is not to say that it is impossible to obtain reliable, repeatable data supporting these claims, but merely that it is not currently evident. Lacking such evidence, holistic nursing researchers would do well to draw more cautious conclusions from their work. Certainly one should refrain from making excuses for a lack of hard data, such as "a fuller appreciation and understanding [of psychic readings] may rest not so much in the accumulation of more data as in an enlightened shift in our cultural mores,"[54] or "all past medical research, denying the effect of consciousness on the body, may be hopelessly flawed."[55]

WHY HOLISM ENJOYS SUCCESS IN NURSING

Notwithstanding the lack of hard data, large numbers of nurses seem willing to accept the teachings of the holists and to adopt their practices. Perhaps this is because there is a ring of truth to much of what the holists are saying. I believe that this faith has its origins in what nursing believes to be its unique caring role, its historical orientation toward promoting wellness, and its concern for distinguishing itself from medicine as a profession. In addition to these considerations, many nurses lack the necessary knowledge and skills to evaluate scientific research. These four factors result in a profession ripe for successful conversion to holism. I will now discuss each in greater detail.

The Belief that Nursing is Unique

As noted earlier, nursing's traditional belief has been that it alone as a profession cares for the whole patient. Nurses do try to care for the needs of the mind and spirit as well as the body. But many believe this concern to be unique to nursing. In 1983 the American Nurses' Association published a white paper on the transition of the profession to a nursing model for practice. In this paper it was observed that "the physician views the client from the perspective of disease, reviews organ systems, and does laboratory tests to determine absence or presence of disease and to plan therapy. The dietician focuses on nutritional needs, the physical therapist on mobility needs, the social worker on roles and functions in society. *In contrast* [my italics], the nurse has a holistic view."[56] It has never been demonstrated that caring is unique to nursing, or that the nurses care for the whole patient in contrast to other health professionals. Nonetheless, these beliefs are repeated with such fervor in nursing education circles and in the literature that they are held to be truths.

Orientation toward Wellness

An orientation toward health and wellness can be identified in the writings of Florence Nightingale; thus, nursing has long concerned itself with helping the patient to heal himself. Codes for nursing speak of the "patients' right to appropriate instruction or education from health care personnel so that they can achieve an optimal level of wellness and an understanding of their basic health needs."[57] There is also a trend in nursing research away from studies of acute care and toward those of prevention and health promotion.[58] Current nursing theories emphasize that health exists independently of disease, and that it is possible to achieve wellness despite a pathologic condition that might otherwise be labeled as illness.

Concern for Differentiation from Medicine

The nursing profession's concern with differentiating itself from medicine is readily apparent to anyone who has studied the nursing literature or attended its professional meetings.[59] There is within nursing a strong need for a professional identity separate from that of medicine. This is altogether appropriate, but to many nurses this difference is embodied in the tenets of holism. Reductionism, or mind-body-spirit separation, is seen as a characteristic of Western medicine, but not of nursing.[60]

In addition, nursing considers itself to be more of a "caring" profession than a "curing" one, like medicine. This sentence from a university nursing catalog is typical: " . . . the science of caring . . . sets the nursing profession apart from other professions in its ability to combine the discipline and knowledge of science with the intangible qualities involved in human care."[61]

In its attempt to be recognized as a profession distinct from the medical model, nursing has increasingly looked to the behavioral and social sciences for its theoretical base and research decisions, rather than to the biological sciences. A review of theses and dissertations of nursing graduate schools will reveal this to be the case. In addition, nursing is actively engaged in developing its own diagnostic classification and has adopted its own euphemistic jargon different from that of medical terminology. Thus patients are referred to as clients, and pain is considered an alteration in comfort.

Nursing's attempt to separate itself from medicine is due to several factors. Certainly there is a dissatisfaction with the status of nurses compared to that of physicians. Nursing has long-standing and legitimate grievances with the medical profession. In the face of a dominating profession, the search to gain recognition and credibility has intensified as nurses become more highly educated and seek to exercise more control over nursing practice.

There is a widespread belief among nurses that physicians don't listen to what patients say, don't care for what they say, and don't meet the patient's total needs. It is felt that the analytic nature of modern Western medicine has resulted in a disregard for patients' complaints about their illness.[62] In addition, the medical profession can be ungenerous in its attitude toward nursing's role in patient care.

There is also a genuine concern shared by nurses for the need to develop a caring environment in the face of a health care delivery system that is increasingly technological. Many feel that the medical community ignores multiple causation factors for diseases and ill health (particularly environmental and psychological causes). Medicine is said to be concerned with pathology and nursing with health, as if the two concerns were either/or. As a result, holism is embraced not on the basis of good reasons and evidence, but rather as a way of differentiating between nursing and medicine.

Lack of Research Skills

Finally, many nurses have been swayed by holistic arguments due to a lack of sophisticated scientific skills and an inability to evaluate the quality of the research presented. In spite of serious attempts to be recognized as members of a scientific profession, nurses as a group lack a rigorous background in traditional science and its criteria for research.

Although the trend toward the baccalaureate degree as the minimal credential has increased, the majority of the profession does not have a full college degree. Even those with a degree may have had little exposure to research. Only five percent of nurses have either a master's or doctorate degree. Still worse, additional education beyond two years of technical nursing training may emphasize holistic themes, specialized jargon, and nontechnical social science rather than biomedicine. In addition, a very small percentage of practicing nurses subscribe to or understand research journals.[64] This dearth of research knowledge among nurses results in a tendency for many to accept the spurious claims of the holists, to ascribe more cause-effect relationships than are warranted by the data, and to accept testimonials or anecdotal reports as scientific fact.

CONCLUSION

It has been shown that holism influences nursing practice, education, and research and that it takes many forms. Much of holism is simply a restatement of nursing's traditional belief about its proper role in patient care. Nursing has always attempted and will continue to attempt to care for the "whole" patient, but this ideal is far from reality, since human needs reach beyond our ability to meet them. Yet few nurses openly question this holistic approach, because to do so gives the appearance of denying nursing's sacred allegiance to total patient care.

There are aspects of holism that are worthy and of obvious proven benefit, but it is already included in the practice of any reasonable nurse. Surely no one will fault the laudable goals of health education, disease prevention, and adoption of more healthful lifestyles. Clearly, many patients need to assume more responsibility for their own health and to be given the opportunity to participate more fully in their care. No thoughtful health care provider separates the body from the mind, knowing that each influences the other and at variable levels and varying times. These "holistic" ideas are neither new nor unique to nursing.

Nursing must resist uncritical adoption of unorthodox practices, meaningless and banal jargon, and unsupported claims of efficacy derived from poor data. Not to question the dubious claims and pronouncements of self-styled holistic nurses hinders the profession's long and continuing struggle to be recognized as a scientific discipline whose members derive their foundations for practice from a reasonable and supportable base of knowledge. Intuitive knowledge and faith are fine, but they should not be confused with scientific reason. We would do well to refer to the ANA Code for Nurses, [65] which clearly admonishes nurses to protect the public from misinformation and misrepresentation and to maintain the integrity of nursing.

Nursing is healing, but it is not sorcery. Most of all, beware of those who label themselves holists. Good nursing can include all the worthy elements of holistic nursing without the label.

NOTES

1. F. Nightingale, *Notes on Nursing-What It Is and It Is Not.* Facsimilie of 1859 edition. (Philadelphia: J. B. Lippincott, 1946), 79.

2. V. Henderson, *The Nature of Nursing* (New York: Macmillian Co., 1966), 15.

3. American Nurses Association, *Nursing: A Social Policy Statement* (Kansas City, Mo.: American Nurses Association, 1980), 9.

4. L. Kelly, *Dimensions of Professional Nursing,* 4th ed. (New York: Macmillian Co. 1981), 159.

5. H. Yura and M. Walsh, *The Nursing Process,* 3rd ed. (New York: Appleton-Century-Crofts, 1978), 197. See also J. Quinn, "Client Care and Nurse Involvement in a Holistic Framework," in D. Krieger. *Foundations for Holistic Health Nursing Practices: The Renaissance Nurse* (Philadelphia: J. B. Lippincott, 1981), 197–203.

6. G. Francis, "Gesellschaft and the Hospital: Is Total Care a Misnomer?" *Advances in Nursing Science* 2(1980):9.

7. F. Mastal and H. Hammond, "Analysis and Expansion of the Roy Adaptation Model: A Contribution to Holistic Nursing," *Advances in Nursing Science* 2(1980):72.

8. P. Chinn and J. Jacobs, *Theory and Nursing: A Systematic Approach* (St. Louis: C. V. Mosby, 1983), 38.

9. Ibid.

10. B. Blattner, *Holistic Nursing* (Englewood Cliffs, N.J.: Prentice-Hall, Inc. 1981), viii.

11. American Holistic Nurses Association. Membership Brochure (Telluride, Col.: American Holistic Nurses Association).

12. S. Narayan and D. Joslin, "Crisis Theory and Intervention: A Critique of the Medical Model and Proposal of a Holistic Nursing Model," *Advances in Nursing Science* 2(1980):35–36.

13. J. Luckmann and K. Sorensen, *Medical-Surgical Nursing: A Psychophysiologic Approach,* 2nd ed. (Philadelphia: W. B. Saunders, 1980).

14. M. Kinney, (ed.), *AACN'S Clinical Reference for Critical Care Nursing* (New York: McGraw Hill Book Co., 1981), 12.

15. C. Kenner, C. Guzzetta, and B. Dossey, *Critical Care Nursing: Body, Mind, and Spirit* (Boston: Little Brown and Co., 1981).

16. Ibid., xiii.

17. Ibid., 917–36.

18. D. Krieger, *Foundations for Holistic Health Nursing Practices: The Renaissance Nurse* (Philadelphia: J. B. Lippincott, 1981); Blattner, op. cit.; and P. Flynn, *Holistic Health: The Art and Science of Care* (Bowie, Md.: Robert J. Brady Co., 1980).

19. Krieger, op. cit., 89.

20. *Journal of the Holistic Nurses Association* 1(1983):42.

21. *Beginnings* (Telluride, Col.: American Holistic Nurses Association, 1982), vol. 1, no. 1, 3.

22. Ibid., 1.

23. Texas Womens University Catalog (Denton, Texas: Texas Womens University, 1980–82), 208.

24. Northwestern State University of Louisiana, College of Nursing (Shreveport, La.: 1983).

25. American Association of Critical-Care Nurses, *Proceedings of National Teaching Institutes, 1983–84* (Newport Beach, Calif.: AACN).

26. *Nursing Times* vol. 80, no. 18, (1984).

27. L. Talabere, "The Child with a Tracheostomy: A Holistic Approach to Home Care," *Topics in Clinical Nursing* 2(1980):27–44. See also S. Hosteadt, and G. Wolfarth, "The Child as a Psychobiological Being—Implications for Health Care," *Topics in Clinical Nursing* 3(1982):29–34; D. Alford, "Expanding Older Person's Belief Systems," *Topics in Clinical Nursing* 3(1982): 35–44; V. Hine, "Holistic Dying: the Role of the Nurse Clinician," *Topics in Clinical Nursing* 3(1982):45–

-54; and C. Clark, "Women and Arthritis: Holistic/Wellness Perspectives," *Topics in Clinical Nursing* 4(1983):45-55.

28. B. Dossey, "Holistic Nursing: How to Make it Work for You," *Journal of Holistic Nursing* 1(1983):32.

29. S. Cafoncelli, "Body as a Hologram," *Beginnings*, vol. 1, no. 11, (1982):3.

30. E. Ercolano, "Caring for Patients Who Use the Gerson Method—An Unorthodox Nutritional Program of Cancer Management," *Journal of Holistic Nursing* 1(1983):27.

31. Ibid., 29.

32. Ibid., 30.

33. Krieger, op. cit., 83.

34. J. Achterberg and F. Lawlis, "Imagery and Health Intervention," *Topics in Clinical Nursing* 3(1982):58.

35. D. Box, "Made in Japan," *Nursing Times* 80(1984):39.

36. L. Kolkmeier, "Biofeedback-Relaxation Therapy for Hypertension," *Topics in Clinical Nursing* 3(1982):68.

37. N. Lovejoy, "Biofeedback: A Growing Role in Holistic Health," *Advances in Nursing Science* 2(1980):92.

38. D. Ryman, "The Sweet Smell of Success?" *Nursing Times* 80(1984):48.

39. Krieger, op. cit., 146.

40. Ibid., 138.

41. Ibid.

42. Ibid., 146; see also New York University College of Nursing, *A Report to the Profession: Nursing Research Emphasis Grant for Doctoral Programs in Nursing.* (NYU School for Education, Health, Nursing, and Arts Professions, Division of Nursing), 8.

43. J. Quinn, "Introduction to the Therapeutic Touch," lecture presented at AACN National Teaching Institute (American Association of Critical-Care Nurses: Dallas, May, 1984).

44. Blattner, op. cit., 84.

45. Krieger, op. cit., 141.

46. P. Clark, and M. Clark, "Therapeutic Touch: Is There a Scientific Basis for the Practice?" *Nursing Research* 33(1984):39.

47. Ibid., 37.

48. Blattner, op. cit., 88.

49. Clark and Clark, op. cit., 40; see also G. Randolph, "Therapeutic and Physical Touch: Physiological Response to Stressful Stimuli," *Nursing Research* 33(1984):35; and R. Heidt, "Effect of Therapeutic Touch on Anxiety Levels of Hospitalized Patients," *Nursing Research* 30(1981):32.

50. J. Quinn, op. cit.

51. J. Brown, C. Tanner, and K. Padrick, "Nursing's Search for Scientific Knowledge," *Nursing Research* 33(1984):29.

52. Chinn, op. cit., 41.

53. P. Winsteadt-Fry, "The Scientific Method and its Impact on Holistic Health," *Advances in Nursing Science* 2(1980):5.

54. Krieger, op. cit., 92.

55. K. Prist, "Healing Crisis: Emergence of the New Medical Model," *Beginnings,* vol. 2, no. 5, (1983):3.

56. American Nurses Association, Division of Medical-Surgical Nursing Practice, Transition to a Nursing Model for Practice: An Opportunity to Clarify, Control, and Improve Nursing Practice (Kansas City, Mo.: ANA, 1983), 2.

57. Kelly, op. cit., 181.

58. Brown, op. cit., 28.

59. J. Rogers, "Toward Professional Adulthood. For Nursing or Against Medicine: A Group Replay of the Second Indviduation Process," *Nursing Outlook* 29(1981):478.

60. ANA, "Transition to a Nursing Model," op. cit., 7.

61. University of California, San Francisco, School of Nursing, Information Brochure, *The Science of Caring: 1983*.

62. Krieger, op. cit., 46.

63. American Nurses Association, "Facts About Nursing 82–83," (Kansas City, Mo.: ANA, 1983), 2.

64. Kelly, op. cit., 258.

65. American Nurses Association. *Code for Nurses with Interpretive Statements* (Kansas City, Mo.: ANA, 1976).

Part II

Examining Holistic Philosophy

Austen Clark, Ph.D.

Psychological Causation and the Concept of Psychosomatic Disease

Holism starts with a profound dissatisfaction over the explanations provided by orthodoxy, offers what it proposes to be a superior account, and on that basis argues for sweeping changes in current practice. In many ways a focus of this dissatisfaction is the traditional medical understanding of psychosomatic disease. Orthodox medicine, the charge goes, fails to understand the role of the mind in disease and in cure; and, furthermore, it cannot understand that role—its concepts and methods are simply inadequate to cope with psychological causation. Only a new holistic paradigm can set things aright. This new paradigm will provide radically new modalities of treatment that will harness the curative powers of the mind for the first time.

Rhetorically, this gambit often yields dividends, for in truth orthodox medicine seems uncomfortable with psychosomatic phenomena. To suggest that mental states cause lesions (such as those found in a perforated duodenal ulcer) seems to smack of occult energies and magic. To diagnose a disease as "psychosomatic" appears to admit etiological factors that are outside the scope of biomedical investigation and whose mechanism of action is unknown. Some practitioners feel that such a diagnosis somehow carries the implication that the disorder is not real, or (confusingly) real only in the patient's mind. In these and other ways talk of the mind leads to a queasy feeling of metaphysical trespass. Indeed, so often has the mind been the traditional home of the occult, parapsychological, and spiritualistic that traditional medicine feels an understandable reluctance to be seen anywhere in the neighborhood.

I will examine the concept of psychosomatic disease and the use to which it is put by holists. I hope to provide an analysis of psychosomatic phenomena that relieves some metaphysical distress and stakes out some clear property lines between itself and the occult. The holists' charge of conceptual inadequacy can easily be defeated, and I will show how their account of mind-body relations suffers from debilitating incoherencies.

THE HOLISTIC ARGUMENT ABOUT PSYCHOSOMATIC DISEASE

"Psychosomatic disease" is a critical concept for the holists. Consider, for example, the definition of holistic medicine offered by Kenneth Pelletier, one of the most articulate spokesmen of the movement:

> Drawing upon numerous sources, it is possible to formulate several criteria for a fundamental working definition for holistic medicine. First, all states of health and all disorders are considered to be psychosomatic.[1]

or

> . . . all disorders are psychosomatic, in the sense that both mind and body are involved in their etiology.[2]

It is clear, then, that the claim that "all diseases are psychosomatic" is important; it is unclear, however, what the claim *means*. Just what is the holistic argument concerning the role of the mind in disease? What sort of evidence is taken to support such claims? What sort of implications are drawn from them? In this section, I shall describe the holistic position in as strong and convincing a form as can be found. Later sections will be concerned with analyzing its import. I shall focus on the version presented by Kenneth Pelletier in *Mind as Healer, Mind as Slayer* because it is well articulated, influential, and representative of the movement. Pelletier is by no means alone in ascribing central significance to the concept of psychosomatic disease; these arguments are found in many different holistic sources, and parallels will be noted as appropriate.[3]

Pelletier begins by examining diseases currently labelled psychosomatic (or stress-related) such as peptic ulcer, asthma, essential hypertension, colitis, arthritis, and others.[4] These disorders share two characteristics: (1) their physiological etiology is unknown and (2) psychological factors seem to be implicated in their genesis. For them Pelletier proposes a standard diathesis-stress model,[5] in which

> a neurophysiological imbalance is precipitated by stressful life events and channeled through a particular personality configuration, resulting in a specific disorder.[6]

"Stress" is universal in such diseases, and is the precipitating cause of the disorder.[7] Diathesis (constitution) determines which disorder and which symptoms will result from that stress.

What justifies the (critical) move from the claim that stress is involved in *some* disease to the claim that it is involved in *all* disease? The key to generalizing this model lies in the mechanism proposed for the effects of stress. Pelletier cites classic psychosomatic studies[8] to argue that stress affects resistance to infection. Suppose psychologically identified stressors suppress the ability of the body to resist infection. If that is so, then (assuming a relatively constant level of pathogens in the environment) more of the variation in whether and when one becomes ill is explained by the changing status of one's endocrine and immuno-logical systems than by variations in that relatively constant assault. Ability to resist disease is in turn to be explained by the level of stress that one has recently undergone.

The various "life change" studies of R. H. Rahe and others seem to support this notion; they found high correlations between the amount of stress and serious illness even among a collection of naval personnel on the same ship.[9] Since the naval personnel were presumably all exposed to essentially the same infectious agents, what explains a sailor's illness at a certain time is not primarily the infectious agent he encountered, but rather the state of his immunological system as affected by recent life changes. In that sense, then, stress is the critical variable, and not the presence or absence of a pathogen. Psychological factors explain who gets sick and when in a way that biochemical and orthodox medicine cannot; they explain some variance left unexplained by traditional medicine. On the grounds that this is true of all diseases, then, all diseases are psycho-somatic.[10]

Pelletier cites estimates of the role of psychological factors in disease from a "conservative" 50-to-70 percent to a full 100 percent, then he says:

> A basic assumption in the latter estimate is that all psychological, psychosomatic, and physical disorders and illnesses are either caused or aggravated by psycho-physiological stress, and that therefore all illness and disease is comprised of the interaction of psychological and physical factors.[11]

Since bodily systems for fighting infection are critically important in all illnesses, and stress suppresses such systems, we have a psychological factor (stress) impli-cated in the etiology of all disease.

Now even if this claim were true it would not demonstrate an irremediable conceptual insufficiency in traditional medicine or a need to overhaul completely its concepts of treatment. After all, psychosomatic medicine has coexisted with orthodox medicine. But the holists employ the concept of psychosomatic disease to build a much broader indictment of orthodox medicine.

Pelletier and other holists argue that traditional medicine has an inadequate account of psychosomatic disease and that its concepts and methods make such a failure inevitable. Traditional medicine describes the anatomical, physiological, and biochemical states of a person, and does not include mental states in its theories of etiology. To do so requries a new conceptual paradigm—the holistic one—which can treat the totality of a person, and not just his or her bodily parts. This new view of the cause of disease is our only hope for successful treatments:

> Attempts to curb the incidence of psychosomatic disease through traditional medical methods are likely to be ineffective, since their alleviation requires the adoption of a new paradigm of mind/body interaction that is oriented toward health.[12]

To many holists, psychosomatic disease demonstrates a limitation on the concepts and methods of traditional medicine. To overcome that limitation requires not merely adding etiological factors within the conceptual framework of orthodox medicine, but rather modifying that framework itself and providing new ways of understanding and explaining disease—a new "paradigm" for medicine.[13]

What is the limitation? The etiological factors addressed by traditional medicine describe some physical property of some part or the whole of the patient's body. "Stress" and "life change" are nowhere found among those factors. Hence, some holists argue, orthodox medicine can only deal with physiological factors; it ignores the role of the mind. But since stress and other psychological factors are important in explaining the incidence of disease, orthodox medicine fails to adequately explain disease. Its conceptual framework has no resistance, so to speak, but collapses immediately when confronted by stress.

This is one source of the holistic slogan that a person is more than the sum of his parts, and that traditional medicine only deals with the parts. One might wonder what is left over after a full inventory of those parts; the holistic response is that such a list leaves out the *mind.*

Along with major changes in understanding disease, the holistic paradigm proposes radical revision in treatment regimens. The argument is that if psychological factors play a significant role in the etiology of $D,$ then any treatment for D must include some component for manipulating those psychological factors. To "treat the whole person, and not just his parts" means in this context also to treat his mind; or, more generally, to treat whatever psychological factors are contributing to the disease. In effect, all medical treatment must include a psychotherapeutic element: an intervention intended to alter psychological functioning.[14]

Now if the holistic view were merely that treatment has psychological effects and that some aspects of treatment are intended to secure some of those effects, then it would trivially apply to current practices, and no change at all would be needed. The claim, however, is much stronger than that; it is that psychological processes are *etiological* (and not merely ancillary) in whatever malady the physician is treating; and that those psychological aspects of treatment are therapeutic in just the same way as an antibiotic or a surgical intervention. They have a direct causal impact on the pathogenic factors leading to symptoms. The medical student is then faced with the daunting task of becoming not only a physician, but a psychotherapist as well.

SOME INITIAL DISTINCTIONS

To evaluate the preceding argument, the first task is to clarify the import of the term "psychosomatic." One can distinguish at least three different characteristics of cases to which that term is applied. Some of these characteristics may in some cases overlap; others are mutually exclusive. Much of the conceptual difficulty over "psychosomatic" disease is due to these ambiguities. Some practitioners question the medical legitimacy of all the categories. I do not wish to prejudge the latter question, but at the outset merely describe their logical features.

A. Distortion in Symptom Reporting

Sometimes the term "psychosomatic" is meant to imply that patient reports concerning symptoms and complaints are inaccurate and do not obey ordinary norms of patient-physician communication. This is not a euphemism for lying; cases in which patients know their complaints are false and intend to deceive are "malingering," not "psychosomatic disorder." However, there are cases in which patients believe their reports and have no intent to deceive, yet their descriptions of symptoms do not correspond to observable indices in any ordinary way. In some cases there may be *no* corroborating physical evidence for a problem reported by a patient. Instead the patient seems to employ different standards of severity for terms used to report pain and other symptoms. An example is hypochondriacal complaints. One denies the severity or occurrence of reported symptoms; this is the sense one uses when they are said to be "only" psychosomatic.

How does one discount reported symptoms, and instead identify the problem as the reporting behavior? There is no corroborating physical evidence of structural or functional change. The patient may report severe pain yet manifest none of the insomnia, elevated heart rate, sweaty palms, and so on that usually accompany it. History may be inconsistent, and syndromes may fail to correspond to any known disorder. Regimens appropriate to the complaint yield no symptom relief. One may find some motive for the continued visits: a need for attention, insecurity, and so on.

In such a case there is no medical problem; instead, the problem is exactly that visits nevertheless continue. The problem is comprised of distorted communication with the physician, unconventional semantics, inaccurate avowals, and unnecessary and wasteful visits to health care providers. In such a case the physician is helpless to cure the psychosomatic disorder since there is no such disorder to be cured. Since the problem is behavioral, there is a clear implication that some nonmedical intervention (perhaps psychotherapy) is required to deal with it.

To call this sort of case "psychosomatic" is essentially a euphemism for a behavioral problem whose locus happens to be the medical profession. While euphemisms are useful, literally speaking no disease *can* be psychosomatic in this sense. There is no psychosomatic disease in this category, for the simple reason that this sense of the term "psychosomatic" carries the implication that there is no *disease* present.

B. Inadequate Physiological Etiology

For some "psychosomatic" disorders, however, one does not deny the reality or the severity of symptoms, and one admits a genuine alteration or loss of certain functions, so unlike cases of distortion in symptom reporting, we admit both the symptomatology and the alteration of function generally associated with disease. However, for these disorders there is no known organic basis: one discovers no structural change, lesion, or damage in tissue that causes the reported disorder. Asthma and colitis are examples. Disorders in which there is loss of function with no known structural change are also sometimes called "functional" diseases.

The critical difference between cases of A and B is that for B one finds corroborating evidence for alteration of function. Without clear alteration of function, the absence of organic signs may lead one to discount the patient's reports of symptoms, and the case collapses into A. The simplest explanation for the hypochondriac who complains of pain, yet shows normal tissue function and none of the concomitants of pain, may be that "it doesn't hurt that much" and so the symptoms are denied. In other cases there is an admitted malfunction or loss of function in tissue, and one does not deny presence of a disease.

An interesting conundrum emerges if the main evidence for alteration of function is that of patient reports, as in some cases of "hysterical" anesthesias. A behavioral test that shows sensitivity is present—despite patient denials—would immediately classify the "disorder" as psychosomatic in sense A rather than B. A hysterically "blind" individual who can successfully navigate around misplaced furniture has no loss of visual function, but rather reports that visual function in a distorted way.

The fact that there is no known organic basis for a disease does not imply that it has no organic basis, but merely that if there is one, it is as yet undiscovered. That colitis is a functional disorder means simply that its etiology is unknown, not that it has no physiological cause. Perhaps the alteration in structure is at the molecular level, and simply escapes detection. In any case, the single characteristic of "no known organic basis" is surely insufficient to classify a disease as psychosomatic, as it would imply that all diseases of unknown etiology are psychosomatic. "Psychosomatic" in this case functions as a euphemism for "unknown etiology." To obtain some legitimate taxonomic principle we need to consider a third category.

C. Psychological Contribution to Etiology

A major class of cases called "psychosomatic" add to the characteristics of B—alteration of function with an inadequate physiological etiology—the characteristic that psychological factors make a significant contribution to etiology. There may or may not be an organic change or structural alteration involved in the loss of function; in duodenal ulcers one finds a lesion, while in conversion hysteria there may be no structural change. Similarly, there may or may not be known physiological factors in the etiology; allergies may involve both psychological and physiological factors, while some disorders (conversion hysteria) may have no known physiological basis.

This sense of "psychosomatic" is, I submit, the central concept. An ulcer is psychosomatic in that psychological factors contribute to its genesis. There is no implication that an ulcerated patient exaggerates or in any way distorts reports of symptoms. Nor do we rule out structural alterations in tissue or physiological factors in its etiology. The central concept of psychosomatic disease, as illustrated by the ulcer, is a disease to which psychological factors contribute.

Psychological causation is also the sense intended by holists when they claim that all diseases are psychosomatic. As Pelletier notes:

> In traditional medicine, the term "psychosomatic" refers to a disorder which persists in the absence of clearly diagnosed organic pathology. Despite the apparent absence of organic pathology, the symptoms and the individual's complaints of distress continue unabated. In cases such as this, it is quite common for many practitioners to assume that the disorder is nonexistent, imaginary, hypochondrical, or, in short, has no real basis. These disorders are termed "psychosomatic," which has become synonymous with "imaginary." However, in the context of a holistic model of health care, and in this book, the term "psychosomatic" has quite a different meaning. Here it is used to convey the concept of a fundamental interaction between mind and body which is involved in all diseases and all processes affecting health maintenance.[15]

Pelletier here claims the traditional concept combines senses A and B, inferring distortion in patient reports and an absence of genuine symptoms from inability to discover some structural alteration of tissue. This claim seems dubious; there are clear syndromes of type B that are not type A.

In any case, the sense in which all diseases are psychosomatic is clearly intended to be neither A nor B, but rather C. It is clearly false to claim that all patients report nonexistent symptoms, or that all diseases have an inadequately understood physiological etiology. The holistic claim then is that psychological factors contribute to the etiology of all disease.

This claim is so often confused with other ones that it will be useful to distinguish it immediately from some of its near relatives.

First, many diseases have psychological side effects, and some have psychological effects that are immediate consequences of the morbid process defining the disease. Korsakoff's syndrome and tertiary syphilis have profound effects on psychological processes because of their effects on brain tissue. Cancer has a side effect of depressing many patients.

It is important to distinguish psychological side effects *of* disease from psychological effects *on* disease. The former are incidental to the particular morbid process that defines the identity of the disease. One can treat the depression resulting from cancer without treating cancer. So even spectacular changes in psychological functioning of patients fail to demonstrate any psychological cause of the disease.[16] One must show that the given psychological factor contributes to cause the morbid process itself. It must help cause the *disease.* Demonstrating an impact on the psychological side effects of that process does not suffice to show this.

Similarly, to show a curative power of the mind, one must show that the given psychological factor causes an alteration in the tissue pathology. In all of the vast literature of miraculous cures, placebo effects, and so on, it is extremely rare to find any documentation of a change in the pathological process of a disease, as opposed to change in the patient's mood, outlook, or behaviors—that is, in psychological side effects of the disease.

Now of course ordinary medical practice has powerful psychological effects (in terms of patient expectations of cure, trust in the physician, emotional concomitants of disease and treatment, and so on); and furthermore many of the ancillary aspects of treatment (e.g., reassuring the patient and communicating confidence in the success of treatment) are employed precisely because of their psychological effects. Traditional medicine accepts a clear responsibility to treat psychological side effects of disease, such as depression following a heart attack or a cancer diagnosis. Such treatments must clearly be distinguished from treatments affecting the disease itself.

A second psychological effect that is irrelevant to the thesis is any one that alters patient beliefs and reports concerning symptoms. Innumerable psychological processes are involved in the patient's perception of the severity of disease and the reporting of symptoms. Pain perception is a species of perception, after all, and has been shown to be sensitive to psychological processes, such as context effects, beliefs, suggestion, the focus of attention, and so on.[17] These processes can alter the severity of felt pain, and it is presumably processes such as these that are at work in hypochodriacs and others in our type A "psychosomatic" disease above.

Quite apart from the perception of discomfort, the formation of beliefs concerning symptoms and the reporting of those beliefs in an interview require flawless function in numerous other psychological capacities: a grasp of the semantics of terms employed, an ability to categorize and identify, as well as judgment, memory, and comparison. Alteration in these functions can drastically alter the reported severity of symptoms. For this reason changes in a patient's felt discomfort and reported symptoms do not themselves suffice to show any effect on the disease process. One may simply influence the psychological processes involved in pain perception and the reporting of symptoms.

Presumably such effects are *not* the ones holists have in mind. All diseases are psychosomatic not in the sense that their reported severity depends on such psychological processes (a truism) but rather in the sense that psychological processes can affect the morbidity process itself. There is a causal link between states of mind and the process of ulceration, for example. One's mental set does not merely influence the severity of pain, or one's reports of its severity, or the psychological concomitants of having an ulcer: it affects the ulcerative process itself.

Some further clarification is needed concerning the notion of 'cause' invoked by the holists. What does it mean to say that psychological factors "contribute to the etiology" of some disease?

Etiology is of course the sum of knowledge concerning the causes of disease; and to say that psychological factors contribute etiologically is to say that they contribute to the causation of the disease. But there is a great deal of confusion in the holistic literature over the meaning of this latter phrase. Holists complain, for example, that no disease can be explained in a simple "cause and effect" manner and that traditional medicine suffers from an overemphasis on single identifiable causes of disease.[18] Holists claim that no disease has a single cause; every disease must be explained by a combination of factors, some physiological and some psychological.

Now if this latter claim means simply that for no disease D can one find a single factor X that invariably causes it, then the holists are correct; but the traditional concept is in no way committed to such an oversimplification. There are always other background conditions that are presumed present and necessary for factor X to have an effect. Such conditions are "necessary" conditions for the effect in the sense that their absence prevents the effect. Even swallowing some acutely infectious toxin causes death only if the person does not immediately afterwards have his stomach pumped and has not recently ingested an antidote. If we let C stand for all those other conditions, then to say "the cause of death was ingestion of the toxin" is to say that given conditions C, ingesting the toxin was a sufficient condition for death, and that every condition in C, as well as X itself, was necessary for death.

Similarly, to say that some psychological factor P contributes to the etiology of some disease D in a particular patient is to say that in that patient there is a set of conditions C under which P is necessary and sufficient for D. That patient would not have had disease D if he had not had psychological factor P, and he has D because of P. To say "Joe's anxiety caused his ulcer" is to say that there were conditions C in Joe that were not alone sufficient for the ulcer, all of which were, however, necessary for the development of the ulcer, and when combined with his anxiety sufficed to lead to the ulcer. Even given those conditions C, Joe would not have gotten an ulcer had he not been so anxious.

Such at least is the standard "regularity" view of causation.[19] It can cope quite easily with holistic hackles concerning multiple causal factors. To say that psychological factor P contributes to the etiology of disease D is on this line to be analyzed as asserting that:

(1) there is a set of conditions C each of which is necessary for D yet none of which alone or in combination are sufficient for D; and

(2) under those conditions C, D occurs just in case P does (P is a necessary and sufficient condition for D).

Conditions C for a gastric ulcer may require the patient to have an abnormally thin stomach wall. They may include characteristics of the functioning of the vagus nerve, levels of hydrochloric acid secretion, dietary considerations, and so on. But for any patients in whom conditions C are present, whether or not they get an ulcer depends on whether or not they manifest P. For them, given conditions C, P is both necessary and sufficient for D.

Notice that any of the factors included in C meet all the conditions specified for the cause P. Just as Joe would not have had an ulcer had he not been so anxious, so he would not have had an ulcer had he not had a vagus nerve. Why not say the cause of his ulcer is the presence of the vagus nerve? The reason has more to do with the pragmatics of explanation than with any logical priority among the clusters of conditions. That is, when explaining the ulcer in Joe one takes for granted those conditions constant for Joe. The presence of the vagus nerve is a given; it was present both before and after the time Joe got his ulcer; and it does not help to explain what changed between those times. Any factor common to situations in which one does and does not observe the effect can be allowed to recede in this way into the "causal background" or "causal field," which is presumed in such explanations.[20] Those are conditions necessary for the occurrence of the effect, yet they cannot explain the change.

A particular instance I of disease D might be caused by P even though other cases have different causes. It is logically permissible to ascribe anxiety as the cause of Joe's ulcer even though one admits that in other individuals there are other combinations of factors that lead to ulcers. Perhaps some of those combinations of factors include nothing psychological.

Because of this possibility, we get a strong and a weak reading for the holistic claim that "all diseases are psychosomatic." The strong reading is that for every instance I of every disease D there is some psychological factor F such that if F had not occurred then that instance I of D would not have occurred. On the strong reading, every cluster of factors sufficient to lead to a disease includes a psychological component as a necessary part.

The strong reading is certainly strong; it is also certainly false. Surely some instances of some diseases have no psychological component in their etiology. Infections during coma, infantile diseases, and genetically transmitted disorders seem to leave little or no room for the mind to make a difference. Often the mind is not even present at the scene. Even if it is, some pathogens seem potent enough to make anyone sick, regardless of their state of mind. In those instances of disease, psychological factors make no difference.

A weaker reading is possible, however. "All diseases are psychosomatic" may be taken to mean that for every disease D there is some instance I of D for which there is some psychological factor F that caused I (so that I would not have occurred had F not occurred). This weaker reading would require that every disease has some instance that would not have occurred were a certain psychological factor absent. However, the weaker reading allows that there can be combinations of factors sufficient to lead to disease in which no psychological component exists. So, for example, "ulcers are psychosomatic" would in effect mean "some instances of ulceration are psychologically caused" while allowing that some other instances of the disease might be produced by a combination of factors that does not need to contain anything psychological. It may be that in some individuals with hypersecretion of gastric acid, a particular set of enzymes, and a thin stomach wall, ulceration will occur whatever their psychological attitude, be it ever so tranquil.

On this weaker reading, for every disease there must be cases in which psychological factors are the critical ones for disease: where the combination of factors C is insufficient for D, yet the addition of P "makes the difference" and yields D. In those cases the disease would not have occurred but for the presence of the psychological factor P. Is there yet a weaker reading, according to which a disease can be psychosomatic even though in none of its cases is a psychological factor in this way critical? Such a possibility can, I believe, be refuted on logical grounds. In effect this weakest reading would have us accept a disease D as psychosomatic even though in none of its instances do psychological factors make the difference between the presence or the absence of the disease. Hence, in all cases the set of factors C sufficient to bring about D includes no tint of the psychological; we need never mention a psychological factor to give a sufficient explanation for the occurrence of the disease. And if it is *never* necessary to cite psychological factors to explain an occurrence of D, what possible reason could there be for claiming D is psychosomatic? So the weakest reading can be ignored. At the very least, to show disease D is psychosomatic, one must show that there are some cases in which the presence or absence of some psychological factor makes the difference between the presence or absence of the disease.

EXPLAINING PSYCHOLOGICAL CAUSATION

The upshot is that to show that a disease is psychosomatic, one must show that a psychological state (such as anxiety) causes a physical state (such as ulceration). This implication has been taken by many to be a *reductio ad absurdum* of the very idea of psychosomatic disease. How can a state of mind cause a lesion? Doesn't this suggestion fly in the face of orthodox physiology by requiring occult energies dabbling in the digestive tract?

To this question many holists respond with an enthusiastic affirmative, and in effect say "so much the worse for orthodoxy" (as I will show below). But are mind/body causal relations incompatible with orthodox medicine? The implications of causal relations between mind and body depend entirely on one's theory of the mind; in particular, on one's interpretation of the meaning of the term "psychological factor." That term has all this time been lurking unmolested in our definitions, and it is now time to scrutinize its credentials.

For all the eeriness one can invoke over claims causally relating mind and body, such claims are extremely commonplace. Anger causes the face to flush. Teenage drunkenness causes traffic accidents. Your decision to pick up a loaf of bread caused you to turn left at the intersection. Just as commonplace are connections from the body to the mind. Fever caused the delirium. A condition of neurons in your retina caused that yellowy-orange afterimage. Fibers firing in fingertips caused a burning sensation. Do all these claims of causal commerce between mind and body infest our bodies, hospitals, and highways with occult energies?

It all depends on one's theory of the mind, and in particular on one's theory of the relationships between mental events and physical events. These problems lead into a tangle of philosophical theories and concepts, and before entering the fray it is necessary to provide some initial orientation.

Some Definitional Landmarks

What exactly is the oddity of supposing that a state of mind can cause a lesion? It might be put as follows. One typically thinks that lesions are results of various physiological processes, and that their genesis can be entirely explained by citing those processes. For a state of mind to enter such a list of causes seems to imply the intervention of some additional external factor (the mental state) that causes changes typically brought about by physiological means. One ordinarily assumes that explanations of physiological events need only cite physiological antecedents. The addition of psychological factors seems to violate that assumption, and adds a new kind of antecedent. So "anxiety caused the ulcer" is odd because it seems "anxiety" is no physiological antecedent. This view—that "anxiety" is not a physiological state, or more generally that no mental state is a physiological state—is known as dualism. More formally:

DUALISM: No mental state is identical to a physical state.

By "identical to" I mean "is the same thing as" (more on this in a moment). The dualist claims that the mind is something distinct from the body, which can perhaps survive the death of the body. A person is made up of a combination of two things: mind plus body.

Much of the confusion concerning this claim derives from the notion of identity. To say "x is identical to y" is to say that the name "x" and the name "y" are both names for the same thing. The names "x" and "y" both refer to, identify, or pick out just the same individual or thing. For example, "The fortieth president of the United States is identical to the former star of 'Lone Cowboy'" implies that the person picked out by the term "fortieth president of the United States" is just the same person as the one picked out by "the former star of 'Lone Cowboy,'" namely, Ronald Reagan.

Two logical features of identity claims are critical to understanding their import. First, two descriptions can both refer to just the same thing even though the descriptions have different meanings. For example, "gene" and "DNA nucleotide sequence" mean very different things, in that "gene" is defined by a Mendelian theory of the inheritance of traits, while "DNA nucleotide sequence" is a term derived from molecular biochemistry. The techniques one employs to identify a particular gene require inheritance studies, and differ markedly from the techniques employed to identify a particular DNA nucleotide sequence—which requires biochemical assay. Yet a gene is identical to a DNA nucleotide sequence: the two terms refer to just the same thing. Notice that this identity claim was a significant empirical *discovery;* like many identities, it is not vacuous or true by definition, but requires investigation. So even though identity claims link two expressions in a language, and assert that those two expressions refer to the same thing, such claims are *not* established by linguistic stipulation, but may require empirical investigation.

Second, if x is identical to y, then all the properties of x are shared by y (and conversely). The reason is simply that "x" and "y" name the same thing, and so all the properties of that thing can be truly ascribed both to x and to y. The second planet in our solar system is Venus, so all the properties of the second planet are properties of Venus. If the second planet has mass k, then Venus has mass k. The atmosphere of the second planet has the same thickness and composition as that of Venus, since they are the same atmosphere.

These points should help to clarify the import of the denial of dualism,[21] namely,

MATERIALISM: Every mental state is identical to some physical state.

The materialist does not think that mind is distinct from body, but instead that mental functioning is (identical to) some subset of physiological functioning. So, for example, an attack of anxiety is identical to some physiological event. To the objection that "anxiety" does not mean the same as any physiological term, the materialist will respond that his thesis does not require that it should, just as "gene" and "DNA nucleotide sequence" can have different meanings yet turn out to refer to just the same stuff. The materialist points to other examples of scientifically discovered identities as examplars of the import of the mind/body identity claim. For example, lightning is identical to electrostatic discharge, even though the terms have different meanings and the claim required empirical investigation. Water is identical to H_2O, even though one term is defined in English and the other in chemistry.

The materialist urges that mental function is identical to some as-yet-to-be discovered features of brain function. This claim is put forward as a reasonable scientific hypothesis, not a thesis about our language. It cannot be defeated by showing differences in meaning of the terms.[22]

Dualism and materialism cut the philosophical terrain neatly in two; a cross cut is required to cover views on the causal relations between mind and body. On one hand we have:

INTERACTIONISM: Some mental events cause some physical events.

An interactionist is one who accepts some causal traffic from mind to body. On the other hand we have:

EPIPHENOMENALISM: No mental event ever causes a physical event.

An epiphenomenalist denies the existence of mental causes for physical effects.[23] An "epiphenomenon" of x is a phenomenon that occurs with x yet has no effects on x. For example, a shadow is an epiphenomenon of a walker, in that it covaries with the walk yet has no effect on it. Mental states are here claimed to be epiphenomena of brain states.

Of this latter pair interactionism is the candidate overwhelmingly favored by common sense. Why would one deny the prima facie obvious claim that mind and body interact?

The contrast between interactionism and epiphenomenalism is important primarily for dualists, who (as will be seen) have difficulties in explaining causal relations between mind and body. Materialists have no such problem; for them mental states are just physical states, and the problem of understanding causal relations between those physical states (the mind) and other physical states (the body) is no more difficult than understanding causal relations just among physical states. For this reason a materialist has no difficulties in endorsing the common sense view that sometimes states of mind cause bodily events; for him all such causation is just a species of physical causation.[24]

Note that "interactionism" is in some ways an unfortunate label for a materialist, as it sometimes carries the implication of two distinct things influencing one another. This connotation should be avoided; as I am using the term, "interaction" applies to anyone, dualist or materialist, who allows causal relations from mental states to physical states. For a materialist, the "interaction" is a relation between some subset of physiological processes (the ones we happen to refer to with our psychological terms) and others; there are not two things, but just different states of one thing, named with different terms.

A dualist who wishes to endorse interaction has difficulties, however, as will be argued below. Some dualists respond by retaining the dualism and dropping interaction. Although it certainly appears that mental events sometimes cause physical events, such theorists hold that appearance to be an illusion: the changes are merely correlated with one another. How can one explain why it so persistently seems as if mental states cause bodily events? Epiphenomenalists rely on the correlations between mental and physical histories. The raised leg of the shadow does not cause the walker's foot to fall; it may give that appearance, but only because the shadow so persistently covaries with the cause—that is, the walker. As the appeal of that explanation waned, so did dualistic epiphenomenalism. The contenders left on the field are in practice all of the interactionist persuasion, and are divided between dualists and materialists, lately with the latter favored.

The Theory of Mind of the Holists

Armed with these distinctions, we can now specify the theory of mind underlying the holistic concept of psychosomatic disease. It is abundantly clear that holists are interactionists, and they claim that interactionism distinguishes them significantly from traditional medicine. Many holists accuse orthodox medicine of a failure to recognize the causal role of the mind. For example, Pelletier notes that many of the contemporary healing professions employ "a philosophical and clinical orientation that essentially dismisses all psychological factors in disorders and considers both disease and health maintenance to be based upon purely physical considerations."[25] Pelletier proposes to replace this epiphenomenalistic view with

> the equally tenable hypothesis that mind and body are engaged in inextricable interaction. Setting aside philosophical arguments, this position is highly viable as a pragmatic means of approaching such phenomena as psychosomatic disorders and in related areas of medicine wherein the negative effects of that putative interaction would seem to be vividly manifested.[26]

He claims that evidence of interaction is incompatible with the current "paradigm":

> Each day, researchers make new discoveries, but some of these are rejected because they point to interactions that are considered unacceptable under the dominant scientific paradigms. Examples of these anomalies are the role of psychological factors in disease, interactions between physicists and fundamental particles of their experiments, and evidence of genuine parapsychological phenomena. . . . [T]here is a substantial body of data that modern science does not consider because the phenomena do not lend themselves to systematic scrutiny by traditional methods.[27]

Norman Cousins makes quite dramatic statements of interactionism:

> The placebo is proof that there is no real separation between mind and body. Illness is always an interaction between both. It can begin in the mind and affect the body, or it can begin in the body and affect the mind, both of which are served by the same bloodstream.[28]

The "real separation" which Cousins denies here is causal isolation, or epiphenomenalism.

It is clear, then, that holists are interactionists. Are they dualists or materialists? The answer to this question is much less clear, as evidenced perhaps in the last citation. The issue is further muddied by the holistic claim that traditional medicine is dualistic, while (presumably) holistic medicine is not: ". . . a progressive division between mind and body has dominated recent Western medicine, and in the last century emphasis has been placed on the body. . . ."[29] Further:

In Western culture, man has been conceptualized as having a separate body, mind, and spirit. This body-mind-spirit division is readily evidenced in the structure of the healing professions. Physicians are dedicated to the treatment of the body; psychiatrists and psychologists are concerned with treating the mind. . . .[30]

Lewis Mehl reiterates this claim:

To separate general medicine and psychology is to maintain the mind/body dualism and to claim that events in the body are unrelated to the psyche. A complex interaction clearly exists between the psyche and soma. . . .[31]

Dualism is identified as the source of the failure of traditional medicine to understand psychosomatic phenomena, since "imprisoned as it is in the Cartesian mind-body dualism, Western medicine has considerable difficulty in conceptualizing the nature of these phenomena."[32] These claims betray a misunderstanding of the terms defined in the last section. It seems implausible to claim that contemporary medicine is "imprisoned," "dominated," or in any way committed to the claim that mental states are not identical to the physical states. How could a philosophical position enunciated in the seventeenth century have such drastic effects on a contemporary scientific discipline? The real point of the holistic objection is instead that traditional medicine ignores the causal import of psychological states in disease; that is to say, that traditional medicine is *epiphenomenalistic.*

This can be clearly seen when one considers the evidence cited by holists to show that traditional medicine is "dualistic." Their main support for this claim is that all of the etiological factors cited in traditional medicine are physiological factors.[33] As Pelletier says,

Medical research focused increasingly on minute aspects of biological processes and systematically excluded psychological and psychosocial variables. . . . Biological models of medicine arbitrarily exclude considerations of emotions, consciousness, and psychosocial variables in order to focus upon specific areas such as the biochemistry of infectious diseases.[34]

E. K. Ledermann (who accurately accuses traditional medicine of "monistic mechanistic materialism") writes:

Monistic mechanistic materialism derives the mental features also from the physico-chemical constitution, i.e., denies their existence as mental features. In other words, this form of materialism denies the existence of psychology as well as of biology, . . . the mind is replaced by the brain. . . .[35]

He later claims that "the mind is denied existence in its own right."[36] Presumably to accept the existence of "mental features" is to accept the distinctness of mind and body.

The fallacy here is rather subtle, connected as it is with the concept of identity. Biological models *exclude* psychological variables only if one assumes that psychological variables are *not* biological. Only for a dualist will the fact that a factor is physiological imply that it is *not* psychological. Only for a dualist will restricting consideration to physiological factors thereby *exclude* psychological ones.[37]

By claiming that traditional medicine "only" considers physical conditions within the body, and thereby "leaves out" the mind, holists are tacitly assuming that mental functioning is something other than physical functioning of the body. So the mistaken charge that modern medicine is "dualistic" (by which they really mean epiphenomenalistic) is itself based on a dualistic premise.

A much more accurate map of the territory is provided, I believe, by the following analysis. *Both* traditional medicine and holistic medicine accept interactionism, allowing causal relations between psychological and physical states. They differ in that holistic medicine is, in fact, *dualistic* (claiming that psychological factors are *not* identical to physiological ones), while traditional medicine (insofar as it has any position on the question) is *materialistic* and assumes that the interaction between psychological states and physical státes is just an interaction between physical states. Holists pride themselves on not being dualists, by which they really mean that they accept interactions between psychological and physiological processes. They also pride themselves on not being materialists— yet not to be a materialist *is* to be a dualist. The remainder of this and the next section will be taken up with providing evidence for this somewhat surprising analysis.

One reason has already been given for thinking that holists are dualists: namely, their argument that traditional medicine "ignores the mind" relies on a dualistic assumption. This claim can be backed by numerous explicit dualistic statements. For example, Pelletier says, "Wilder Penfield's observation that consciousness and the physical brain are discrete but in interaction seems increasingly probable."[38] He argues that "support for the study of the nonphysical properties of mind comes from modern physics,"[39] and at another place he points out how "nonphysical entities" such as the "phenomenology of consciousness" are postulated in many advanced sciences.[40] Pelletier calls the processes of attention and volition "intangibles" that interact with "biological matter."[41]

> . . . the phenomena of consciousness cannot be totally explained by the activity of the brain. In fact, it seems evident that the brain can be likened to a computer that must be programmed and operated by the independent agent of mind.[42]

The independent agent is of course mind, distinct from body.

Even without explicit claims that mind is distinct from body, there is a third kind of evidence for dualistic holism. Whenever a theorist ascribes different properties to mental states and to physical states, dualism is a logical consequence. If "mind" and "matter" have any differences in properties, then they cannot be identical. Recall that identity implies sameness in all properties. If Jones is bald and the chairman of the hospital board is not, then Jones cannot be the chairman of the hospital board. So for any property P, if a mental state is P and a physical state is not, then that mental state is not identical to that physical state. We get implicit denials of identity in statements such as:

> Mind is matter, and yet it is more. Mind is both within physical reality and beyond it. . . . My concept suggests that the inseparable duo of mind and body are part of the same tissue substance, and yet there are undeniable differences.[43]

Taken at face value this passage is self-contradictory; it is logically impossible for mind both to be matter and to have any differences from matter. Any difference in properties commits one to dualism. For example:

> The body can be known, as it is finite and can be observed by a single observer. The mind, however, cannot be known, for it is infinite . . . the two realms are totally different, one has a spatial and a temporal extension, the other only a temporal extension. The mind is private, the brain is public.[44]

Ledermann also notes that "the two components are different in kind."[45] Even if he did not explicity reject identity of mind and body (which he does[46]) these comments are sufficient to commit Ledermann to a dualist position.

Problems with Interaction

The fourth and in some ways best kind of evidence for attributing dualistic inter-actionism to holists has to do with their explanation of the interaction between mind and body. The key difficulty with the view that mind and body are distinct is and always has been that of obtaining an intelligible account of the nature of the interaction between the two. If the mind has no physical properties, how can it cause changes in physical properties? As will be explained below, any such interaction seems to contradict the law of conservation of energy. I will argue that to the extent the latter law is well confirmed (which needless to say is rather high) it is unreasonable to accept dualistic interactionism.

Change in the structure of a tissue (even at the molecular level) requires work, and work requires energy. If a mental state is to change tissue, then, the mental state must have the capacity to do work. This again is no problem for the materialist (the energy is just that of the chemical state the mental state happens to *be*) but it is problematic for the dualist, for whom the mental state is no physical state, and so cannot have any of the forms of energy of matter. Hence it is quite consistent to find dualist interactionists proposing new kinds of energy to fulfill this role. (For purposes of discussion I shall label all the various new kinds of energy "psychical energy.") A theorist who argues that some new kind of energy is *required* in order to account for psychosomatic effects employs an implicit dualistic assumption.

Pelletier, for example, chides biomedical researchers for "their longstanding neglect of psychological and psychosocial energies."[47]

> Among the most fundamental challenges to the present mechanistic belief system is the concept that consciousness is primary to matter. . . . In all meditative systems, consciousness is regarded as primary. The potential of visualization, hypnosis, dreams and meditative practices to heal physical disorders requires such a perspective. From a purely materialistic, mechanistic stance, these phenomena are given little credence, since the minute quanta of energy involved are not considered capable of having an effect upon a large system such as the body.[48]

The effect of visualization is to be explained via "minute quanta of energy."

> Experimental research by [Sir John] Eccles and other neurologists has yielded data permitting great refinement of the concept of ephemeral mind acting upon static matter. Theirs is a model of ineffably subtle interactions among infinitesimal energy fields occurring in quantum space.[49]

Those quantal effects are active, purposeful, and serve to coordinate functions of the physical brain.[50]

Holists claim that traditional medicine treats the body as a physical mechanism causally isolated from psychological effects. It is a machine, and all its workings can be predicted from earlier physical states of the device. A recurrent holistic analogy is that traditional medicine treats the mind as if it were the driver of a car, and disease as a mechanical breakdown in the car (to be repaired by the application of specialized knowledge, engineering techniques, and high technology). Stephen Black describes this analogy as follows:

> You have to look after it, of course, and drive it well—and the ideal on the roads is "a good driver in a good car": or *mens sana in corpore sano* in the words of Juvenal. In these terms physical illness is the equivalent of a blameless brake failure, or a puncture—according to severity. You can, of course, "drive the car too hard" and "blow a big end"—or work too hard and "get a coronary." And if you have bad driving habits—like "riding the clutch"—these too can precipitate a temporary mechanical failure. . . .[51]

Physical states of the car are isolated from psychological states of the driver.

Holists replace the image of the car whose mechanical operations are causally isolated from the driver's moods (dualistic epiphenomenalism) with the image of a car whose operations are sensitive to psychical energy emanating from the driver. They keep the dualistic metaphor, but simply add the premise that the driver can causally influence states of the car. While traditional medicine "viewed the body as a machine that could be analyzed in terms of its parts,"[52] holistic medicine treats it as a system open to ineffably subtle influences from the mind. As Norman Cousins puts it,

... the mind can govern the ability of the body not just to overcome pain but to regulate such functions as respiration, digestion, circulation, and even the way cells reproduce . . . .[T]he mind is regarded not just as a biological switchboard but a center for total mangagement. And it is recognized that the mind must not be bypassed or underestimated in any effort to deal with breakdowns, whether from stress or pathological organisms.[53]

He later points out that "the mind can carry out its ultimate functions and powers over the body without the illusion of material intervention."[54] The idea of "powers over the body" is dualistic; for a materialist there are only powers of the body.

Some holists reintroduce classic spiritualistic ideas such as "energy fields" and "life force." William Tiller, for example, states that "there are energies functioning in Nature completely different from those known to us via conventional science," and he identifies "mind forces" with some of these new nonphysical energies.[55] Tiller suggests that psychic healers have the capability of "transmitting" these energies, and he offers some speculations concerning the bandwidth and kilowatts required.[56]

Another sort of psychical energy is identified by Ledermann as a "holistic force" or power. He writes:

The medical scientist should not deny the existence of a force which is responsible for the existence and the operation of the various regulative and homeostatic mechanisms . . . . For the therapist, the concept stands for an entity which he must not ignore.[57]

What makes the proposition dualistic is the suggestion that, as Karl Popper puts it, "something totally different from the physical system acts in some way on the physical system."[58] Ledermann claims that there is an "unbridgeable gap" between mind and body,[59] and that the relationship between the two can never be known. Such a claim is clearly dualistic; a materialist sees no more "gap" between mind and body than there is between Ronald Reagan and the fortieth U.S. president.

Some holists link psychosomatic phenomena directly to the paranormal energies:

If we are able to accept the existence of paranormal phenomena such as psychosomatic illness, voluntary control of autonomic functions through biofeedback training, clairvoyance, telepathy, telekinesis, and extrasensory perception, even though we do not presently understand them, perhaps new modes of héaling will be allowed to surface.[60]

New modes of healing will indeed "surface" from such a mix. Psychosomatic illness is thrown in the same kettle as telekinesis because both are presumed to show nonphysical energies causing changes in matter. Indeed, once one accepts a dualistic interactionist view of psychosomatic disease, it is hard to see how one can cavil at telekinesis. (Perhaps psychical energy respects bodily boundaries?) The paranormal fringe of holism feels no such compunction:

> When we begin to accept that our body is only one form of our energy, then it isn't hard to begin to see that health is more than that which we can see and measure. It's a spirit quality, an energy flow, not just bodily functions. . . . When we begin to understand that our body is only one form of our energy, then it isn't so anti-scientific to begin to consider the influx of the spirit, the miraculous healings, and the resurrection of the dead promised in the Judeo-Christian scriptures. . . we see that nothing is against the laws of nature—only against our understanding of those laws.[61]

Some will be delighted and others appalled that the explanation proposed for psychosomatic illness can be extended so readily to account for psychic healing and the influx of the spirit.

What of Tubesing's claim that the principles do not violate any scientific canons, but merely current understandings of those laws? It is not necessarily irrational to propose new kinds of energy; if it were, it would have been irrational to propose electric fields in the nineteenth century or strong nuclear force in the twentieth. The holists are free to propose new kinds of energy. The difficulty lies in finding any evidence for them. In fact any such effects would require exceptions to the law of conservation of energy as currently formulated, and no exceptions have thus far been observed. The conservation laws are extremely well validated, and since the psychical energy version of dualistic interactionism contradicts them, there is a very low probability that it is true.

Suppose psychical energy causes some structural change in a tissue. That the energy *causes* the change implies that the change would not have occurred without that energy. Hence the total physical energy in the tissue beforehand must have been insufficient to cause the change. This in turn implies that without the psychical energy there is less energy in the tissue before than after; and that if we measure merely the known physical energies, there will be a net gain. That implication is never borne out. The law of conservation of energy is framed in terms of currently known physical energies, and among them gains always equal losses. No molecular changes are found in which physical energy present is insufficient to cause a reaction.

Oddly enough, the dualistic interactionist is committed to the claim that physiology cannot explain everything that goes on in the brain; that some events within it are exceptions to the known laws of chemistry; and that one must cite psychological factors to explain what is going on within the organ. There must be a failure of physical laws in explaining brain function. If psychological factors sometimes cause physical events, then they are a necessary part of the conditions leading to some event *E*. If psychological factors are not themselves physical events, then a necessary element in the cause of *E* is not a physical event. So reference to physical events, no matter how comprehensive, will necessarily fail to explain E—since no such combination of merely physical events suffices to produce E. Hence there must be a failure in physical laws in explaining E. Some part of the brain is given the privilege of exemption from physical law and the responsibility of communication with another (viz., mental) world. Events in that "liaison area" cannot be explained physiologically.[62]

Holists who posit new kinds of energy are following a desperate course, for their thesis requires exceptions to the conservation laws, and there is no evidence of any such exceptions. One must give such an hypothesis an extremely low prior probability. A safer course is to somehow endorse dualistic interactionism while preserving the conservation laws. One relatively recent suggestion of how to do this, adopted by some holists, appeals to quantum effects.[63] The suggestion is that the law of conservation of energy has only a statistical validity, and that brief exceptions to it are licensed by Heisenberg's uncertainty principle.[64] Over very short time intervals energy measurements are uncertain. Random fluctuations of energy are therefore possible, up to a limit imposed by the uncertainty principle, even though such fluctuations briefly violate the conservation of energy. Indeed, quantum theory predicts energy fluctuations that violate conservation laws for short intervals, such as the creation of virtual positron-electron pairs.[65] If the effects of the mind are always found among such quantum fluctuations, dualistic interactionism can be rendered consistent with the (statistically interpreted) conservation of energy.

Pelletier adopts the suggestion that the energy fluctuations caused by the mind are quantum phenomena. He calls quantum events in the brain "the fundamental interactions between mind and matter"[66] and says:

> Those researchers who have attempted to penetrate the ultimate mystery of mind in interaction with matter have focused upon quantum events occurring in and among the neurons of the brain.[67]

The mind purportedly determines the magnitudes of quantum energy fluctuations. Now if the mind is to determine physical states of the brain, the brain must be sensitive to such quantum fluctuatons. Pelletier endorses this implication:

> . . . it becomes possible to hypothesize that there is sufficient energy even at small quantum magnitudes to affect a large system such as the brain. . . .[I]nfinitesimal size is by no means a limitation on considering consciousness as interacting consequentially with matter at a quantum level.[68]

Finally, the small magnitude of the effects purportedly renders them consistent with energy conservation. The energy fluctuations caused by the mind are simply always of smaller magnitude than the minimum uncertainty given by Heisenberg's uncertainty principle.[69]

The quantum junket is successful only if it shows that interactionism is consistent with physical law, including quantum laws; and the latter question involves immensely complicated issues such as the interpretation of the uncertainty principle, the statistical nature of conservation laws, the possibility of local hidden variables, and the indeterminism of quantum fluctuations. These issues are addressed elsewhere in this volume,[70] and holistic misinterpretations of quantum physics are there detailed. Here I wish to make the simple point that even if their interpretation of such effects were consistent with quantum physics, it would not solve the dilemma for dualistic interactionism.

As in any form of dualistic interactionism, the quantum account requires there to be physiological events E that cannot be fully explained by physiological antecedents. The reason for this explanatory gap is not that E violates conservation laws, but rather that among its antecedents are some quantum energy fluctuations that are physically indeterminate. This makes brain state E physically indeterministic, as it is caused by a quantum event. While it may be possible for quantum events to affect entire brain states,[71] it is utterly implausible to expect such determination in every situation in which the mind has an effect.

Furthermore, the dualist makes the mind into a subquantum determinant of those quantum energy fluctuations; they occur because of the influence of the mind. Such fluctuations presumably occur not only in poised neurons, but also in cloud chambers and other physical systems. One must therefore produce some explanation for why the mind plays a role in some quantum fluctuations but not others. Dualists have not done this, and it may be inconsistent with quantum physics to suppose that it can ever be done.[72] Even worse, the fluctuations in question are in principle unobservable, due to their minute energies and brief lifespan. The only differential predictions that quantum dualism could make are in principle impossible to observe. While this conveniently prevents any experimental refutation of the theory, it does not give cause for confidence in the predictive profits yielded by postulating a nonphysical mind.

In short, dualistic interactionists are committed to a strange view of the explanatory role of appeals to psychological states. They presume that there is some failure in physiological explanation of brain events, and that the gap is plugged by appeal to the mind. A mental hiatus accounts for physical anomalies. Let us waive the lack of evidence for any such anomalies, and suppose that there were such gaps. How could appeal to a second kind of stuff—mental stuff— rectify them, given that description of the first kind of stuff—physiological stuff—cannot? *This* question is simply never addressed by dualists. What exactly does the mind do, during the hiatus? How does its composition enable it to do those things? Why cannot ordinary matter fulfill the same function? Quite apart from issues concerning the explanatory *need* for positing mental substance, it has never been made clear how such a posit would be *sufficient* for explanation. We have never been provided details of how a different kind of *stuff* helps explain phenomena that are physically inexplicable.

While the holists often insist that they wish only to add to current medical understanding, and are in no way antagonistic to its insights, in their account of mind/body interaction they are committed to *contradicting* the orthodox physico-chemical account of tissue function.

Now of course it is possible that there are exceptions to the currently formulated law of conservation of energy; the fact that none have been found does not imply that there are none. But it seems a desperate measure to base a theory of mind on some phenomenon for which there is no evidence, and against which evidence continually accumulates. We find that the brain is a physical system. There are no mysterious exceptions or "gaps" in its physiological functioning. Activity at a synapse is dependent on molecular factors that can be detailed, and that jointly suffice for the production of later effects. What goes on inside is a function of chemical and electrical laws. The synapse is no exception.

This argument is not conclusive; it does not demonstrate that the holistic view of the mind is false, but merely that there is no good reason to believe it. It is perfectly legitimate for a scientist to propose principles inconsistent with currently accepted explanations. Furthermore, if there is good evidence of an anomaly, and a more coherent alternative explanation, there may even be good reason to abandon the current account and replace it with the new one. Unfortunately for dualistic interactionism, however, neither condition is met. They must provide some phenomenon that cannot be explained with known physical laws, such that the most reasonable modification in our current understanding of how the brain works is to modify conservation of energy or quantum physics, and add a new version taking into account psychical energy. And holists have not produced any such evidence.

To this charge one might respond by pointing to the facts of psychosomatic illness. Do not such effects demonstrate a failure in physiological causation? Are not they sufficient reason to posit psychical energy? It is critical to address this question and to determine whether the conceptual framework of traditional medicine cannot cope with psychosomatic illness, as the holists charge. How can a materialist account for psychological causation?

A Materialistic Account of Psychosomatic Disease

A logically conclusive refutation of the claim that psychosomatic disease demonstrates a conceptual inadequacy in orthodox medicine can be had by providing an account of psychosomatic disease that is consistent with orthodox medicine. I hope to provide such an account in this section.

This account should, incidentally, help disarm a *bad* argument that sometimes surfaces in orthodox discussions of psychosomatic phenomena:

If psychological factors contribute to the etiology of disease, then purely physiological accounts are inadequate, and nonphysiological factors would be required in explanations. But to allow the contribution of nonphysiological factors violates known physico-chemical laws (as well as the conservation of energy). Hence, psychological factors do not contribute to the etiology of disease.

This argument denies interaction on the grounds that it implies *dualistic* interaction, and the latter (as argued above) is unacceptable. But must all interactionists be dualists? It seems just as desperate to deny evidence for psychological causation as it is to posit psychical energy and violations in known physical laws. Is there some alternative that avoids both?

Difficulties over psychological causation of bodily events only arise if one thinks that psychological events are *not* (identical to) bodily events. Current evidence makes dualistic interactionism an unreasonable modification of known physical laws; let us see then if a more reasonable theory can be provided by abandoning dualism and retaining physical law and interactionism. This view accepts the materialistic thesis that every psychological event is identical to some physical event. Mental states can cause physical change, but in no more mysterious a manner than is implied by ordinary physical causation, of which it is a species.

Materialism immediately disarms the above argument, for the entry of a psychological factor into an etiological list is *not* the entry of a nonphysical factor. As long as one holds to a materialist account, admitting psychological causation is in no way inconsistent with physiological causation. So admitting psychological factors in no way shows physiological accounts are inadequate.

What then does it show? What is a psychological factor on this account? For the materialist, psychological terms are not labels for a different kind of stuff; they are just different kinds of terms for describing the same stuff. To call a term "psychological" is to make a comment about our vocabulary, not about the things that vocabulary describes. It is to ascribe to that term particular semantic and epistemological features: characteristic ways of coming to know whether the term applies, classes of evidence relevant to its ascription, and kinds of inferences allowed, given truthful ascription of the term. While the semantics of the terms differ, the things described are just the same as those described by physiological terms.

Those semantic differences largely derive from the fact that psychological terms are used to explain *behavior*. Evidence to ascribe a psychological term generally involves some combination of stimulus factors; implications of such terms are behavioral. Physiological terms, on the other hand, are used to explain different phenomena, including those having to do with tissue structure and function. Evidence required for such ascriptions may include physiological assay, and the ascription may have no implications for how a person acts.[73]

A psychological construct identifies its referent in terms of its role in the genesis of behavior—in terms, that is, of the processes intervening between stimulus input and behavioral output. Evidence that bears on an ascription comprises descriptions of environmental stimuli and descriptions of behavior. It generally does not imply anything about the state of a tissue, but rather something about potential responses to different sorts of stimulus situations. Terms called "psychological" are just ones having these (and perhaps other) epistemological features.

The label "psychosomatic" is epistemological as well. It reflects the way in which we come to describe, predict, and control the etiology of the disorder, and *not* any difference in substance, or extra-physiological causation. A psychosomatic disease has a cause identified psychologically. To call a disease *D* "psychosomatic" is not to say that *D* has a different kind of cause than ordinary diseases (that is, some nonphysiological cause) but merely that we have a different way of assessing evidence for and drawing inferences from descriptions of the causes. It marks no essential difference in kind. It describes a difference in our way of knowing about the etiology of the disorder.

What does it mean to use different *kinds* of terms to pick out causes and effects? To dispel any remaining sense of mystery about psychological causation, an analogy may be useful.

A recent suggestion is that the relation between mind and brain is like the relation between a computer program and the hardware on which it "runs." Psychological vocabulary has been likened to the abstract vocabulary used to describe programs. Every execution of a program instruction *is* just an instance of some hardware event, yet nevertheless talk about programs means something different from talk about machine instructions. A program is a sequence of instructions that maps an input to an output; the variables involved in the process are defined in terms of their role in that transformation. The claims that a variable has a certain value, or that a subroutine call occurred at a given point, say something about the "place" of a given event within that transformation.

Similarly, the mind maps stimulus inputs into behavioral outputs, and much of our psychological vocabulary identifies events by the role they play in that transformation. Psychological terms for perception, memory, and thinking are on this view biological analogs of cybernetic processes of input, data storage, and computation.[74] I suggest that other cybernetic processes provide a conceptually pristine analogy for psychosomatic disease.

It is possible for programs to physically damage hardware. A badly written routine for reading data from floppy diskettes, for example, can cause the "head" that reads data to bounce against the surface of the diskette. Such a "head crash" destroys data on the diskette and can damage the disk drive itself. The hardware thereafter manifests pathological function and an alteration in structure. It shows "psychosomatic" symptoms—a malfunction caused, in this case, by software.

Now suppose there is some program that sometimes causes head crashes, and we wish to understand the "etiology" of this symptom. We have a set of conditions *C* that are common to the moments when the head does and does not crash (such as the hardware configuration, power line status, and so on); and while each such condition is necessary for the symptom to appear, they are not jointly sufficient. We proceed to diagnose (debug) the program. We may first find that a head crash occurs only when subroutine GETDATA is exited, but that it does not always occur when GETDATA is exited. What makes the difference? Further work with the debugger reveals that the head crash occurs when GETDATA is exited just in case variable Z has a nonzero value. So,

> Under conditions C, whenever subroutine GETDATA is exited with non-zero Z, a head crash occurs; and it would not have occurred, were it not for exiting GETDATA with nonzero Z.

In other words, the cause of the head crash under conditions C is exiting GETDATE with nonzero Z.

Our malfunction is "psychosomatic" in that its etiology includes a "software" description, instead of a pure "hardware" description. That etiology includes a description of software entities such as subroutines and variables, and of a particular program state defined by a variable having a certain range of values. We may have no means of determining the full set of hardware factors that are jointly sufficient to produce the malfunction; perhaps the only way we can describe the conditions that lead to the problem is in terms of certain software events. We may not know what hardware events underly them.

Does such a finding imply that the program is infested with occult energies that cause changes in the chips? Or that the program is a causal factor over and above hardware that should be considered in all disease?

The software cause for a hardware fault can be described without committing oneself to computer dualism or software energies. Clearly there is some hardware condition described by "exiting GETDATA with nonzero Z," and that condition (the same one we describe with our "mental" term) is the cause of the malfunction. We may simply be unable to determine what that hardware condition is, so that our only description of it is a software description. (It may take special electronics gear to determine the exact electrical configuration before a crash, or the chip may be inaccessible to measurement, or in a complicated system it may be too difficult to determine which hardware states correspond to the program condition.) There is nothing supernatural or occult in attributing a malfunction to an abstractly described program condition. We should not conclude that a new set of factors for explaining the workings of a computer have been found—factors that have been ignored or suppressed by maintenance electricians. It would not follow that the internal states of the device cannot be explained by physical laws. Nor need we posit new kinds of computer energy, quantum interactions, or a new paradigm for understanding hardware.

I submit the situation is similar with psychosomatic disease. In attributing a disease to some psychological cause, one presumes that there is some underlying physiological state thereby described psychologically. One may not know what that state is, and our only access to the conditions jointly sufficient to yield symptoms may be via a psychological description. The terms used to specify that condition clearly mean something different from physiological terms, even though they refer to a physiological state. Far from implying a failure or an inadequacy in physiological causation, attribution of a psychological cause requires there to be an underlying physiological mechanism. We simply do not know what that mechanism is, and must describe it by behaviorally salient effects.

Techniques for isolating software conditions are distinct from those for isolating a hardware condition. The procedures, measurements, and tests proceed differently, and the sorts of evidence relevant to an ascription are quite distinct. One uses the error statements and listings of a debugger to probe software; the other employs voltmeters and chip testers to analyze circuits. Nevertheless, the software condition leading to malfunction is just some hardware condition or other; one only has access to it via software tests, and one may not know what that hardware condition is.

Perhaps the biggest difference between dualist and materialist accounts of psychosomatic disease is the knowledge-relative nature of the latter. For a dualist, a disease with a psychological cause cannot be explained physiologically, and the disease must always be explained psychologically. "Psychosomatic" diseases are a different kind of disease. For a materialist, however, the "psychosomatic" label reflects the state of our knowledge of etiology, and no essential difference in kind. That a disease has a psychological cause, in particular, does not show that all physiological accounts of that disease must be inadequate.

The psychosomatic diseases of computers show this knowledge-relative character. We may well come to discover that "exiting GETDATA with non-zero Z" corresponds to a particular condition of voltages in registers controlling the disk-driver circuitry, and that the voltage pattern causes an overload that crashes the head. Our knowledge of the head crash disease changes: where previously ignorance confined us to a software-level description of its cause, we can now, if desired, employ a hardware description.

Similarly, for the materialist there is always a possibility of discovering a physiological description for etiological factors, which, until then, could only then be described psychologically. If psychological factor P contributes to peptic ulcers, we may come to discover what corresponds physiologically to P; and then a purely physiological explanation for ulcers could be provided. At that point we would no longer be forced to employ a psychosomatic description of peptic ulcers. Of course relabelling the cause in no way changes its character; it would not imply that ulcers no longer have a psychological cause. However, we could thereafter work entirely with a physiological vocabulary; such a possibility demonstrates that there is no essential difference in kind between psychosomatic diseases and others.

HOW TO ESTABLISH PSYCHOLOGICAL CAUSATION

In the computer analogy for psychosomatic disease, it is quite clear how to go about identifying a software cause for hardware problems: one identifies the current execution point in a sequence of instructions and the values of program variables at that point. The methods and tools one employs to do this are clearly distinct from those used to determine hardware problems. Unfortunately, this aspect of the analogy does not mimic features of psychologically caused diseases very well, for in the latter it may be quite unclear how to go about identifying a psychological factor, and what methods and tools are used to do this. We need to consider this latter question in order to evaluate the holistic claim that psychological factors are involved in every disease.

How does one identify a psychological factor? What evidence is required to show that it bears a causal relation to a disease? In this section I will address these questions and consider how well holists meet such requirements. On both counts there are surprising gaps in the evidence for holistic claims that particular diseases are psychosomatic. I will argue that quite apart from the conceptual difficulties discussed in the last section, there are simple failures in the evidence purportedly supporting claims for psychological causation. An understanding of what is required to demonstrate such a link will show this.

Identifying a Psychological Factor

To evaluate a claim for psychological causation, one must have a sufficiently detailed understanding of the psychological factor in question to be able to assess when it is present and when it is absent, as otherwise one cannot relate any experimental or correlational data to the claim. One details the conditions under which a factor is present or absent by specifying the antecedent conditions that bring it about and the consequences it has on the remainder of a person's psychology. Since at least some of the antecedents or consequences may be unobservable, such propositions are typically theoretical. In that case, to be able to attach data to the claim for psychological causation, the theory as a whole must be sufficiently well developed so that one can determine what it predicts, and determine whether observations agree or disagree with those predictions.[75]

By far the favorite psychological variable among holists is "stress." Does the evidence cited concerning "stress-related" disorders demonstrate psychological causation of disease?

It is clear that stress is not a characteristic of stimuli, but of how an individual reacts to those stimuli. It is not an observable characteristic of behavior, since the initial effects of stress may be suppressed. It is an internal reaction that may or may not be evidenced in behavior.

Stress purportedly depends on the idiosyncracies of an individual. What is a stressor to one individual might not be to another. The individual factors affecting stress include: current incentives and motives, plans, cognitive categories, social supports, personality type, age, current emotional state, and so on. Many of these variables are transient characteristics and are themselves difficult to measure. Put another way, "stress" is a hypothetical term and not an observable. Since it is hypothetical, it is critical to determine whether the theory of stress-related disorders is sufficiently well formulated to allow experimental test.

To be testable, the psychological theory underlying the ascription of "stress" must be sufficiently detailed so that one can determine from it what evidence would be required in order to (a) test whether or not a particular individual was stressed, (b) set up control groups differing in stress levels from a treatment group, (c) manipulate stress levels in some group, (d) measure stress levels, and (e) test a stress measurement for accuracy. Note that the theory need not guarantee success in any of these enterprises (it may imply, for example, that the variables controlling stress levels cannot easily be manipulated in an experiment), but it must be formulated clearly enough so that one can determine whether or not success has been achieved. We should be able to tell what sort of evidence is relevant and required in order to make such a determination.

Unfortunately the holistic theory of stress fails to do this. What one finds instead is an intuitive model built on psychological platitudes. There are no clear statements of the parameters that affect stress or of the individual differences in mechanisms of its effect. For example, Pelletier says,

> Unfortunately, most stress-inducing stimuli in a modern environment consist of noise or air pollution, subtle social or business pressures, familial problems, food, toxins such as caffeine or white sugar, environmental contaminants such as lead and excessive hydrocarbons which irritate the lungs, and other ambiguous or abstract stressors . . . . Very few contemporary stressors are immediate or identifiable, and individuals are left with a physiological state of arousal for which they have no cognitive label.[76]

This account makes "stress" a catch-all term for anything anyone finds unpleasant or harmful. Of course it may be true that all these events have some theoretically significant similarity, and that they all have effects on some single factor, which one calls "stress." While this may be true, the theory does not provide the wherewithal to determine whether it is true. The theory is never developed clearly enough so that one can determine what the relevant similarity is, or what events do and do not increase "stress." If white sugar is a stressor, for example, is brown sugar as well? Are moderate hydrocarbons not a stressor? There is no means to determine an answer.

If we are to show that stress is a cause of disease, we must define a single variable in the disease model corresponding to stress. (Otherwise tests of the hypothesis may conflate two or more factors whose influence is sometimes additive, sometimes antagonistic.) That we have just one variable (and no more) implies in turn that one finds univariate effects: effects that can be explained in terms of variation of just one construct within a theory. This is the problem with catch-all constructs. There is no plausible psychological model in which one variable is both the function of so many different antecedents and a determinant of so many different effects.

One cannot avoid doing the work of specifying such antecedents and of detailing the conditions under which a construct does and does not have certain effects. The reason is simply that vague common-sense generalizations are readily disconfirmed, as they conflate theoretically significant distinctions, and ignore the mediating conditions under which a given effect is found. For example, does stress aggravate all disease? There is animal evidence that stressors only make a difference to infection rates within a middle range of pathogen dosages.[77] A low pathogen dosage was so easily combated immunologically that no amount of stress (electric shock preceded by a warning light) affected infection rates. A high dosage was so infectious that stress again made no difference to rates. Furthermore, some stressors have been found to increase resistance to some infections while decreasing it to others.[78] The unqualified claim that all diseases are aggravated by stress is simply not borne out by the evidence.

A second startling example of the perils of vague generalization is provided by results indicating that in some conditions both acute and chronic stress actually *improve* resistance to infection. The effects of acute stress on resistance to infection depend largely on the order of events. In animals, stressors lead initially to immuno-suppression, but that is often followed by a period of immuno-elevation. Animals stressed *after* exposure to a pathogen had elevated infection rates compared to controls, while those stressed *before* exposure to the pathogen had lower rates than controls.[79] In short, acute stress can *improve* resistance to infection, provided it occurs before exposure to pathogens. And there is evidence that chronic stress can enhance immunological function.[80] Unless one states mediating variables with some care, these critical temporal relationships are simply ignored.

The studies providing these surprising findings concerning stress all employed animal models. "Stress" can be defined in a way that allows experimental investigation; in animal studies it is usually defined as a conditioned or unconditioned negative reinforcer.[81] It is clear when such terms apply, and when they do not; one can readily devise experimental procedures to manipulate and measure stress. The objection to holistic accounts of "stress" is not simply that some of the key generalizations in it are shown to be false by such models, but more importantly that the holistic account is so vague that it cannot be applied directly to human data. It is totally unclear when an individual is or is not stressed, what the antecedents of stress are, and what functional relations exist between those antecedents and the construct. That a causal factor is psychological gives no license for sloppy theorizing; such factors can and should be defined as rigorously as any biochemical or physical factor.

Demonstrating Causality

After formulating a testable theory and devising empirical tests and measures for some psychological variable within it, one must then demonstrate causal relations between that variable and disease. The best evidence for the role of stress in disease comes from animal experimentation, in which one can show that randomly assigned stressed animals have significantly higher infection rates than unstressed controls.[82] Given that such experimentation with humans is unethical, how have holists extrapolated from animal data to humans? What sort of human data could support such a claim?

Note in regard to the first question that animal models of stress do not involve the cognitive, motivational or attitudinal aspects of human stress described by holists. Stressors for rats include, for example, swimming in ice water, placement in the middle of an "open field" arena, and exposure to a cat. One can state the relevant similarity between these conditions: they are all conditioned (or unconditioned) negative reinforcers for that species. But this crisp test for "stress" (demonstrate that it is a negative reinforcer) cannot be applied to the holistic models of stress in humans.

Extrapolation to humans is empirically warranted to the extent that one can demonstrate *in humans* mechanisms with the same effects controlled by the same variables.[83] Since animals simply do not possess the motivational states, beliefs, and attitudes of humans, that route to testing holistic claims is barred. What sort of human data can be used instead?

Although it cannot be conclusive, the best remaining evidence is epidemiological. Consider the hypothesis that every instance of disease D has a contributing psychological cause P, which is not alone sufficient for D but which must act in concert with background conditions C, every one of which is necessary for occurrence of the disease. Such a model would predict that the disease rate among individuals with P is higher than the disease rate among individuals without P.

Unfortunately, much of the research cited for psychosomatic effects is logically confused and employs the wrong rates. Instead of examining the entire population, and determining rates of disease among those with and without P, the typical study examines those with the disease and tries to determine what psychological factor P they all share. Even if the latter strategy is successful, it is irrelevant to the demonstration of a causal claim. Suppose we show that all patients with peptic ulcers are orally dependent.[84] No inferences can be drawn from such a finding: perhaps *everyone* is orally dependent, or at least would pass the tests employed by such studies. Switching diagnoses, suppose we show that more anxious individuals are ulcerated than are not. That evidence is also inconclusive. One must also determine the ulceration rate among the tranquil. One may have a higher number of anxious individuals among the ulcerated without having a higher ulceration rate among the anxious. It is the latter rate that is critical, not the former.

Failure to substantiate a prediction of differential rates would show the "strong" version of psychological causation to be incorrect. But there are other causal models one may propose (in particular, a "weak'" multifactorial version) that do not entail differential rates. For this reason, failure to substantiate the prediction does *not* rule out all causal relations between psychological factors and disease, but merely rules out the "strong" version. The logic is further complicated by the fact that substantiating the prediction does not show the strong (or any) model to be correct. There is first the drearily familiar motto that correlations do not demonstrate causality, and furthermore the prediction could be explained in other ways.

I said early on that the strong reading of the holistic claim is simply implausible, and that it is certain that some instances of some diseases involve no psychological cause. Consider then how one might test the weaker reading, to the effect that every disease has some instance whose etiology includes some psychological factor, but that not all instances include that factor.

The weaker reading is much more difficult to test epidemiologically. If one allows multiple causation (that is, a disjunction of distinct sufficient conditions) then one need not find anxiety among all the ulcerated patients, even though anxiety does in some patients cause ulceration. So failing to find P among all D cases does not rule out a causal claim between P and D.

Predictions depend on the exact formulation of one's theory of the conditions necessary and sufficient to produce D. The situation is complicated by suppressor variables. A suppressor variable Z is one which is found among some causal conditions of D and which is negatively correlated with P.[85] It "suppresses" the appearance of a P effect by cancelling the addition of P effects to Z cases, resulting in equal rates of D among the P cases and among the non-P cases. If suppressor variables are at work among the combinations of factors causing D, a causal relation between P and D is consistent with the complete absence of a correlation between P and D. The incidence of D may be no higher among those with P than those without, even though in some instances P causes D. Without filling out the model, one can draw no inference positive or negative about incidence rates of disease.

A simple example will show this. Suppose P is anxiety, D ulcers, and Z some abnormal condition relating to prolonged digestion, which also causes ulcers. Z occurs among the nonanxious individuals and causes ulceration in ten percent of the cases. Anxiety, however, suppresses prolonged digestion so that Z never occurs among the anxious, of whom ten percent get ulcers. Then anxiety will not be correlated with ulceration, even though in some cases anxiety does cause ulceration.

To be able to test the claim that some but not all instances of disease D include a psychological component in their etiology, it is therefore absolutely critical that the etiological model for D be detailed. One cannot draw any epidemiological predictions from the model unless the various combinations of factors that are sufficient for D are described, as well as the various relationships *between* those factors. The latter is required in order to rule out suppressor variables, which if present may reverse epidemiological predictions.

Such details are notably lacking from holistic claims concerning the etiology of disease. Correlations and epidemiological data cannot be attached to the sweeping claim that "all diseases are psychosomatic" unless details of the model are provided. As Jan Palmblad puts it in his review of studies relating stress to infection: "If it was not for the other kinds of studies that are available, the present epidemiologic material would not allow any conclusions regarding the relationship between stress and infection."[86] At the very least we require a specification of what combinations of factors suffice for disease and of the relationships of those factors. Without such details, even the "weak" version of the claim is untestable: it may imply (for example) higher ulceration rates among the anxious, or it may imply lower rates. So while this key premise of holistic medicine is currently immune from refutation, it is empirically vacuous as well, and survives only by remaining isolated from data.

IMPLICATIONS FOR TREATMENT

Suppose, contrary to fact, that it were both meaningful and true to claim that all diseases are psychosomatic. What would follow from that finding? Would it justify the sweeping changes in treatment hawked by holists?

Finding a psychological cause for D does not imply all treatments for D must be psychotherapeutic. Nor need successful treatments for D manipulate or alter any aspect of psychological functioning. The pathogenic effect of P only occurs in combination with constitutional and biochemical conditions C that are also necessary for occurrence of the disease. It is conceivable (and, in fact, often observed) that treatment for D proceeds more efficiently by attacking one of the biochemical conditions C, instead of the typically recalcitrant psychological factor P.[87] For example, instead of attempting to alter those character factors within an individual that lead to ulcers (a thankless and probably futile task), a cure might more easily be obtained through surgery or administration of an acid blocker. Surgery does sometimes cure peptic ulcer; psychotherapy is not inevitably required.

More strongly, psychotherapy may not be at all useful. Take "psychotherapy" to mean (in this context) any procedure that causes change in whatever psychological factor P contributed to the etiology of some case of D. Even though P caused the disease, altering P may not cure it. That psychological factors are causal does not imply that they are curative. Once a pathological process is established, there may be no psychological mechanism sufficient for its cure. Peptic ulcers provide a simple example. One may require physiological interventions, even though the disease was established partly by psychological cause.

Psychosomatic disease in computers can sometimes be treated by debugging software, but often the resulting hardware malfunctions can be much more readily fixed (and prevented) by adding the correct sorts of jumpers or circuit grounds. It certainly does not follow that *only* debugging can cure head crash. Furthermore, if the hardware pathology is sufficiently extensive, software remedies may be totally inadequate to restore the computer to good health. Even though it is true that the head crash would not have occurred, were it not for that particular software condition, the damage to hardware may be beyond the powers of a programmer to remedy, and may require the attention of an electrician.

These distinctions may seem somewhat unfair to the facts. While it is conceivable that effective physical interventions against peptic ulcer, insomnia, or migraine can be found, in fact currently successful interventions are almost exclusively behavioral. If the main factor determining whether and when an individual becomes ulcerated is his or her response to stress, then that response should clearly be the first target of an intervention, and manipulating the physiological concomitants necessary for ulceration is likely to be of little use. While behavioral treatments are not logically mandated by a psychosomatic diagnosis, perhaps as a matter of fact they are the only ones likely to succeed.

The important issue is whether such treatments imply a conceptual overhaul of contemporary medicine. While behavioral therapy or biofeedback is clearly a different modality of care, does it follow that such therapy somehow contradicts the assumptions of orthodox medicine?

In fact it is easy to reconcile the effectiveness of such treatments with biochemical materialism. Perhaps behavioral techniques are simply the only means to manipulate the relevant physiological variables. It is difficult to cause specific changes in the central neural, endocrinological, and immunological parameters that seem to mediate psychosomatic symptoms. Perhaps the best way to cause such changes is to train patients to do it "from the inside"; that is, to employ behavioral and stress reduction techniques to train the patients themselves to cause the changes in their physiology. (Behavioral techniques do have such effects.) It is conceivable that behavioral techniques are the optimal *physiological* means of manipulating such factors. For a materialist, there is no significant difference in kind between behavioral techniques and traditional regimens. The effectiveness of such treatments does not demonstrate curative energies distinct from the familiar physical ones.

Prospects for such a reconciliation may provide an explanation for why holists tend to be dualists. The holistic view is that the physician should consider etiological factors that have not previously been considered, and are outside the conceptual province of orthodox medicine. Furthermore, treatments that affect such factors must be a new *kind* of treatment—since they affect the mind. This project falls flat if it is shown that the factors are not new, and that the effects of treatment are just the ordinary physical ones. If the new treatment factors that holists propose were identical to the physiological variables manipulated by orthodox regimens, then there would be no distinction in kind between orthodox and holistic cures. The psychological aspect of treatment would lose its autonomy.

Dualism safeguards the autonomy of these treatments. For a dualist the mind is independent of the body, so that the effects in question can only be had by some new kind of therapy—one which affects the mind. It is independent of the illness and provides a distinct set of untapped antecedents that can be independently manipulated to alter the course of disease. To retain such interaction while rejecting identity forces one into an implausible dualism.

CONCLUSION

I hope to have shown that one can give a clear analysis of the concept of psychosomatic disease; that the concept of psychological involvement in disease etiology is not necessarily occult, and that it is consistent with orthodox physiology; that one can devise rigorous and well designed experiments to test such effects; and that such evidence can support carefully formulated generalizations linking psychological factors to disease.

The danger in the holistic interpretation of psychosomatic disease is that it squanders these hard-won insights. It promulgates a murky view of the role of the mind, embraces an occult view of mind/body interaction, commits itself to contradicting current physical science, and abandons the enterprise of developing precise theories and rigorously formulated tests. Psychosomatic research has had a dubious status within medicine, and the holistic interpretation of psychosomatic effects unfortunately and undeservedly reinforces that bad reputation. It is a disservice to past and present investigators to suggest that the insights of psychosomatic research can only be accepted after one rejects orthodox physiology and traditional scientific method. Such a view threatens to freeze the development of our knowledge of psychosomatic effects, and hand its future over to mystics and cranks.

Notes

1. Kenneth Pelletier, *Mind as Healer, Mind as Slayer* (New York: Delta Books, 1977), 18.

2. Ibid., 13.

3. For example, the following writers define holistic medicine as implying the claim that psychological factors are involved in all disease: Norman Cousins, in his introduction to Kenneth Pelletier, *Holistic Medicine* (New York: Delacorte Press, 1979), xiv; Lewis Mehl, *Mind and Matter: Foundations for Holistic Health* (Berkeley: Mindbody Press 1981), 155; E. K. Ledermann, *Philosophy and Medicine* (London: Tavistock Publications, 1970), xv; Donald Tubesing, *Wholistic Health* (New York: Human Sciences Press, 1979), 82–83; Herbert A. Otto and James W. Knight, "Wholistic Healing: Basic Principles and Concepts," in Herbert A. Otto and James W. Knight (eds.), *Dimensions in Wholistic Healing* (Chicago: Nelson Hall, 1979), 8; Walter Strode, "An Emerging Medicine: Creating the New Paradigm," in idem., 74; James Fosshage, "Introduction," in James Fosshage and Paul Olsen (eds.), *Healing: Implications for Psychotherapy* (New York: Human Sciences Press, 1978), 16; James S. Gordon, "The Paradigm of Holistic Medicine," in Arthur C. Hastings, James Fadiman, and James S. Gordon (eds.), *Health for the Whole Person* (Toronto: Bantam Books, 1980), 17.

4. See Pelletier, *Mind as Healer, Mind as Slayer*, op. cit., 7.

5. On the diathesis-stress model see Linda Gannon, "The Psychophysiology of Psychosomatic Disorders," in Stephen N. Haynes and Linda Gannon (eds.), *Psychosomatic Disorders: A Psychophysiological Approach to Etiology and Treatment* (New York: Praeger Publishers, 1981), 1–31; David Graham, "Psychosomatic Medicine," in Norman S. Greenfield and Richard A. Sternbach (eds.), *Handbook of Psychophysiology* (New York: Holt Rinehart, 1972), 839–924.

6. Pelletier, *Mind as Healer, Mind as Slayer*, op cit., 157.

7. While stress is the holists' favorite psychological variable, some writers cite other con-

structs. Lewis Mehl, for example, cites "belief systems" as potential pathogens (*Mind and Matter*, op. cit., 149, 155). Ledermann favors a "teleological principle" or purposiveness (*Philosophy and Medicine*, op. cit., 24–25, 35). "Emotional disorder" has often been identified as a cause of psychosomatic disease; Tubesing (*Wholistic Medicine*, op. cit., 82) cites "loneliness" and "guilt." Others cite various (new) forms of mental energy (see section entitled "Problems with Interaction" below).

8. Hans Selye, *The Stress of Life* (New York: McGraw-Hill, 1956); Walter B. Cannon, *The Wisdom of the Body* (New York: W. W. Norton, 1932); A. T. Simeons, *Man's Presumptuous Brain* (New York: Dutton and Co., 1961).

9. See E. K. E. Gunderson and R. H. Rahe (eds.), *Life Stress and Illness* (Springfield, Ill.: Charles C. Thomas, 1974).

10. Pelletier provides a biochemical rationale for implicating the mind in all disease; other holists provide different rationales, or none at all. Some, for example, seem to argue that because a person is an "indissoluble unity" of mind and body, mind permeates the body, and therefore any bodily event (including therefore diseases) involves the mind. (See Mehl, *Mind and Matter*, op. cit., 3; William A. Tiller, "Rationale for an Energy Medicine," in Otto and Knight [eds.], *Dimensions in Wholistic Healing*, op. cit., 166). Other holists provide no rationale, and simply rely on the unwarranted inference from "Some diseases are psychosomatic" to "All diseases are psychosomatic."

11. Kenneth Pelletier, *Toward a Science of Consciousness* (New York: Delacorte Press, 1978), 185.

12. Pelletier, *Mind as Healer, Mind as Slayer*, op. cit., 19.

13. It is an extremely common claim among holists that psychosomatic phenomena demonstrate a *conceptual* inadequacy in traditional medicine, and that new concepts, methods, and treatments are required. Pelletier reiterates this claim throughout his *Toward a Science of Consciousness*, op. cit. See Lewis Mehl, *Mind and Matter*, op. cit., xv, 165, and *passim;* Tubesing, *Wholistic Health*, op. cit., 29–32, 74–87; Ledermann, *Philosophy and Medicine*, op. cit., 16–28; Otto & Knight (eds.), in *Dimensions in Wholistic Healing*, op. cit., 6–8; Walter S. Strode, in Otto & Knight (eds.), *Dimensions in Wholistic Healing*, op. cit., 67–74; James S. Gordon, in Hastings, Fadiman, and Gordon (eds.), *Health for the Whole Person*, op. cit., 3–27.

14. A (perhaps extreme) example of the psychologizing of treatment is found in Mehl, *Mind and Matter*, op. cit., 31–142, where insight psychotherapy is claimed to be efficacious against diabetes, asthma, allergies, and gynecological disorders.

15. Pelletier, *Mind as Healer, Mind as Slayer*, op. cit., 12–13.

16. For a careful treatment of such psychological concomitants see Leonard Zusne and Warren H. Jones, *Anomalistic Psychology* (Hillsdale, New Jersey: Lawrence Erlbaum, 1982), 18–42.

17. See Ronald Melzack, *The Puzzle of Pain* (New York: Basic Books, 1973).

18. See Pelletier, *Mind as Healer, Mind as Slayer*, op. cit., 42; Mehl, *Mind and Matter*, op. cit., 158–59.

19. An excellent analysis can be found in J. L. Mackie, *The Cement of the Universe* (Oxford: Clarendon Press, 1974).

20. See ibid., 34–36.

21. Strictly speaking the denial of dualism (as defined) is "Some mental states are identical to some physical states." The materialist makes the stronger claim that *all* of them are.

22. For two classic articles on this position, see U. T. Place, "Is Consciousness a Brain Process?" and J. J. C. Smart, "Sensations and Brain Processes," both in C. V. Borst (ed.), *The Mind-Brain Identity Theory* (London: Macmillan, 1970).

23. Both definitions are less restrictive than is traditional. In traditional definitions both "interactionism" and "epiphenomenalism" are dualist positions, and they both accept causal relations from body to mind. The difference between them is that the interactionist accepts, and the epiphenomenalist denies, causal relations from mind to body. I am stipulating the latter difference as definitive, so that the terms can apply whether or not an individual is dualistic or denies causal relations from body to mind.

24. Although it is a logically possible position, materialistic epiphenomenalism would be a very strange view, and in practice all materialists are interactionists.

25. Pelletier, *Toward a Science of Consciousness*, op. cit., 25; see also Pelletier, *Mind as Healer, Mind as Slayer*, op. cit., 10–11.

26. Pelletier, *Toward a Science of Consciousness*, op. cit., 35.

27. Ibid., 15.

28. Norman Cousins, *Anatomy of an Illness as Perceived by the Patient* (Toronto: Bantam Books, 1979), 56.

29. Kenneth Pelletier, "The Mind in Health and Disease," in Hastings, Fadiman, and Gordon (eds.), *Health for the Whole Person*, op. cit., 111.

30. Pelletier, *Toward a Science of Consciousness*, op. cit., 24; see also Pelletier, *Holistic Medicine*, op. cit., 25.

31. Mehl, *Mind and Matter*, op. cit., 4, 145.

32. Jerome Frank, "Psychotherapy and the Healing Arts," in Fosshage and Olsen (eds.), *Healing*, op. cit., 37.

33. "Physiological" should be construed broadly throughout this discussion, as encompassing not merely physiological terms, but also anatomical, cytological, biochemical, molecular, and any other physical terms.

34. Pelletier, *Holistic Medicine*, op. cit., 25.

35. Ledermann, *Philosophy and Medicine*, op. cit., 5.

36. Ibid., 50.

37. For a materialist, there is a critical distinction between naming what in fact is a psychological state (perhaps using a physiological term to do so) and describing it *as* a psychological state (in which case one must use psychological vocabulary to do the job). Biological models can "include" psychological factors in the former sense, but not in the latter. The materialist claim is that some of the physical terms used to describe the system will turn out to name psychological states, even though we may not know it now.

38. Pelletier, *Toward a Science of Consciousness*, op. cit., 140.

39. Ibid., 139–40.

40. Ibid., 132.

41. Ibid., 144.

42. Ibid., 67.

43. Mehl, *Mind and Matter*, op. cit., 3.

44. Ledermann, *Philosophy and Medicine*, op. cit., 50–51.

45. Ibid., 49.

46. Ibid., 63.

47. Pelletier, *Holistic Medicine*, op. cit., 26.

48. Pelletier, *Mind as Healer, Mind as Slayer*, op. cit., 33–34.

49. Pelletier, *Toward a Science of Consciousness*, op. cit., 135.

50. Ibid., 141.

51. Stephen Black, *Mind and Body* (London: William Kimber, 1969), 73–74.

52. Pelletier, *Holistic Medicine*, op. cit., 31

53. In his introduction to ibid., xiv.

54. Cousins, *Anatomy of an Illness*, op. cit., 67.

55. William A. Tiller, "Rationale for an Energy Medicine," in Otto & Knight (eds.), *Dimensions in Wholistic Healing*, op. cit., 166, 168.

56. It is interesting to note in this regard how close dualistic interactionism is to parapsychology. Both typically posit "new energies"; while the dualist restricts their effects to within one body, the parapsychologist adds further capabilities and properties to the energy—such as transmission across distance or time. This theoretical alliance is evident in several anthologies of holistic/parapsychological speculations. See Otto and Knight (eds.), *Dimensions in Wholistic Healing*, op. cit.; Fosshage and Olsen (eds.), *Healing*, op. cit.; Nicholas Regush (ed.), *Frontiers of Healing: New Dimensions in Parapsychology* (New York: Avon Books, 1977).

57. Ledermann, *Philosophy and Medicine,* op. cit., 35.

58. See Karl R. Popper and John C. Eccles, *The Self and Its Brain* (London: Routledge & Kegan Paul, 1977), 472.

59. Ledermann, *Philosophy and Medicine,* op. cit., 51.

60. Walter S. Strode, "An Emerging Medicine: Creating the New Paradigm," in Otto & Knight (eds.), *Dimensions in Wholistic Healing,* op. cit., 74.

61. Tubesing, *Wholistic Health,* op. cit., 84.

62. The term "liaison area" is from John Eccles in Popper and Eccles, *The Self and Its Brain,* op. cit., 361–70.

63. Ibid., 539–47, 564–65.

64. Ibid., 541.

65. Most college-level physics texts explain these phenomena. See for example Richard T. Weidner and Robert L. Sells, *Elementary Modern Physics* (Boston: Allyn and Bacon, 1968), 474–89. A popular account is found in Heinz R. Pagels, *The Cosmic Code: Quantum Physics as the Language of Nature* (New York: Bantam Books, 1983), 244–47.

66. Pelletier, *Toward a Science of Consciousness,* op. cit., 66.

67. Ibid., 132–33.

68. Ibid., 59.

69. Ibid., 58–59, 134.

70. See Douglas Stalker and Clark Glymour, "Quantum Medicine," in this volume.

71. The best evidence for this comes from visual psychophysics. Under optimal conditions, one can visually detect absorption of from two to ten photons in retinal receptors. The energy involved is apparently within bounds for quantum fluctuations, and yet it suffices to change the brain from a "no" report to a "yes." Absorption may however require much longer time intervals than those allowed for quantum fluctuations. See Tom Cornsweet, *Visual Perception* (New York: Academic Press, 1970), 25–26.

72. Some interpretations disallow any possibility of a subquantum theory, which would restore determinism to quantum phenomena—as quantum dualism would do. See Stalker and Glymour, "Quantum Medicine" (this volume), and Max Jammer, *The Philosophy of Quantum Mechanics* (New York: John Wiley, 1974), 252–340.

73. These contrasts are further described in Austen Clark, *Psychological Models and Neural Mechanisms* (Oxford: Clarendon Press, 1980), chapter 5, 155–79.

74. Many authorities think this is much more than an analogy, and that psychological processes are literally computational: manipulation of symbolic codes by instructions built into the system. See Jerry Fodor, *Representations* (Cambridge: MIT Press, 1981); Zenon Pylyshyn, *Computation and Cognition* (Cambridge, MIT Press, 1984); Alan Newell and Herbert A. Simon, *Human Problem Solving* (Englewood Cliffs, N.J.: Prentice-Hall, 1972). The idea of software faults damaging hardware may be more than a mere analogy.

75. On the problems of defining theoretical terms see Austen Clark, "Hypothetical Constructs, Circular Reasoning, and Criteria," and "Functionalism and the Definition of Theoretical Terms," both in *Journal of Mind and Behavior* 4 (1983): 1–12, 339–53.
1971).
letier, *Toward a Science of Consciousness,* op. cit., 196.

77. See S. Michael Plaut and Stanford B. Friedman, "Psychosocial Factors in Infectious Disease," in Robert Ader (ed.), *Psychoneuroimmunology* (New York, Academic Press: 1981), 5.

78. Ibid., 16, 19.

79. See Jan Palmblad, "Stress and Immunologic Competence: Studies in Man," in Ader (ed.), *Psychoneuroimmunology,* op. cit., 252. Palmblad cites three corroborating studies.

80. Andrew A. Monjan, "Stress and Immunologic Competence: Studies in Animals," in Ader (ed.), *Psychoneuroimmunology,* op. cit., 210–12. Monjan cites six corroborating studies for temporal effects.

81. See Jeffrey Gray, *The Psychology of Fear and Stress* (London: Weidenfeld & Nicolson,

82. See the review by Andrew A. Monjan, "Stress and Immunologic Competence: Studies in

Animals," in Ader (ed.), *Psychoneuroimmunology*, op. cit., 185–227.

83. See Austen Clark, "The Logic of the Comparative Approach," *The Behavioral and Brain Sciences* 7 (September 1984).

84. Such was the interpretation of F. Alexander, *Psychosomatic Medicine* (New York: W. W. Norton, 1950).

85. See Hurbert Blalock, *Causal Inferences in Nonexperimental Research* (Chapel Hill: University of North Carolina Press, 1964).

86. Jan Palmblad, "Stress and Immunologic Competence: Studies in Man," in Ader (ed.), *Psychoneuroimmunology*, op. cit., 242.

87. Psychological change is probably *more* difficult to bring about than biochemical change. While traditional medicine has an armory of biochemical procedures that are demonstrably more effective than a placebo, it is questionable whether psychotherapy has *any*. See S. J. Rachman and C. T. Wilson, *The Effects of Psychological Treatment*, 2nd enlarged edition (Oxford: Pergamon Press, 1980).

Douglas Stalker, Ph.D., and Clark Glymour, Ph.D.

Quantum Medicine

INTRODUCTION

Writers on holistic medicine have a lot to say about modern physics, especially about the quantum theory. They have a lot to say as well about philosophy, especially philosophy of science, and their remarks on the former subject are entwined with their remarks on the latter. Their claim comes down to this: The new physics and its philosophy together show that holistic therapies work and are in tune with modern science.

On the face of it, a reader should be puzzled as to why advocates for any new medical therapy should spend a great deal of their time talking about quantum mechanics, or about philosophical notions such as "reductionism," "dualism," "multiple causality," and the like. If you pick up any respected medical journal and examine papers intended to defend specific therapies, whether vitamin C therapy or bypass surgery, you will not find discussions of the interpretation of quantum mechanics, or philosophical disquisitions on reductionism. Presumably the authors of such essays on medical research do not think quantum mechanics or philosophy have any bearing, one way or the other, on such questions as to whether bypass surgery relieves angina, or whether vitamin C prevents colds or cures cancer. Holists, in contrast, really do seem to think that quantum mechanics and philosophy of science have a bearing on whether Rolfing, acupuncture, visualization, chiropractic, iridology, homeopathy, and the like, cure or prevent disease. The holists occupy themselves with such matters for one simple reason: In their eyes, quantum physics establishes something *general* about scientific procedure and about the nature of the world science tries to investigate, and these general things show that traditional medical therapy and traditional medical research are fundamentally in error, while holistic therapies are on the right track. In this vein, Kenneth Pelletier writes the following:

Holistic approaches to health parallel the insights of quantum physics in that both supplant the Newtonian reductionist view of the world with the quantum perspective of a dynamic universe. From this new paradigm derive the philosophical and scientific roots for the practice of holistic medicine.[1]

And Fritjof Capra, the *doyen* of quantum holists, says:

... while biomedical scientists elaborated mechanistic models of health and illness, the conceptual basis of their science was shattered by dramatic developments in atomic and subatomic physics, which clearly revealed the limitations of the mechanistic world view and led to an organic and ecological conception of reality. . . .

The conceptual revolution in modern physics foreshadows an imminent revolution in all the sciences and a profound transformation of our world view and value.[2]

These are sweeping pronouncements, but what are the specifics? In what ways does quantum physics show that medical science has gone wrong, and how does it lead to a new conception of reality that requires holistic medicine? Holists seek support from quantum physics for three principal themes: one about consciousness, one about "reductionism," and one about causality. Quantum theory teaches us, holists claim, that human consciousness shapes reality. Pelletier again:

Intraphysic and psychosocial factors influencing states of disease or health do not exist as identifiable objects and because of this they are given second-class status in a purely biomedical orientation to health care. Yet from modern physics has come a clear mandate for the necessity of considering the variables of human consciousness in attempting to comprehend fully the nature of reality.[3]

And from another holist, Larry Dossey, reflecting on a theorem of the quantum theory first derived by J. S. Bell:

... human consciousness and the physical world cannot be regarded as distinct, separate entities. What we call physical reality, the external world, is shaped—to some extent—by human thought.[4]

The quantum theory teaches us as well that big things cannot be reduced to little things, and that the properties of big things, like people, cannot be explained by the interrelations of our physical parts. Human mental properties, especially, cannot be reduced to physical properties of our tissues, or so the holists contend. Fritjof Capra makes this general claim: "Quantum theory thus reveals a basic oneness of the universe. It shows that we cannot decompose the world into independently existing smallest units."[5] Pelletier then draws the following medical moral:

Just as the physicist approaches the limits of Newtonian physics when dealng with subtle energy systems, biomedical researchers confront these same limits and need to revise their long-standing neglect of psychological and psychosocial energies. Just as properties of quantum objects cannot be defined independently of preparation and measurement, people cannot be separated from their context and interactions with others.[6]

Finally, quantum mechanics shows that medical science proceeds with the wrong conception of causal relations. Professor Pelletier once more:

According to the assumptions of Newton and Galileo in prequantum physics, man was simply another mechanism. By applying the laws of classical physics, the causes of a man's actions could be traced to their source. From this root assumption the notion evolved that research on human behavior would ultimately lead to that behavior being totally predictable. Yet according to the uncertainty principle, the very act of measurement or observation transmits sufficient energy to alter the system that is observed, thus precluding total predictability.[7]

And Dossey elaborates:

Molecular theories of disease causation are now seen in a different way than in the traditional biomedical model. For we recognize in the new view that isolated derangements at the level of the atoms simply do not occur. The modern rule is that all information is everywhere transmitted. Crisp, causal events that were once thought to characterize each and every human disease fade into endless reverberated chains of happenings. In the new view we see the molecular theory of disease causation as an outmoded, picturesque description. Discrete causes never occur in individual bodies because of the simple reason that discrete, individual bodies do not themselves exist.[8]

This is only a sampler. The three themes are intertwined repeatedly in holistic writings.

New developments in physical science have always been used to justify new therapies, or to explain the supposed efficacy of old ones. Most of the therapies were ineffective or crank; most of the science good or important. In the seventeenth century, the heyday of the mechanical philosophy, Robert Boyle argued for the curative powers of amulets from the hypothesis that matter is made up of corpuscles. The eighteenth-century interest in magnets generated magnetic cures, and the nineteenth-century interest in electrical phenomena brought about all manner of electrical cures. None of them worked, but their promoters did a good business. Is the holistic appeal to quantum mechanics more of the same— intellectual crankery mixed with medical crankery—or is it more serious, more informed, more likely to be right?

In what follows we will argue for two claims: (1) The holists have no understanding of the scientific process; their claims about the structure of contemporary and recent physical science, and the conclusions that can reasonably be drawn from that science, are false and absurd. (2) There is no alternative holistic paradigm for scientific medicine. There is only an insistence on abandoning every feature of scientific medicine, including experimental controls and experimental design generally, careful statistical analysis, use of the best relevant conclusions drawn from other sciences, and the practice of rational criticism and response to arguments.

WHAT IS QUANTUM MECHANICS?

The quantum theory of radiation emerged at the very beginning of this century in the work of Max Planck and Albert Einstein. Initially the theory was developed to explain thermodynamic properties of electromagnetic radiation, such as "black-body" radiation, but Einstein used it to explain a number of other puzzling phenomena involving light and other forms of radiation. About 1913, Niels Bohr developed a quantum theory of the structure of matter. Bohr's theory was intended to explain the motions of subatomic particles, and to account for the interactions of atoms and electromagnetic radiation. Bohr's theory was developed and modified for over a decade until, in the 1920s, it was displaced by a new and radically different quantum theory of matter and radiation. The new quantum theory was developed principally by Erwin Schrödinger and Werner Heisenberg, although a great many other first-class physicists contributed to the elaboration of the theory. This "new" quantum theory, now sixty years old, has in turn been modified in many ways by later theoretical developments (Schrödinger's and Heisenberg's theory, for example, had to be modified to be made consistent with special relativity). But the essential features of the "new" quantum theory have been retained in later modifications, and holists appeal to these features in claiming that the quantum theory has refuted orthodox medicine and requires holistic medicine instead.

Quantum theory applies to any physical system, but to apply it the structure and parts of the system, as well as the forces they exert on one another, must be specified. Thus the quantum theory can be applied to a system consisting of an atomic nucleus and the atom's electrons. The theory explains and predicts the behavior of the electrons. For any such physical system, appropriately described, the theory determines a differential equation describing how the physical *state* of the system changes with time. These differential equations are typically beyond our ability to solve, except for the very simplest of systems. In practice, physicists and physical chemists who use the quantum theory usually do not solve the equations exactly. Instead, they rely on *approximate* solutions, obtained in various ways.

For a physical system such as an atom and its component parts, there are many *dynamical variables* that are important. If we are studying the behavior of an atom's electrons, for example, these variables include the position of the electron, its momentum, its angular momentum, its energy and its spin. It is the value of these variables that we measure, directly or indirectly, when we do experiments on the atomic system.

In Newtonian physics, the state of a physical system implies unique values for all of the dynamical variables of the system. In quantum theory, the state of a physical system does not determine a unique value for every dynamical variable of the system. Different possible states will determine unique values for different collections of dynamical variables. But no one state determines a unique value for all of the dynamical variables that could be measured. Thus a quantum state that determines a unique value for the position of an electron will not determine a unique value for the momentum of the electron, and a quantum state that determines a unique value for the momentum of an electron will not determine a unique value for the position of the electron. If a state determines a unique value for a variable, then the state is said to be *eigenstate* for that variable. If a quantum state is an eigenstate of a variable, then the state determines a unique value of the variable, and that value is said to be an *eigenvalue* of the quantum state.

What does the quantum theory say about the values of variables such as momentum when the system is not in an eigenstate of momentum? While the theory does not determine a unique value for variables if the system is not in an eigenstate of those variables, it does say something important about their values. If the state of a system is not an eigenstate of a variable, the state determines a *probability distribution* for the possible values of the variable. That is, for any value or measurable set of values of the variable, the state of the system determines the probability that the variable has that value or has a value in that set of values. Thus, if a system were not in a spin eigenstate, the theory would still determine a probability for each of the possible values of the spin variable. The quantum theory's predictions about the probabilities of values of dynamical variables can be tested experimentally, and are thus far strongly confirmed.

While the state of the system and the general quantum theory together only determine a probability distribution for some variables, the theory also determines *relationships* among the probability distributions for different variables. The most famous of these relationships is the Heisenberg Uncertainty Relation. Consider two variables, such as position and momentum, which do not have a common eigenstate.[9] Any quantum state will determine a probability distribution for the momentum of a particle and a probability distribution for the position of the particle. Probability distributions can be more or less spread out. That is, all of the probability can be concentrated in one or in a small set of values, or, alternatively, the probability can be more widely distributed among many possible values. In probability theory, the spread-outness of a probability distribution in a variable X is measured by the *variance* of the distribution. The variance is defined by the formula

$$VAR(X) = \sum (X-\hat{X})^2 Prob(X)$$

In this formula "VAR(X)" stands for the variance of the probability distribution of X, "$\sum$" stands for summation over all possible values of X, "$\hat{X}$" stands for the mean or average of all of the X values, and "Prob(X)" stands for the probability of any X value. So the formula says that the variance of X is the sum, over all possible values of X, of the squared difference between each value and the average value of X, multiplied by the probability of that value of X.

The Heisenberg Uncertainty Relation specifies a relationship between the variances of the probability distributions of any two dynamical variables in any quantum state. It says that for any two dynamical variables P and Q (e.g., momentum and position)

$$VAR(P)VAR(Q) > 0.527 \bullet 10^{-34} \text{ joule-sec}$$

The number on the right is *very* small. The Uncertainty Relation says that the product of the spread-outnesses of the two probability distributions cannot be less than this number. Put another way, this relationship puts a limit on how precisely we can predict the simultaneous values of two variables that do not share a common eigenstate. In the case of position and momentum this relationship is usually expressed as

$$\Delta q \ \Delta p > 0.527 \bullet 10^{-34} \text{ joule-sec}$$

A joule is a unit of energy, and a joule-second is a unit of "action." The important thing to understand is that the uncertainty relationshps are only of significance for very, very small objects. For a two hundred pound man, the uncertainty relations permit the determination of his position to within much less than a trillionth of an inch, and the simultaneous determination of his momentum to within much less than a trillionth of a pound-foot per second. That is a great deal more precise than we require in order to know, in everyday terms, where someone is and how he is moving.

The Schrödinger equation of the quantum theory specifies how the quantum state changes through time. The Schrödinger equation is deterministic: For a given initial quantum state, it specifies a *unique* quantum state at any later time. The Schrödinger equation correctly describes the time evolution of the quantum state of a system only if the system is *isolated,* that is, only if there are no other forces acting on the system besides the forces considered in the Schrödinger equation for that system. If other forces intervene, the Schrödinger equation will not correctly predict the state of the system. In reality, of course, no system is completely isolated. The electrons in atoms, for example, are subject to gravitational forces from one another and from other particles. But these gravitational forces are so small compared to electromagnetic forces that they are ignored in the Schrödinger equation. Neglecting gravitation makes no detectible difference in any of the experimental outcomes. There is an important moral here: *Physics proceeds by approximation. If every bit of every force always had to be taken into account exactly, no calculations or predictions could be made at all.*

In large systems, such as planets and people, the amount of energy required to measure dynamical variables can be reduced to a miniscule fraction of the energy of the system. The system can therefore be regarded as approximately isolated even during the process of measurement. In quantum systems, however, the energies that must be introduced into the system in the process of measurement, or extracted from it, are a significant fraction of the energy of the system as a whole. We therefore cannot expect that the Schrödinger equation applied to an electron, say, will accurately predict how the state of the electron will change with time when the electron is subjected to a measurement of some kind. If we make the electron interact with another particle, as in cloud chamber measurements, there will be energy transfers between the other particle(s) and the electron. If we make the electron interact with radiation, there will be similar energy transfers. How does the state of a quantum system change when we measure a dynamical variable?

The question of the behavior of a subatomic system when measured may seem remote, but it is the source of the claim that modern physics has something special to say about consciousness. The holists' frequent references to quantum physics and consciousness depend on rather technical features of the quantum theory. The merit (or demerit) of their claims cannot be understood unless one has at least a glimpse of how measurement is treated in quantum theory. Essentially, the quantum theory has a problem because it has two different ways of predicting the state of a physical system, such as an electron, and these two ways need not always agree. When a theory has two ways of predicting a quantity, such as the state of a system, and the predictions do not agree, then the theory is inconsistent, unless some rule can be found that says when each of the conflicting predictions are appropriate. The notion that consciousness has something to do with physical phenomena derives from the conjecture that it is the presence or absence of a conscious mind that determines which of the two ways of calculating the state of a quantum system is the appropriate one. With that point in mind, let us look more closely at measurement in quantum theory.

John von Neumann, who provided the elegant mathematical foundations of the quantum theory, treated the question this way.[10] When a measurement is made, he assumed, the measured value that is found for the variable in question is always an eigenvalue for *some* quantum state of the system, although in general it will not be an eigenvalue of the quantum state the system was in directly before measurement. After a measurement is made, he postulated, the state of the quantum system is changed. The original quantum state is "projected" onto another quantum state, which represents the state of the system immediately after the measurement interaction. *The latter state is always an eigenstate of the measured variable, and has the measured value of the variable as an eigenvalue.* This assumption is known as the *Projection Postulate,* and it is an integral, if sometimes controversial, part of the quantum theory.

So in quantum mechanics there are two distinct rules for describing how the quantum state of a system changes with time. One rule, the Schrödinger equation, applies to isolated systems. The other rule, the Projection Postulate, applies to systems undergoing a measurement interaction. The existence of two distinct rules for determining the development of quantum states has led to the measurement problem of quantum theory, which has both a technical aspect and a philosophical aspect. To understand the latter one must first understand something about the former.

The technical problem is this. The quantum theory can be applied to any system. In the process of measurement, an atomic or subatomic system is not isolated because some other source of energy, whether matter or radiation, interacts with the system. We could, however, apply the quantum theory to the larger system that includes the other source of energy—photons or particles—and write a Schrödinger equation for that larger system. We could regard the larger system as effectively isolated and use the quantum theory and the Schrödinger equation to predict the state of the system during and after the measurement process. From the state of the system after the measurement process, we could predict the probabilities of subsequent measurements of other dynamical variables or even of the same variable that was measured in the first instance. This procedure makes no use of the Projection Postulate. On the other hand, we could treat the original quantum system by the Schrödinger equation and derive its state just before measurement. We could then use the Projection Postulate to determine the state of the quantum system after measurement. Knowing the state of the quantum system after measurement, we could again apply the Schrödinger equation to derive its state at a later time, and thus predict the probabilities of subsequent measurements of the same or different dynamical variables. The technical aspect of the measurement problem lies in showing that these two ways of calculating the results of a sequence of measurements are consistent, that is, always give the same results. Research suggests that in general they do not.

The philosophical aspect of the measurement problem derives from the following reflection. Suppose we let the quantum system, an electron say, interact with other particles in order to measure its position. That is roughly what is done in a cloud chamber in which an electron interacts with other particles to ionize them, and droplets of water form around the ionized particles to leave a cloudy image of the path of the electron through the apparatus. If we treat the electron and the particles it interacts with as an isolated system, we must somehow do something to *that* system in order to detect where the ions are located in space. So theoretically, we must apply the Projection Postulate to the combined system consisting of the electron and the particles it interacts with. But in order to locate the positions of the ions, we have water vapor liquify around them. We could treat the electron, the particles, and the water vapor as an isolated system. But to measure the position of the water droplets in the cloud chamber, we must somehow interact with those droplets. Theoretically, again, we could apply the Projection Postulate to the larger system consisting of the electron, the particles and the water vapor, and thus determine the state of the total system after measurement. But in order to locate the position of the water droplets in the cloud chamber, we look at it, or take a photograph of it. In either case, light must interact with the water droplets to form an image, either on the camera film or on our retinas. Once again we can consider the larger total system consisting of everything we had before plus the light rays, and we can apply the Projection Postulate to that system. Suppose we are looking at the cloud chamber with our eyes. Then we could consider the still larger system consisting of our retina, the light rays, the water vapor, the particles, and the electron as an isolated system to which the Schrödinger equation applies, and we could apply the Projection Postulate to that system. We need not stop there. For us to know about the position of the electron, the retinal image must be transmitted along the optic nerve and be processed (somehow) by our central nervous system. So we could add our central nervous system to the system being considered, and we could apply the Schrödinger equation to the system consisting of the electron, the particles, the water vapor, the light rays, our retina, and our central nervous system.

Where is the right place to draw the line? When should we stop applying the Schrödinger equation and use the Projection Postulate? What should we treat as the system under study and what should we treat as the measuring apparatus that is not included within the Schrödinger equation? Von Neumann's answer is that it doesn't matter: If the theory is correct we should get the same answer wherever we draw the line, so we may draw it where we please. All that matters is that we use the Projection Postulate somewhere.

Suppose now that the technical measurement problem in quantum theory has no solution, which means that we will, in general, get different answers about the results of a sequence of measurements if, on the one hand, we apply the Schrödinger equation to the object system, then apply the Projection Postulate, then apply the Schrödinger equation to the object system again; or if, on the other hand, we include the measuring apparatus within the object system and apply the Schrödinger equation alone to the combined system. In that case either the quantum theory, as von Neumann developed it, is inconsistent or else there must be some one appropriate place at which to apply the Projection Postulate. But how can there be? For any division we allow between measuring apparatus and quantum system, the quantum theory always permits us to enlarge the system described by the Schrödinger equation to include all or any part of the measuring system itself.

Eugene Wigner considered this question in a number of papers, and his solution was to suppose that there *is* a privileged way of making the division between a system described by the Schrödinger equation, and an observing system.[11] But according to Wigner that division cannot be into two different *physical* systems, for the reasons just given. The observing system, the system that causes the quantum state to be projected into an eigenstate of the measured observable, must be something nonphysical, something to which the Schrödinger equation cannot be applied. What could that something be? Wigner proposed that it be consciousness. The entire sensory system of the human observer can be included in the system described by the Schrödinger equation, and so can the human brain, but consciousness cannot be. On Wigner's view, physical systems evolve in complex ways according to the Schrödinger equation, and after a mere *physical* interaction with a measuring system the quantum state of atomic systems is not necessarily in any eigenstate of the measured variable. But when a human becomes conscious of a measurement result, somehow, mysteriously, in that very instant the state of the atomic system is projected into an eigenstate of the measured variable. Thus, everything works just as if we had applied the Schrödinger equation to the atomic system alone, and had used the Projection Postulate.

Wigner's solution is not the only possible one, and it is not even a very popular one among experts on the interpretation of the quantum theory. Other approaches are to deny the universal validity of the Projection Postulate, or to deny that the Schrödinger equation can be applied to macroscopic systems (such as the entire human central nervous system). Still another approach is to admit that the quantum theory *is* inconsistent, but that the inconsistency is of no practical consequence, since we know how to *use* the theory to get consistent experimental results. The last interpretation is not at all bizarre. Physicists are used to dealing with theories that give good predictions of experimental results but are internally inconsistent. Classical electrodynamics could not explain, for example, why electrons are not torn apart by their own electric fields. Quantum field theories had difficulties with the infinite self-energy of the vacuum, and various "renormalization" procedures were developed to permit the theories to give consistent results. Theoretical inconsistencies can be challenging problems to theorists, but they need not interfere with the usefulness of a scientific hypothesis in explaining and predicting the outcomes of experiments.

If we accept Wigner's interpretation of the quantum theory, however, we must understand how little power consciousness has. On Wigner's account, consciousness causes quantum states to change, but it has no power to determine *how* they change, or with what frequency they change. The observer's psychological state, his preferences, tastes, desires, fears, hopes, wishes, have no effect on the measured values that we observe. Those values must occur with the frequency that is predicted by giving the appropriate Schrödinger equation for the atomic or subatomic system, and applying the Projection Postulate for the variable measured. There is only one power of consciousness on Wigner's interpretation: to determine what measured variables it becomes aware of. The probabilities of the various possible values of the measured variable are determined by physical law, and states of mind are impotent to alter them.

There are other controversial features of the quantum theory that are still under active discussion by physicists and by professional philosophers of science. One of these issues concerns whether, even though quantum states do not permit us to *predict* exact values for all dynamical variables, we can still consistently suppose that quantum systems *have* exact values for all of their dynamical variables at once. A system might, we could suppose, have simultaneous, exact values for all of its dynamical variables, even though not all of those values can be predicted. It turns out that there is no clear answer to this question. The answer obtained depends on what counts as a dynamical variable. In a famous paper (famous, that is, among real physicists and real philosophers of science; the paper is apparently unknown to holist writers) two mathematicians, Simon Kochen and Ernst Specker, showed that on one straightforward interpretation of what counts as a dynamical variable, it is mathematically impossible to assign exact values to all such variables at once.[12] However, another mathematician, Stanley Gudder, showed that with a different account of the variables it is possible for all dynamical variables of a quantum system to have simultaneous, exact values.[13] Gudder's way of counting variables is more generous than that of Kochen and Specker. Where the latter count one dynamical variable, Gudder counts several—all of which may have different values. To date, there is no clear resolution as to which way of counting dynamical variables is correct.

Holistic writings about quantum mechanics sometimes mention a proof attributed to J. S. Bell.[14] Just why they cite it is unclear, since the proof has nothing to do with consciousness or the like. Quantum physics retains many of the conservation laws of classical physics. Angular momentum, for example, is a conserved quantity in quantum mechanics, as are many other quantities. Some quantum systems consist of parts that have correlated dynamical variables. Thus a system might consist of two electrons that have opposite spins. The sum of their spins is zero, and that sum must be conserved. Again, photons may have correlated polarizations. If a system consisting of correlated parts (e.g., two photons) is produced, and the parts move away from one another and become spatially separated, we can perform measurements on each separately. Typically, there are many different dynamical variables we could measure on each system, and each variable is bound by a conservation law to a dynamical variable of the other system. If we measure any such variable on subsystem one, the conservation laws tell us what the measured value must be for that variable on subsystem two. In principle (and to some extent in practice) we can actually do such measurements, and collect data about the correlations of values of variables on the two subsystems. Now for such a quantum system, consisting of two correlated parts, one could adopt either of two hypotheses: for each subsystem there is a physical state that determines the values of all of the dynamical variables of that subsystem, or else there aren't such states. Bell showed with an easy argument that if you assume there is such a state, different predictions about the correlations of the measured variables are obtained than the predictions given by the quantum theory. Experimental work has confirmed the quantum theory's predictions about the correlations. There has been considerable discussion about just how to interpret Bell's theorem and related results. One view, for example, is that the quantum subsystems do not *have* values for their dynamical variables (or at least not for many of them) until a measurement is made; but when a measurement is made on one such subsystem, the other subsystem instantaneously acquires the appropriate value (appropriate that is, to agree with the conservation laws) for its corresponding variable. One trouble with this interpretation is that it threatens to make the quantum theory inconsistent with special relativity. If the choice of measurements to be made on one system can have an instantaneous effect on a remote system, then it would seem to be possible in principle to establish a code, so that the choice of measurements in one place could be used to send a message to another place more rapidly than the speed of light.

WHAT IS QUANTUM SILLINESS?

Holists maintain that quantum mechanics shows consciousness to be an important variable in determining the course of illness and cure, and that conventional scientific medicine is hopelessly flawed by its neglect of this important variable. Thus Larry Dossey writes:

> The possibility that patients actually influence the course of their own illness as well as their response to therapy through the impact of their consciousness on the physical world—which contains their own bodies—must be seriously considered, unless we wish to ignore the theoretical considerations and the experimental data of quantum physics.[15]

We have seen that on one very controversial interpretation of quantum theory, i.e., Wigner's, consciousness does have a role in determining quantum states, but even on that interpretation consciousness can only determine what variables the quantum state is an eigenstate of. It cannot have any effect on the *value* of those variables. "Emotions and feelings," Dr. Dossey's human factors, make no difference to quantum phenomena, not even on Wigner's account.

Holists also claim that quantum theory shows, owing to the role it assigns to consciousness, the importance of subjectivity in science. Although they do not put it so bluntly, what they imply is that quantum theory shows that what there is can be determined by what you want there to be, or how you feel about things. Thus Dr. James Gordon intones:

> Today health care professionals whose scientific education has been shaped by the implications of relativity theory and quantum mechanics are emphasizing the inherent subjectivity of all diagnostic judgements, including those based on the most advanced of our technologies. They are suggesting that we may, simply by observing and defining it, shape the nature, course, and outcome our patients' health and illness.[16]

And Professor Pelletier:

> As physicists probe into an invisible, subatomic universe where time is reversible and matter must be annihilated and created in billionths of a second, they find it no longer possible to adhere to their traditional conventions of objective research, for what is readily observable by anyone is highly tenuous.[17]

And finally Dr. Dossey:

We find natural the idea that the world exists apart from us, that it occupies an independent existence in its own right. Scientists are able to approach this kind of world, make observations from it at a distance, extract valid and meaningful data, and then retreat to make sense out of these observations. The objective world is what makes science possible.

This idea of doing science, however, belongs to the eighteenth century, not to our own. This belief has been challenged in our time by quantum physics. The notion of science as an objective endeavor was most forcefully shaken by Heisenberg's Uncertainty Principle.[18]

This is noxious falsehood. The quantum theory has nothing to do with the "subjectivity of all diagnostic judgements." The "conventions of objective research" have not been altered by the quantum theory. The uncertainty relations limit predictability—they are limitations on the powers of mind, not enhancements of it. Theoretical physics has not become touchy-feely—anything goes, you have your particles, I'll have mine—pseudoscience. Ask the teams of physicists who spend tens of thousands of hours, and millions of dollars, designing reliable apparatus, reproducing experimental results, checking for errors in calculations and in physical arrangements. Ask them if they have abandoned the "conventions of objective research."

Moreover, quantum theory has not led physicists to place any emphasis on "consciousness" as a causal factor in experimental outcomes. States of consciousness do not appear as variables in any of the papers published in the *Physical Review* nowadays. Physicists have not found that in order to do particle physics they must first do psychology. Consciousness plays only a minor role in one rather implausible solution to the measurement problem; and even if that solution is embraced, there is nothing to be learned about the physical structure of the universe from speculations about the mind.

The second holistic theme concerns "reductionism." Biomedical scientists investigate biochemical pathways of disease processes; and because they do, we have an enormously enriched understanding of genetic disorders, infectious diseases, and immunological processes. The holistic thesis is that quantum mechanics shows all of this to be a grave mistake, because it depends on "reductionism," a view that the holists invariably denounce by appealing to the quantum theory. Part of what they mean is just consciousness again. The "reductionism" of biomedical science holds that all properties of people can ultimately be explained by the physical properties of matter. The holists' version of quantum mechanics requires consciousness to have irreducible powers to affect the course of nature. Real quantum mechanics does no such thing, as should be plain from what we have said before.

Another part of what the holists mean in denouncing reductionism has to do with the very idea of breaking large things down into smaller things. The holistic version of quantum theory says that there is no such thing as individual, separate entities: no electrons, no protons, no mesons, no molecules, no macromolecules. Only a tangled Oneness. Hence, biomedical science is not just leaving something—consciousness—out of consideration. Worse, biomedical science proceeds on the false assumption that large things are made up of separate small things, an assumption that is contradicted by the revelations of quantum theory. Clinical medicine makes the same mistake, says Dr. Dossey:

The word "patient" is as misleading as the word "particle." All mental images of human beings as isolated, fundamental, clinical units are bound to be as wrong as the notions of subatomic particles as spatially separated particulate bits. . . . [H]uman beings are essentially dynamic processes and patterns that are fundamentally not analyzable into separate parts—either within or between each other. Like health and disease, they are spread through space and time, and it is their interrelatedness and oneness, not their isolation and separation, which is most important.[19]

Well, suppose the holists are right and in literal truth there are no distinct entities. We find, nonetheless, that physicists proceed very well by dividing the world into various kinds of distinct entities: mesons, pions, photons, electrons, positrons, and quarks. Indeed, if we look at quantum theory as it is practiced, we realize that the theory *cannot even be applied* without treating various systems as approximately isolated, and without describing systems such as atoms as composed of distinct parts between which forces operate. We find that chemists, the scientists whose work is closest to the atomic level, proceed very nicely by supposing that they are dealing with discrete objects, molecules, made up of discrete atoms, which are in turn made up of discrete elementary particles. It is not just that these assumptions are the very bedrock of chemical theory and enable chemists to predict and explain the properties of materials. Without these assumptions there is, quite simply, no chemistry at all. So if the holists are correct, and all is Oneness, still the Oneness turns out to be very unimportant in predicting, understanding, and explaining the world we find around us. The Distinctness turns out to be very important for all of these things. The world, whether subatomic, atomic, or macroscopic, behaves very much as if there are distinct entities, some distinctly localized in space/time, some spread out through vast regions. The hypothesis that the world is full of distinct entities may be false in detail, but it is very close to the truth, and it is the only hypothesis that makes understanding and the very activity of science—any science—possible.

Distinctness does not imply unrelatedness. Distinct objects can have relationships to one another. Another part of the holist denunciation of reductionism alleges that quantum theory shows everything to be related to everything else. Biomedical science, woe to it, fails to take account of this profound fact. In truth, however, the notion that everything in the universe affects everything else is a Newtonian conception: it is the very core idea of universal gravitation. The remotest pebble on the remotest planet exerts a tug on your heartstrings and on mine. Contrary to the holists' fanciful accounts of the history of physics, it is with *general relativity* that we find a gravitational theory within which the possibility arises that some parts of the universe may have no effect on other parts, because no causal process can reach from one region of space/time to the other. Contemporary quantum theory and general relativity have not yet been merged into a consistent and well confirmed generalization, but if they are we can expect that the resulting theory will share a statistical version of the localization possibilities implicit in general relativity.

When the holists go on about the Oneness, they betray an ignorance of the first principle of physics: that some relationships are more important than others. Some forces and some effects are too small to be of any practical consequence. The more spatially remote the source, the less important the effect is likely to be, other things being equal. Quantum physicists studying nuclear resonances with earthly cyclotrons happily ignore the goings on of remote stars. For science, the interrelatedness of all things is a happy (but probably false) reflection, not a guide to understanding.

The third holistic theme from quantum mechanics concerns causality. Biomedical science makes a profound error, holists claim, in attempting to detect causal pathways. The errors alleged are several: first, quantum mechanics is contradicted when the assumption is made that there are any causal relations at all between distinct entities or events; second, biomedical sciences err in assuming that for each effect there is a unique cause, when in truth quantum mechanics shows us that everything effects everything else; and third, biomedical sciences err in assuming that causal relations are deterministic while quantum theory shows they are indeterministic. Sometimes holists put these complaints in a phrase: the biomedical sciences have a "mechanistic" conception of causality, and that contradicts quantum mechanics.

Holists voice these complaints repeatedly in their writings about quantum mechanics. Thus Fritjof Capra alleges:

> The conceptual problem at the center of contemporary health care is the biomedical definition of disease, according to which diseases are well-defined entities that involve structural changes at the cellular level and have unique causal roots. The biomedical model allows for several kinds of causative factors, but researchers tend to adhere to the doctrine of "one disease, one cause." . . .
>
> These mechanisms, rather than the true origins, are seen as the causes of disease in current medical thinking, and this confusion lies at the very center of the conceptual problem of contemporary medicine.[20]

Capra prepares the reader to recognize this "conceptual problem" with some remarks about quantum mechanics:

> In quantum theory individual events do not always have a well-defined cause. For example, the jump of an electron from one atomic orbit to another, or the disintegration of a subatomic particle, may occur spontaneously without any single event causing it . . . . The behavior of any part is determined by its nonlocal connections to the whole, and since we do not know these connections precisely, we have to replace the narrow classical notion of cause and effect by the wider concept of statistical causality. . . . Whereas in classical mechanics the properties and behavior of the parts determine those of the whole, the situation is reversed in quantum mechanics: it is the whole that determines the behavior of the parts.[21]

And Dr. Dossey points to the same "problem" when he says: "Just as the older physical models of the universe wrongly attributed causal and independent qualities to the universe, the current medical models impart the same qualities to man."[22]

Let us take these theses one by one. First of all, is it true that biomedical science assumes that for each disease there is one and only one causal factor? Of course not, and to claim otherwise is just silly. All sorts of causal factors, at various levels, are detailed for many disease processes. Consider AIDS (Acquired Immune Deficiency Syndrome), a disease that has in recent years killed more than five thousand people. Causal factors in *contracting* AIDS include: hemophilia, homsexuality, promiscuity (especially homosexual promiscuity), intravenous drug abuse, and being Haitian. But biomedical science does not stop with the articulation of alternative causal factors. It also looks for common bases for the several causal factors, and the likeliest suggestion is that the various practices and living conditions associated with these causal factors all increase the probability of transmitting bodily fluids from one person to another. The transmission of fluids is likely to transmit the disease if the fluids contain some infectious agent or agents that contribute to the disease. Biomedical scientists have isolated and identified an AIDS virus, and conclude that this virus is transmitted from one AIDS victim or carrier to another.

Does this mean that, so far as AIDS is concerned, biomedicine has proceeded on the assumption that there is one and only one causal factor? Exactly the reverse. Not only is the virus a causal factor, but so are all of the practices and living conditions that contribute to its transmission. Not only are the virus and the transmission routes causal factors, but so is the frequency of transmission and the degree of exposure to the virus. Not only are all of these factors causally relevant, but so are unknown features that vary widely from person to person in the population. Scientists know that a great many more people have been exposed to the virus than have contracted the disease.

Why does biomedical science concentrate on the virus; why is it termed the "specific cause" of AIDS? This is to some extent just standard medical terminology. In medicine "specific cause" does not mean, and never meant, "unique cause." "Specific cause" means that variable factor (or factors—specific causes do not have to be unique) without which the disease never occurs. The virus is a specific cause of AIDS because, without exposure to the virus, the disease does not occur. Scientists focus on the virus, on seeking tests to identify it and vaccines against it, because that is the one *ethical* means they have to attempt to prevent the spread of the disease, and very likely the most effective means as well. We could try to stop the spread of AIDS in lots of other, more "holistic" ways. We could isolate Haiti and deport all Haitians. We could stop giving blood transfusions to hemophiliacs (or anyone else)—that way, people might die, but they wouldn't get AIDS from blood transfusions. We could make homosexuality illegal, punishable by death, and vigorously enforce the law. Or we could tell everyone to use their "consciousness" and just *hope* that AIDS does not continue to spread. We prefer the route of biomedical science.

What about the charge that biomedical science uses an erroneous deterministic view of causality, or fails to understand the quantum fact that the whole determines the part, not vice-versa? We have seen that the indeterminism in quantum theory is very small, and has no significance even on the micro-biological level. There are biological effects in which quantum effects are important, but when such effects and processes are studied, biologists do what they should do: they use the quantum theory. There is no determinism of the part from the whole in quantum theory. It is not the whole of the universe that determines whether or not an atomic nucleus will decay in a given moment: *nothing* determines it. On some interpretations of the theory, what quantities we decide to measure determine whether or not a quantum system has a value for a particular variable, but our decision has no effect on what value the quantum system has, if it has a value.

Finally, what about the charge that biomedical science errs in assuming that there are any causes at all? We think this is not a thesis holists should want to press very hard, since every holistic therapist claims that his therapy "works," and this is at best euphemistic talk for the claim that the therapy *causes* desired effects. But even so, nothing in quantum theory prohibits or contradicts our notions of causal relations. Quantum theory does make us realize that some subatomic events have no deterministic causes, and so makes us think of causal relations as sometimes relations that merely increase or decrease the probability of effects. Philosophers of science, medical scientists, and social scientists have thought that way very comfortably for many years.

WHAT IS REALLY GOING ON?

There is a pattern to holistic writing about quantum mechanics. Some half-truth about the theory is vaguely stated, some controversial interpretation is taken as the settled judgment of the scientific community, the half-truth is wildly exaggerated, and the exaggeration is used to justify an absurdity about biomedical research and clinical practice. The repeated litany is that orthodox medicine is in error because it is not *consistent* with this exaggerated and distorted account of fundamental physics. Fritjof Capra makes this appeal in a typical way:

> Among the sciences that have been influenced by the Cartesian world view and by Newtonian physics, and will have to change to be consistent with the views of modern physics, I shall concentrate on those dealing with health in the broadest ecological sense: from biology and medical science to psychology and psychotherapy, sociology, economics and political science. . . . Scientists will not need to be reluctant to adopt a holistic framework, as they often are today, for fear of being unscientific. Modern physics can show them that such a framework is not only scientific, but is in agreement with the most advanced scientific theories of physical reality.[23]

Capra's talk of consistency is bluff. Any medical researcher can call the bluff with one challenge: *Give us a single quantum mechanical calculation that contradicts our biomedical findings.* Holists cannot and do not do it, exactly because—save in rare cases—quantum mechanics simply cannot be applied to the levels at which biomedical researchers work. No one knows how to apply the theory, or approximations of it, to bacteria and viruses. When the theory can be applied, it is taken account of in conventional scientific practice.

This concern for consistency is misplaced for another reason. Science works by approximation; it never was, and perhaps never will be in theory or in practice, a single consistent piece. Our fundamental theories of the universe have always had their difficulties, their internal incoherencies and their inconsistencies with one another. Scientists try to iron them out, but typically ironing out the details of logical tensions results in the replacement of the theories by better theories, with still other conceptual problems. Even when theories are consistent, science proceeds in applications by rearranging and contradicitng them. We do not calculate the orbits of satellites using general relativity. Instead, we use Newtonian celestial mechanics, even though that theory contradicts general relativity. We do so because the Newtonian theory is simpler to apply and because we know that, in the circumstances we wish to apply it, Newtonian theory approximates general relativity as closely as we could wish. As for scientists who do physiology, sociology, organic chemistry, fluid dynamics, and biomedicine without regard to quantum mechanics, they are not betraying scientific standards or being illogical or old-fashioned. They are doing science the way it is supposed to be done, and the only way it can be done. It does not improve science to substitute conjecture and rhetoric about frontier sciences for the careful work of scientists concerned with macroscopic phenomena. It only abuses science.

We do not believe that the holists are really concerned to make science consistent with quantum theory. Instead, their aim is to establish their credentials on the cheap. It usually requires a lot of work to establish new therapies, new sciences, and new approaches to old and well investigated problems. They must be shown, by the usual canons of evidence and argument in science, to explain better and to predict better. In medicine the standard is found in the clinical trial, which requires careful design, careful selection of subjects, accurate and specific descriptions and definitions, and close statistical analysis. Holistic practitioners do not really care to provide any of these things. Nor do they even care to provide weaker forms of scientific evidence such as statistical *ex post facto* studies. They rely instead on attempting to undermine the very concept of rational science, and present their holism as the only apparent alternative. Were they to succeed, the result would not be better and more exciting science. It would be no science at all.

NOTES

1. K. Pelletier, *Holistic Medicine: From Stress to Optimum Health* (New York: Dell, 1979), 23–24.
2. F. Capra, "Foreword," in L. Dossey, *Space, Time & Medicine* (Boulder, Colo.: Shambhala, 1982), x.
3. Pelletier, *Holistic Medicine*, 30–31.
4. Dossey, *Space, Time & Medicine*, 116.
5. F. Capra, *The Tao of Physics* (New York: Bantam Books, 1975), 57.
6. Pelletier, *Holistic Medicine*, 26.
7. K. Pelletier, *Toward a Science of Consciousness* (New York: Delacorte Press, 1978), 50.
8. Dossey, *Space, Time & Medicine*, 144.
9. More precisely, two variables represented by noncommuting operators.
10. J. von Neumann, *Mathematical Foundations of Quantum Mechanics* (Princeton, N.J.: Princeton University Press, 1955).
11. E. Wigner, *Symmetries and Reflections* (Bloomington, Ind.: Indiana University Press, 1967), chs. 12–14.
12. S. Kochen and E. Specker, "The Problem of Hidden Variables in Quantum Mechanics," *Journal of Mathematics and Mechanics* 17 (1967): 59–87.
13. S. Gudder, "Systems of Observables in Axiomatic Quantum Mechanics," *Journal of Mathematical Physics* 8 (1967): 2109–13.
14. J. Bell, "On the Einstein Podolsky Rosen Paradox," *Physics* 1 (1964): 195–200.
15. Dossey, *Space, Time & Medicine*, 212.
16. J. Gordon, "The Paradigm of Holistic Medicine," in A. Hastings, J. Fadiman, J. Gordon (eds.), *Health for the Whole Person: The Complete Guide to Holistic Medicine* (New York: Bantam Books, 1980), 12.
17. Pelletier, *Toward a Science of Consciousness*, 42–43.
18. Dossey, *Space, Time & Medicine*, 194–95.
19. Ibid., 113–14.
20. F. Capra, *The Turning Point* (New York: Bantam Books, 1982), 150.
21. Ibid., 86.
22. Dossey, *Space, Time & Medicine*, 222.
23. Capra, *The Turning Point*, 49.

Robert N. Brandon, Ph.D.

Holism in Philosophy of Biology

Why should one interested in holistic medicine concern himself with philosophy of biology? There are several reasons. First, the term *holism* was coined by J. C. Smuts in the context of a dispute within philosophy of biology. Proponents of holistic medicine often mention this bit of history without giving any indication of understanding it. Second, the dispute continues today and advocates of holistic medicine write of holism versus reductionism or holism versus mechanism as if these "isms" were all perfectly clear. They are not, and clarifying them falls within the province of philosophy of biology. Finally, the resolution of the dispute is a matter of philosophy of biology. It is true that putative resolutions of this dispute have been applied to medical matters. That they are so applicable should not be surprising. Human beings are biological creatures. Disputes about the proper methods for the scientific study of life are obviously relevant to medicine, but the disputes themselves are parts of the philosophy of biology proper. My aim is to clarify the sense in which current philosophy of biology is and is not holistic. But to do that I think it is best to first survey the modern history of the concept of holism.

It is usual in tracing the history of ideas in biology to start with either Aristotle or Darwin. But to understand the rise of holism in twentieth-century biology one needs to turn first to Descartes. As is well known, Descartes thought that there was a fundamental difference between humans and other animals. Nonhuman animals were simply machines, mechanical devices. Humans were machines too, but not simply machines. In addition to their mechanical bodies, humans, Descartes argued, had souls (or minds). Although Mayr has recently argued that no knowledgeable biologists found Cartesian dualism persuasive, it did provide a working hypothesis for mechanistic physiology.[1] Physiologists could investigate humans and other animals by the same methods since the mental side of man was beyond the realm of physiology. Within biology challenges were raised to Cartesian dualism from the very beginning, but it was Darwin who dealt this form of dualism its death blow.

The Darwinian revolution was not completed until the "evolutionary synthesis" of the 1930s and 1940s.[2] Nevertheless, soon after the publication of *The Origins of Species* the Darwinian idea of evolution by common descent was almost universally accepted among biologists. (His mechanistic explanation of evolution—natural selection—was not so widely accepted.) Although there was (and still is) disagreement over just how gradual the evolutionary process is, the theory of evolution by common descent made it highly implausible that man and only man had a soul. Given the overwhelming evidence Darwin marshaled for this aspect of his theory, Cartesian dualism ceased to be a viable hypothesis shortly after 1859.

The mutual implausibility of evolution by common descent and Cartesian dualism presents what Laudan calls a conceptual problem.[3] It is this conceptual problem that gave rise to the philosophical controversies of the 1920s and 1930s to which we now turn.

HOLISM IN THE 1920s AND 1930s

One way of avoiding the aforementioned conceptual problem is to draw a line not between man and other animals, but between living things and inanimate matter.[4] Vitalists do just that. They claim that what differentiates living beings from inanimate matter is that the former have, in addition to their corporeal bodies, an immaterial "vital force" or "vital principle." This, in a sense, gives Cartesian souls to all plants and animals. Although its egalitarian spirit is to be admired, vitalism was clearly perceived to be unscientific, and by the 1920s no biologist, no matter what his philosophy, wanted the term "vitalist" hung around his neck.

J. C. Smuts and J. S. Haldane were two of the leading proponents of holism during this period. As I have already mentioned, Smuts coined the term *holism* in his 1926 book, *Holism and Evolution*. J. S. Haldane (father of the geneticist J. B. S. Haldane) expounded a view similar to Smuts's in a number of books.[5] After reading *Holism and Evolution* Haldane used 'holism' to describe his own views. Both writers went to great lengths to disassociate themselves from vitalists. Although vitalism avoids the conflict with the Darwinian hypothesis of evolution by common descent, it has other serious conceptual problems. Cartesian dualism posits causal interactions between material and immaterial substances. It has never been clear how such interactions would work, as they seem to violate the physical principle of the conservation of mass and energy. Vitalism also posits such interactions. Haldane and Smuts clearly saw this and rejected vitalism for that reason.[6] Smuts, for example, made the point plainly when he remarked:

> As Descartes formulated it, there is the *res cogitans* in the *res extensa;* there are two distinct separate *res* or entities, and the difficulties and contradictions arise

from their mutual assumed interaction. The theory of Vitalism or the vital force seems simply to repeat and to emphasize this dualism. But if we wish to overcome these difficulties and contradictions we have to probe more deeply than these popular views.[7]

According to its proponents, then, holism was not vitalistic. But the main target of Smuts's and Haldane's critical writings was mechanism, not vitalism. Unfortunately, here their arguments become more diffuse. At one point Haldane rejects mechanism, because, as of 1935, no complete mechanistic explanation of all life processes existed.[8] This clearly is not a good reason to reject a mechanistic approach to biology. More generally, both Smuts and Haldane seem to saddle mechanism with a singularly impoverished view of mechanisms (just as some current holists would saddle mechanists with Newtonian, or even Cartesian, physics). Having so characterized mechanism, they then went on to argue that self-regulating, homeostatic processes—processes they considered characteristic of life—were in principle incapable of being explained mechanistically. This will be discussed more fully in the next section, but for now let me just point out that advances in cybernetics make this argument much less plausible than it was in the 1920s and 1930s.[9] In the next section we shall see that it was not all that plausible even then.

The holism of Smuts and Haldane was on the one hand a reaction to vitalism and on the other a reaction to a crude sort of mechanism. For Haldane, the importance of holism as a positive doctrine was that it stressed the interconnectedness of living things. Not only are parts of wholes—e.g., parts of organisms—interconnected in such a way that the study of the parts in isolation will not reveal their working *in vivo,* but also organisms are connected with their environment in a way that makes the separation of the two impossible.[10] Smuts stressed that the whole is more than the sum of its parts, but not something added to those parts (contra vitalism): "A whole is not some *tertium quid* over and above the parts which compose it; it is these parts in their intimate union and the new reactions and functions which result from that union."[11] Indeed, the primary project of *Holism and Evolution* was to explain how evolution can be creative, that is, how higher levels of wholes (e.g., life) can emerge from lower levels (e.g., matter). Like Haldane, Smuts argued that the synthesis of parts into a whole changes those parts so that they no longer function as they would in isolation.

THE MECHANISTIC RESPONSE TO HOLISM IN THE 1920s AND 1930s

Before turning to a critical appraisal of holism and its role in current philosophy of biology, I want to examine the criticisms of a contemporary of Smuts and Haldane, Lancelot Hogben. In 1929, Hogben joined Smuts and Haldane for a symposium on the nature of life. He was highly critical of their holistic views, and in 1930 he published his criticisms in *The Nature of Living Matter*. Aside from their historical interest, Hogben's criticisms foreshadow much of what I will have to say in the final section of this paper. Three major points may be gleaned from Hogben's discussion of the holism-mechanism dispute.[12] They are:

1. The dispute is best seen as a methodological dispute.

2. Mechanism is not the same thing as reductionism. In particular, a mechanistic explanation in biology need not be given in physico-chemical terms.

3. Interconnections among the objects of study are not incompatible with a mechanistic point of view. But interconnections are to be discovered and explained mechanistically, not postulated *a priori*.

These points are all nicely illustrated by Hogben's discussion of T. H. Morgan's work on the genetics of Drosophila. Space does not permit a detailed discussion of this episode, but in what follows I shall try to hit the highlights.

Holists claim that the parts of wholes are interconnected in such a way that they cannot be studied in isolation—at least not if one wants to know how they behave in the whole. What is the methodological message in this? It is not clear, but whatever it is it would not have served genetics well. Mendel studied characters in peas, such as stem length, flower color, and seed shape, as independent characters. So, for example, stem length and flower color could be ignored in studying crosses between wrinkled and round peas. Of course, we now know that Mendel's characters are determined by genes located on different chromosomes and that is *why* they are independent (i.e., segregate independently). Characters determined by genes located on the same chromosome do not assort independently (i.e., do not obey Mendel's second law).

Morgan used the lack of independence among characters (linkage) to provide chromosome maps for Drosophila. He found that the characters studied fell into four linkage groups. This number matched the number of chromosomes in Drosophila. He also found that for any three characters within a linkage group, *A*, *B*, and *C*, the probability of *A* and *C* separating equals either the sum of the probabilities *A*–*B* and *B*–*C* separating or their difference. This was explained by the hypothesis that genes are aligned in a linear manner on chromosomes, and are separated when homologous chromosomes intertwine during reduction division and crossing-over occurs (i.e., a chromatid from each of the two homologous chromosomes breaks off and one replaces the other). If chromosomes are equally likely to break at any point, then it follows that the frequency of crossing-over between any two linked genes will be proportional to the distance between them. Using cross-over frequencies, Morgan was able to map the genes of his study onto the four chromosomes. This mapping gave the linear sequence of the genes as well as their relative distances. This obviously goes well beyond Sutton's theory that genes are located on chromosomes, and was a great advance in genetics.

Hogben persuasively argues that Morgan's methodology is thoroughly mechanistic. By mapping the location of genes on chromosomes Morgan provided a mechanistic explanation (based on accepted cytological observations and some plausible assumptions) of linkage groups and cross-over values. If methodologies are judged according to their results, then Morgan's work is surely a point in favor of mechanistic methodology. But is the holism-mechanism dispute a methodological one? Hogben points out that it is not generally so perceived:

> [I]n any discussion between the two [mechanist and holist], the combatants are generally at cross purposes. The mechanist is primarily concerned with an epistemological issue. His critic has always an ontological axe to grind. The mechanist is concerned with how to proceed to a construction which will represent as much about the universe as human beings with their limited range of receptor organs can agree to accept. The vitalist or holist has an incorrigible urge to get behind the limitations of our receptor organs and discover what the universe is *really* like.[13]

Clearly the prospects for resolving *that* sort of debate are grim. So, Hogben suggests, the debate should be construed as a methodological (or epistemological) one. Here the mechanist wins hands down. There are numerous examples of successful applications of mechanistic methodology: the holist offers no positive alternative.[14]

The example of Morgan's work was chosen not simply because Morgan was successful; what is particularly striking about this example is that it clearly shows that mechanism in biology is not to be identified with physico-chemical reductionism. The term *reductionism* is used in many ways by philosophers of science.[15] The most straightforward usage has to do with formal relations between theories.[16] More interesting, but less clear-cut, are the associated doctrines of ontological and explanatory reductionism. The ontological reductionist picks out some base-level entities and processes and claims that all higher-level entities and processes are nothing more than certain combinations of these base-level entities and processes. Associated with this doctrine is the claim that one can, in principle, explain all higher-level events and processes in base-level terms. In biology this typically gets expressed as the view that all biological events and processes can be explained in physico-chemical terms. As far as I can tell, Hogben was agnostic with respect to these two doctrines. He saw Morgan's work as interesting in this regard precisely because, as of 1930, we had virtually no knowledge of the physico-chemistry of chromosomes and their behavior during meiosis.

Morgan's mechanistic explanation is given totally in *biological* terms. Linkage groups and cross-over frequencies were determined by the statistical behavior of phenotypic traits in mass breeding experiments. These observed values were explained in terms of a hypothetical process suggested by the observable behavior of chromosomes during the reduction division of meiosis. Thus, to give a mechanistic explanation is not necessarily to give a physico-chemical explanation.

An important corollary of this point is, as Hogben puts it,

> The principle of mechanism or experimental determinism is compatible with the recognition of different levels of complexity or wholes, for what is analysable is complex, and what is complex consists of interrelated parts which together constitute a whole.[17]

A mechanist is no more prevented from recognizing organisms or, for that matter, groups of organisms as organized wholes than he is from recognizing automobiles as organized wholes.

The final point to emerge from Hogben's discussion of Morgan's work is that the mechanistic conception of wholes is completely compatible with the existence of complex interconnections among parts. Mendel had the good fortune (or duplicity) of studying seven independently segregating traits in a species whose chromosome number is seven. Morgan studied many more traits. Some segregated independently, others were linked. As we have seen, Morgan offered a mechanistic explanation of these observations. But what I think is most important here is that Morgan neither assumed that all traits segregate independently (as Mendel's second law would have it), nor that all traits were linked together in some inseparable holistic union. He was willing to observe the degree to which various traits were linked.

HOLISM AND MECHANISM IN CONTEMPORARY PHILOSOPHY OF BIOLOGY

Any mature and relatively complete philosophy of science will make both ontological and epistemological (or methodological) claims. If this philosophy is coherent the ontology and methodology will complement one another. That is, the methods will be appropriate for the entities and processes of the ontology, and the ontology will reflect what reliable methods have revealed. Philosophy of biology has yet to reach its senescence, but it has matured considerably in the last few years. In what follows I shall briefly explore the ways in which contemporary philosophy of biology is holistic and the ways in which it is mechanistic.

Although it is somewhat artificial to separate ontology and methodology—indeed, one of the points I wish to make is that such a separation is artificial—I shall begin by discussing biological methodology. Mayr has argued that the fundamental division in biology is between functional biology and evolutionary biology:

> The functional biologist is vitally concerned with the operation and interaction of

structural elements, from molecules up to organs and whole individuals. His ever-repeated question is "How?" How does something operate, how does it function? . . . The evolutionary biologist differs in his method and in the problems in which he is interested. His basic question is "Why?"[18]

Mayr illustrates his distinction by means of an example, a warbler beginning its migration from New Hampshire in late August. The functional biologist seeks the *proximate* causes of the start of migration. He asks, "What is the mechanism and how is it triggered?" The evolutionary biologist seeks the evolutionary, or *ultimate,* causes. He asks, "How and why has this mechanism evolved?" These two sorts of questions may be asked of almost all biological phenomena, and answers to both are necessary for a complete understanding of the phenomenon.

I think it is fairly obvious that the methodology of the functional biologist is thoroughly mechanistic. When a functional biologist studies warbler migration, Mendel's first law, the development of a species-specific song in birds or whatever, he seeks to explain the phenomena in terms of some underlying mechanism. While I agree completely with Mayr's distinction and have myself argued that there is an important difference between evolutionary explanations and other biological explanations,[19] I think that the evolutionary half of biology is no less mechanistic than its functional brother.

Evolutionary biology itself is traditionally divided into the study of the diversity and distribution of species ("the origin of species") and the study of adaptations. When concerned with the origins and distribution of species, evolutionary biologists are thoroughly mechanistic. For example, if someone wanted to argue for the possibility of speciation without geographical isolation (sympatric speciation) one would do so by presenting a model of a mechanism that could lead to sympatric speciation.[20] The widely accepted conclusion that sympatric speciation does not occur is based on the argument that no mechanism consistent with known facts of population genetics could lead to such an event.[21] Similarly, ever since Darwin, explanations of the biogeographical distribution of species have been mechanistic.[22]

In the above mentioned articles,[23] I think Mayr and I both had in mind the evolutionary explanation of adaptations. Perhaps here biologists depart from their mechanistic approach. In practice, some surely have. Some have been content to "explain" adaptations by inventing "just so" stories showing how the adaptation benefits its possessor. This practice has been rightly criticized by Gould and Lewontin.[24] But properly conceived, the program of explaining adaptations by means of the theory of evolution by natural selection has little to do with such storytelling and is thoroughly mechanistic.[25] Perhaps the best substantiation of this point comes from the fact that, during the last twenty years, concern over the problem of altruism in nature has led to a great deal of theoretical work on possible *mechanisms* for the evolution of altruism (e.g., kin selection and group selection).[26]

I have argued that biological methodology is thoroughly mechanistic. What can holism contribute here? To answer let me distinguish extreme holism from a more moderate variant. The extreme holist claims that wholes are unanalyzable, the parts of wholes are so changed by their integration into a whole that no analysis of the whole in terms of its parts will yield knowledge about the whole. The methodological implications of this view would seem to be that the description of the behavior of wholes is possible, but mechanistic analysis of this behavior is impossible and so should not be attempted. There is no *a priori* reason to deny this holist vision (unlike some physicists, I do not believe that the world was created so that we might do science); but the success of mechanistic science gives us ample reason to reject it.

I hope, but am not sure, that I have spent the last paragraph attacking a straw man. In any case, it is useful to set out the extreme position in order to contrast it with a more moderate holism. The methodological prescription from the moderate holist is rather simple and completely salutary. It is not that one ought to reduce or eliminate mechanistic analyses, but rather that organized wholes may occur at various levels, so mechanistic analyses may have to be given at various levels of organization. For example, if a population biologist recognizes that certain population structures can give rise to higher levels of selection, then he will be sure to record population structure rather than ignore it.[27] In this case, that is an important corrective to a reductionist inspired methodology (as might be suggested in G. C. Williams's 1966 work entitled *Adaptation and Natural Selection*).

As we have seen in the two previous sections, the holists of the 1920s and 1930s were concerned primarily with ontological matters and took mechanistically oriented biologists as their main opponents. This was a mistake—a mistake that I suspect has been repeated many times since—based on confusing mechanism with the doctrines of ontological and explanatory reductionism. The holist's picture of a world populated by a hierarchy of wholes is opposed, not by mechanism, but by the austere ontology of the reductionist who presents a picture of a world populated by a single basic level of entities. Although the pictures are opposites, they have something in common—their method of development. Both have been developed in a largely *a priori* manner.

When Haldane or Smuts described various levels of wholes (e.g., matter, life, consciousness, personality, society and on to the Holistic Ideals of Truth, Beauty and Goodness[28]), they gave no empirical evidence for the levels, nor did they give any indication how one might gather evidence for or against their theory. What they gave us was pure metaphysical speculation. Similarly, when a reductionist claims that all biological processes are explainable in terms of quantum mechanics, he bases his claim not on empirical evidence, but on some deeply held feeling about how the world *must* be. Metaphysicians, both holist and reductionist, may make all the "must-y" pronouncements they like; nature, I am confident, pays no attention.

When holism removes itself from the realm of metaphysics and becomes empirically based it can become a valuable part of philosophy of biology.

When one compares the ontological visions of holists and reductionists, it must be admitted that the holist's view comes closer to the view held by most current philosophers of biology than does that of the reductionist. We have learned from the recent history of biology, especially the history of the units of selection controversy,[29] that there are various levels of organization in biology, but knowledge of these levels comes only from careful theoretical reasoning in conjunction with observation and experimentation, not from metaphysical speculation. I also think that we would all agree that a structured biological whole is more than the sum of its parts. It is so in the sense that a functioning Jaguar XKE is more than a complete pile of XKE parts. But this more is due to structure and is to be explicated in mechanistic terms. Finally, I hope we have learned to follow Morgan's example with regard to the interrelations of parts within a whole. We should be willing to observe the degree of dependency among parts without prejudice, and aim for a mechanistic explanation of the observed degree of dependency.[30]

In sum, philosophy of biology can embrace a moderate, empirically based holism while maintaining its thoroughly mechanistic point of view.

NOTES

1. E. Mayr, *The Growth of Biological Thought* (Cambridge: Harvard University Press, 1983), 97.
2. See E. Mayr and W. B. Provine, *The Evolutionary Synthesis* (Cambridge: Harvard University Press, 1980).
3. L. Laudan, *Progress and Its Problems* (Berkeley: University of California Press, 1977).
4. Since life is supposed to have evolved from inanimate matter one might think this just pushes the problem further back. But earlier evolutionists did not have much to say about the origins of life, so this problem would be less acute.
5. See J. S. Haldane, *Mechanism, Life and Personality* (New York: E. P. Dutton, 1923); *The Sciences and Philosophy* (Garden City, N.Y.: Doubleday, Doran and Co., 1929); *The Philosophical Basis of Biology* (Garden City, N.Y.: Doubleday, Doran and Co., 1931); and *The Philosophy of a Biologist* (Oxford: Clarendon Press, 1935).
6. Haldane, *The Philosophy of a Biologist,* 35; J. C. Smuts, *Holism and Evolution* (New York: Macmillan, 1926), ch. 12. They had other reasons as well. Haldane, in effect, argued that vitalism is not holistic enough in that it separated the organism from its environment (see *The Philosophical Basis of Biology,* 29 and *The Philosophy of a Biologist,* 35). Smuts argued that the vitalistic hypothesis was unnecessary, that his theory of holism satisfactorily explained the phenomena of life.
7. Smuts, op. cit., 161.
8. Haldane, *The Philosophy of a Biologist,* op. cit., 37.
9. A. Rosenbleuth, N. Weiner, and Bigelow, J., "Behavior, Purpose, and Teleology," *Philosophy of Science* 10 (1943): 18–24.
10. See for example Haldane, *The Philosophical Basis of Biology,* 29; *The Philosophy of a Biologist,* 35.
11. Smuts, op. cit., 122.

12. For further discussion of these matters and a more detailed exposition see R. N. Brandon, "Grene on Mechanism and Reductionism: More than Just a Side Issue," *PSA 1984*, volume 2, 1985.

13. L. Hogben, *The Nature of Living Matter* (London: Kegan Paul, Trench, Trubner and Co., 1930), 100.

14. Ibid., 297–98.

15. W. C. Wimsatt "Reduction and Reductionism," in H. Kyburg and P. Asquith (eds.), *Current Problems in Philosophy of Science* (East Lansing, Mich.: Philosophy of Science Association, 1978).

16. See E. Nagel, *The Structure of Science* (New York: Harcourt, Brace and World, 1961).

17. Hogben, op cit., 297.

18. E. Mayr, "Cause and Effect in Biology," *Science* 134 (1961): 1520; and *The Growth of Biological Thought,* op. cit.

19. R. N. Brandon, "Biological Teleology: Questions and Explanations," *Studies in History and Philosophy of Science* 12 (1981): 91–105.

20. J. Maynard Smith, "Sympatric Speciation," *American Naturalist* 100 (1966): 637–50.

21. E. Mayr, *Animal Species and dvolution* (Cambridge: Harvard University Press, 1963).

22. See C. Darwin, *On the Origins of Species* (London: John Murray, 1859), chs. 11 and 12.

23. E. Mayr, "Cause and Effect in Biology," and R. N. Brandon, "Biological Teleology: Questions and Explanations."

24. S. J. Gould and R. Lewontin, "The Spandrels of San Marco and the Panglossian Paradigm: A Critique of the Adaptationist Programme," *Proceedings of the Royal Society of Land., Bulletin of Biological Science* 205 (1979): 581–89.

25. See R. N. Brandon, "Biological Teleology: Questions and Explanations," and "Adaptation Explanations: Are Adaptations for the Good of Replicators or Interactors?" in B. Weber and D. Depew (eds.), *Biology and the New Philosophy of Science* (Cambridge: MIT Press, 1984); and E. Mayr, "How to Carry Out the Adaptationist Program?" *American Naturalist* 121 (1983): 324–34.

26. R. N. Brandon and R. M. Burian (eds.), *Genes, Organisms, Populations: Controversies Over the Units of Selection* (Cambridge: MIT Press, 1984).

27. See D. S. Wilson, *The Natural Selection of Populations and Communities* (Menlo Park, Calif.: Benjamin Cummings, 1980).

28. Smuts, op. cit., 106–107.

29. See R. N. Brandon and R. M. Burian, *Genes, Organisms, Populations* for a collection of some of the most important articles in this area of controversy.

30. Incidently, there is no *a priori* reason to believe that mechanisms underlying the relative independence of parts will be simpler than mechanisms underlying the relative dependence of parts. For instance, the independent rear suspension of a Jaguar XKE is one of the most complicated mechanisms in automotive history. It, of course, allows the vertical travel of one rear wheel to be relatively independent of the other. In contrast, the solid rear axle of a Triumph TR 4 is an extremely simple mechanism. With it, the vertical travel of each of the rear wheels is tightly linked to that of the other.

Daniel Wikler, Ph.D.

Holistic Medicine: Concepts of Personal Responsibility for Health

Are individuals personally responsible for their health? Holists think so. Some holists even say that this concept defines their approach and is the fundamental difference between holism and orthodox medicine. However, despite its putative importance, holists have not provided a detailed, coherent account of personal responsibility for health. The concept is almost always presented as if its precise meaning were clear to all and its implications self-evident. This is certainly not the case. Holists do not agree among themselves over its meaning, and there is much debate over its clinical and social significance.

Is this lack of clarity an important problem? It is if we are to take seriously the holists' claim that personal responsibility is the foundation of their discipline. The holistic approach cannot be evaluated, much less accepted, if its basic propositions cannot be understood. But there are larger issues at stake here as well. The social significance of holistic medicine is not merely that of a handful of new or rediscovered medical therapies. The holists also claim that their movement aims to change some basic attitudes about health and about the relation of individuals, the professions, and the state. The holists' treatment of the personal responsibility issue is an important indicator of the social role of holism itself and some trends in social policy on health care.

WHAT IS "PERSONAL RESPONSIBILITY FOR HEALTH?"

Is the meaning of "personal responsibility" really so unclear? Definitely. A story devised by the philosopher H. L. A. Hart shows how much the meaning of "responsible" can vary according to context:

As captain of the ship, X was responsible for the safety of his passengers and crew. But on his last voyage he got drunk every night and was responsible for the loss of the ship with all aboard. It was rumored that he was insane, but the doctors considered that he was responsible for his actions. Throughout the voyage he behaved quite irresponsibly, and various incidents in his career showed that he was not a responsible person. He always maintained that the exceptional winter storms were responsible for the loss of the ship, but in the legal proceedings brought against him he was found criminally responsible for his negligent conduct, and in separate civil proceedings he was held legally responsible for the loss of life and property. He is still alive and he is morally responsible for the deaths of many women and children.[1]

What is telling about Hart's story, of course, is that these different sorts of responsibility do not covary; the captain was responsible in some senses of the term and not in others. He *was* responsible for the death of passengers in that he caused their death; he *was not* responsible in the sense that he had not been duly ordered to bring about their deaths (as the responsibility of an executioner is to kill the condemned); he *was* responsible for their deaths in that he was found criminally negligent; and so on.

Holists who insist that we are responsible for our health, then, should tell us what they mean. It is no help to be told, as we are in a holistic nursing text,[2] that "Definitions of responsible include: accountability . . . reliability . . . trustworthy . . . in ethics, having the character of a free moral agent." These are obviously related but likewise obviously distinct.

This essay does not pretend to offer an exhaustive survey of holistic uses of the phrase "personal responsibility for health," but it is possible to distinguish a few major themes. The discussion will proceed from the abstract, conceptual level to the practical world of social policy.

An initial question is how seriously we ought to take the holists' insistence on personal responsibility. Personal responsibility can be the subject of rigorous theory, as in the debate over responsibility for actions in criminal law, and in such a case we have some idea of what the arguments are and what standards to use in evaluating them.

The writings of the holists are different. Much holistic writing is to standard expository prose what holistic medicine purports to be in relation to orthodox medicine. It deals with the whole person, not just the cognitive faculty; it soothes, massages, inspires, deals with the "spiritual" as well as the empirical and the material—and denies the reality of these distinctions.

It is no surprise, then, that many of the references to personal responsibility are simply hortatory. When the proposition "Health care is not only everybody's right but everybody's responsibility"[3] appears in a list of "principles," without accompanying argument, the author is simply urging people to take better care of themselves. This use of the notion of personal responsibility is agreeably unpretentious and, on balance, innocuous. Most of us *would* be better off if we took better care of ourselves, and there would be little to criticize in an approach to medicine that emphasized the importance of doing so.

Perhaps this is all that holists mean when they claim that personal responsibility is the key to their approach. Many of their pronouncements, however, indicate otherwise. One indication is that the holists usually insist that individuals *are* responsible for their health, not merely that they should become so (in the sense of doing more to stay healthy). This suggests a more substantive claim—and the need for supporting argument. What sort of claims are made, then, when responsibility for health is ascribed to that diverse and weighty group called "the individual"? We can begin with the least substantive.

CAUSAL RESPONSIBILITY

In one sense of the term, individuals are often responsible for their health (and illness) in that their actions are among the causes of particular health states. To "accept responsibility" for health, in this minimal sense, is merely to acknowledge that one's actions do have health-related consequences; to act on this realization is to take care of oneself. This seems to be what Kenneth Pelletier means when he states that the advent of holism involves "the increasing recognition that health care is a matter of individual responsibility."[4] When he reports that a holistic program "stresses that the individual should take responsibility for his own health,"[5] he seems to be saying that people should realize how much they could do to keep healthy and that they should act accordingly. Similarly, the statement of purpose published in the *Journal of Holistic Medicine* holds that its approach "particularly focuses upon patient education and patient responsibility for personal efforts to achieve balance." Assuming that this last term is some sort of synonym for health, the journal can be understood to be concerned with what patients can do for themselves rather than what can be done to or for them. Responsibility in this sense, then, is *activity,* or effort.

Saying that people *are* responsible for their health, then, would mean nothing more than that they are actively trying to stay healthy. This cannot be what holists mean, since it is the *lack* of such activity that they are addressing with their healing approach. The best one can make of this language is that holists want us to *become* "responsible" (i.e., active). But nonholists surely do not disagree with this on the level of principle. Perhaps they can be faulted for slighting this aspect of therapy, but there is no significant difference here in doctrine.

What is controversial is not the concept of responsibility but the holist's account of what actions lead to what consequences. Holists endorse a host of unorthodox (and often nonspecific) therapies and preventive practices that others hold in low esteem. Thus, though all can agree that patients should be urged to take care of themselves, holists and nonholists may differ over what measures patients should take. The debate is not over whether people are, or should become, responsible, but over how this responsibility can most effectively be discharged.

The holist gets into deeper water when the commonplace observation that a person can take measures to stay healthy is conjoined with the proposition that the patient's health status depends *only* on what the patient does. Actually, this latter (and obviously false) claim is not stated baldly in holistic writing. But there is a persistent tendency in its direction. This is due in part to the hortatory function of some of the literature: If the author is trying to motivate the reader, it makes some sense to speak only about what the patient might do.

CAUSATION AND AUTONOMY

The discussion so far does not, however, satisfactorily explain the holists' preoccupation with the individual's role. They feel that orthodox medicine, in its concern with what disease agents do *to* the patient and what medicine can do *for* the patient, has put its emphasis in the wrong place. Their reasons for this stance deserve extended discussion, for they help to explain why the holists make such heavy use of the concept of responsibility.

To some extent, the difference between holists and others in this regard can be ascribed to divergent empirical beliefs. Since holists generally have more faith in the efficacy of the unorthodox regimens, they naturally have greater faith that the patient can influence events by adopting them. Often the dispute is not over which steps lead to health in a given context, but whether any are really known to do so. Those who insist that we do not yet know the causes of most illnesses are less likely to endorse the proposition that a particular set of "unhealthy" actions is causally responsible for illness.

Similarly, holists and nonholists may differ over how much disease is ultimately psychosomatic. Holists vary among themselves on this score, but some are quite bold. One holistic nursing text, written by Barbara Blattner, teaches that "Illness occurs when people don't grow and develop their potentials or when they become blocked by a crisis or a series of events which stunt and twist their growing images of themselves."[6] Others are not far behind. If the mind causes all physical disease, then perhaps a change of mind will prevent or cure disease.

At this point, however, the difference between holists and traditionalists becomes more than empirical, more than a dispute over the causes of disease and the efficacy of certain cures. Though the holists ascribe much more causal power to behavior and the mind than traditionalists do, they are also staking out a moral and philosophical position that sets them apart. What is contested is not only what causes what, but which causes should be slated for change; who should be asked to ensure that the changes are made; what value there is in trying to make the changes, and what wrong there is in not trying.

To put a label on the holistic concept, what is at issue is the value of *positive autonomy*. This is another sort of personal responsibility. The basic idea here is that of active, purposive, effective direction of one's personal affairs.

Holists seem to find this to be not only efficacious in preventing and curing illness, but good in itself. This is one respect in which holists can rightly be said to recommend a style of life rather than one or another particular mode of therapy. We can best characterize positive autonomy, both generically and in the holists' writings, by contrasting it with other concepts. We can begin, naturally enough, with *negative autonomy.*

Autonomy is, literally, self-governance. It is sometimes used synonymously with "freedom." Philosophers have long debated what freedom and autonomy amount to. One standard answer is that a person is free so long as he is not hindered from accomplishing his ends by interference or restrictions from others. Freedom in this sense is the *absence* of constraint, a "negative" characterization. This sort of freedom is most often what is at stake in discussions of civil liberty. To many theorists, however, negative autonomy is only a part of the picture—and perhaps the lesser part. A person is not "genuinely free," on this view, even if unconstrained, when he acts like a passive object, wandering listlessly and without direction throughout his life. He may answer only to himself in such a case, but there will be little governing going on. To the absence of constraint these theorists would add a requirement that the free, autonomous individual be actively taking part in the direction of his affairs. He must be knowledgeable, or at least seeking knowledge; he must actively attempt to discover all the options of action; he must exert strong efforts to overcome obstacles and accomplish his ends; and he must reflectively construct a plan of life that puts his various projects in some sort of rational order, ranked according to priority and made consistent.

Many holistic writers endorse this kind of existence. Donald Ardell, in his *High Level Wellness,* blames much illness on the lack of "an ethic of self-responsibility for our own health." He urges the reader to "investigate the alternatives to dependency, overcome the social obstacles to a wellness lifestyle. . ."; to "go for positive happiness, wellness style . . ."; to "stop, examine, and choose"; to realize that "you are in charge of your own life"; to ask "Have I consciously set up the patterns I follow, or did things just develop as they are?"; and so on.[7] Blattner's nursing text asserts that "every human being, no matter how defenseless or dependent, has a natural desire and tendency for self-direction and self-determinism. Holistic nurses recognize self-responsibility as a basic developmental task. . . . The definition of self-responsibility will be broadened to mean the reflective response of the self to freely choose from a variety of alternatives."[8]

Assuming that we are justified in interpreting the talk of "natural tendencies" as an endorsement, these representative passages seem to value positive autonomy for more than its effect on health as ordinarily conceived. In the holistic vocabulary, it *is* health. The emphasis on personal responsibility in this sense simply recapitulates the basic claim of holism to be a movement concerned with health. To those who maintain a narrower concept of health, holism is in this respect a "philosophy of well-being"—what academic philosophers would call a theory of the good—rather than an approach to medicine. This is, of course, precisely what some holists have insisted on.

This vision of the good life—either including or apart from its health consequences—is an appealing one. It is closely connected to political ideals of democracy and popular sovereignty. It calls for people to make the fullest use of those faculties that make them uniquely human. Some contemporary philosophers have identified the capacity to reflect and revise personal values and goals as the individual's highest interest.[9] It assigns a welcome role to the therapist or healer, that of educator, of "consciousness-raiser," one who helps the individual understand and make use of all the powers he might have for shaping his life in desirable ways.

However, this stance cannot be adopted without difficulty or cost. It carries, perhaps unnoticed, perhaps denied, certain sorts of ideological freight. It may presuppose a kind of indeterminism that cannot be sustained, and it is closely linked to concepts of liability, fault, blame, and desert, which have serious social implications. These problems have to be identified and debated.

DETERMINISM AND FREEDOM

A classical problem with the notion of positive autonomy is the plausibility of determinism. The picture of a self-governing individual leaves out, in the opinion of many philosophers, the fact that our behavior is determined by genetic, constitutional, and environmental factors over which we have no control. Independent considerations supporting the determinist thesis have convinced some that positive autonomy simply does not exist.

This problem bothers some holists. According to Dr. Larry Dossey:

> The problem is particularly important in the holistic health care movement, for its credo is anchored in the concept of self-responsibility. And self-responsibility is an empty principle in a physically determined universe. The holistic health care movement, then, should rise or fall on how the ancient problem of free will versus determinism is answered.[10]

This is not the proper occasion to examine Dossey's solution to this problem (unconvincing to this writer). We might, however, ask whether he is correct in tying holism's fate to indeterminism. If he is, his approach to healing is in jeopardy. In any case, he is not. Whether or not all of our actions are determined by genes and environment, it is indisputable that our behavior is malleable. New information, new urgings and advice, new ways of looking at things become determinants themselves, causing us to change our ways. Biofeedback, if it works, is better suited to a deterministic universe. So is health education. What matters is not whether our actions are caused, but what the causes are.

The difficulty holists must face is not that all choices are determined but that some are. Or, rather, that some changes seem to be beyond the ability of some individuals, however well-motivated. Holists provide constant reassurance that individuals can do whatever they want, make any decisions that might benefit them, regardless of heritage or environment. Some holists are rather shrill on this subject:

> We are responsible for ourselves. . . . We are responsible and are accountable for our feelings, thoughts, beliefs, morality, ethics, behavior, and actions in relation to others. We can control and change these. . . .[11]

> You're in what could be called a trap of nonresponsibility if you believe you cannot change your diet, your destructive habits and patterns, your inability to engage in vigorous exercise for pleasure and fitness, your stress levels, or the environment in which you live. You created that trap by your own limiting definitions of your possibilities and potentials. . . .[12]

It is difficult to know how to evaluate these claims. What would count as evidence against them? Could it be the failure of countless highly-motivated individuals to make the changes that the holists insist can be made simply by deciding to do so? Apparently not. The holistic insistence on the reality (or at least possibility) of positive autonomy in all circumstances must, then, be either mystical or false. Or, what is equally likely, hortatory: If you tell patients over and over that they can change their habits by deciding to, perhaps they eventually will.

RESPONSIBILITY AS LIABILITY

There is a price to be paid for this kind of exhortation, however beneficial its occasional effect. As Hart's story illustrates, the most common meaning of "responsible" has less to do with cause or positive autonomy than with *fault, liability,* and *desert* (and their antonyms). In particular, the person who is responsible for harm may be found at fault, judged undeserving of praise or other benefits, and deserving of and liable for sanctions. In addition, to find that person responsible for the harm may be to let other causal agents off the hook. In the context of holistic medicine, the difficulty is that the notion of personal responsibility for health will be understood as grounds for blaming the victim, exonerating the environmental factors that made him sick, and excusing medical intervention that failed to restore health.

Holists differ with respect to their attitudes toward these implications of the claim of personal responsibility for health. Some seem comfortable with them: A paper championing several of these positions by the late John Knowles, then president of the Rockefeller Foundation, is quoted favorably by many holistic writers.[13] Other holists, however, are aware of the problem and fight against it. Dr. Gordon speaks directly to these concerns and indeed fixes part of the blame on traditional medicine (quoting "leftist critics": "our medical system diverts attention from the political and social origins of illness by focusing on the proximate causes in the bodies of those who become ill . . .").[14] Others seem not to be bothered by the tension. ("We can . . . know that we are strong *and* we have limits. We are responsible for our choices and can choose to be positive *and* negative, optimistic *and* pessimistic, open *and* closed. Each of these seeming opposites can be seen in a yin-yang symbol of both, rather than either-or.")[15]

Whatever the level of discomfort with these implications of the personal responsibility doctrine, they cannot be wished away. Readers will make these inferences because they are reasonable ones to make. If we really could avoid all illness by deciding to, why *shouldn't* we be blamed for becoming ill? And if we could become wholly independent and self-reliant if we chose to, why should orthodox medicine be faulted for not catering better to our needs?

To be sure, there are specific reasons for saying that individuals should not be blamed, even when choice is possible, as I have explored elsewhere.[16] But the fine points of these arguments may carry little weight when compared to some large-scale social forces that make use of holistic ideology for its other ends. Robert Crawford[17] and others have argued that the holistic emphasis on the individual's role is conducive to the conservative reaction against entitlements to health care, brought on especially by the cost crisis in health care finance. The holistic rhetoric is appropriated by those who argue for cutbacks in benefits and for reduction of environmental and workplace protection against hazards. Knowles's proposal that the notion of "a right to health care" be *replaced* by that of a "responsibility for health" was not an idle one. Holists routinely quote this very passage from that paper, which suggests either that they do not take it seriously or that they endorse it. Either possibility is a matter of some concern.

RESPONSIBILITY AS DUTY

We come finally to a different conception of personal responsibility, that of duty to specific parties. In ordinary circumstances we do not think of ourselves as having the duty to try to stay healthy; perhaps a professional athlete could have contractual obligations to that effect, but most of us do not. Nonetheless, this represents one way to interpret the holists' insistence on personal responsibility. The immediate question is: duty to whom? There are two conceivable answers, neither of which, in the end, is sustainable: one's nation and oneself.

The idea that the nation or state has a right to your health is in fact an old one (answering to a doctrine called "cameralism"), but is rarely defended as such in contemporary debate. It is recalled, however, in the suggestion by writers like Knowles that those who fail to avoid illness act irresponsibly. One person's illness inflicts on others the loss of his productivity and, perhaps more significantly, the cost of care. This argument could conceivably be useful to the holists, but has not generally been adopted. Perhaps this is because the portrayal of health as a public duty is most naturally tied to justifying public intervention:

prohibitions, taxes, and other constraints on unhealthy choices. The holists, with their emphasis on personal autonomy and individualism, have not warmed to these ideas.

A more natural stance for holists is the notion of duties *to the self*. This view is not often expressed as such either, but perhaps it underlies some of the holists' exhortations. If holists were to appropriate this reading of their doctrine of personal responsibility, however, they would be obliged to face a number of difficulties posed by philosophers critical of the concept. The chief problem is that a duty can usually be erased by a waiver of the person to whom the duty is owed. In the case of a duty to the self, that party is the same as the one who has the duty. Thus the duty could be erased if the individual decided to do so. The essence of duty, however, is that it stay in force even in the absence of inclination.

Even worse for the holists' case, individuals sometimes have good reason to disregard this duty to the self. Sometimes staying healthy is not worth the cost, and adopting a "healthy lifestyle" makes one worse off overall than continuing to take risks. How could this be so? Perhaps the steps required to remove risk factors from one's life—quitting a job, or moving to a new climate—would lead to more harm overall than good. Risk-avoidance is sometimes opportunity-avoidance; mountain climbers would insist on this, but there are many everyday examples as well. Some people are even better off sick, as a generation of potential draftees decided not long ago. These elementary facts are almost never addressed in the holistic literature, but they are potentially devastating to the construal of personal responsibility as a duty to the self. What would be the point of a duty to the self that made the self worse off?

CONCLUSIONS

The notion of personal responsibility for health is, out of context, multiply ambiguous. It has received several interpretations in the holistic literature, but the differences are rarely noted and seldom explained. Nor has there been a serious effort to take notice of the difficulties inherent in each concept of personal responsibility and to argue convincingly for the claim. Absent such argument, the holistic concept of personal responsibility that is most acceptable is the rhetorical, hortatory one, precisely that which is least deserving of being taken seriously. Holists might yet be able to make a claim for a more substantial theory of personal responsibility, but this will require a sustained argument of the sort that has so far been lacking.

NOTES

1. H. L. A. Hart, *Punishment and Responsibility: Essays in the Philosophy of Law* (Oxford: Oxford University Press, 1968), 211.

2. Patricia Flynn, *Holistic Health: The Art and Science of Care* (Bowie, Md.: Robert J. Brady Co., 1980), 24.

3. Tom Ferguson, "Medical Self-Care: Self-Responsibility for Health," in Arthur C. Hastings, James Fadiman, and James Gordon (eds.), *Health for the Whole Person* (New York: Bantam, 1980), 102.

4. Kenneth Pelletier, *Mind as Healer, Mind as Slayer* (New York: Dell, 1977), 302.

5. Ibid.

6. Barbara Blattner, *Holistic Nursing* (Englewood Cliffs, N.J.: Prentice-Hall, 1981), 35.

7. Donald B. Ardell, *High Level Wellness* (Emmaus, Pa.: Rodale, 1977), 102, 105, 106, 108, 109.

8. Blattner, op. cit., 34.

9. John Rawls, "Social Unity and Primary Goods," in A. K. Sen and Bernard Williams (eds.), *Utilitarianism and Beyond* (Cambridge: Cambridge University Press, 1982), 159–85.

10. Larry Dossey, *Beyond Illness* (Boulder, Col.: Shambhala, 1984), 124.

11. Flynn, op. cit., 26.

12. Ardell, op. cit., 110.

13. John H. Knowles, "The Responsibility of the Individual," in John H. Knowles, *Doing Better and Feeling Worse* (New York: W. W. Norton, 1977), 57–80.

14. James Gordon, et al., op. cit., 13.

15. Flynn, op. cit., 26.

16. Daniel Wikler, "Persuasion and Coercion for Health: Ethical Issues in Government Efforts to Change Life-Styles," *Milbank Memorial Fund Quarterly* 56 (1978): 303–38.

17. Robert Crawford, "You Are Dangerous to Your Health: The Ideology and Politics of Victim-Blaming," *International Journal of Health Services* 7 (1977): 663–80.

Part III

Examining Holistic Methodology

Daisie Radner, Ph.D., and Michael Radner, Ph.D.

Holistic Methodology and Pseudoscience

It is often said that holistic medicine is not meant to replace traditional scientific medicine but to work together with it. The holistic approach is usually contrasted with the "biomedical model" or "mechanistic view," but the contrast— so it is said—does not imply that the techniques and modalities of scientific medicine are incompatible with the holistic approach. Most reputable practitioners of holistic medicine are willing to give "mechanistic" medicine its due in combatting infectious diseases, in surgically removing tumors, and so on. The trouble with the biomedical model, as they see it, is that it tends to ignore psychological, social, environmental, and spiritual factors, and it focuses upon the eradication of disease rather than promoting and maintaining positive states of health. Ideally, the holistic approach should take the best of modern medical science and incorporate it into a broader model for health care.[1]

One of the basic principles of holistic medicine is that any diagnostic technique or modality of treatment that works should be used.[2] That includes surgery, antibiotics, and other achievements of scientific medicine. It also includes a large assortment of unconventional practices such as acupuncture, homeopathy, naturopathic medicine, chelation therapy, psychic diagnosis, Rolfing, colonic irrigation, yoga, meditation, psychic healing, and the laying-on-of-hands. There is some difference of opinion about which unconventional practices work and which do not. Dolores Krieger, the professor of nursing who developed the technique of therapeutic touch, includes iridology in her list of popular holistic health practices, describing it without critical comment,[3] whereas psychologist Lawrence LeShan calls it "nonsense."[4] C. Norman Shealy, M.D., director of the Pain Rehabilitation Center in La Crosse, Wisconsin, reports that he has found palmistry useful in medical diagnosis and advocates the teaching of astrology in medical schools.[5] As for acupuncture, however, he declares that it is "almost worthless" for the treatment of disease, though he has found it effective for pain.[6]

Some advocates of the holistic approach are sensitive to the problem of quackery. In *The Holistic Way to Health and Happiness* Bloomfield and Kory note that the emphasis on unconventional modalities is "one of the most exciting yet most potentially dangerous aspects of holistic medicine. . . . Certainly, the public must beware of quackery and faddism."[7] How is the public to tell that someone is a quack? On the holistic approach, the answer lies not in the nature of the therapy but in the attitude of the therapist toward standard medical treatment. LeShan writes in *The Mechanic and the Gardener: "Any intelligent and responsible treatment of disease involves the care of a physician. If a health specialist says, 'Leave all medical treatment and follow my path,' he is a dangerous charlatan and belongs in jail."[8] The implication is that even if the treatment is on LeShan's list of "carefully developed and time-tested methods" (for example, meditation and Rolfing), the therapist is a quack if he or she advocates abandoning conventional medical treatment.

Suppose, however, that a therapist tells you to continue to see your doctor and take your medication but also to follow a course of treatment that is *not* on the list of "time-tested methods"—for example, sleeping under a pyramid. According to LeShan, "some of the specific techniques are the sheerest kookiness and magical thinking (such as 'pyramid energy,' or 'copper contact') and may be dismissed without further investigation."[9] Presumably these would not qualify as proper adjunctive modalities in a holistic health care program, no matter how honest and eclectic the therapist. The criterion for quackery, then, is not enough; we also need a criterion for "kookiness."

Writers on holistic health are curiously reluctant to tell their readers how to separate the wheat from the chaff in the alternative techniques of health care. Many do not admit that there is any chaff at all, and the few who do (such as LeShan) stop short of telling us how to spot it. The prevailing attitude in the holistic health field is one of laissez faire. If one looks at the kinds of reasons given *in support of* particular modalities, one begins to understand why this is so. The reasoning is often pseudoscientific. Few techniques are explicitly rejected, because there are few that cannot be supported by the standard pseudoscientific arguments.

In our book *Science and Unreason* we list nine marks of pseudoscience.[10] These are styles of argument or methods of reasoning based upon misconceptions of what science is and how it proceeds. Our list was gleaned from a survey of well-known pseudosciences such as flat earth, ancient astronauts, creationism, biorhythm, and the like. We do not claim to have provided a complete list of all forms of pseudoscientific reasoning, for there are innumerable ways to distort the methods of science. If a discipline exhibits none of our nine marks, it does not necessarily follow that the discipline is scientific. The presence of any one mark, however, is sufficient to establish that something pseudoscientific is going on. Most pseudosciences exhibit more than one mark, but it would be very rare indeed to find a single pseudoscience clearly exhibiting all of them.

The nine marks, briefly, are the following: anachronistic thinking, looking for mysteries, appeal to myths, a grab-bag approach to evidence, putting forth irrefutable hypotheses, argument from spurious similarity, explanation by scenario, research by exegesis, and refusal to correct in light of criticism. We shall not discuss all of them in detail here, only the four that most directly apply to the arguments for alternative health care practices.

Holistic advocates may try to head us off at the pass by reminding us that the practice of medicine is not a science but an art. True, but modern clinical medicine is firmly grounded in science. The holistic advocates may counter by saying that they do not restrict themselves to the narrow confines of the biomedical model. So be it; but if they claim to be expanding rather than rejecting scientific medicine, then they must be willing to submit their practices to scientific scrutiny. The reasons they offer in support of their techniques must be the kind that carry weight in the scientific arena. Indeed, a number of people in the holistic health field openly acknowledge the need for scientific research into the alternative modalities. Dolores Krieger has performed experiments on therapeutic touch, and there is a fairly large body of research on meditation. The layperson is not likely to be in a position to evaluate these experimental studies, any more than he or she is likely to be able to judge technical articles in the standard medical journals. Nonscientists may not be able to tell bad science from good, but they can, with a little practice, learn to spot pseudoscientific reasoning.

ANACHRONISTIC THINKING

To resurrect a previously discarded idea without addressing the reasons for its rejection in the first place is to engage in anachronistic thinking. Sometimes science does return to notions cast aside long ago, but only if a way has been found to make them work where they did not work before. This usually involves putting them in a wholly new context.

Let us illustrate with an example from astronomy. Copernicus revived the ancient Pythagorean doctrine that the earth moved—a doctrine that had been out of favor for over a thousand years. But Copernicus's moving earth occupied a different position from the one the Pythagoreans assigned to it. In the Pythagorean universe the earth, the moon, the sun, the five visible planets and the fixed stars all revolved around a central fire. Between the earth and the central fire was another planet called the counter-earth. Neither the counter-earth nor the central fire was observable by people on earth, because the earth revolved with its inhabited side always facing away from them. One of the main reasons that the Pythagorean scheme was rejected in the first place was that it postulated unobservable bodies. When Copernicus combatted the Ptolemaic geocentric scheme, he rearranged the universe in such a way that the original objections to the Pythagorean scheme no longer applied. Copernicus was doing science. Were someone to come along now and return to the Ptolemaic system, ignoring the modern objections to it, that person would be doing pseudoscience.

Whenever a health care specialist advocates revival of a technique drawn from an outmoded theory, without providing updated support for the technique, he or she is guilty of anachronistic thinking. Calls for return to ancient modes of treatment should be viewed with suspicion, especially when the treatment is to be done precisely as the ancients did it. We say only that one should be suspicious in such cases, not that they automatically indicate anachronistic thinking; for it is possible that the ancients did hit upon some techniques that fit our ideas exactly. Nevertheless, it is reasonable to suppose that in most cases the valuable practices of old will need substantial modifications to bring them in line with current theories and up to current standards. Herbal remedies provide a case in point. The American Indians and country folk of past eras were on the right track when they treated fevers with a decoction made from the bark of the willow tree, for willow bark contains salicyclic acid, which is related to acetyl-salicylic acid, better known as aspirin. Modern physicians, however, prescribe aspirin, not willow bark, since the purity and dosage are better controlled in the synthetic product, and it is much less irritating.

Acupuncture is a practice that dates back to the second millenium B.C. in China. It consists of inserting needles into the skin at points along invisible meridians, of which there are twelve. The life force, called "Ch'i," flows through them in a certain sequence. Illness is due to an imbalance of Yin and Yang, the negative and positive elements of the life force. The insertion of the needles is supposed to correct the imbalance by increasing or decreasing the flow of energy.

Acupuncture, as currently practiced in the West, is basically the same as that described in the classical Chinese writings. The points and meridians are taken from ancient sources. Aside from concessions to modern hygiene and the occasional use of electric stimulation, the techniques of inserting and manipulating the needles have remained essentially unchanged. The specific points used for treating various conditions are based upon ancient formulas.[11]

Many advocates of acupuncture seem quite comfortable with the philosophical concepts of Chinese medicine. Whether these concepts are compatible with Western scientific medicine seems to be of little or no concern to them. The Sinologist Manfred Porkert offers a neat way to reconcile the irreconcilable: the two points of view are "mutually exclusive yet equally true."[12] Not only does this dictum serve to reconcile Eastern and Western medicine, it can also be used to dissolve the contradictions within oriental medicine itself. Marc Estrin notes that one school of acupuncture holds that the lefthand pulses of a man are equivalent to the righthand pulses of a woman and vice versa, whereas another school asserts that the positions of the male and female pulses are the same. "The only way I have been able to come to grips with these contradictions," he says, "is to assume that all the experts are right, and that their techniques work for *them*—in part, because they and their patients believe in them. This is not quackery or placebo effect, but a clear application of the mind affecting Ch'i flow."[13] Not only does your mind affect your Ch'i flow, but your therapist's mind affects it too!

Some acupuncturists admit that it would be better if the therapy could be explained and perhaps even modified in terms of modern scientific principles; but rather than wait for the scientific rationale, they proceed on the basis of the traditional Chinese concepts. The British husband and wife team of G. T. and N. R. Lewith illustrate this attitude. In the introduction to their book *Modern Chinese Acupuncture* the Lewiths write: "We do not decry the scientific approach to acupuncture, quite the contrary; ultimately it may indicate a more physiological approach to point selection, but at the moment such indication is not available. It seems logical, then, that until it is available we should use the empirical clinical experience that has been obtained from many centuries of work by the Chinese." Lest the reader think that the Lewiths mean to divorce the clinical experience from the Chinese framework for explaining it, they go on to say: "The Chinese have rationalized their clinical experience into a detailed system and, by using this system, the acupuncturist can benefit from their experience and obtain better therapeutic results."[14] In other words, until modern scientific medicine makes room for acupuncture, one should forget about modern scientific medicine and go with the Ch'i flow.

ARGUMENT FROM SPURIOUS SIMILARITY

According to some writers, the ancient Chinese theory behind acupuncture, far from being inimical to modern science, is actually in harmony with the most up-to-date scientific thinking. This view is expressed by David E. Bresler, M.D., director of the UCLA Pain Control Unit, in his book *Free Yourself from Pain:* "In a sense, the early Chinese philosophers antedated Einstein's theory of relativity, for they recognized that matter and energy are just two different manifestations of the same thing."[15] The theory of meridians may not conform to the narrowly mechanistic viewpoint of orthodox medicine. No one has ever observed meridian ducts under a microscope. (About twenty years ago, a Korean scientist named Kim Bong-Han claimed to have discovered them, but other researchers were unable to confirm his findings.[16]) The "organs" governed by the meridians ("heart," "spleen," etc.) do not correspond to the structures of Western anatomy. Nevertheless, the Chinese theory is more in tune with the latest science than the biomedical model is. Physics teaches that objects are systems of energy and that on the quantum level the observer and the observed are inextricably linked. Yet orthodox medicine continues to view the body as a machine and illness as a phenomenon that can be studied independently of its psychological component.[17]

Those who argue in this manner cannot be accused of anachronistic thinking, for they are addressing the question of how to fit the ancient theory into the current framework. This method of reasoning falls under another mark of pseudoscience, one which can be used for new theories as well as old.

The argument from spurious similarity is an attempt to gain scientific status for a theory on the grounds of its alleged likeness to a recognzed scientific theory. The form of the argument is as follows: (1) Theory X employs principles similar to those of theory Y; (2) theory Y is part of current science; therefore, (3) theory X is consistent with current science. In Bresler's version, theory X is the Chinese theory explaining acupuncture and theory Y is Einstein's theory of relativity. The principle in X that is similar to one in Y is "matter and energy are two forms of the same thing."

Another practice often defended by this type of argument is homeopathy. Founded by Samuel Hahnemann (1755–1843), the homeopathic system of treatment is based on three laws: the Law of Similars, the Law of Single Remedy, and the Law of Minimum Dose. The Law of Similars states that the cure for a given disease is that substance which, when administered to a healthy person, produces symptoms exactly like those of the disease. Quinine, for instance, when taken by a healthy person, produces symptoms identical to certain cases of malaria. The procedure of administering a substance to a healthy person to bring on the symptoms is called "proving" the medicine. In matching the disease symptoms with those of the provings, the totality of symptoms must be considered, including the minor and idiosyncratic ones. The Law of Single Remedy says that only one remedy should be administered at a time. The proving is only of a single substance, hence a combination of remedies may produce unpredictable results. The Law of Minimum Dose says that only a minute dose of the medicinal substance is needed to bring about a cure. In fact, the more diluted the medicine, the more potent it is. Dilutions of 10^{-200} or more are common. Such doses are decidedly ultramolecular: it is highly probable that not even a single molecule of the medicinal substance is ingested by the patient. The claim is that the energy or "vital force" of the medicine is released throughout the solvent by succussion (rapping the vial against the palm of the hand), and that repeated dilutions and succussions release more and more energy.

Like Chinese medicine, homeopathy posits an energy field or "vital force." Disease is a disorder of the body's energy field, and the way to cure it is to manipulate that field. The energy field of the medicine stimulates the body's own fluid to induce healing. As with Chinese medicine, it is maintained that the energy fields are similar to those of modern physics. Again the principle cited is the interchangeability of matter and energy.[18]

The argument from spurious similarity is an illegitimate combination of two legitimate forms of scientific reasoning. One has to do with the defense of a new proposal. When a scientist wishes to defend a new avenue of research, it is good strategy to argue that it is consistent with current scientific knowledge. A new proposal needs far less elaborate argumentation if it is compatible with current science than it would if it were truly revolutionary. For example, it has been argued that research into biofeedback should be conducted according to the principles of instrumental conditioning, since previous research seemed to establish that even visceral functions are open to that type of modification.[19] Along with the assertion of consistency goes the insistence that current knowledge should guide the research.

The other form of scientific reasoning is the use of analogy to get clear about a certain area. It is quite legitimate and often very fruitful to look at one class of phenomena in light of concepts developed for another class. The oscillations of electric current in a circuit are precisely analogous to the vibrations of a weight hanging from a spring. This correspondence helps the physicist to solve problems in electricity by looking at mechanics, and vice versa. Scientists recognize that they must spell out the analogy in detail, noting exactly the agreements and differences. Otherwise the relationships discovered in one area cannot properly be applied to another.

Scientists, then, do defend new proposals on the grounds of their compatibility with current scientific knowledge. They also use analogies. But they do not argue that a new proposal is consistent with current science *because* it is similar to something else already accepted. They do not argue in this way because the argument is invalid. The similarity may be just verbal. Such is the case with homeopathy and Einstein's theory of relativity. Einstein asserted that an inertial mass is equivalent to a certain amount of energy (mc^2). The homeopaths claim that matter and energy are interchangeable. This is supposed to help explain how the miniscule doses can be effective. With each dilution and succussion more energy is released, and this process continues, even after the last molecule of the substance has left the vial. But Einstein's theory of relativity plays no role at all here. The $E = mc^2$ energy of the medicinal substance stays right in the molecules and leaves the solution when they leave. The homeopathic account makes no scientific sense with or without Einstein.

GRAB-BAG APPROACH TO EVIDENCE

When all attempts at theoretical justification fail, one can always fall back on the evidence. By far the most common defense of alternative health practices is by appeal to their efficacy. "We don't know how it works, but it works" is the familiar refrain. Here is an illustration from a work on homeopathy. The author writes: "When asked how he can be sure that his theory is valid, the homeopathic physician will respond that it has served for 150 years as the basis for the successful homeopathic treatment of disease. . . . And if the homeopathic physician *can* cure his patients consistently and methodically on the basis of this theory, this set of assumptions, who is to say that it is wrong? Practice is the only test."[20] A similar claim is often made about acupuncture. Typical is the remark by Louis Moss, M.D.: "This type of treatment has been traditional in China for many thousands of years. How it works we do not know. It is empirical."[21]

Certainly there is nothing wrong with defending a scientific hypothesis on the grounds that the evidence supports it. The more evidence there is for a hypothesis, the greater its degree of confirmation; and the better confirmed it is, the more it demands acceptance. The criteria for assessing the degree of confirmation of a hypothesis include the following: (1) the number of confirming instances (in general, a large number is better than a small number); (2) the variety of confirming instances (a small number observed under a variety of conditions is better than a large number observed under identical conditions); (3) disconfirmation of competing hypotheses (the evidence yields a higher degree of confirmation for the hypothesis if it also at the same time disconfirms a competing hypothesis); and (4) successful prediction (confirming instances observed after the hypothesis has been proposed offer better support than those observed before).

These criteria tell how much weight to assign to a whole set or collection of instances. The use of the term "confirming instance" to refer to the items in the set carries with it the implication that each item taken individually is a sound piece of evidence. With a large collection, of course, some unsound data may sneak in, but they must not be numerous enough to weaken the overall support for the hypothesis. If most or all of the instances are questionable, then no matter how large their number or how great the variety of conditions, they will not confirm the hypothesis. Unless unreliable data are constantly guarded against and weeded out, the hypothesis may come to be accepted on the basis of support that it really does not have.

It is a mark of pseudoscience to think that sheer quantity of evidence makes up for any deficiency in the quality of individual pieces of evidence. Yet this is precisely the sort of reasoning exhibited by Louise Oftedal Wensel, M.D., in her account of a three-year study conducted by the Washington Acupuncture Center. Dr. Wensel writes: "Although the methods for collecting this information were not entirely objective and scientific, this is the largest study of acupuncture treatment results that has ever been made in the United States." She then goes on to present the data "to give an indication of the effectiveness of acupuncture for treating the conditions listed."[22]

One type of questionable evidence especially favored in the holistic health field is anecdotal evidence. Pick up any book on herbal medicine, iridology, foot reflexology, Rolfing, Edgar Cayce readings, or psychic healing and you will find it in abundance. Dr. Robert Leichtman, a physician and psychic who uses clairvoyance in diagnosis, gives a spirited defense of anecdotal evidence in the *Journal of Holistic Health:* "I want you to understand that I am giving you a method to verify the reality of psychic phenomena and its significance in your practice. If you wait for parapsychologists to do laboratory experiments to give you enough evidence to accept this field, I'm afraid you'll be three thousand years old before it's done. If you'll just look around at your friends, your enemies, your clients, your relatives, your patients, they'll teach you how real these things are. . . ."[23] If your brother-in-law once had a hunch that turned out to be right, you have evidence enough for the existence of PSI. If your mailman had one too, so much the better.

Another believer in the power of the anecdote is Norman Cousins, the former editor of *Saturday Review,* who managed to parlay his experience as a patient into a faculty position at a major medical school. Cousins has proposed a methodological principle that deserves to be recorded in the annals of pseudoscience. It can be stated as follows: two pieces of anecdotal evidence constitute a replication. This principle is found in *The Healing Heart,* the medico-autobiographical sequel to *Anatomy of an Illness:* "My heart attack gave me the opportunity to find out whether the same approach and technique that had worked so well before might work again. I had a chance to graduate from the anecdotal to the reproducible. The essence of the scientific method is reproducibility."[24]

Reproducibility means that anyone who performs the experiment according to the specified conditions will get the same results. It makes no sense to speak of reproducibility unless the conditions of the experiment have been set down. Otherwise how is one to know whether one has in fact reproduced the original experiment? Suppose, for example, that a person manifests psychic phenomena under relaxed and uncontrolled conditions. It makes no difference how often he does so. There is no replication in the scientific sense since proper controls are absent. The same is true of Cousins. It is not that Cousins somehow "cheated," but simply that he had his experiences in the ordinary course of life, where no one—himself included—sorted out the significant factors.

REFUSAL TO CORRECT IN LIGHT OF CRITICISM

In order to correct one's mistakes, one must first know what they are. One of the best ways to discover them is to listen to criticism and take it to heart. Criticism is essential to science, for science is by nature open-ended and self-corrective. At no time is it assumed that science has all the answers. Theories are proposed, argued for, enlarged upon, eventually refuted and replaced by other theories. Experiments are designed and performed, attempts are made to replicate them, flaws in experimental design are uncovered, new controls are imposed. Criticism is welcome at every step.

It is a mark of pseudoscience to think that being on the right track scientifically means never having to change your mind about anything. If all reasoned criticism by experts seems somehow misguided or beside the point, this is not a sign that all is well with your theory. On the contrary, it indicates something very wrong with it.

In the holistic health care field, the refusal to accept criticism shows up especially on the issue of double-blind studies. Dr. Wensel offers two reasons for rejecting double-blind studies on acupuncture. The first applies to all such studies: "Unfortunately, double-blind experiments are not appropriate for acupuncture evaluation because patients can easily tell whether the needles have been inserted into acupuncture points or elsewhere." The second applies to studies conducted in the United States that have yielded results unfavorable to acupuncture. This research, says Dr. Wensel, "has only demonstrated that the people inserting needles for experiments were not skilled acupuncturists."[25]

In *The Chelation Answer* Morton Walker, D.P.M., advocates EDTA (ethylene diamine tetraacetic acid) chelation therapy for a variety of conditions, including hardening of the arteries, premature senility, diabetic gangrene, and macular degeneration. Walker also gives two arguments against double-blind experiments. The first is basically the same as one of Dr. Wensel's: "Performing double-blind tests with EDTA chelation therapy can't be done, because patients are aware of the drug's action in their body from various symptoms. . . ." The second is an ethical argument: "While placebo testing is standard procedure for trials with new drugs on terminal patients, chelation physicians don't consider it justified to give a placebo to someone dying from vascular disease who could be saved by giving him the real EDTA."[26]

Each of these arguments is an exercise in begging the question. Take first the argument that a double-blind study cannot be conducted because the patient knows when he is getting the real thing. How does he know? Because the real thing—EDTA or needles inserted into acupuncture points—produces effects that are not produced by the placebo. But the question of whether the effects are unique to the therapy is the very question the double-blind study is designed to answer. To say at the outset that the effects cannot be caused by a placebo is to assume what is to be proved. Next, consider Wensel's assertion that if acupuncture is not effective in a given study, that only proves it was not done correctly. Why does it prove this? Because acupuncture is effective, of course. So again she assumes what is to be proved. Finally, there is Walker's argument that it is unethical to withhold chelation therapy from a seriously ill patient. The argument has two premises: (1) that it is unethical to withhold an effective therapy, and (2) that EDTA chelation therapy is effective for the conditions cited. No one would quarrel with the first premise, but the second cannot be assumed since it is precisely what is at issue.

The marks of pseudoscience uncover a kind of order in the eclectic chaos of holistic medicine. Each unconventional modality seems at first to bear its own unique rationale; but upon closer examination, certain recurring patterns of reasoning emerge. The various subfields share family resemblances. Acupuncture, for example, is like folk remedies in its anachronism, like homeopathy in its spurious similarity to current scientific theory, like psychic diagnosis with respect to the quality of evidence in support of it, and like chelation therapy with respect to its practitioners' rejection of double-blind studies. The marks of pseudoscience can be used in conjunction with traditional ways of assessing claims, such as looking for inconsistencies and checking statistics, to help the layperson see through the confusing array of holistic health care practices.

NOTES

1. Harold H. Bloomfield and Robert B. Kory, *The Holistic Way to Health and Happiness* (New York: Simon and Schuster, 1978), 46–47; Kenneth R. Pelletier, *Holistic Medicine: From Stress to Optimum Health* (New York: Delacorte, 1979), 14–15.

2. Bloomfield and Kory, op. cit., 55; C. Norman Shealy, *Occult Medicine Can Save Your Life* (New York: Dial Press, 1975), 163.

3. Dolores Krieger, *Foundations for Holistic Health Nursing Practices* (Philadelphia: J. B. Lippincott, 1981), 90–91.

4. Lawrence LeShan, *The Mechanic and the Gardener: Making the Most of the Holistic Revolution in Medicine* (New York: Holt, Rinehart and Winston, 1982), 130.

5. Shealy, op. cit., 105–106, 118.

6. Ibid., 117.

7. Bloomfield and Kory, op. cit., 55.

8. LeShan, op. cit., 93.

9. Ibid., 129–30.

10. Daisie Radner and Michael Radner, *Science and Unreason* (Belmont, CA: Wadsworth, 1982), chapter 3.

11. Louis Moss, *Acupuncture and You* (Secaucus, N.J.: Citadel, 1964), 47–48.

12. Manfred Porkert, "Chinese Medicine: A Traditional Healing Science," in *Ways of Health,* David S. Sobel (ed.), (New York: Harcourt Brace Jovanovich, 1979), 168.

13. Marc Estrin, "A Bird's-Eye View of Oriental Medicine," in *Body, Mind and Spirit,* eds. Peter Albright and Bets Parker Albright (eds.), (Brattleboro, Vt.: The Stephen Greene Press, 1980), 261.

14. G. T. Lewith and N. R. Lewith, *Modern Chinese Acupuncture* (Wellingborough, Northamptonshire: Thorsons, 1980), 7–8.

15. David E. Bresler, *Free Yourself from Pain* (New York: Simon and Schuster, 1979), 174.

16. Louis Oftedal Wensel, *Acupuncture for Americans* (Reston, Va.: Reston Publishing Company, 1980), 84.

17. Pelletier, op. cit., 25–26.

18. Jeffrey Arthur Migdow, "An Introduction to Homeopathic Medicine and the Utilization of Bioenergies for Healing," *Journal of Holistic Medicine* 4 (1982): 137–45.

19. A. H. Black, A. Cott and R. Pavloski, "The Operant Theory Approach to Biofeedback Training," in *Biofeedback: Theory and Research,* G. E. Schwartz and J. Beatty (eds.), (New York: Academic Press, 1977), 89–127.

20. Harris L. Coulter, "Homeopathic Medicine," in *Ways of Health,* Sobel (ed.), 293.

21. Moss, op. cit., 15.

22. Wensel, op. cit., 143.

23. Robert Leichtman, "Clairvoyant Diagnosis," *Journal of Holistic Health* 2 (1976): 39.

24. Norman Cousins, *The Healing Heart* (New York: W. W. Norton, 1983), 48–49.

25. Wensel, op. cit., 10.

26. Morton Walker, *The Chelation Answer* (New York: M. Evans, 1982), 87.

Thomas C. Chalmers, M.D.

Scientific Quality and the
Journal of Holistic Medicine

Evaluations of the scientific quality of the publications related to therapeutics in clinical journals have been reported a number of times (1-6). All of them have the same general conclusion: the quality is nowhere near as good as it should be. The *Journal of Holistic Medicine,* official journal of the American Holistic Medical Association, is no exception—except that the scientific quality is worse than usual.

Before going into details, two definitions are needed: scientific method and holistic medicine. The dictionary definition of the scientific method is "a method of research in which a problem is identified, relevant data are gathered and a hypothesis is formulated from these data, and the hypothesis is empirically tested." A straightforward definition of a scientific fact is that attributed to Dr. L. J. Henderson, co-discoverer of the Henderson-Hasselbalch equation. Henderson said to a class at Harvard University something like the following: "Science is the gathering of reproducible facts." That is the essence of trials of new therapies. The better the design of the experiment, especially with regard to the control of bias and the measurement of biological variability, the more reproducible will be the conclusion. The patient benefits most from receiving a therapy that has been reproducibly shown to be effective in the disease from which that particular patient suffers. The randomized control trial is generally recognized as the most, if not the only, scientific method available for comparing one diagnostic maneuver or treatment with another.

Holism is defined in philosophy as the theory that whole entities, as fundamental components of reality, have an existence other than as the mere sum of their parts. Stedman's *Medical Dictionary,* published in 1982, defines "holism" only in psychology terms: "holistic psychology, the approach to the study of a psychological phenomenon through the analysis of the phenomenon as a complete entity in itself."

Four volumes of the *Journal of Holistic Medicine,* consisting of two issues each from 1980 through 1982, have been reviewed. One gets the impression from the tenor of the editorials and in some of the articles that holistic medicine is more concerned with the unconventional or unusual types of medical diagnosis and therapy rather than with those that can be strictly defined as holistic. There is a naturopathic element to some of the articles. There is a lengthy historical article defending homeopathy, and at the same time, possibly toxic megadoses of vitamins are espoused—examples that there are not only unconventional but extreme ends of the therapeutic spectrum.

The following is a rough distribution of these forty-seven articles, excluding short notes, editorials, and book reviews. The most common essays are overviews of therapeutic remedies, usually of the "nonconforming" type. None of these are meta-analyses in which data are actually analyzed by the reviewer. Only three of them seem to recognize the importance of controls in the evaluation of therapies, and only one, an evaluation of vitamin E (7), maintains a conservative tone in its conclusions about efficacy.

The second largest group of articles, fourteen in number, may be classified as philosophical reviews that relate in one way or another to holistic medicine but address a wide range of subjects. Three of these emphasize the importance of religion in the activities of the holistic physician. Three are readable analyses of what makes a good physician from the standpoint of listening to and understanding the patient, rather than applying the scientific method.

There are seven uncontrolled trials of various therapies such as EDTA, silence, diets for headaches and arthritis, and biofeedback for the control of hypertension. In each of these the patient acts as his own control for a variable period of time. There is no blinding of the assessment of symptomatic responses, but the hypertension study does suggest some response of the biofeedback sort, something that has been demonstrated elsewhere in controlled trials (8). There are two reasonably well done physiological studies of patients, although none of the measurements are made in a blinded fashion.

The seven miscellaneous articles include a diatribe against the peer review system and one against those who oppose megadoses of vitamin C for a variety of disorders. There is a report of conservative economics, a review of data on hair analyses, and a competent review of what insecticides are doing to the soil in agricultural practice.

Only two of the forty-seven articles are randomized control trials, both by the same author (9, 10). These are competent studies that would receive an above-average score by most quality-assessing systems (11). One is a demonstration that acupuncture-induced mood changes can be reversed by the narcotic antagonist naloxone, and the other correlates the effects of acupuncture on the response of patients to pain and with rises in serum beta endorphin and cortisol.

The expressed views of the editor make it unlikely that well-controlled trials will appear very often in this journal. In reviews of the efficacy of EDTA chelation therapy in occlusive arterial disease (12), Cranton, the editor, referred to an uncontrolled evaluation of the effects of EDTA on renal function in patients with "chronic degenerative disorders" (13). Fifty-seven patients received EDTA and also a multi-vitamin trace mineral agent in doses five to ten times that recommended for adults. There was no blinding of the measurements, no simultaneous controls, and no separation of the investigative agents. Fifty of these fifty-seven patients were said to have improved and seven worsened. It appears that the editor assumes that any study making before and after measurements is a controlled trial.

The following words appear at the end of the review (12): "entirely satisfactory double-blind studies of EDTA chelation therapy are probably impossible due to the multi-factorial nature of the ideal total therapy. When studying occlusive arterial disease, a scientific community may be compelled to revamp its collective thinking and begin to accept a new scientific method and positive functional results as proof of effectiveness." Responses that depend on functional results are the very essence of the need for blinded randomization and assessment of therapies. Such a study is no more expensive or difficult than an uncontrolled series, and the claim that the millions of dollars required are not available is not applicable.

In summary, in this series of articles there are two well-done, randomized control trials and three uncontrolled measurements of physiologic responses without adequate blinding.

The Journal of Holistic Medicine has a long way to go to achieve the same standards of scientific reporting as the more orthodox medical journals, bad as they may be.

REFERENCES

1. R. H. Fletcher and S. W. Fletcher, "Clinical Research in General Medical Journals: A 30-year Perspective," *New England Journal of Medicine* 301 (1979): 180–83.

2. J. A. Freiman, T. C. Chalmers, H. Smity, Jr., et al., "The Importance Beta, the Type II Error and Sample Size in the Design and Interpretation of the Randomized Control Trial: Survey of 71 'Negative' Trials," *New England Journal of Medicine* 299 (1978): 690–94.

3. R. I. Horwitz and A. R. Feinstein, "Methodologic Standards and Contradictory Results in Case Control Research," *American Journal of Medicine* 66 (1979): 556–64.

4. G. Moskowitz, T. C. Chalmers, H. S. Sacks, R. M. Fagerstrom, and H. Smith, Jr., "Deficiencies of Clinical Trials of Alcohol Withdrawal," *Alcoholism* 7 (1983): 42–46.

5. B. A. Blackburn, H. Smith, Jr., and T. C. Chalmers, "The Inadequate Evidence for Short Hospital Stay After Hernia or Varicose Vein Stripping Surgery," *Mount Sinai Journal of Medicine* 49 (1982): 383–90.

6. R. DerSimonian, L. J. Charette, et al., "Reporting on Methods in Clinical Trials," *New England Journal of Medicine* 306 (1983): 1332–37.

7. J. Bland, "Vitamin E (Tocopherol) Therapy in Clinical Medicine," *Journal of Holistic Medicine* 2 (1980): 55–75.

8. G. Andrews, S. W. MacMahon, A. Austin, and D. G. Byrne, "Hypertension: Comparison of Drug and Non-drug Treatments," *British Medical Journal* 284 (1982): 1523–26.

9. P. M. Toyama, "Acupuncture Induced Mood Changes Reversed by the Narcotic Antagonist, Naloxone," *Journal of Holistic Medicine* 3 (1981): 46–52.

10. P. M. Toyama, C. Popell, J. Evans, and C. Heyder, "Beta-endorphin and Cortisol Measurements Following Acupuncture and Moxibustion," *Journal of Holistic Medicine* 4 (1982): 58–67.

11. T. C. Chalmers, H. Smith Jr., B. Blackburn, et al., "A Method for Assessing the Quality of a Randomized Control Trial," *Controlled Clinical Trials* 2 (1981): 31–49.

12. E. M. Cranton, and J. P. Frackelton, "Current Status of EDTA Chelation Therapy in Occlusive Arterial Disease," *Journal of Holistic Medicine* 4 (1982): 24–33.

13. E. W. McDonagh, C. J. Rudolph, and E. Cheraskin, "An Oculocerebrovasculometric Analysis of the Improvement in Arterial Stenosis Following EDTA Chelation Therapy," *Journal of Holistic Medicine* 4 (1982): 21–23.

Part IV

Examining Holistic Practices

Russell S. Worrall, O. D.

Iridology: Diagnosis or Delusion?

For centuries the eye has been said to be the mirror of the body and the soul. Terror and love are expressed through the eyes; and the general state of health can be reflected in the eyes, as in the vacant, glassy stare of the gravely ill. Today, a more precise analogy would be to describe the eye as a window rather than a mirror. The eye is an optically clear porthole that allows one to view body tissues, such as blood vessels and nerves, in their undisturbed state. The subject of this paper, iridology, proposes a more elaborate analogy—specifically, that the iris of the eye is a gauge registering the condition of the body's various organs; or, as Jessica Maxwell describes it in her book *The Eye/Body Connection,* the iris is "an organic Etch-a-Sketch" (Maxwell 1980, p. 12).

Iridology, pronounced "eyeridology," is the "science" of reading the markings or signs in the iris (the colored part of the eye) to determine the functional state of the various components of the body. It is not unique; other, equally sophisticated systems of belief exist utilizing the soles of the feet, the ear, the palm, and the spine. A common theme unites these varied techniques. They are noninvasive (you do not have to be punctured or sliced into!) and they each involve a specific area of the body's surface, which when read by a "well-trained" practitioner reveals your innermost health problems. Elaborate charts (suitable for framing) that guide the practitioner and impress the patient are the centerpiece of each method.

Iridology may have its origins in antiquity, or more recently in Russia, as suggested by the *National Enquirer* (1978), but Dr. Ignatz von Peczely, of Hungary, is generally held responsible for developing and promoting the modern

Reprinted from *Skeptical Inquirer* 7 (1983):23–35 by permission of the publisher.

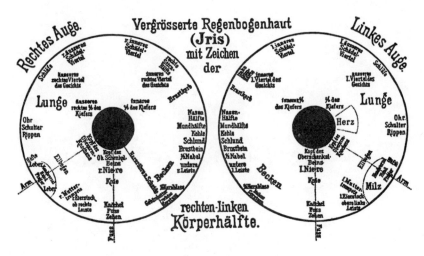

FIGURE 1. An iris chart developed by von Peczely.

"science" of iris diagnosis. According to the story, the miraculous discovery of the iris-body connection came when, as a boy of ten, Ignatz accidently broke the leg of an owl and a black stripe spontaneously appeared on the owl's iris. He went on to develop charts based on his clinical observations (see Figure 1) and published a book on the subject (von Peczely 1866).

In the United States, Bernard Jensen has been the most influential proponent of iridology. His book, *The Science and Practice of Iridology* (Jensen [1952] 1974), has been the authority on the subject since its publication in 1952. His new book, *Iridology: The Science and Practice in the Healing Arts,* vol. 2

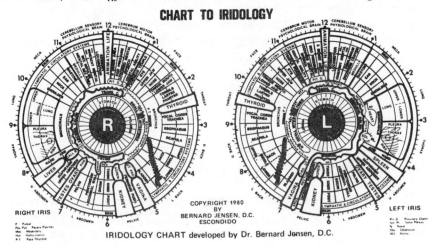

FIGURE 2. Iridology chart by Jensen (Jensen, *Iridology Simplified*, Iridologists International, 1980).

(Jensen 1982), is a 580-page epic detailing the history, "science," and application of iridology. Dr. Jensen's updated charts (see Figure 2) are the standard in the United States. European charts, though more detailed and exacting, follow the same general format as illustrated by Kriege's (1975) Bone Zone Chart (Figure 3) and Korvin-Swiecki's charts (Figure 4) shown in *The Eye-Body Connection* (Maxwell 1980). This pseudoscience has been popularized by many recent books and articles, including a story in the *National Enquirer* (1978) with a typically dramatic headline: "Do-It-Yourself Eye Test That Can Save Your Life." All these reports are blandly neutral or, more commonly, outright enthusiastic about this purportedly marvelous diagnostic procedure. Only two papers present a critical view based on controlled scientific studies, the results of which are not astonishing to the skeptical inquirer.

The philosophical, scientific, and clinical ramifications of iridology are succinctly stated by Harri Wolf (1979, pp. 7-8), founder of the National Iridology Research Foundation, in the introductory remarks of his *Applied Iridology:*

Now wouldn't it seem *logical* [emphasis added] that through some creative design, or evolutionary process (whatever the reader's preference), the human body would be equipped with a metering device functioning as a gauge in regard to the health of the individual?

Each of us is, *in fact* [emphasis added], equipped with just such a miniature recording screen—the iris. Via the direct neural connection of the surface layers of the iris with the cervical ganglion of the sympathetic nervous system, impressions

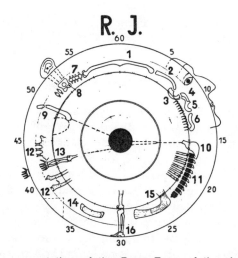

FIGURE 3. Schematic representation of the Bone Zone of the right eye by Kriege: (1) Cranial bone. (2) Frontal bone. (3) Orbit. (4) Nasal bone. (5) Upper Jaw and teeth. (6) Lower jaw and teeth. (7) Cervical vertebrae. (8) Ear. (9) Shoulder and clavicle. (10) Scapula. (11) Spine and ribs. (12) Sternum and ribs. (13) Hand and arm bones. (14) True pelvis. (15) Pelvic crests. (16) Foot and leg bones. (*Fundamental Basis of Iris-diagnosis,* trans. Priest, Fowler Co., London, 1975, p. 102.)

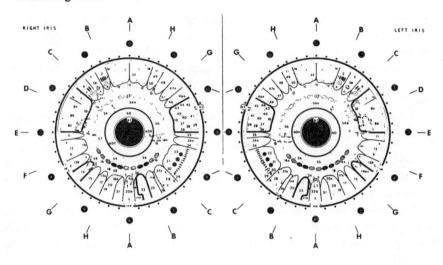

FIGURE 4. Basic European Iridology chart by Korvin-Swiecki. Some examples from the chart: (1) Cerebrum. (2) Cerebellum. (5) Ear. (6) Neck, throat. (8) Lungs. (9) Heart. (B) Aorta. (14) Liver. (16) Pancreas. (23) Kidneys. (27A) Uterus. (42) Larynx. (53) Autonomic nervous system. (54) Ascending colon. (58) Appendix. (59) Gallbladder. (60) Stomach. (61) Central nervous system. (62) Circulatory and lymphatic system. (Jessica Maxwell, *The Eye/Body Connection*, Warner Books, New York, 1980, pp. 60-63.)

from all over the body are conveyed to the iris. Thus is established the neuro-optic reflex.

Iridology, as the study of the neuro-optic reflex is known, is the art/science of *revealing* [emphasis added] pathological, structural and functional disturbances in the body.

THE PHILOSOPHY AND LOGIC

The claim that iridology is a logical, natural system is central to iridology philosophy. As Jensen (1981a, p. 2) writes, "We must realize that iridology represents a law of nature that cannot be changed. I believe that it is just as immutable and unchangeable as any of the laws that govern the universe." When viewed from a critical perspective, the logic in iridology begins to fade. First, a gauge or metering system has to be read and understood to be useful. The iris of the eye is certainly inaccessible to all of earth's creatures, including man (unless he happens to have a mirror handy). Further, the iris signs are so complex as to be unintelligible to all but those who have been enlightened by von Peczely's theories. In short, here is no logical evidence to support a claim of functional utility for this complex biological system purported to exist in many diverse organisms, including man.

This apparent lack of utility to the organism exposes a more fundamental flaw in the logic of iridology when it is considered in the context of the evolutionary process. A physiological subsystem such as the suggested iris-body connection would be developed and refined under the gradual pressures exerted by natural selection. For such a system (more properly the gene pool that codes for the system) to have evolved in many diverse species, a distinct survival advantage had to be present for the organisms with this system. This is an assumption for which I can offer no logical arguments. Certainly the saber-toothed tiger derived little benefit from this amazing metering system, nor does today's modern owl.

THE SCIENCE

A second theme in iridology is that, as Wolf states, the neuro-optic relfex exists "in fact." The facts supporting the existence of the neuro-optic reflex are tenuous at best. It is postulated by Wolf (1979, p. 7) that the sympathetic division of the automatic nervous system mediates the iris response. D. Bamer (1982, p. 22) includes the parasympathetic division in his theory and offers an anatomical diagram to support his claim (see Figure 5). In a gross anatomical sense the autonomic system does interconnect and enervate almost every segment of the body, including the eye. However, anatomical interconnection does not imply functional connection any more than having a telephone in your home is proof of the proposition that you receive all of the calls intended for the president of the United States. Further, the autonomic nerves supplying the eye are of small caliber and would not seem to have adequate numbers of nerve fibers to handle the volume of information presumed to reach the iris. Anatomical, physiological,

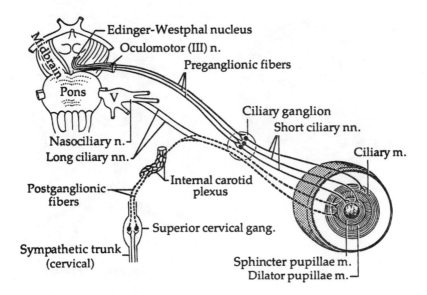

FIGURE 5. Anatomical diagram by Bamer (*Applied Iridology and Herbology*, BiWord Publishers, Orem, Utah, 1982, p. 22).

and clinical studies have eloquently demonstrated the functional neural pathways involved in many of the eye's control and response mechanisms, but published studies report no evidence in support of a functional iris-body connection (Moses 1975; Last 1973). Though these investigations were not specifically looking for a neuro-optic reflex, given the quality and quantity of information postulated to appear in the iris it is curious that even accidental detection of this elaborate system has eluded researchers.

One aspect of the functional theory, as expressed by Jensen, is especially interesting in light of well-established neurological evidence. Anatomists and physiologists have long known that as a general rule the central nervous system is functionally split, with each side controlling and monitoring the opposite side of the body. In iridology it has also been "established" that each eye "sees" its own side of the body. Thus a conflict is created for iridologists in explaining the flow of information over the autonomic pathways that cross to the opposite side as they travel through the central nervous system. To explain this apparent difficulty. Jensen proposes that the optic nerve serves as the final link between the autonomic system and the iris (see Figures 6 and 7). Since the optic nerve crosses between the eye and the brain, information from an organ would make a second crossing on its way to the iris and register on the same side that it originated from. Jensen (1980, p. 3) also infers that the large size of the optic nerve would provide the needed transmission capacity to account for the flow of information to the iris. Thus, with Jensen's assumptions, iridology theory seems to agree with anatomical evidence!

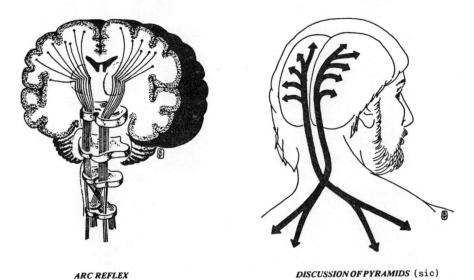

ARC REFLEX   *DISCUSSION OF PYRAMIDS* (sic)

FIGURE 6. The first crossing in the autonomic system according to Jensen. (*Iridologists International Manual for Research and Development,* Iridologists International, Escondido, Calif., 1981, p. 25).

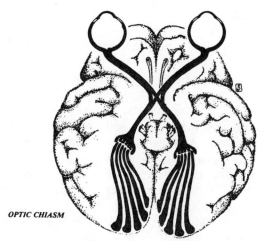

OPTIC CHIASM

FIGURE 7. The second crossing in the optic nerve according to Jensen (*Iridologists International Manual for Research and Development,* Iridologists International, Escondido, Calif., 1981, p. 27).

The assumption that the optic nerve mediates the final leg of the neuro-optic response solves the iridologists' theoretical dilemma by creating a double cross, but at the same time the assumption raises serious questions by anyone familiar with the tremendous body of literature published on the visual pathways. The visual system (including the optic nerve) is probably the most intensively studied and best understood neural system in the body. The Nobel Prize recently awarded to Hubel and Wiesel was the result of many years of work on this intriguing system. All of the accumulated research unequivocally demonstrates that the mammalian optic nerve is primarily an afferent pathway, that is, one in which the signals travel from the eye to the brain. There is no evidence suggesting that any fibers from the optic nerve make connections with the iris. This, combined with the fact that only half of the fibers in the optic nerve cross, makes the proposition that the optic nerve is the final link to the iris untenable (Moses 1975, pp. 367–405).

This double-cross hypothesis is characteristic of the "scientific" evidence presented in Jensen's new text. This volume contains countless misinterpretations of established anatomical and physiological knowledge and includes references to many pseudosciences, such as Kirlian photography and personology (Jensen 1982, pp. 88, 491).

This pseudoscience rises to the level of the ridiculous with the proposition that the iris can communicate information back to remote organs. D. Hall (1981, pp. 210-11) describes the "removal of function" following the surgical removal of a piece of iris tissue in glaucoma or cataract surgery. She says, "As sure as eggs, the iris zones affected will be down in function and maybe in structure too." As D. Stark (1981, p. 677) points out, "This can only be the case if the iris not only reflects but also controls bodily function, which is patently absurd."

CLINICAL CONSIDERATIONS

Though the gossamer theoretical structure that underlies iridology is apparent to the critical inquirer, proponents and practitioners continue to sell iridology as a "valid" clinical procedure. As Wolf (1979, pp. 7–8) states, iridology as a clinical tool reveals "pathological, structural and functional disturbances in the body." Jensen (1981a, p. 2) adds that "iridology is unique in its ability to make a subclinical evaluation, whereas the medical point of view only recognized lab test verification of dysfunction." Although Jensen mentions "diagnosis" in many of his writings, he qualifies this by stating (1981b, p. 16) that "iridology does not diagnose disease in the sense that Western medicine does, nor does it label combinations of symptoms with disease names." A paper by Fernandiz appearing in the same journal (published by Jensen) is titled "Hemicrania (Migraine) and Its Diagnosis by Means of the Iris"! Such double talk does not cover the reality of the fact that iridology is a clinical technique purported to determine functional states within the body for the purpose of recommending a course of corrective treatment.

Confusion is the first order of business in the clinical application of iridology; for, as Stark (1981, p. 677) notes, there are many iris charts (more than 19) and this "presents the first diagnostic dilemma—which chart to choose." Although most charts are in general agreement on major landmarks, such as the leg area being represented at the six-o'clock position, there are also many differences in both location and interpretation of iris signs (compare Figures 2–5).

Acknowledging the lack of objective clinical evidence, in a recent article Jensen (1981a, p. 1) says, "At the present time, we have no exact way of proving anything other than in a phenomenological manner that what we know and see is true." Thus, in support of the efficacy of iridology, proponents have published endless numbers of anecdotal case reports.

Medicine has long used clinical observation to support claims of observed phenomena even when detailed knowledge of the underlying functional processes are not fully understood. To ensure reliable reproducible results, clinical investigators have adopted strict rules in the form of controlled clinical studies. The controls are chosen to remove, to the extent possible, the inevitable bias of both the patient and the practitioner, to isolate the procedure or medication, and to provide subject groups of adequate size to make statistical comparisons. The controlled clinical study is not, as promoters of iridology suggest, a tool developed by Western medicine to attack unorthodox procedures (Jensen 1981b, p. 20), but in fact it is universally accepted and applied in all areas of scientific inquiry.

The design of a controlled clinical study of iridology would at first appear relatively simple, especially in light of Jensen's (1974, p. 2) comment that "iridology can diagnose a patient for the doctor if he has a perfect colored photograph showing three-dimensional depth of the patient's eye. The patient need not be present." Utilizing photographs in a study effectively isolates the iridologist from the patient, thus limiting the data available to only that obtained from the iris appearance. This eliminates the possibility that direct observation might provide information from general physical appearance and also prevents items of pertinent history from being inadvertently divulged, as is commonly observed in "cold readings" by psychics. The difficulty develops when a standard criterion for the diagnosis of the condition in question is established, as illustrated in the following discussion.

Establishing a standard diagnosis with which to compare the validity of iridology may well be impossible. First, as was quoted above, iridology claims to be able to make a subclinical diagnosis, that is, before symptoms or measurable signs develop. In addition, Jensen (1974, p. 12) adds: "Many times the conditions revealed in the iris today will not be apparent in the body for years to come, but time will inevitably show the analysis to be correct." Thus the proponents of iridology have an excellent but inherently unprovable explanation for the high rate of overdiagnosis (false positives) in controlled studies.

There is also little common diagnostic ground, because many of the conditions detected by practitioners of iridology are "diseases" whose existence has been disputed or discredited by scientific investigation. A common finding is a toxic bowel settlement (which is treated with procedures of questionable value, such as colonic irrigation!); however, the toxic settlement theory of disease was soundly discredited in the early part of this century (Ratclift 1962, p. 52). Thus from a critical perspective it would be difficult to agree on a standard diagnosis where the existence of the disease itself is in dispute.

Though the clinical application of iridology is widespread, the results of only two controlled clinical studies have been published. At the University of Melbourne (Australia), D. Cockburn compared iridology evaluations with known medical histories. The most interesting phase of his study had iridologists evaluate before-and-after iris photographs of subjects who developed an acute disease. He asked the iridologists to determine if a change in the iris had occurred and, if possible, to tell which organ was affected. The only set of photographs determined to have changes was a set taken as a control on the same subject two minutes apart! Cockburn (1981, p. 157) states, "It must be concluded that, at least for the subjects of the prospective trial and for the acute stage of the disease states represented, there were no detectable iris changes of the type depicted in the commonly used iris diagnosis charts."

At the University of California, San Diego, A. Simon, D. Worthen, and J. Mitas (1979) compared the accuracy of iridology based on the reading of color slides for the detection of kidney dysfunction. A blood chemistry test (creatinine level) was used as the standard for assessment of kidney function. Photographs of 143 subjects (48 with kidney disease) were read by three iridologists and three ophthalmologists. The overall record for hitting a correct determination was no better than chance when the number of incorrect and correct determinations were compared. In conclusion the authors state, "Clearly, none of the six observers in this study derived data of clinical importance or significance" (p. 1389).

Jensen, one of the iridologists participating in the San Diego study, has written several critical commentaries on the results. His first criticism was the poor quality of the photographs; however, at the time of the study he did not decline to read them. He also disputes the validity of the creatinine test as an indication of kidney function, though it is widely accepted and routinely used by orthodox practitioners. He asserts that the creatinine test has been around for 10 to 12 years, whereas iridology has been in use for more than 125 years (Jensen 1981c, p. vi). Jensen seems oblivious to the fact that the amount of time a test has been in existence has no relevance to its validity.

As further evidence of the clinical value of iridology, Jensen cites the work of Romashov and Velkelvor of the USSR (*National Enquirer* 1978), who reported a 95-percent accuracy in 1,273 subjects with diagnosed disease. He also states that Deck in Germany has reported a 92-percent efficiency in the detection of kidney disease through iris diagnosis (Jensen 1981c, p. 19). Jensen does not describe the details of these investigations, the nature of the controls, or the standards used for diagnosis. These are important, because one iridologist in the San Diego study also could boast of having correctly identified 88 percent of those with kidney disease. Unfortunately, he reported that 88 percent of the normal subjects included in the study as a control were also suffering from kidney disease (Simon, Worthen, and Mitas 1979, pp. 1387-88). Therefore, without specific details of the design, the use of these studies is of no value when offered in support of iridology.

To enhance the image of iridology by association with an accepted clinical technique, Jensen (1981c, p. i) writes: "The fundus examination, which has been accepted by ophthalmologists, reads the arterial circulation. Similarly, iridology reads the iris stroma. . . ." The word "similarly" is loosely applied in this analogy. The fundus examination is a routine medical procedure using a special optical instrument (ophthalmoscope) that provides a view of the interior lining of the eye through the pupil. Body tissues, including blood vessels, can be studied undisturbed, an opportunity not afforded elsewhere on the body. The changes in arterial appearance in the eye represent a local manifestation of a more generalized vascular disease. No specific reflexive communication with remote body organs needs to be postulated to explain this or any of the many other observed phenomena in a traditional fundus examination.

SCIENCE OR RHETORIC

In his rhetorical war with "Western" medicine Jensen (1980, p. 2) writes: "Iridology is based on scientific observation. It is the kind of science that cannot be related through scientific tests, for it does not provide clinical information." If this non sequitur does not deter all of those inclined to subject iridology to controlled clinical studies, Jensen (1981c, p. vi) adds the ultimate argument used by practitioners of all unorthodox procedures. He writes: "Iridology can only be judged by those who use it properly. Iridology has not been properly used by those who have criticized and say it fails the test." In other words, you have to be "sensitive" to the technique to ensure favorable results!

Even though proponents may have used iridology "properly" since von Peczely published his theories in 1866, they have failed to publish even one well-documented study to support the validity of any of the information presented on their iris charts. Since efficacy has not been established, the ultimate question faced by practitioners of iridology is one of ethics in their relationship with patients.

HARMLESS FAD OR HEALTH HAZARD?

It is clear from a logical, theoretical, and clinical perspective that iridology is a pseudoscience of no clinical value. Unfortunately, the use of iridology by unorthodox practitioners is all too common today, and the unsuspecting and often vulnerable patient in the clinical application of the "science" is the recipient of its presumed benefits. In my private practice and as a member of the faculty of the School of Optometry at the University of California, Berkeley, I have been increasingly alarmed by the growing popularity and acceptance of iridology as a diagnostic tool. This is an area of great concern to everyone in the health professions, because acceptance of this pseudoscience can lead an individual to delay needed treatment when a false-negative diagnosis is made (i.e., when a disease is present but not detected). This would appear inevitable given Jensen's recent advice on the differential diagnosis of appendicitis. He writes: "When trying to distinguish between appendicitis and cecal inflammation, we must carefully examine the area at five o'clock in the right iris. Many cases of cecal inflammation have been incorrectly diagnosed as appendicitis, but the iris reveals the location of the inflammation" (Jensen 1982, p. 235). (Remember Jensen claims not to diagnose!) A delay created while treating "cecal inflammation" could prove fatal if appendicitis is the correct diagnosis. On the other hand, when a false-positive finding is reported (i.e., when a disease is "detected" but not present) to a naive patient, extreme mental anguish can result. In addition, the patient may expend large sums of money on unneeded treatments or (if they are skeptical) on traditional diagnostic tests to confirm the reported nondisease.

THE FORMULA FOR SUCCESS?

It would seem that the false-positive diagnosis of subclinical disease is the underlying key to the popularity and success of iridology. The bulk of the diseases reported are vaguely stated conditions in organs, such as an "underactive" pancreas or "chronic weakness" in the lungs. Such vagueness permits clinicians to capitalize on any improvement in the way a patient "feels" as proof that the treatments are doing some good. Under those conditions the cure rate and patient satisfaction in a clinical practice can be very high.

Though the validity of the diagnosis and treatment may rest on false premises, many patients appear to experience a positive change in their health. This is understandable since these programs often include a good diet and moderate exercise, a formula that would do all of us some good! However, as the following two cases will illustrate, the false-positive diagnosis can also have a negative impact on the patient.

A well-educated accountant, whom I have seen routinely for eye care, was experiencing lower back pain. He consulted a local chiropractor, and during the course of treatment an iridology workup was recommended. The results indicated, among many other health problems, the presence of cancer. Overwhelmed, the patient spent the day in torment. Unable to consult his family physician, who was out of the office, or his wife, who was at work, he finally sought my advice late in the afternoon. After a lengthy discussion I was able to allay his fears and he began to understand, in a more critical way, the complexities of a medical diagnosis. He wondered how an intelligent person like himself could be caught up in such a deep emotional web over such a diagnosis. This story fortunately had a pleasant ending. However, the outcome could have been much more serious since this patient is also suffering from a heart condition, which was not noted on the iridology evaluation!

Another patient in my office related her recent experience with an herbalist and iridology. Based on her iris photographs, she was given a list of herbs and advice supposedly needed to correct a long list of low-grade chronic conditions. The prescription for this long list was a total of over $200 worth of herbs. Considering herself to be healthy, she was skeptical and decided to save her money. This case also had a happy ending, but it leads me to wonder how many naive patients are investing in questionable treatments based on the results of questionable diagnostics?

A more humorous episode occurred recently when an investigative reporter had an iridology workup. She was told that "a whitish color emanating from the iris shows a lot of acidity and mucus throughout the body and could be from eating a lot of meat, bread and milk products. When told the reporter is a vegetarian, [the iridologist] said the acidity could be a reverse effect from eating too much fruit and vegetables." A classic example of clinical nonsense. (Meyer 1982, p. 81).

DELUSION OR DIAGNOSIS?

It seems that the pseudoscience of iridology has deluded both patient and practitioner alike. The surge in popularity that iridology and its fellow pseudodiagnostic sciences are enjoying is not surprising. Iridology is "amazing," relatively simple to learn, and painless and, most important, it has that mystical attraction on which unorthodox theories and practices have thrived over the centuries.

REFERENCES

Bamer, D. 1982. *Applied Iridology and Herbology.* Orem, Utah: BiWorld Publishers.

Cockburn, D. 1982. "A Study of Validity of Iris Diagnosis." *Australian Journal of Optometry* (July).

Hall, D. 1981. *Iridology: How the Eyes Reveal Your Health and Personality.* New Canaan: Keats Publishing.

Jensen, B. 1974. *The Science and Practice of Iridology* (1952). Escondido, Calif.: Jensen.

———. 1980. *Iridology Simplified.* Escondido, Calif.: Iridologists International.

———. 1981a. "An Eye for the Future." *Iridologists International Manual for Research and Development* 2-11/12.

———. 1981b. "Reply to Western Medicine's Study of Iridology." *Iridologists International Manual for Research and Development* 2-11/12.

———. 1981c. "Answer to an Article Appearing in the Journal of the American Medical Association Evaluating Iridology." Insert to *Iridologists International Manual for Research and Development* 2-11/12.

———. 1982. *Iridology: The Science and Practice in the Healing Arts,* vol. 2. Escondido, Calif.: Jensen.

Kriege. T. 1975. *Fundamentals of Iris Diagnosis.* Trans. A. Priest. London: Fowler Co.

Last, R. J. 1973. *Wolf's Anatomy of the Eye and Orbit,* 6th ed. Philadelphia: W. B. Saunders.

Maxwell, J. 1980. *The Eye/Body Connection.* New York: Warner Books.

Meyer, Norma. 1982. "Do Your Eyes Really Speak?" *Daily Breeze* (Torrence, Calif.). September 5.

Moses, R. A. 1975. *Adler's Physiology of the Eye.* New York: C. V. Mosby.

National Enquirer. 1978. "Do-It-Yourself Eye Test That Can Save Your Life" (May 23).

Ratclift. 1962. "America's Laxative Addiction." *Today's Health* (November).

Simon, A.; Worthen, D.; and Mitas, J. 1979. "An Evaluation of Iridology." *Journal of the American Medical Association* (September 28).

Stark, D. 1981. "Look into My Eyes." *Medical Journal of Australia* (December 12).

Von Peczely, I. 1866. *Discovery in the Realm of Nature and Art of Healing.* Budapest: Druckeree der Kgl.

Wolf, H. 1979. *Applied Iridology.* San Diego: National Iridology Foundation.

Petr Skrabanek, Ph.D.

Acupuncture: Past, Present, and Future

"A chief obstacle in the way of scientific investigation of [this phenomenon] is the difficulty of finding any solid footing in the quagmire of error, self-delusion, and downright imposture . . . even in the hands of medical men of high character the proportion of truth to mere error is as Falstaff's halfpenny worth of bread to his intolerable deal of sack." Thus spoke a discerning hypnotist in the heyday of hypnotism nearly a hundred years ago.[1] The same holds good for present-day acupuncture.[2]

Reading through a representative selection of about four hundred articles and two dozen books of the acupuncture literature, I have found that the bulk of it consists of writings by converts, impervious to any criticism, who preach a hermetic doctrine in their own esoteric jargon, liberally peppered with Chinese words. Naturally, financial spoils of a fashionable cure also attract swarms of shady operators and unscrupulous opportunists, who rarely bother to go to print. A minority of acupuncture practitioners, mainly those with medical degrees, are anxious to maintain a link with the main body of the medical profession; they try, often successfully, to present acupuncture to their uninitiated colleagues in a matter-of-fact way as a valuable contribution to the therapeutic armamentarium of orthodox medicine; they use moderate language and the terms of modern medicine. This critical review is mainly concerned with the arguments of these apologists.

I see little point in arguing against patent absurdities, e.g., that acupuncture cures acute bacillary dysentery, that it is effective in controlling fever, or that it enhances "antiphlogistic[!] . . . antishock, and antiparalytic abilities of the body," or that it is of value in the treatment of conjunctivitis, central retinitis, myopia, and cataract—miracles that have the *imprimatur* of the World Health Organization (WHO).[3]

THE HISTORY OF ACUPUNCTURE

The ancient origins of acupuncture are regularly used by the acupuncture apologists as evidence for its intrinsic value. If it is realized that there has been no conceptual development in the theory of acupuncture for the last two thousand years, its antiquity is also its undoing. Lu and Needham[4] have provided a scholarly exposition of the history of acupuncture, and it is a pity that their book is marred by an uncritical acceptance of pseudoscientific claims made by modern acupuncturists, and the text is replete with the marvels of acupuncture hagiography. The attitude of the authors can be judged from a naive admission of one of them who witnessed "her mother's cholera in 1909 surmounting the crisis by the aid of acupuncture." The free mix of fantasy and historical facts in this authoritative book is a trap for the unwary.

In its early stages (the third to the first centuries B.C.), acupuncture was used as a form of bloodletting in a magico-religious ritual during which the malevolent spirit of disease was allowed to escape. The humoral concept was soon replaced by the concept of vital energy *(pneuma, Qi)*.

Qi is said to flow in channels beneath the surface of the body. The surface markings of these channels are known as "meridians." The acupuncture points (acupoints) are located along these meridians in sites where the *Qi* channels can be directly tapped by the needle. Originally there were 365 such points, corresponding to the days of the year: the human microcosm mirroring cosmic time. The stimulation of acupoints may not only release an excess of *Qi,* but also correct a deficiency, thus maintaining harmony between the opposing metaphysical principles of *Yin* and *Yang*.[5]

The only development in the last two millenia has been a gradual increase in acupoints, which now exceed two thousand. (This proliferation has been skillfully exploited by the acupuncture apologists to obfuscate negative results from controlled trials—since any random point is more likely than not to be an acupoint, "the impossibility of choosing placebo points" precludes the possibility of objective evaluation of acupuncture![6])

Acupuncture reached Europe in the seventeenth century and has since been rejected, rediscovered, and forgotten again in four major waves.[7] In the last two decades of that century, acupuncture was fairly well established in Europe, though many physicians, including Thomas Sydenham, were skeptical.[8] Several prominent French physicians and surgeons (Dujardin, Vicq-d'Azyr, Berlioz, Cloquet) advocated acupuncture in the eighteenth and nineteenth centuries, but other, equally prominent doctors were not impressed. For example, Trousseau and Pidoux in their *Traité de Thérapeutique* (1836) accused Dr. Louis Berlioz (the father of the composer) of resurrecting an absurd doctrine from well-deserved oblivion.[9] Electroacupuncture, so popular today, was first used by Sarlandière before 1825.[10] Soulié de Morant, a French diplomat in China, fascinated by acupuncture as a cure for cholera, published his influential book *L'Acupunture Chinoise* in 1939.

While France and Germany were the principal European countries under the spell of acupuncture, periodic upsurges were also noticeable in nineteenth-century England. In 1829, the editor of *Medico-Chirurgical Review* wrote: "A little while ago the town rang with 'acupuncture,' every body talked of it, every one was curing incurable diseases with it; but now not a syllable is said upon the subject."[11] In 1871, Teale quoted a friend from Birmingham: "We used to stick half-a-dozen needles into the deltoid . . . with sometimes 'wonderful' results."[12] There were many other enthusiastic reports.[13]

Much of this needling was practiced by doctors who had no knowledge of Chinese acupuncture, but results were equally spectacular among believers. Needling the "trigger" points in painful musculoskeletal disorders was found to be beneficial. This so-called "needle effect" was rediscovered recently but it has received little attention, presumably because it is devoid of Oriental mystique.[14]

It is ironic that while Europeans were flirting with needles, the Chinese banned acupuncture, first in 1822, and then a number of times later, the last rejection being issued by the Kuomintang government in 1929. The fate of acupuncture was similar in Japan, where the practice was officially prohibited in 1876. What was the reason for this change in attitude toward a practice revered for thousands of years? Lu and Needham, unwilling to accept the possibility that acupuncture is of little use, tried to explain this sudden devaluation of acupuncture by "a strange Victorian prudery" of the ultra-Confucian moralists.[15] The truth seems to be more prosaic, and grains of it can be found in the Chinese Communist rhetoric: "trampling upon the cultural legacy" and "the cultural aggression" of Western imperialists in nineteenth-century China means, among other things, the introduction of Western medical knowledge, including vaccination; the teaching of anatomy, surgery, anaesthesia; and autopsies.[16]

Huard and Wong cite from a note written in the nineteenth century by some Chinese doctors who had just witnessed an autopsy on two English sailors: "We are overcome by your kindness but everything we have just seen is in complete disagreement with the teaching of our books."[17]

After the victory of the Communists in 1949, acupuncture, together with other forms of traditional Chinese medicine, was revived on Mao's orders. It was a pragmatic political solution to the problem of providing health care for a population of over half a billion, when there were only twenty to thirty thousand doctors who had been trained in Western medicine and who looked mainly after the rich and foreign clientele in cities.[18]

The first European echo of this revival was heard in the Soviet Union, following the return of Soviet doctors from China where they attended courses in *chen-chiou* therapy (acupuncture and moxa) in 1956–1957.[19] However, after the break in political relations, acupuncture publications in the Soviet Union and its satellites tapered off. The strongest official rejection of acupuncture in the Soviet sphere of influence came from the Academy of Sciences of the German Democratic Republic.[20] Enthusiastic reports from Eastern Europe in the 1960s did not go unnoticed in the West,[21] but the Western acupuncturists in general kept a low profile until after Nixon's visit to China in 1972.

ACUPUNCTURE "ANAESTHESIA"

In 1958, during the Great Leap Forward, the Chinese invented acupuncture anaesthesia, and by the time the Western cultural and scientific delegations started arriving, the scene was set for breathtaking spectacles of patients operated upon without any anaesthetic, who were smiling, sucking mandarin oranges, and chatting with the delegates, while their brain tumors, goitres, lungs, or stomachs were being removed. The delegations were provided with propaganda material, films, and souvenir needles to take home with them. A typical scene was described by one of the flabbergasted Western observers who witnessed a thyroid adenoma being removed from a Chinese patient: "The patient sat up, had a glass of milk, held up his little red book, and said in a firm voice: 'Long live Chairman Mao and welcome American doctors.' He then put on his pajama top, stepped to the floor and walked out of the operating room."[22]

The same scene is described in Chinese propaganda booklets: "The smiling Hu Shu-hsuan sat up on the operating table and, facing a portrait of Chairman Mao, cheered, 'Long live Chariman Mao!'"[23] Curiously, many Western observers have been adamant that acupuncture has nothing to do with hypnosis, suggestion, or brainwashing.

Compare these stories with an account of an American patient undergoing thyroidectomy under hypnoanalgesia in 1956: "The patient talked amiably to the surgical team throughout the surgery, had a glass of water immediatley after the operation, jumped off the table. . . ."[24] Such reports were ignored because hypnosis was old hat, whereas Chinese acupuncture created a stir because it was a novelty for many.

Windsor recalled how on one occasion in 1973 in Beijing (Peking) he performed a pulmonary lobectomy on a young man, who, on being shown the excised tissue, clapped his hands, and after the operation was over, sat up, shook hands with everybody, lifted his tubes and bottles, and walked out.[25] (What was in the bottles?) Close reading of such "eyewitness" reports reveals important pieces of information. The patients were carefully selected, indoctrinated, underwent "ideological preparation," and moreover, they were given premedication, local anaesthetic for skin incision, and parenteral analgesia during the operation, *in addition to* acupuncture.

The credulous acceptance of the Chinese propaganda extolling the merits of acupuncture analgesia (used in "ninety percent" of operations; effective in "ninety-eight percent" of patients) and the parrotting of such claims by "eyewitnesses" reminds me of some reports by the Western visitors at the purge trials in the Soviet Union in the 1930s—in their eyes the admission of guilt by the victim was "genuine."

Bonica calculated that even during the zenith of acupuncture anaesthesia in

China, it was used in no more than 5 percent of operations,[26] or "more like 1% or 2%."[27] Nevertheless, following meetings between Nixon's personal physician (who was one of the eyewitnesses) and the director of the National Institutes of Health (NIH), a special committee was set up and funds provided to investigate this wonder.[28] The will to believe was stronger than the willingness to pause and think. "Highly respected scientists, though well-meaning, did not have the expertise to critically evaluate their observations."[29]

It has been known for a long time that, with or without hypnosis, some patients can be operated upon without anaesthesia and find the pain is tolerable. Intensity of pain is not directly related to the nature or extent of the wound, but strongly depends on the mental state of the patient and on what pain means to the patient.[30] Mesmerism had been used for surgical operations in England since 1837 and was intensely studied by Elliotson, who was also interested in acupuncture. In France, another acupuncturist, Jules Cloquet, carried out mastectomies on hypnotized patients. Esdaile made a reputation by operating on mesmerized patients in India.[31]

Formal hypnosis, however, is not necessary. Parker operated on many patients in China without any anaesthesia (or acupuncture) and was astonished by their apparent insensibility to pain. In 1843, he performed a mastectomy on a patient, who, when the operation was over, "raised herself from the table without assistance, jumped upon the floor and made her bow to the gentlemen present, in the Chinese style, and walked into another room as though nothing had occurred."[32] Similar observations were made by other Western surgeons in China, such as Lockhart, McPherson, and others. "The manner in which they bear the pain of an operation is perfectly astounding," wrote Gordon in 1863, "a large proportion of those upon whom operations were performed had no chloroform . . . some did not even clench their hands or teeth, but lay upon the table perfectly motionless, while their muscles were being cut by the knife and their bones divided by the saw."[33] In Europe, doctors had similar experiences. Lennander published a series of articles describing major operations being carried out painlessly with local anaesthesia only. Mitchell (1907) performed limb amputations, thyroidectomies, mastectomies, and other major surgery without general anaesthesia.[34]

When I read Dimond's paper I was reminded of a French soldier who cried "Vive la Nation!" when his leg, in which a huge Prussian ball had lodged, was amputated without anaesthetic in 1793.[35]

One of the operations believed to be particularly suitable for acupuncture anaesthesia is thyroidectomy.[36] In Berne before 1898, Theodor Kocher carried out 1600 thyroidectomies: "The danger in complicated cases has been diminished since general anaesthesia was abandoned. An injection of 1% solution of cocaine is made for the skin incision and intelligent patients, after this has been made painless, bear the remainder of the operation without difficulty."[37] Professor H. E. Ackerknecht kindly brought to my notice a letter by Harvey Cushing written in 1900 in which Cushing expressed his utter astonishment on seeing César

Roux operating on goitres in Valois peasants with no anaesthesia.

The Chinese inventors of acupuncture anaesthesia used initially more than fifty needles, but the number gradually dropped to one or two. Would the same effect be achieved with no needles whatsoever? Those who dared to ask such awkward questions were branded as "counter-revolutionary revisionists."[38]

The widely quoted figure of "ninety percent" effectiveness of acupuncture anaesthesia must be seen in the context of the meaning of the word "success" in Chinese propaganda: Grade I ("excellent"—30 percent of patients), Grade II ("good"—30 percent of patients), and Grade III ("fair"—30 percent of patients) comprise "success." In Grade IV the operation has to be abandoned or a general anaesthesia used. To get a glimpse of what this scale actually means, I shall cite from a recent report, published in a reputable journal, on women who were sterilized under local anaesthesia *and* acupuncture anaesthesia: patients in Grade II were "moaning and groaning," and in Grade III "struggling and otherwise interfering with the operation."[39] Success? Yes, the authors concluded that the method was simple, safe, and economical!

When Bonica asked two Chinese doctors (a surgeon and an anaesthetist) whether they themselves, if undergoing a hernia repair, would choose acupuncture anaesthesia, the virtues of which they were extolling, both expressed a preference for chemical anaesthesia.[40] The lie of acupuncture anaesthesia was exposed in the Chinese press more recently.[41]

The doyen of the British acupuncturists, Felix Mann, found that acupuncture would be "just adequate" for surgery in only ten out of one hundred patients. He used electroacupuncture and the pain of stimulation itself was "so severe that, even though lying horizontally, the patients sometimes feel that they are almost fainting. Interestingly, despite this severe pain, they can carry on an animated conversation and even smile."[42] (I suspect that they could suck an orange as well.) Mann thought that "even if it is unintentional, something allied to hypnosis may be taking place." Other Western experimenters fared no better. Wallis et al. reported that none of their twenty-one obstetric patients obtained adequate analgesia by means of acupuncture.[43] Even in China the anaesthesia could not be adequate since a special fast-cutting technique ("the method of flying knives") had to be developed to minimize the pain of skin incisions.

The acupuncture apologists believe that reports on acupuncture anaesthesia in animals are clear proof that there is something more to it than hypnosis, since animals cannot be influenced by words or political propaganda. They ignore the extensive literature on animal "hypnosis" or "still reaction." Animals undergoing operations under acupuncture anaesthesia have to be tied down firmly[44]—the fear and restraint induce anaesthesia.[45] Acupuncture alone does not produce significant changes in pain tolerance in animals, but pain tolerance is increased in frightened, restrained animals, or in animals in the immobility-reflex-like state.[46]

CRITICAL STUDIES OF ACUPUNCTURE IN MAN

Acupuncture does not induce physiological analgesia since sensory discrimination remains unimpaired. However, the psychological attitude of subjects undergoing acupuncture makes them more reluctant to report pain.[47] Dey et al., in a well-controlled study, failed to demonstrate any effect of acupuncture on pain perception or on galvanic skin responses.[48] Li et al. found acupuncture inferior to hypnosis; acupuncture did not increase pain tolerance.[49] Levine et al. found that in chronic pain, acupuncture was more likely to be effective in patients with high scores for anxiety and depression.[50]

The dissociation of pain perception and pain reporting was documented by Modell et al. in a patient who had undergone augmentation mammoplasty (breast enlargement through plastic surgery) under acupuncture anaesthesia: she found that the skin incision "really hurt" and that cauterization felt as if she were "being touched with a soldering iron." Yet, she did not complain during the operation and two anaesthetists who watched her did not detect any evidence of pain.[51]

What was believed to be the "stoicism" of Chinese patients in the face of pain was their conditioning and not a racial reaction. Knox et al. found no difference in response to pain (with or without acupuncture) between Oriental subjects and North American subjects.[52]

The complexity of pain perception and the difficulty of separating the psychological from the physiological components are the main reasons for the persistence of irrational beliefs in acupuncture. In disorders in which changes in pathophysiology can be objectively determined, "acupuncture and its theories have long been recognized for the crass unmitigated nonsense they are."[53] Critical observers, however, also find acupuncture useless in painful conditions. Sweet summarized his experience of the value of acupuncture in trigeminal neuralgia (painful spasms of the fifth cranial nerve): in only 9 out of 97 patients treated with acupuncture was there any temporary amelioration of pain, while 6 other patients were sure they got worse.[54] In another study of 100 patients with chronic pain, long-lasting relief was reported by 3 patients, though none of them had reduced their intake of analgesics![55]

The leading British acupuncturist, George T. Lewith, suggested in an editorial in the *British Medical Journal* that objective scientific studies of acupuncture would require a relatively small number of patients since the "predicted" response rates for acupuncture and placebo differ widely—60 percent and 30 percent, respectively.[56] This belief is shared by the pain expert Melzack.[57] This is a fundamental misunderstanding of placebo. Placebo response can range from 0 percent to 100 percent, depending on circumstances.[58] Even in the studies cited by Lewith, the placebo response varied from 0 percent to 70 percent. The average response of 30 percent applies to ordinary placebos. It is well known that the placebo response to new "therapies" is initially of the order 70 to 90 percent in the enthusiasts' reports and gradually decreases to a 30 to 40 percent baseline in reports of the skeptics.[59] This is why Trousseau advised the medical tyros that they should treat as many patients as possible with the new drug while it still has the power to heal. The Chinese figures of 99 percent success of acupuncture in various disorders[60] are fictional and on a par with election results in totalitarian countries.

In his editorial, Lewith misinformed his readers when he suggested that "the results [of controlled trials] give an overall impression that acupuncture has an analgesic effect in about 60% of patients." This is wishful thinking. The studies in question can be divided into two groups: (1) major studies published in journals of high repute, showing no difference whatsoever between acupuncture and placebo; and (2) observations in lesser-known journals or in acupuncture periodicals, claiming up to 100 percent effectiveness for acupuncture. Surely it is unjustifiable and meaningless to pool the results of these two groups in order to obtain the 60 percent mean.

It has been shown in many studies that acupuncture points are nonspecific and that the same results can be obtained by inserting needles in other sites, not listed in acupuncture atlases.[61] In chronic pain, controlled studies showed that acupuncture was no better than conventional therapy or placebo.[62]

HOMUNCULAR ACUPUNCTURE

What has been said about acupuncture in general holds true also for the many acupuncture variants, such as moxibustion (burning cones of powderized dried leaves over acupoints), acupressure (pressure over acupoints), homeoacupuncture (injection of homeopathic solutions into acupoints), and others. The most popular variant of acupuncture is auricular acupuncture, based on a bizarre notion that the human external ear corresponds point by point to the inner organs and functions of the human body. This is represented by drawings of an inverted homunculus (the body in dwarf form) snugly fitting within the outline of the pinna (outer ear). (Similar representations of the body within the nose, face, hand, or foot have also been described and used for "treatment.") I mention auricular acupuncture only because this mediaeval lunacy occasionally creeps into reputable medical journals[63] and books.[64] The main difficulty with ear acupuncture is that the French homunculus and the Chinese homunculus are markedly different[65] so that the organ allegedly stimulated from the ear will change with the change of the homuncular map used.

The American Journal of Medicine recently published a paper[66] purporting to show that auricular acupuncture is effective against smoking addiction. The reason for publishing this paper by a reputable journal remains obscure. The study was uncontrolled and the patients were subjected to antismoking indoctrination in addition to acupuncture. The authors discovered the "antismoking" ear point by chance when two overweight nurses were treated for obesity by a needle in the ear and suddenly stopped smoking. If the "antiobesity" point was identical with the "antismoking" point, one would expect that over-weight smokers thus treated would lose weight. No data on weight loss were given in the 514 patients studied. (The effectiveness in the treatment of obesity was such that one patient was said to have lost six pounds over a weekend!) The authors claimed a success rate of 88 percent. Of 514 patients presented for treatment only 339 were "evaluable." Of these 339 self-selected patients, 297 stopped smoking after four weeks (this is the 88 percent) but we were not told how many of them relapsed, because only 220 patients were "available" at a follow-up; of these, 31 percent had resumed smoking. Thus, the total of patients who resumed smoking, assuming that those lost or excluded also resumed smoking, would be 362, i.e., 70 percent treatment failure. Controlled studies showing that acupuncture for smokers is no better than indoctrination were not cited.[67] Editors of medical journals should be particularly vigilant when dealing with such partisan reports.

THE ENDORPHIN HYPOTHESIS

Following conflicting reports that the opiate antagonist naloxone abolished acupuncture analgesia,[68] it has become a new dogma of acupuncturists that acupuncture analgesia is mediated by endogenous opiates (endorphins). The endorphin hypothesis has brought acupuncturists and biological psychiatrists together. The latter believe that an imbalance of endorphins is a cause of mental disease and could be corrected by bloodletting.[69] The endorphin theory of mental disease is modelled on the Yin-Yang doctrine, and acupuncture has been used for treatment of mental disease both in China and the United States.[70] Recently *The Lancet* published an acupuncture article in which it was claimed that acupuncture improved chronic pain *and* psychiatric symptoms. The study was uncontrolled and the difference in the mean pain score was only 26 percent, based on self-reporting by patients "experiencing serious psychiatric difficulties."[71]

The endorphin "explanation" of acupuncture has put the cart firmly before the horse. Two simple questions would have to be asked and then answered before appealing to endorphins. First, do endorphins correlate with clinical pain? Second, does acupuncture release endorphins?

There is no good evidence that acupuncture-induced pain relief is mediated by endorphin release.[72] There is no correlation between plasma endorphin levels and pain; even patients with ß-endorphin levels 300-600 times the normal had no impairment of sensitivity to pain.[73] Intravenous injections of ß-endorphin have no analgesic effect in man.[74] Studies usually quoted by acupuncture apologists in support of acupuncture-induced release of endorphins are either inapplicable to acupuncture in humans (e.g., electrostimulation of brain areas in animals) or conflicting.[75]

The endorphin hypothesis has also been repeatedly invoked in the use of acupuncture as a treatment for opiate addiction. This "treatment" was based on uncontrolled or seriously suspect studies. Gossop et al. found that acupuncture failed to suppress withdrawal symptoms and was markedly inferior to methadone treatment. Several addicts found no difference between the use of acupuncture and withdrawing "cold turkey" (a sudden opiate withdrawal).[76]

It appeared for a time that the endorphin hypothesis could salvage acupuncture, even if acupuncture were a form of placebo, since placebo itself might be mediated by endorphins. This hope was shattered by experiments conducted by Gracely et al., who demonstrated that naloxone does not antagonize the placebo.[77]

While many acupuncturists are gradually coming to terms with the weakness of the endorphin hypothesis, the possible speculations on the humoral (fluid) basis of acupuncture, originating mainly from Communist China, are endless, though of no clinical significance.[78]

WHY DOES ACUPUNCTURE WORK?

There is no denying that acupuncture is effective in some patients with functional and psychosomatic disorders. So is placebo. It is also a fact that the acupuncture effect is unpredictable and unreliable. Results depend on the faith. "Negative findings . . . may reflect negative attitudes on the part of the experimental subject."[79]

The simple explanation for a better average response to acupuncture than to more conventional placebos is its very unconventionality, the mystique surrounding an ancient Oriental ritual, and the magic of model mannikins and golden needles. Once these trappings are removed and the veil of the mystery lifted, acupuncture will again be relegated to its original place among counter-irritants,[80] such as cupping, sinapisms (mustard plasters), bee stings, vesicants, cautery (moxa), and setons (known in the modern acupuncture terminology as "thread acupuncture"), or more recently, vibration, electrostimulation, and temperature changes.[81] By discussing acupuncture in terms of placebo, distraction, suggestion, and hypnosis, and taking into account the natural history of self-limiting and functional disorders that acupuncture is supposed to cure, it will lose its attraction, its novelty, and its power over the mind of the gullible.

The gullible include scientists. A plea for investigation of acupuncture was made by a medical historian: "No matter how bizarre a therapy is, how lacking in rationale, and how uncertain its value, it is concerned with patients and hence it is a phenomenon which must interest the world of medicine."[82] While skeptical inquiry is safer than an outright dogmatic rejection, it is disheartening to see serious scientists conducting incompetent investigations. To use an analogy from parapsychology: scientists did not find the explanation of the Uri Geller phenomenon by studying bent spoons under the microscope; they found the answer by studying Uri Geller himself. The question was not how the spoon bent, but how Geller made the scientists believe that it bent on its own.

Similarly, when studying the phenomenon of acupuncture, the minute bio-chemical analysis and the search for endorphins in acupunctured subjects is misdirected, since the problem is not biochemical but psychological and cultural. Just as a student of the Geller "mental" bending would be well advised to consult a professional magician, so a student of acupuncture will profit from the expert advice of a stage hypnotist.

Kroger, who is experienced in hypnoanalgesia, pointed out the similarities between acupuncture and hypnosis: conditioning, ritual, indoctrination, auto-genic training, misdirection, autosuggestion.[83] In China, the strong traditional belief in the power of needles was further augmented by sociopolitical rewards for good behavior during acupuncture. Kroger knew from his experience that scientists unfamiliar with the phenomena of suggestion and autohypnosis would not believe that the patient is hypnotized without a formal induction and without falling asleep.

For obvious reasons, the possibility of hypnosis or suggestion is strongly resisted by acupuncture apologists. They even twist the evidence. For example, Lewith commented on a study of Moore and Berk[84] as follows: "They demon-strated that suggestibility did not affect the outcome in their study." Yet Moore and Berk wrote: "The average improvement in discomfort scores, as well as the percentage of those who achieved 60% or more relief increased with hypnotic susceptibility [from 29% to 55%]." "In demonstrating . . . a possible link between response to treatment and susceptibility to hypnosis, we are challenging those who believe that acupuncture offers a unique approach to pain control."

Chaves and Barber suggested six tentative headings under which acupunc-ture anaesthesia could be investigated: (1) strong belief, (2) concomitant use of other analgesia, (3) overestimation of surgical pain, (4) distraction produced by needles, (5) special preparation and indoctrination, (6) suggestion.[85] Excluding points 2 and 3, the headings are equally applicable for other acupuncture treatments.

THE FUTURE OF ACUPUNCTURE

In the last few years the gap between acupuncture practitioners and rational medicine has widened and will continue to do so. In the keynote address at the founding convention of the American Association of Acupuncturists and Orien-tal Medicine in Los Angeles in 1981, R. A. Dale announced the coming of the great age of holistic harmony in which acupuncture will pay a pivotal role. Since his remarks represent the mainstream of acupuncture ideology, they are worth our attention: "Acupuncture is a part of a larger struggle going on today between the old and the new, between dying and rebirthing, between the very decay and death of our species and our fullest liberation. Acupuncture is part of a New Age which facilitates integral health and the flowering of our humanity."[86]

Dale differentiated five attitudes of the medical profession to acupuncture:

(1) "the reactionary extreme," which should be ignored, isolated, and exposed; (2) "the conservative opposition," which should be supplied with data and statistics ("although the American Medical Association will not be convinced by such arguments, some of its members will be"); (3) "the liberal support," whose members are "usually cautious not to discuss their views with their colleagues from Groups 1 and 2," but they are "excellent candidates" for Group 4, "the progressive support"; (5) "support by medical heretics," who are "excellent candidates not only for active membership in our association but for leadership roles."

The tactic and strategy to be adopted by the acupuncturists when dealing with the public are, according to Dale's advice, as follows: (1) undermine their faith in modern medicine and science, (2) educate them in their need for alternative medicine, and (3) explain to them that what they need is not a medical specialist but an acupuncture generalist.

The openness of this document is disarming. Let us note, however, that Dale's "New Age" is matched only by the WHO's messianic rhetoric of "health for all by the year of 2000." Unreal promises and false hopes raised by the medical profession, no less irrational than the illusions of "alternative" medicine, deserve to be criticized as mercilessly as the deceptive fancies and will-o'-the-wisps of the holistic prophets and quackupuncturists.

NOTES

1. E. Hart, *Hypnotism, Mesmerism and the New Witchcraft*, 2nd ed. (London: Smith & Elder, 1896), 168.

2. P. Skrabanek, "Acupuncture and the Age of Unreason," *Lancet* 1 (1984): 1169–71.

3. R. H. Bannerman, "Acupuncture: The WHO View," *World Health* (December 1979): 24–29.

4. G-D Lu and J. Needham, *Celestial Lancets: A History and Rationale of Acupuncture and Moxa* (London: Cambridge University Press, 1980).

5. D. C. Epler, "Bloodletting in Early Chinese Medicine and Its Relation to the Origin of Acupuncture," *Bulletin of the History of Medicine* 54 (1980): 337–67.

6. S. J. Liao, "Recent Advances in the Understanding of Acupuncture," *Yale Journal of Biology and Medicine* 51 (1978): 55–65.

7. E. H. Ackerknecht, "Zur Geschichte der Akupunktur," *Anaestetist* 23 (1974): 37–38; E. H. Ackerknecht, "Akupunktur—Gestern, Heute, Morgen," *Schweizerische Aerztezeitung* 33 (1972): 1067–68.

8. Lu and Needham, op. cit., 292

9. J. Lacassagne, "Le docteur Louis Berlioz—Introducteur de l'Acupuncture en France," *Presse Médicale* 62 (1954): 1359–60.

10. Anon., *Edinburgh Medical and Surgical Journal* 27 (1827): 190–200; 334–49.

11. Anon., "Acupuncturation," *Medico-Chirurgical Review (London)* 11 (1829): 166–67.

12. T. P. Teale, "On the Relief of Pain and Muscular Disability by Acupuncture," *Lancet* 1, (1871): 567–68.

13. J. Elliotson, "Acupuncture," in J. Forbes, A. Tweedie, and J. Connolly, (eds.), *The Cyclopaedia of Practical Medicine*, vol. 1. (London: Sherwood, 1833), 32–34; Anon., "When

Acupuncture Came to Britain," (editorial) *British Medical Journal* 4 (1973): 687–88; G. Lorimer, "Acupuncture and Its Application in the Treatment of Certain Forms of Chronic Rheumatism," *British Medical Journal* 2 (1885): 956–58; Anon., "Employment of Acupuncture as a Counter-irritant," *Practitioner* 1 (1868): 371–72; see also Skrabanek, note 2.

14. K. Lewit, "The Needle Effect in the Relief of Myofascial Pain," *Pain* 6 (1979): 83–90; F. A. Frost, B. Jessen, and J. Siggaard-Andersen, "A Control, Double-blind Comparison of Mepivacaine Injection versus Saline Injection for Myofascial Pain," *Lancet* 1 (1980): 499–501.

15. Lu and Needham, op. cit., 160.

16. P. Huard and M. Wong, *Chinese Medicine* (London: Weidenfeld & Nicolson, 1968).

17. Ibid., 135.

18. Ibid., 159.

19. Ibid., 150.

20. Anon., "Statement Regarding Acupuncture by the Medical Council of the Academy of Sciences of the German Democratic Republic," *Zeitschrift fuer Experimentelle Chirurgie* 14 (1981): 67. For a critical review of German literature, see W. Mattig and A. Gertler, "Akupunktur: Scharlatanerie oder therapeutische Bereicherung?" *Innere Medizin* 10 (1983): 208–12; 247–52.

21. I. Veith, "Acupuncture Therapy—Past and Present: Verity or Delusion?" *Journal of the American Medical Association* 180 (1962): 478–84.

22. E. G. Dimond, "Acupuncture Anaesthesia: Western Medicine and Chinese Traditional Medicine," *Journal of the American Medical Association* 218 (1971): 1558–63.

23. Anon., *Acupuncture Anaesthesia* (Peking: Foreign Languages Press, 1972), 9.

24. W. S. Kroger, "Acupunctural Analgesia: Its Explanation by Conditioning Theory, Autogenic Training, and Hypnosis," *American Journal of Psychiatry* 130 (1973): 855–60.

25. H. M. Windsor, "Cardiac Surgery in China," *Medical Journal of Australia* 1 (1984): 599–602.

26. J. J. Bonica, "Acupuncture Anesthesia in the People's Republic of China: Implications for American Medicine," *Journal of the American Medical Association* 229 (1974): 1317–25.

27. T. M. Murphy and J. J. Bonica "Acupuncture Analgesia and Anesthesia," *Archives of Surgery* 112 (1977): 896–902.

28. B. J. Culliton, "Acupuncture: Fertile Ground for Faddist and Serious NIH Research," *Science* 177 (1972): 592–94.

29. Murphy and Bonica, note 27 above.

30. H. K. Beecher, "Relationship of Significance of Wound to Pain Experienced," *Journal of the American Medicial Association* 161 (1956): 1609–13.

31. G. Rosen, "Mesmerism and Surgery: A Strange Chapter in the History of Anaesthesia," *Journal of the History of Medicine* 1 (1946): 527–50.

32. D. A. Johnson, "History and the Understanding of Acupuncture Anaesthesia," *Southern Medical Journal* 76 (1983): 497–98.

33. Ibid.

34. J. F. Chaves and T. X. Barber, "Acupuncture Analgesia: A Six-factor Theory," in S. Krippner (ed.), *Psychoenergetic Systems* (New York: Gordon & Breach Science Publishers, 1979), 169–78.

35. Anon., "An Incident of Pre-anaesthetic Surgery," *Medical Press* 2 (1890): 239.

36. S. B. Cheng and L. K. Ding, "Practical Application of Acupuncture Analgesia," *Nature* 242 (1973): 559–60.

37. Anon., "600 More Goitre Operations," *Medical Press* 2 (1908): 624.

38. See note 23.

39. P. L. R. Dias and S. Subramanium, "Minilaparotomy Under Acupuncture Analgesia," *Journal of the Royal Society of Medicine* 77 (1984): 295–98.

40. See note 26.

41. X. Gan and N. Tao, in the Shangai daily *Wen-Hui-Bao* (October 22, 1980).

42. F. Mann, "Acupuncture Analgesia: Report of 100 Experiments," *British Journal of Anaesthesiology* 46 (1974): 361–64.

43. L. Wallis, S. M. Shnider, R. J. Palahniuk, and H. T. Spivey, "An Evaluation of Acupuncture Analgesia in Obstetrics," *Anesthesiology* 41 (1974): 596–601.

44. A. Macdonald, *Acupuncture: From Ancient Art to Modern Medicine* (London: Allen & Unwin, 1982), 126.

45. Kroger, note 24.

46. C. Galeano and C. Y Leung, "Has Acupuncture an Analgesic Effect in Rabbits?" *Pain* 4 (1978): 265–71; C. Galeano, C. Y. Leung, R. Robitaille, and T. Roy-Chabot, "Acupuncture Analgesia in Rabbits, " *Pain* 6 (1979): 71–81.

47. W. C. Clark and J. C. Yang, "Acupunctural Analygesia: Evaluation by Signal Detection Theory," *Science* 184 (1975): 1096–98; W. C. Clark, J. C. Yang, and W. Hall, "Acupuncture, Pain, and Signal Detection Theory," *Science* 189 (1975): 66–68.

48. R. L. Day, L. M. Kitahata, F. F. Kao, E. K. Motoyama, and J. D. Hardy, "Evaluation of Acupuncture Anesthesia: A Psychophysical Study," *Anesthesiology* 43 (1975): 507–17; R. L. Day, "Acupuncture," *Lancet* 2 (1984); 175.

49. C. L. Li, D. Ailberg, H. Lansdell, M. A. Gravitz, T. C. Chen, C. Y. Ting, A. F. Bak, and D. Blessing, "Acupuncture and Hypnosis: Effects on Induced Pain," *Experimental Neurology* 49 (1975); 272-80.

50. J. D. Levine, J. Gormley, and H. L. Fields, "Observations on the Analgesic Effects of Needle Puncture (Acupuncture)," *Pain* 2 (1976): 149–59.

51. J. H. Modell, P. K. Y. Lee, H. G. Bingham, D. M. Greer, and M. B. Habal, "Acupuncture Anaesthesia: A Clinical Study," *Anaesthesia and Analgesia* 55 (1976): 508–12.

52. V. J. Knox, K. Shum, and D. M. McLaughlin, "Response to Cold Pressor Pain and to Acupuncture Analgesia in Oriental and Occidental Subjects," *Pain* 4 (1977): 49–57.

53. W. H. Sweet, "Some Current Problems in Pain Research and Therapy (Including Needle Puncture, 'Acupuncture')," *Pain* 10 (1981): 297–309.

54. Ibid.

55. Murphy and Bonica, note 27.

56. G. L. Lewith, "Can We Assess the Effects of Acupuncture?" *British Medical Journal* 288 (1984): 1475–76.

57. R. Melzack, "Acupuncture and Musculoskeletal Pain," *Journal of Rheumatology* 5 (1978): 119–20.

58. Anon., "Shall I Please?" (editorial) *Lancet* 2 (1983): 1465–66.

59. H. Benson and D. P. McCallie, "Angina Pectoris and the Placebo Effect," *New England Journal of Medicine* 300 (1979): 1424–28.

60. *National Symposia of Acupuncture and Moxibustion and Acupuncture Anaesthesia* (Beijing: Foreign Languages Press, 1979); *passim; Essentials of Chinese Acupuncture* (Beijing: Foreign Languages Press, 1980); *passim.*

61. A. C. Gaw, L. W. Chang, and L-C. Shaw, "Efficacy of Acupuncture on Osteoarthritic Pain: A Controlled, Double-blind Study," *New England Journal of Medicine* 293 (1975): 375–78; P. K. Lee, T. W. Andersen, J. H. Modell, and S. A. Saga, "Treatment of Chronic Pain with Acupuncture," *Journal of the American Medical Association* 232 (1975): 1133–35; B. Lynn and E. R. Perl, "Acupuncture Analgesia of the Skin in Relation to the Traditional Meridian Map," *Journal of Physiology (London)* 245 (1975): 83P–85P; M. Weintraub, S. Petursson, M. Schwartz, T. Barnard, J. P. Morgan, J. Gluckman, and R. H. Geertsma, "Acupuncture in Musculoskeletal Pain: Methodology and Results in a Double-blind Controlled Clinical Trial," *Clincial Pharmacology and Therapeutics* 17 (1975): 248; M. Y. Moore and S. N. Berk, "Acupuncture for Chronic Shoulder Pain: An Experimental Study with Attention to the Role of Placebo and Hypnotic Susceptibility," *Annals of Internal Medicine* 84 (1976): 381–84; G. Edelist, A. E. Gross, and F. Langer, "Treatment of Low Back Pain with Acupuncture," *Canadian Anaesthetists' Society Journal* 23 (1976): 303–306; C. M. Godfrey, and P. Morgan, "A Controlled Trial of the Theory of Acupuncture in Musculoskeletal Pain," *Journal of Rheumatology* 5 (1978): 121–24; L. L. Co, T. H. Schmitz, H. Havdala, A. Reyes, and M. P. Westerman, "Acupuncture: An Evaluation in the Painful Crises of Sickle-cell Anemia," *Pain* 7 (1979); 181–85; P. E. Hansen, J. H. Hansen, and

O. Bentzen, "Acupuncture Treatment of Chronic Unilateral Tinnitus: A Double-blind Cross-over Trial," *Clinical Otolaryngology* 7 (1982): 325–329; O. K. W. Chow, S. Y. So, W. K. Lam, D. Y. C. Yu, and C. Y. Yeung, "Effect of Acupuncture on Exercise-induced Asthma," *Lung* 161 (1983): 321–26.

62. L. Fernandes, H. Berry, R. J. Clark, B. Bloom, and E. B. D. Hamilton, "Clinical Study Comparing Acupuncture, Physiotherapy, Injection, and Oral Anti-inflammatory Therapy in Shoulder-cuff Lesions," *Lancet* 1 (1980); 208–209; G. T. Lewith, J. Field, and D. Machin, "Acupuncture Compared with Placebo in Post-herpetic Pain," *Pain* 17 (1983): 361–68.

63. R. Melzack and J. Katz, "Auriculotherapy Fails to Relieve Chronic Pain: A Controlled Crossover Study," *Journal of the American Medical Association* 251 (1984): 1041–43; G. T. Lewith, J. Field, and D. Machin, "Acupuncture Compared with Placebo in Post-herpetic Pain," *Pain* 17 (1983): 361–68; C. V. Dang, "The Ear Lobe Crease, Chromosomes, Acupuncture, and Atherosclerosis," *Lancet* 1 (1984): 1083; D. S. J. Choy, L. Lutzker, and L. Meltzer, "Effective Treatment for Smoking Cessation," *American Journal of Medicine* 75 (1983): 1033–36; T. D. Oleson, R. J. Kroening, and D. E. Bresler, "An Experimental Evaluation of Auricular Diagnosis: The Somatotopic Mapping of Musculoskeletal Pain at Ear Acupuncture Points," *Pain* 8 (1980): 217–29.

64. Lu and Needham, op. cit., 164f.

65. T. D. Oleson and R. J. Kroening, "A Comparison of Chinese and Nogier Auricular Acupuncture Points," *American Journal of Acupuncture* 11 (1983); 205–23.

66. D. S. J. Choy, L. Lutzker, and L. Meltzer, "Effective Treatment for Smoking Cessation," *American Journal of Medicine* 75 (1983): 1033–36.

67. Y. Lamontagne, L. Annable, and M-A. Gagnon, "Acupuncture for Smokers: Lack of Long-term Therapeutic Effect in a Controlled Study," *Canadian Medical Association Journal* 122 (1980): 787–90.

68. Anon., "Endorphins Through the Eye of a Needle?" (editorial) *Lancet* 1 (1981): 480–82.

69. P. Skrabanek, "Naloxone in Schizophrenia," *Lancet* 2 (1982): 1270; P. Skrabanek, "Haemodialysis in Schizophrenia–déjà vu or idée fixe?" *Lancet* 1 (1982): 1404–1405.

70. J. Kane and W. J. Di Scipio, "Acupuncture Treatment of Schizophrenia," *American Journal of Psychiatry* 136 (1979): 297–302.

71. R. S. Kiser, M. Khatami, R. J. Gatchel, X-Y. Huang, K. Bhatia, and K. Z. Altshuler, "Acupuncture Relief of Chronic Pain Syndrome Correlates with Increased Plasma Met-enkephal in Concentrations," *Lancet* 2 (1983): 1394–96; P. Skrabanek, "Acupuncture and Endorphins," *Lancet* 1 (1984): 220.

72. Anon., "Endorphins Through the Eye of a Needle?" (editorial) *Lancet* 1 (1981): 480–82.

73. J. C. Willer, L. Sheng-Shu, X. Bertagna, and F. Girard, "Pituitary ß-endorphin Not Involved in Pain Control in Some Pathophysiological Conditions," *Lancet* 2 (1984): 295–96.

74. U. Hosobuchi and C. H. Li, "Demonstration of the Analgesic Activity of Human ß-endorphin in Six Patients," in E. Usdin, M. E. Bunney, and N.S. Kline, (eds.), *Endorphins in Mental Disease and Research* (New York: Macmillan, 1979), 529–34.

75. See note 72.

76. M. Gossop, B. Bradley, J. Strang, and P. Connell, "The Clinical Effectiveness of Electro-stimulation vs. Oral Methadone in Managing Opiate Withdrawal," *British Journal of Psychiatry* 144 (1984): 203–208.

77. R. H. Gracely, R. Dubner, P. J. Wolskee, and W. R. Deeter, "Placebo and Naloxone Can Alter Postsurgical Pain by Separate Mechanisms," *Nature* 306 (1983): 264–265; Anon., "Shall I Please?" (editorial) *Lancet* 2 (1983): 1465–66.

78. J. S. Han and L. Terenius, "Neurochemical Basis of Acupuncture Analgesia," *Annual Review of Pharmacology and Toxicology* 22 (1982): 193–220.

79. C. R. Chapman, "Psychophysical Evaluation of Acupuncture Analgesia," *Anesthesiology* 43 (1975): 501–506.

80. C. J. B. Williams, "Counter-irritation," in J. Forbes, A. Tweedie, and J. Connolly (eds.), *The Cyclopaedia of Practical Medicine,* vol. 1 (London: Sherwood, 1833), 483–92.

81. G. D. Gammon, and I. Starr, "Studies on the Relief of Pain by Counterirritation," *Journal of Clinical Investigation* 20 (1941): 13–20.

82. See note 21.

83. W. S. Kroger, "Acupunctural Analgesia: Its Explanation by Conditioning Theory, Autogenic Training, and Hypnosis," *American Journal of Psychiatry* 130 (1973): 855–60.

84. G. T. Lewith, "How Effective Is Acupuncture in the Management of Pain?" *Journal of the Royal College of General Practitioners* 34 (1984): 275–78; Moore and Berk, see note 61.

85. J. F. Chaves and T. X. Barber, "Acupuncture Analgesia: A Six-factor Theory," in S. Krippner (ed.), *Psychoenergetic Systems* (New York: Gordon & Breach, 1979), 169–78.

86. R. A. Dale, "The Origins and Future of Acupuncture," *American Journal of Acupuncture* 10 (1982): 101–20.

Edmund S. Crelin, Ph.D.

Chiropractic

For a number of years I have tried with little success or thanks to educate the public about the unscientific cult known incorrectly by an adjective, chiropractic. Proper grammar dictates that it be a noun, chiropraxis, but this is typical of such an unscholarly cult. I first became aware of chiropractic when I was given a "free" spinal adjustment for a generalized bacterial and/or viral infection when I was a teenager. Needless to say I continued to have a high fever, felt lousy, and, in addition, I had a sore back for about a week after the treatment. At that time I never imagined that I would one day be one of only forty international authorities chosen to be a member of a symposium on low back pain, sponsored by the National Institutes of Health and the American Academy of Orthopaedic Surgeons. My expertise centered on the functional anatomy of the lumbosacral spine (1).

My motivation to protect unwary human beings from chiropractic grew very strong when I learned in 1961 that Bradley Straatsma, M.D., an ophthalmologist who had been my fellow student at the Yale University School of Medicine, was prevented from saving the life of an eight-year-old girl by a chiropractor (2). Bradley was to surgically remove the girl's left eye and surrounding soft tissue along with a localized cancer. He was prevented from doing this because the chiropractor insisted that he could cure the child's cancer. He said that the doctors would treat her as a "guinea pig," cut her up, and kill her. The mother took the child out of the hospital and the chiropractor began a daily manipulation of the little girl's spine (a chiropractic adjustment) while providing a large supply of vitamins, minerals, food supplements, and laxatives for her to take. She was taking 124 pills a day, including such items as dessicated ox bile and extract of beef eyes. Although she got her daily adjustment and took her pills the tumor grew swiftly. Twenty-three days later it was the size of a tennis ball and pushed the eye out of the socket and down along the nose. Three months later Los Angeles County Deputy District Attorney John Miner was led to the child's bedside shortly before she died. He said, "Seasoned as I am by observation of many score of autopsies of burned, raped, drowned, strangled, stabbed, shot, accident-mangled, even tumor-ridden bodies, it was all I could do to keep from abruptly leaving the room. The right half of the little girl's face was that of an angel. The left half was covered by a growth so monstrous as to seem beyond nature's capacity to be so cruel and grotesque." The trial judge prohibited the showing of the death pictures to the jury because the photographs were so terrible that they might deprive the jury of the ability to weigh the issues rationally. Although the chiropractor was sentenced to from five years to life in prison for second degree murder, he "got off" on appeal.

My motivation to protect the unwary public from chiropractors was given an outlet when I was asked to volunteer my services to the Bureau of Medical Devices of the Federal Drug Administration. I was aware that chiropractors liked gadgets but never appreciated how much until I became actively involved with the devices they used in their practice (2). Some are very sophisticated and quite expensive, such as the ThermoScribe II made by Murdoch Engineering, Inc., San Leandro, California, for the Doctors Financial Fund, Inc., Independence, Missouri (Figure 1). There is a hand-held, pick-up unit attached to the

FIGURE 1. Top view of the ThermoScribe II device used by chiropractors. A — pick-up unit. B — tracing paper that has passed out of the device.

instrument by a long wire. The chiropractor slowly moves the pick-up unit along the spine of the patient. When it passes over a spinal nerve that is being compressed by the bony spine, it picks up the heat generated by the nerve. This causes an ink pen to deviate from the straight line it is making on a slow-moving roll of tracing paper that passes out of the instrument (Figure 1). When the full extent of the spine has been covered by the pick-up unit the tracing paper is cut free and held up against the patient's spine. The point (or points) where the pen was deflected denotes the level at which the spinal nerve (or nerves) is compressed to cause whatever disease the patient is supposed to have. However, I had the instrument tested by Dr. Subrata Saha, assistant professor in the Yale School of Engineering and Applied Science, and his student, Antony Tin. They found that the pick-up unit could not differentiate between heat or pressure. I had my colleague Rollin Johnson, M.D., Acting Chief of Orthopaedic Surgery at Yale, test the device on three patients who had severe spine and spinal nerve disorders. He found it to be worthless as a diagnostic tool simply because, if a deviation of the pen line occurred at a specific point on the tracing paper, it would not appear there when a second tracing was made, or a third, or a fourth, and so on. Since the pick-up unit could not tell the difference between temperature and pressure, I found I could very carefully move the unit along the full length of a person's spine and end up with a perfectly straight line on the tracing paper. I could repeat this procedure on a perfectly healthy, strong, and robust twenty-one-year-old male while making subtle shifts of my wrists, which were undetected by him but resulted in a pen line tracing that indicated severe compression of nearly all of his spinal nerves (Figure 2). I cringe when I think of how many innocent people have been deliberately deceived by chiropractors using this instrument.

The most recent device I have tested for the Bureau of Medical Devices is the Toftness Radiation Detector (Figure 3). It was "invented" by Irving Toftness, a chiropractor from Cumberland, Wisconsin. The device is a plastic tube with a handle that the chiropractor holds with his hand or a clamp and moves it over the spine of a patient. When the tube passes over a spinal nerve that is compressed by the spine, electromagnetic radiations of 69.5 gigahertz given off by the compressed nerve pass into the plastic tube. The radiations are focused by lenses, often used as ordinary magnifiers, onto a strip of material at the top of the tube, known as the detection plate. The chiropractor uses a finger of his other hand to rub across the detection plate. If 69.5 gigahertz radiations are focused on the plate the chiropractor "feels" it! Better yet, if the chiropractor rubs his finger hard enough across the detection plate a crackling sound like that of a Geiger counter is made. The device is just so much hocus-pocus. First of all, 69.5 gigahertz of radiation penetrates only about one millimeter of body tissue, while the spinal nerves are two to three inches from the body surface. Even if energy of 69.5 gigahertz could be focused at the detection plate, it could not be detected by the fingers. Who said that a compressed spinal nerve emits radiations of 69.5 gigahertz anyway? Only one completely unscientific chiropractor! I wrote my affidavit to ban the Toftness Radiation Detector in 1975, but I fear that people are still being exploited by chiropractors who use this device.

The most notorious chiropractic device I ever tested was the Specific

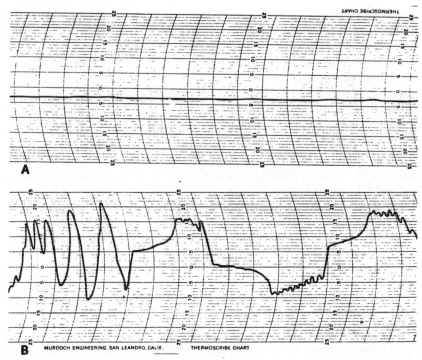

A

B   MURDOCH ENGINEERING. SAN LEANDRO, CALIF.   THERMOSCRIBE CHART

FIGURE 2. Two strips of tracing paper each containing a pen line recorded by the ThermoScribe II device shown in figure 1 when the pick-up unit was passed over the spine of a twenty-year-old healthy male. The top strip (A) was made using a uniform pressure of the pick-up unit against the skin of the back, resulting in a straight pen line. The bottom strip (B) was made by deliberately shifting the pressure to the pick-up unit from side to side, resulting in a very irregular pen line. The pressure shifts were not detected by the individual.

Chiropractic Technique

FIGURE 3. A Toftness Radiation Detector being used by a chiropractor. The fingers of his right hand are being rubbed across the detection plate.

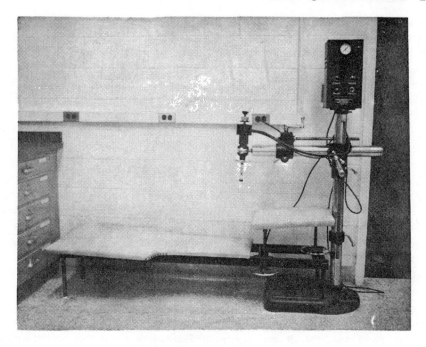

FIGURE 4. A Chiropractic Specific Adjusting Machine. [From Crelin (3)]

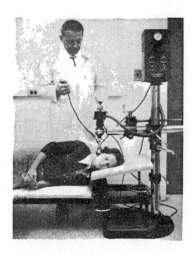

FIGURE 5. The plunger of the Specific Adjusting Machine shown in figure 4 is placed against the neck of the author's secretary, Mrs. Susan Hurst. She is holding her hands in prayer for fear that the author, holding the "firing button," may have forgotten to unplug the device. [From Crelin (3)]

Adjusting Machine (Figure 4) (3). It was "invented" by Arden Zimmerman, a chiropractor from San Jose, California, who disowned all he had been taught at the Palmer School of Chiropractic and came up with his own theory of the cause of all disease, which he believed to be the result of immobilization of the first two cervical vertebrae, the atlas and axis. All he had to do was mobilize these two vertebrae and he could cure your back pain, arthritis, ruptured disc, asthma, stomach ulcers, bursitis, eczema, inflammation, frontal and sinus head-aches, general debility, persistent cough, high blood pressure, rapid heart beat, tuberculosis, pain in the face as well as head, and skin conditions (3). Indeed he could, because the device he made to do this might possibly kill you. The device was essentially an air hammer. With force, a plunger was to make contact with the patient's neck to loosen the supposedly immobile first and second cervical vertebrae (Figure 5). The directions for the device specifically stated the amount of air pressure and depth of thrust of the plunger as follows: 105 pounds and three-fourths-inch for an adult male, 60 pounds and one-half-inch for an adult female, and 20 pounds and one-fourth inch for a child. My tests showed that the above figures would have broken the neck. The figures given for the adult male allowed me to drive nails through wood! Obviously, the chiropractors who used the device only allowed the plunger to barely touch the skin of the neck of their patients. I found the controls of the device to be quite unreliable. Fortunately, the Bureau of Medical Devices confiscated all of these devices before anyone was maimed or killed.

In my early zeal to "stand up and be counted" I appeared on television channel 8 in New Haven, Connecticut, to inform the public about chiropractic. All it did was allow equal air time to the chiropractors, who put on a big free advertising campaign. I figured the best way to convince the public was to attack the chiropractors directly with the facts. So, I accepted a challenge to debate the former president of the American Chiropractic Association, Stephen E. Owens, face to face for two hours on radio station WELI in New Haven. Naively, I walked into the studio with an armful of books and pamphlets loaded with the scientific facts. My opponent walked in with a little book on chiropractic, written and published by a chiropractor, which he never once opened during the broadcast. When I lashed out at him with documented facts derogatory to chiropractic he would deny them in a very calm, meek voice. I then knew how it must be to try and honestly debate the Russians at the United Nations; he said things that were untrue whenever it suited his purposes. I kept an audiotape of the broadcast with the hope that I could get him into a court of law, but he was too smart for that. He did succeed in making me appear to be a part of the monopolistic medical establishment while he appeared as the mistreated under-dog. Although he constantly referred to the American Medical Association as the union of rich medical doctors out to get the downtrodden chiropractors, he found it difficult to make me a part of the association since I am not a physican. Actually, I was really a relatively low-paid basic scientist with no axe to grind but the truth. The only reaction I got from Yale University was a visit from the assistant dean for legal affairs of the medical school who feared that the school might get sued for what I said on the air. The only reaction I got from the public for acting in their interest was a lot of hate mail from chiropractors' patients. At that time there existed a Committee Against Medical Quackery of the Connecticut State Medical Society that met occasionally. I went to one of the meetings and asked if they would take some action against the chiropractors of the state. The members nodded politely and said that they would do all they could and then resumed an active discussion of how to prevent the optometrists from making inroads into the practice of ophthalmology. Of course, to this day the committee has done nothing about chiropractic.

Although it was never official, I have always been considered a member of the Section of Orthopaedic Surgery at Yale; I am listed on its letterhead as a regular faculty member. I found my orthopaedic colleagues to be the only professional people who really understood what I said about chiropractic. I had taught most of the resident physicians as medical students before they went on into the orthopaedic specialty. Therefore, I had acquired over the years an extensive knowledge of the spine from both a basic science and a clinical aspect. Thus, I decided to take time out from a productive and successful research program to devote one last effort to expose chiropractic for what it always was, an unscientific cult.

I designed an experiment to expose the basic tenet of chiropractic to be completely false, that is, the vertebral subluxation—a condition that has been alleged to exist ever since chiropractic began. T. A. Vondarhaar, president of the Northern California College of Chiropractic, recently confirmed this by stating the following:

> Because of the various stresses to which the spine is subject, individual vertebrae can become misaligned. Such misalignments can create pressure on nerve tissue, and thus interfere with the conduction of nerve impulses to other parts of the body. Chiropractors call the condition a *subluxation*.
>
> Nerves travel to various tissues and organs from each vertebra of the spine. A subluxation reduces the nerve signals to the affected tissue or organ, resulting in dysfunction and eventually disease. The subluxation of the spine, because it reduces nerve supply, is considered by doctors of chiropractic to be a main *cause* of disease. The point in the body at which disease becomes apparent is the *symptom*.
>
> Physical trauma is one major cause of subluxations. . . . Mental stress is another cause of subluxation. Tightened muscles resulting from tension can pull the vertebrae out of alignment. Finally, chemical ingestion associated with faulty nutrition or consumption of drugs can cause misalignment of the vertebrae (4).

There are two kinds of chiropractors, the "straights" and the "mixers." The former adhere to a strict notion of chiropractic, i.e., that the vertebral subluxation is the fundamental cause of disease. The latter include with their treatment of spinal adjustments clinical nutrition (mostly vitamins) and physiotherapy (4).

No one, living or dead, has ever seen a chiropractic subluxation. This includes the chiropractors. When in 1964 the National Association of Letter Carriers Health Plan received claims from chiropractors for the treatment of cancer, heart disease, mumps, mental retardation, and many other questionable conditions, the chiropractors were asked to justify such claims by submitting X-rays of their patients showing the subluxations that caused the above disorders (5, 6). In the presence of reputable radiologists the chiropractic officials were unable to point out a single subluxation! Needless to say, the chiropractors were kicked out of the health plan.

The Lehigh Valley Committee Against Health Fraud, Inc., of Lehigh Valley, Pennsylvania, challenged the Lehigh Valley Chiropractic Society to demonstrate ten tests where an X-ray showed a subluxation of a patient that was "reduced" by their spinal adjustment (5). Naturally they refused. In response, chiropractor Ronald Frogley replied, "Chiropractors do not claim to be able to read a specific subluxation from an X-ray film." And yet, Congress included chiropractic under Medicare stating that payment would be made for treatment of "subluxations demonstrated by X-rays to exist." Although none has ever been shown, millions of dollars of taxpayers' money have filled the pockets of chiropractors. Who is looking out for the innocent taxpayer on this score? It surely isn't Congress, because in addition, chiropractors are required to harm their patients unnecessarily with dangerous X-rays: they use the full-spine X-ray, which exposes the sexual organs. It is pathetic that many people who publicly demonstrate against nuclear energy plants willingly submit to harmful irradiation by chiropractors. It is a sin that parents allow their innocent children to receive such irradiation. The physicists and radiologists of this nation are quite aware of the dangers inflicted by the full-spine X-ray. It is 10 to 1,000 times as much radiation as a routine chest X-ray (5). And yet, these morally-bound experts have done nothing significant to prevent chiropractors from harming their patients with irradiation, and the American Medical Association won't help the public either. H. Thomas Ballantine, M.D., a clinical professor of surgery at the Harvard Medical School and a senior neurosurgeon at the Massachusetts General Hospital, did an excellent job speaking out against chiropractic as the chairman of the American Medical Association Committee on Quackery (6). However, when the AMA had to tighten its financial belt a few years ago, the Committee on Quackery was one of the first to get the axe.

For many years my position as an anatomist at the Yale University School of Medicine has provided me with ample opportunity to study the dissection of the human spine in minute detail. Every medical student gets to dissect every muscle, ligament, nerve, and vessel of the spine, in addition to making a complete exposure of the spinal cord and its spinal nerves in a human cadaver. Therefore, I had long known that the chiropractic subluxation was an impossibility. However, I felt that a carefully conducted scientific experiment performed in such a manner that it could be easily repeated, would once and for all settle the question of whether or not there was such a thing as a chiropractic subluxation. I dissected out the intact spines or vertebral columns, with their attached ligaments, from three infants and three adults a few hours after they died. I carefully exposed the spinal nerves as they pass through the intervertebral openings or foramina. I placed the spines in an ordinary drill press (Figure 6). A fine wire was then wrapped around the spinal nerve and another was placed against the side wall of the intervertebral foramen (Figure 7). I then applied a measured force to both the front and back of each vertebra. I also twisted and bent the spines with a measured force (Figures 8 and 9). If the intervertebral foramen became reduced in size to the point that its walls merely touched the spinal nerve passing through it, the wires would also touch and cause a volt-ohm-microampere meter to register it. The forces applied to the spine reached the level where the spine was about to break. In not one instance did the walls of the intervertebral formina impinge upon the spinal nerves passing through them. In order to have that happen I had to break the spine. Here is definite scientific proof that the chiropractic subluxation causing impingement or pressure upon a spinal nerve is a myth! This experiment was published in 1973 (7), and the chiropractic rebuttal came in 1974 (8). One should expect it in the form of a repetition of my experiment showing that I was wrong. However, an unscientific cult can only throw up a smoke screen of verbiage. As expected, the president of the American Chiropractic Association, Stephen Owens, after writing a tirade to discredit my research, could only conclude that my findings were irrelevant because they were done on dead bodies. In one fell swoop he rejected all of the relevant, invaluable medical knowledge acquired from autopsying dead bodies. It probably never occurred to him that if a vertebra could be subluxed to impinge upon a spinal nerve, it would have occurred more readily in a dead body. In a living person there is a reflex response by the powerful spinal muscles to fight or resist any forces that would sublux a vertebra to the degree that it and/or spinal nerves could be damaged. In the spines I tested the only resistance to the displacement of the vertebrae were the attached passive ligaments. Thus, if the impingement on the nerves could not happen in a dead body, it definitely could not happen in a living one. My tests were witnessed by faculty members of the Section of Orthopaedic Surgery at Yale University. It has been twelve years since I published that experiment, and to this day no one has repeated it and published contrary findings.

I participated in a similar experiment that was published in 1975 (9). In that experiment the neck or cervical part of the spine was studied. It was found that the ligaments of the cervical spine control motion within finite limits without jeopardizing spinal cord or nerve root function. The ligaments proved to be exceptionally strong in preventing displacement of a vertebra of a fresh cervical spine removed from an adult. When a force was applied to a cervical vertebra as its numerous ligaments were cut free, the vertebra stayed in place until the last pair of ligaments remained. When they were cut the released vertebra literally flew across the laboratory.

The fact that I had to break the spine before impingement of spinal nerves by the walls of the intervertebral foramen could occur is what should be expected. After all, the vertebral column has been evolving for over 400 million years to support the body and to protect the central nervous system. By a process of natural selection the vertebral column of mammals has evolved into one in which the articulations allow a range of motion so that individuals may func-

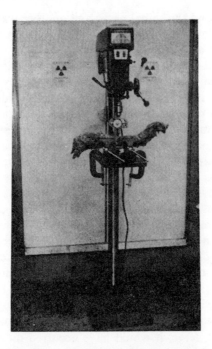

FIGURE 6. The drill press used to exert pressure on human vertebral columns. A force gauge (A) that records the amount of compressive force applied to the vertebral column (B) is attached to the pressure foot of the press. [From Crelin (7)]

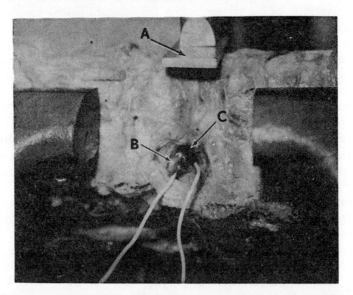

FIGURE 7. The pressure foot (A) of the drill press shown in figure 6 is placed against the body of the tenth thoracic vertebra of an adult human spine. A wire is wrapped around the tenth thoracic spinal nerve (B) and another wire is placed against the side of the intervertebral foramen (C). Both wires are attached to a V.O.M. meter. [From Crelin (7)]

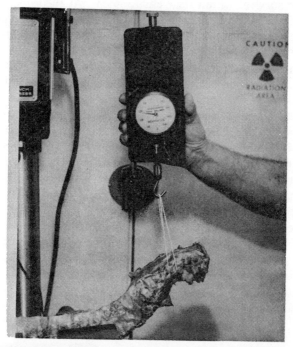

FIGURE 8. The cervical end of an adult vertebral column is attached by a cord to a push-pull gauge. The cervicothoracic part of the column is being maximally flexed. [From Crelin (7)]

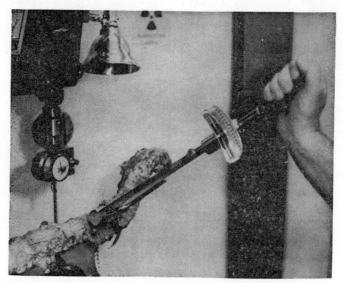

FIGURE 9. An adult vertebral column is held in a vise on the drill press platform. A chain clamp attaches a torque gauge to the midthoracic region of the column so that the degree of twisting force applied to the column can be quanitifed. [From Crelin (7)]

tion well for survival within their environment. At the same time the selective process has favored vertebral columns that have spacious intervertebral foramina in combination with the barest minimum of displacement between adjacent vertebrae—two factors that preclude impingement upon the spinal nerves as they pass through the foramina (1, 7). When the spine is severely injured the intervertebral foramina usually escape damage (Figures 10 and 11). Bony growths known as osteophytes, occurring in osteoarthritis, rarely involve the intervertebral foramina (Figures 12 and 13). Even when the thinned-out bone of osteomalacia in older individuals results in collapse of the vertebral bodies, the intervertebral foramina remain large enough to prevent impingement of the nerves passing through them (Figure 14). Chiropractors and orthopaedists talk a lot about ruptured, herniated, or slipped discs. Actually, this is rarely the cause of back pain (1). The degeneration of the center of the disc, the nucleus pulposus, normally occurs in every human being, beginning around twenty years of age. If, by chance, it protrudes or herniates from its central position in the intervertebral disc near middle age, it most often passes into the bodies of the adjacent vertebrae causing no sensations or disability (Figure 15). Rarely, the nucleus protrudes toward an intervertebral foramen and presses against a spinal nerve. If it does I can say with authority that a chiropractic adjustment is the most illogical and damaging procedure that can be performed on the patient.

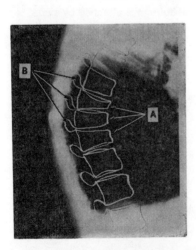 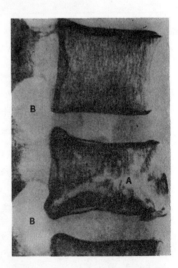

FIGURE 10. *(left)* Radiograph of a lateral view of the thoracic part of the vertebral column of an adult male patient who fell from a third floor window to the ground, landing on his feet. The bodies of three thoracic vertebrae (A) were crushed, however, the patient had no nerve function deficit. All of the intervertebral foramina (B) are spacious.

FIGURE 11. *(right)* A radiograph of a lateral view of the upper lumbar spine of a sixty-seven-year-old male. The body of the second lumbar vertebra (A) was fractured in an accident, however, the intervertebral foramina (B) are spacious. The patient had no neurological deficit.

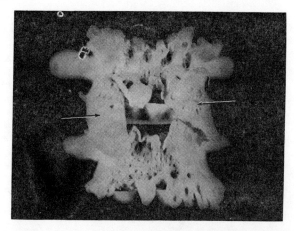

FIGURE 12. Anterior view of the articulated third and fourth lumbar bony vertebrae from an adult male who suffered from severe osteoarthritis of his skeleton. Numerous bony growths known as osteophytes extend from the vertebral bodies. Two large ones (arrows) bridge the joint space to join the two vertebrae together.

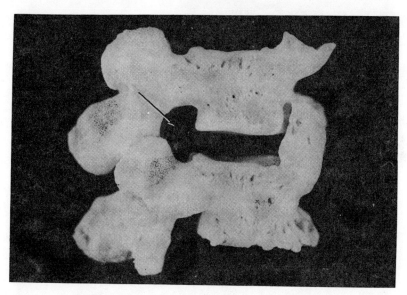

FIGURE 13. Right lateral view of the two lumbar bony vertebrae shown in figure 12. Although the bodies of the vertebrae contain numerous osteophytes, the vertebral arch portion of the vertebrae show little, if any, pathology. The intervertebral foramen (arrow) is spacious and free of osteophytes.

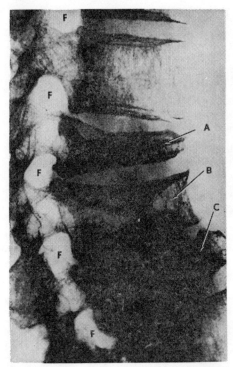

FIGURE 14. A radiograph of a lateral view of the lower spine of a seventy-seven-year-old woman with marked osteoporosis. The bodies of the first (A), second (B), and third (C) lumbar vertebrae are extremely flattened. However, there is no significant protrusion of the intervertebral discs and the intervertebral foramina (F) are relatively spacious. There was no neurological deficit.

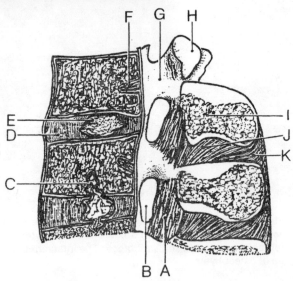

FIGURE 15. A drawing of a midline section of the spine of a middle-aged adult showing a herniation (C) of the nucleus pulposus of the intervertebral disc into the body of the third lumbar vertebra. A — ligamentum flavum. B — intervertebral foramen. D — anulus fibrosus of intervertebral disc. E — degenerated remains of nucleus pulposus. F — bony canal for basivertebral vein. G — pedicle. H — articular process of second lumbar vertebra. I — spinous process. J — interspinous ligament. K — supraspinous ligament. [From Crelin (1)]

FIGURE 16. Carole Crelin subjecting her spine to extreme lateral stress on a gymnastic high beam. No neurological disorders have occurred during the four years after this photograph was taken.

FIGURE 17. Carole Crelin subjecting her spine to extreme extensional bending stress on a gymnastic high beam. She has suffered only an occasional common cold during the four years after this photograph was taken.

Watching my daughter Carole when she was captain of her high school gymnastics team perform on the high beam showed me how silly the chiropractic theory of disease is (Figures 16 and 17). As an amateur she often did a running front flip on the mat and landed hard on her buttocks instead of her feet. The shock waves absorbed by her spine were tremendous! This happened often. If it were true that one can also get a disease from a subluxation caused by merely being upset mentally, Carole should have every disease known to human beings. And yet, she continues to be in the best of health in every way.

When chiropractors are confronted publicly they will deny that they treat conditions such as infectious diseases, allergies, cancer, and others. However, the truth is that they have and will treat any disease (5). There is a chart used in the chiropractors' offices, their schools, and in their advertising (Figure 18A) showing the human spine. The individual vertebrae are pointed out, showing a number of disorders caused by the subluxation of each vertebra, resulting in their impingement on adjacent spinal nerves. The disorders range from head colds and whooping cough to heart conditions and hemorrhoids (piles). Each vertebra is also shown to be directly related to specific body regions and organs. When I volunteered to testify at the trial of a chiropractor, R. T. LeBarre, accused of false newspaper advertising, I felt I could be the most effective if I attacked his use of the spine chart in his advertising. I wasn't going to discuss how ridiculous the notion was that pressure on spinal nerves could have anything to do with causing all of the disorders listed on the chart. Instead, I pointed out that most of the spinal nerves adjacent to the vertebrae directly related to specific regions and organs on the chart did not send any branches to innervate those regions or organs. The chart is a farce! By merely using a high school level anatomy book one can determine how inaccurate the chart is.

The chart La Barre used in his advertising (Figure 18B) was essentially the same as the chart shown in figure 18A. His chart is presumed to be the most accurate since it bears the "Seal of Approval of the L. F. P. Advertising Council," whatever that is. I described in detail the anatomical inaccuracies of the chart, and these were placed in the court records of the trial. Examples of the errors are as follows:

1) An arrow on the left side of the chart (see Figure 18B) points to the first cervical (neck) vertebra that would indicate possible involvement of the first or second pair of cervical spinal nerves. It is labeled "To All Sections of the Head and Face." This is false. No cervical spinal nerves have any branches that supply any type of innervation to the front of the face, both superficial and deep, including the forehead. These regions are supplied by the fifth and seventh pairs of cranial nerves that pass directly from the brainstem and through the skull to their sites of innervation.

2) In the first paragraph on the right hand side of the chart, the arrow points to the first cervical (neck) vertebra, indicating that a slight "pinching" of the first or second pair of cervical spinal nerves could be the cause of the following:

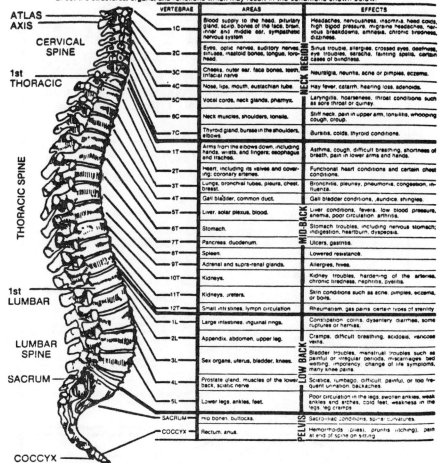

CHART OF EFFECTS OF SPINAL MISALIGNMENTS

"The nervous system controls and coordinates all organs and structures of the human body." (*Gray's Anatomy*, 29th Ed., page 4.) Misalignments of spinal vertebrae and discs may cause irritation to the nervous system and affect the structures, organs, and functions which may result in the conditions shown below.

VERTEBRAE	AREAS	EFFECTS
1C	Blood supply to the head, pituitary gland, scalp, bones of the face, brain, inner and middle ear, sympathetic nervous system	Headaches, nervousness, insomnia, head colds, high blood pressure, migraine headaches, nervous breakdowns, amnesia, chronic tiredness, dizziness.
2C	Eyes, optic nerves, auditory nerves, sinuses, mastoid bones, tongue, forehead.	Sinus trouble, allergies, crossed eyes, deafness, eye troubles, earache, fainting spells, certain cases of blindness.
3C	Cheeks, outer ear, face bones, teeth, trifacial nerve	Neuralgia, neuritis, acne or pimples, eczema.
4C	Nose, lips, mouth, eustachian tube.	Hay fever, catarrh, hearing loss, adenoids.
5C	Vocal cords, neck glands, pharynx.	Laryngitis, hoarseness, throat conditions such as sore throat or quinsy.
6C	Neck muscles, shoulders, tonsils.	Stiff neck, pain in upper arm, tonsilitis, whooping cough, croup.
7C	Thyroid gland, bursae in the shoulders, elbows.	Bursitis, colds, thyroid conditions.
1T	Arms from the elbows down, including hands, wrists, and fingers; esophagus and trachea.	Asthma, cough, difficult breathing, shortness of breath, pain in lower arms and hands.
2T	Heart, including its valves and covering; coronary arteries.	Functional heart conditions and certain chest conditions.
3T	Lungs, bronchial tubes, pleura, chest, breast.	Bronchitis, pleurisy, pneumonia, congestion, influenza.
4T	Gall bladder, common duct.	Gall bladder conditions, jaundice, shingles.
5T	Liver, solar plexus, blood.	Liver conditions, fevers, low blood pressure, anemia, poor circulation, arthritis.
6T	Stomach.	Stomach troubles, including nervous stomach; indigestion, heartburn, dyspepsia.
7T	Pancreas, duodenum.	Ulcers, gastritis.
8T	Spleen.	Lowered resistance.
9T	Adrenal and supra-renal glands.	Allergies, hives.
10T	Kidneys.	Kidney troubles, hardening of the arteries, chronic tiredness, nephritis, pyelitis.
11T	Kidneys, ureters.	Skin conditions such as acne, pimples, eczema, or boils.
12T	Small intestines, lymph circulation	Rheumatism, gas pains, certain types of sterility
1L	Large intestines, inguinal rings.	Constipation, colitis, dysentery, diarrhea, some ruptures or hernias.
2L	Appendix, abdomen, upper leg.	Cramps, difficult breathing, acidosis, varicose veins.
3L	Sex organs, uterus, bladder, knees.	Bladder troubles, menstrual troubles such as painful or irregular periods, miscarriages, bed wetting, impotency, change of life symptoms, many knee pains.
4L	Prostate gland, muscles of the lower back, sciatic nerve	Sciatica, lumbago, difficult, painful, or too frequent urination, backaches.
5L	Lower legs, ankles, feet.	Poor circulation in the legs, swollen ankles, weak ankles and arches, cold feet, weakness in the legs, leg cramps
SACRUM	Hip bones, buttocks.	Sacro-iliac conditions, spinal curvatures.
COCCYX	Rectum, anus.	Hemorrhoids (piles), pruritis (itching), pain at end of spine on sitting

ATLAS
AXIS
CERVICAL SPINE
1st THORACIC
THORACIC SPINE
1st LUMBAR
LUMBAR SPINE
SACRUM
COCCYX

NECK REGION
MID-BACK
LOW BACK
PELVIS

Chart from a brochure distributed in 1979 at a New York Chiropractic College Clinic.

FIGURE 18A. Typical chart of the effects of spinal misalignments used by chiropractors in their schools, offices and advertising. [From Barrett (5), reprinted with permission]

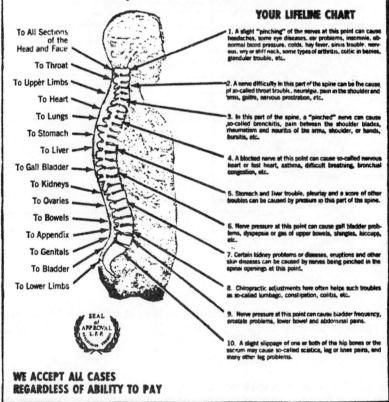

FIGURE 18B. Spinal chart used in an advertisement in the *Globe-Times,* Bethlehem, Pennsylvania, February 17, 1975.

A. *A slight "pinching"* of any of the eight pairs of cervical spinal nerves could never be the cause of any *eye disease* whatsoever. There are no cervical spinal nerve branches that are located anywhere near the eyes, let alone have anything to do with vision, eyeball movements, or sensations.

B. *A slight "pinching"* of any of the cervical spinal nerves could never be the cause of *ear problems* that have anything to do with hearing, and this includes the functioning of the tiny bones of the middle ear and the fluid-filled canals of the inner ear that transmit the original sound vibrations to the proper nerves. If ear problems also include those of equilibrium, which is localized in the inner ear, no cervical spinal nerves could ever be involved. The nerves involved with hearing and the vestibular apparatus of equilibrium arise within the brain and never leave the skull. They are known as the eighth (vestibulocochlear) pair of cranial nerves.

C. It would be impossible for *a slight "pinching"* of the cervical spinal nerves to have anything to do with *glandular trouble* in the head and neck region. The pituitary, pineal, lacrimal, lymph, salivary, mucous, thyroid, parathyroid, and thymus glands do not receive any nerve supply from the cervical spinal nerves whatsoever.

3) An arrow on the left side of the chart, labeled "To Throat," points to the level of the second cervical vertebra, indicating possible involvement of the second or third pair of cervical spinal nerves. This is false. Not one of the eight pairs of cervical spinal nerves supplies the throat (pharynx) with any type of innervation.

4) In the second paragraph on the right hand side of the chart, an arrow points to the third cervical (neck) vertebra, indicating *a nerve difficulty* in *this part of the spine* (second or third cervical spinal nerves) *would be the cause of* the following:

A. Any *so-called throat trouble* could never be the result of *difficulty* of any cervical spinal nerve because the throat (pharynx) is innervated exclusively by the ninth and tenth cranial nerves. These nerves pass through openings in the base of the skull and pass directly to the throat with no relationship whatsoever to the spine or any spinal nerves.

B. *Pain in the arms* could never be the result of *difficulty* of the second or third cervical spinal nerves as the arrow indicates on the chart. The cervical spinal nerves that supply the arms with pain sensation are the fifth to eighth cervical and the first and second thoracic spinal nerves.

C. *Goitre* is an enlargement of the thyroid gland. No cervical spinal nerve branches pass to the thyroid gland.

5) An arrow on the left side of the chart, labeled "To Liver," points to the sixth thoracic vertebra indicating involvement of the fifth or sixth pair of the twelve pairs of of thoracic spinal nerves. This is false. No branches of the fifth or sixth thoracic spinal nerves pass to the liver.

6) An arrow on the left side of the chart, labeled "To Lower Limbs," points to the sacrum. The first, second, third, and fourth pairs of the five pairs of sacral nerves do send branches to the lower limbs. However, the indication that these sacral nerves could ever be involved in a movement or subluxation at the sacral foramina is false because it is impossible. These nerves could never be involved in any movement or subluxation at the sacral foramina since the sacrum is one solid mass of bone.

My testimony took most of one morning in the Northampton County Court-house in Pennsylvania at the trial brought against the chiropractor by the Lehigh Valley Committee Against Health Fraud, Inc. I placed a number of well-known human anatomy textbooks on a table in front of the courtroom for the chiropractor's lawyers to use to rebut all of the simple anatomical inaccuracies I pointed out that are in the spine chart.

I returned to the witness stand for most of the afternoon. The chiropractor who was on trial never appeared. Representing him were two lawyers and a chiropractor whom the lawyers frequently consulted in private. I had difficulty keeping awake along with the court stenographer and reporters from the *Easton Express,* the *Allentown Morning Call* and the *Bethlehem Globe-Times* news-papers as the two lawyers took turns haranguing about everything but the anatomical inaccuracies of the spine chart. Their discourses were punctuated with questions directed to me as to what I had against chiropractors or why I hated them so. Of course, the defendant's attorneys were unable to show I was incorrect in any of my charges of inaccuracy. One of the lawyers concluded his defense with the statement that the chart illustrates a "theory" of anatomy taught by the chiropractic schools that are licensed by Pennsylvania. He went on to say that the defendant is licensed by the State Board of Chiropractors and put in his ads what he was taught in chiropractic school. This was all duly reported in the local newspapers and I quietly returned to Yale. The trial began in 1975 and has yet to reach a legal conclusion.

It was no surprise to me to find that chiropractors were quick to jump on the bandwagon of the new health fad known as holistic medicine. Many did the same thing when acupuncture was the new health craze in the 1970s. When the chiropractors failed to have the law changed to allow them to stick needles into their patients they resorted to applying pressure to the acupuncture sites. A New Haven chiropractor, J. B. Timoner, charged $45 to $50 for a single "puncture-less" acupuncture treatment in 1975 (10). The expensive fee was probably be-cause he used an Accuflex machine to determine the meridians of the body. The machine uses rechargeable batteries and gives the patient a "tingling" sensation. I'm sure the machine is similar to a medical quack gadget I own that was made in the 1920s. How the Accuflex machine is able to determine the meridians of the body but my gadget is not will forever be an unsolvable mystery.

A New Haven holistic medical group has also made a play on words by calling themselves the New England Chiropractic and Wholistic Treatment Center. It is headed by a chiropractor, R. A. Lesnow. To assist him in making his spinal adjustments he uses a hand-held instrument that contains a metal spring (Figure 19). The thrust delivered by the instrument is light and fast. "The thrust delivered by the instrument helps the body reduce the spinal misalignment thus alleviating the irritation to the spinal nerves, and allows your body to operate more efficiently and more comfortably" (Figure 19). If this instrument's thrust could have any effect in shifting the position of a vertebra, the vertebrae would have to be so weakly held together that we would all be crumpled up on the ground.

The chiropractor is assisted by three people with questionable credentials. In the advertising of the center one assistant is listed as a "trained movement analyst." She guides selected patients through a series of strengthening exercises and "relazation" (sic) techniques. Another is a psychotherapist and has a masters degree in "Movement Therapy." He works with movement and more traditional verbal therapy to help the patients become "concious" (sic) of the root causes of their stress, and from there working to alleviate the cause. The third person is a certified Polarity Practitioner/Instructor, certified member of the American

Q. WHAT DOES THE SMALL HAND IN-
STRUMENT DO?

A. The hand held instrument is a new concept in light force and painless adjusting. It has been designed to deliver a controlled, light, fast thrust without undue strain or force to the patient. The thrust delivered by the instrument helps the body reduce the spinal misalignment thus alleviating the irritation to the spinal nerves, and allows your body to operate more efficiently and more comfortably.

FIGURE 19. A chiropractic instrument used at the New England Chiropractic and Wholistic Treatment Center, New Haven, Conn.

Massage and Therapy Association and Member of the Flower Essence Society. Instead of people being impressed by the above degrees and qualifications they should regard them for what they are, a lot of nonsense. To be a member of the Flower Essence Society sounds more like a qualification to sell perfume rather than health.

In advertising distributed by the Wholistic Center (shown in Figure 20) there is a revelation of naiveté when the functioning of the nervous system is described. It contains words such as "biological rheostat," "turning down vital messages," "body function is dimmed." This implies that the nervous system is an electrical switchboard with the nerves acting as copper wires carrying electrical signals to and from it. Vertebral subluxations are supposed to cause "short circuits" by impinging on the spinal nerves. It demonstrates that after attending a chiropractic school for four years the graduates end up with an erroneous understanding of the nervous system. Nerves are living cells. They are gland cells that secrete a hormone which stimulates another nerve cell to secrete its hormone, or induces a muscle cell or fiber to contract or relax. The extensions of the nerve cells, known as fibers, do not conduct electricity (11, 12).

Science has discovered a condition known as **Vertebral Subluxation** which is an interference to function in your body, forcing you to have less than normal health. Forcing you to have less than optimum physical, mental and social well-being; your body, against your will, then becomes fertile ground for diseases and infirmities.

Vertebral Subluxation — The most serious and tragic interference to function in your body that we know of

Vertebral Subluxation is caused by one or more of the bones of your spine becoming misaligned and out of their natural positions. This causes pressure to the vital nerve pathways of the spinal cord (in the center of the spine) and the spinal nerve roots (exiting from the sides of the spine).

This pressure or interference acts as a **biological rheostat**, **"Turning down"** vital messages that pass between the brain and organs of the body.

Thus the nerve system, the main coordinator of **body function** is **"dimmed"**, resulting in **unnatural body function**, **aberrant behavior** and an **early death**.

HEALTH

FIGURE 20. An excerpt from advertising distributed by the New England Chiropractic and Wholistic Treatment Center, New Haven, Conn.

CHIROPRACTIC AND HEALTH

The question is, "What Controls Function?"

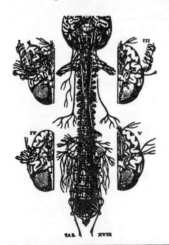
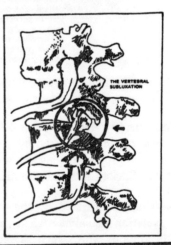

FIGURE 21. An excerpt from advertising distributed by the New England Chiropractic and Wholistic Treatment Center, New Haven, Conn. The vertebral subluxation shown is a complete fabrication.

Figure 21 is also from the advertising distributed by the Wholistic Center. It has an illustration showing a vertebral subluxation causing pressure on a spinal nerve that is reduced in size because of it. The nerve is encircled where it emerges from the intervertebral foramen. This illustration is a deliberate fabrication, which shows that there is no limit to how far chiropractic will go to deceive. To have a vertebra displaced, as the one shown in the illustration, would require a person to subject himself to such trauma that the spine breaks. Not only would the nerves be irreparably damaged at the site of the break, but the contents of the vertebral canal, such as the spinal cord and/or spinal nerve roots, would be crushed so that a person would be permanently paralyzed below that level of the spine. When a so-called health profession has to stoop to such a desperate, deceitful act to justify its basic tenet for existence, it should be outlawed.

I started by stating that my concern for a child strongly motivated me to "stick my neck out" to protect innocent children from chiropractic "treatment." As a father of four children and the grandfather of four I am even more motivated than ever. A few years ago the Lehigh Valley Committee Against Health Fraud sent a healthy four-year-old girl to five chiropractors for a "check-up." The first said that the child's shoulder blades were "out of place" and found "pinched nerves to her stomach and gall bladder." The second said the child's pelvis was "twisted." The third said one hip was "elevated" and that spinal misalignments could cause "headaches, nervousness, equilibrium or digestive problems" in the future. The fourth predicted "bad periods and rough child-birth" if her "shorter left leg" were not treated. The fifth not only found hip and neck problems, but also "adjusted" them without bothering to ask permission. Unfortunately, the adjustments were so painful that the committee decided to postpone further investigation until adult volunteers could be found (5). It was with disgust and disbelief that I read about J. Laverriere, a Canadian chiro-practor who treated a boy with hydrocephaly for seven years (13). This condi-tion is an enlarged head due to a blockage of the cerebrospinal fluid circulation of the brain. The practitioner was found guilty in court for having the boy's mother perform the ridiculous procedure of keeping her son's head wrapped in boiled cabbage leaves to cure the condition.

A lot of intelligent adults have gone to chiropractors and realized on their own that they made a mistake. Likewise, a lot of people really believe they have been helped, even cured, of a medical disorder by a chiropractor. This is under-standable because a quack can't fail completely. At least half of the people with an ache or a pain who go to a witch doctor, a chiropractor, or medical doctor, have a self-limiting disorder that will clear up by itself in time. Even though an M.D. physician is a fallible human being who doesn't know all there is to know about how to treat all of the many diseases humans contract, he has at least been taught how to apply scientifically-based principles in his diagnosis and treatment of a particular disorder. Since the basic tenet of chiropractic is not only unscientific but false, there is no justification for its existence. A person who goes to a chiropractor is not only at risk but being robbed of his hard-earned money.

Science writer Ralph Lee Smith attended a three-day seminar in "practice building" led by a chiropractor, James W. Parker (2). Parker said, "At these sessions, I intend to teach you all the gimmicks, gadgets, and gizmos that can be used to get new patients. . . . Thinking, feeling, acting determine the amount of money you take to the bank. . . . Remember, enthusiasm is the yeast that raises the dough." Smith talked to many chiropractors during the seminar. One of them had attended a number of these sessions. He said, "After the first one my income went up from $2,000 to $4,000 a month." He then told Smith that he was nearing the $100,000 mark. Another chiropractor summarized the situation with graphic simplicity: "We have gone," he said, "from rags to riches." And the chiropractors will continue to do so as long as the courts and the lawmakers continue to support and protect them, and as long as there are unsuspecting people who are willing to let the quacks fleece them of their money. If any adult reads this chapter and is still willing to be treated by a chiropractor, he or she agrees to be cheated and to suffer the consequences. However, he or she should at least have the decency not to permit the chiropractors to treat their innocent children.

REFERENCES

1. E. S. Crelin, "Functional Anatomy of the Lumbosacral Spine," in *Symposium on Idiopathic Low Back Pain* (St. Louis: The C. V. Mosby Co., 1982).

2. R. L. Smith, *At Your Own Risk: The Case Against Chiropractic* (New York: Pocket Books, 1969).

3. E. S. Crelin, "A Lethal Chiropractic Device," *Yale Scientific Magazine* 49 (1975):8-11.

4. T. A. Vondarhaar, "Chiropractic in Theory and Practice," in *The Holistic Health Handbook, edited* by E. Bauman, A. E. Brint, L. Piper, and P. A. Wright (Berkeley: And/Or Press, 1978).

5. S. Barrett, "The Spine Salesmen," In *The Health Robbers,* edited by S. Barrett (Philadelphia: G. F. Stickley Co., 1980).

6. H. T. Ballantine, "Chiropractic and the Protection of the Nation's Health," presented at the Northeast Regional Conference on Health Quackery-Chiropractic, Marriott Motor Hotel, Philadelphia, Penn, 1973.

7. E. S. Crelin, "A Scientific Test of the Chiropractic Theory," *American Scientist* 61 (1973):574-80.

8. S. E. Owens, "Rebuttal: Crelin Spine Test Not Valid," *American Chiropractic Association Journal of Chiropractic* 8 (1974):54-64.

9. R. M. Johnson, E. S. Crelin, A. A. White, M. M. Panjabi and W. O. Southwick, "Some Observations on the Functional Anatomy of the Lower Cervical Spine," *Clinical Orthopaedics* 3 (1975):192-200.

10. N. Thomas, "City Chiropractic Utilizes 'Punctureless' Acupuncture," *The Register* (New Haven, Connecticut) February 2, 1975.

11. E. S. Crelin, "Development of the Nervous System," *Ciba Clinical Symposia.* 26 (1974):1-32.

12. E. S. Crelin, "Embryology," in *Nervous System, Volume 1, Part I: Anatomy and Physiology,* edited by by F. H. Netter (West Caldwell: N.J.: Ciba, 1984).

13. *American Medical News,* page 2, December 13, 1976.

Oliver Wendell Holmes

Homeopathy

It is necessary, for the sake of those to whom the whole subject may be new, to give in the smallest possible compass the substance of the Homoeopathic Doctrine. Samuel Hahnemann, its founder, is a German physician, now living in Paris,[1] at the age of eighty-seven years. In 1796 he published the first paper containing his peculiar notions; in 1805 his first work on the subject; in 1810 his somewhat famous "Organon of the Healing Art;" the next year what he called the "Pure Materia Medica;" and in 1828 his last work, the "Treatise on Chronic Diseases." He has therefore been writing at intervals on his favorite subject for nearly half a century.

The one great doctrine which constitutes the basis of Homoeopathy as a system is expressed by the Latin aphorism,

"SIMILIA SIMILIBUS CURANTUR,"

or *like* cures *like*, that is, diseases are cured by agents capable of producing symptoms resembling those found in the disease under treatment. A disease for Hahnemann consists essentially in a group of symptoms. The proper medicine for any disease is the one which is capable of producing a similar group of symptoms when given to a healthy person.

It is of course necessary to know what are the trains of symptoms excited by different substances, when administered to persons in health, if any such can be shown to exist. Hahnemann and his disciples give catalogues of the symptoms which they affirm were produced upon themselves or others by a large number of drugs which they submitted to experiment.

From "Homoeopathy and Its Kindred Delusions," two lectures delivered before the Boston Society for the Diffusion of Useful Knowledge in 1842 and reprinted in *Holmes' Works,* Volume IX, which is entitled *Medical Essays* (Boston: Houghton, Mifflin and Company, 1892). Holmes used the British spelling of the term "homoeopathy" in his lectures; we have used the American spelling in the title to this selection and elsewhere in this volume.—*Eds.*

The second great fact which Hahnemann professes to have established is the *efficacy of medicinal substances reduced to a wonderful degree of minuteness or dilution*. The following account of his mode of preparing his medicines is from his work on Chronic Diseases, which has not, I believe, yet been translated into English. A grain of the substance, if it is solid, a drop if it is liquid, is to be added to about a third part of one hundred grains of sugar of milk in an unglazed porcelain capsule which has had the polish removed from the lower part of its cavity by rubbing it with wet sand; they are to be mingled for an instant with a bone or horn spatula, and then rubbed together for six minutes; then the mass is to be scraped together from the mortar and pestle, which is to take four minutes; then to be again rubbed for six minutes. Four minutes are then to be devoted to scraping the powder into a heap, and the second third of the hundred grains of sugar of milk to be added. Then they are to be stirred an instant and rubbed six minutes,—again to be scraped together four minutes and forcibly rubbed six; once more scraped together for four minutes, when the last third of the hundred grains of sugar of milk is to be added and mingled by stirring with the spatula; six minutes of forcible rubbing, four of scraping together, and six more (positively the last six) of rubbing, finish this part of the process.

Every grain of this powder contains the hundredth of a grain of the medicinal substance mingled with the sugar of milk. If, therefore, a grain of the powder just prepared is mingled with another hundred grains of sugar of milk, and the process just described repeated, we shall have a powder of which every grain contains the hundredth of the hundredth, or the ten thousandth part of a grain of the medicinal substance. Repeat the same process with the same quantity of fresh sugar of milk, and every grain of your powder will contain the millionth of a grain of the medicinal substance. When the powder is of this strength, it is ready to employ in the further solutions and dilutions to be made use of in practice.

A grain of the powder is to be taken, a hundred drops of alcohol are to be poured on it, the vial is to be slowly turned for a few minutes, until the powder is dissolved, and two shakes are to be given to it. On this point I will quote Hahnemann's own words. "A long experience and multiplied observations upon the sick lead me within the last few years to prefer giving only two shakes to medicinal liquids, whereas I formerly used to give ten." The process of dilution is carried on in the same way as the attenuation of the powder was done; each successive dilution with alcohol reducing the medicine to a hundredth part of the quantity of that which preceded it. In this way the dilution of the original millionth of a grain of medicine contained in the grain of powder operated on is carried successively to the billionth, trillionth, quadrillionth, quintillionth, and very often much higher fractional divisions. A dose of any of these medicines is a minute fraction of a drop, obtained by moistening with them one or more little globules of sugar, of which Hahnemann says it takes about two hundred to weigh a grain.

As an instance of the strength of the medicines prescribed by Hahnemann, I will mention carbonate of lime. He does not employ common chalk, but prefers a little portion of the friable part of an oyster-shell. Of this substance, carried to the sextillionth degree, so much as one or two globules of the size mentioned can convey is a common dose. But for persons of very delicate nerves it is proper that the dilution should be carried to the decillionth degree. That is, an important medicinal effect is to be expected from the two hundredth or hundredth part of the millionth of the millionth of the millionth of the millionth of the millionth of the millionth of the millionth of the millionth of the millionth of the millionth of a grain of oyster-shell. This is only the tenth degree of potency, but some of his disciples profess to have obtained palpable effects from much higher dilutions.[2]

The third great doctrine of Hahnemann is the following. *Seven eighths at least of all chronic diseases* are produced by the existence in the system of that infectious disorder known in the language of science by the appellation of PSORA, but to the less refined portion of the community by the name of ITCH. In the words of Hahnemann's "Organon," "This Psora is the sole true and fundamental cause that produces all the other countless forms of disease, which, under the names of nervous debility, hysteria, hypochondriasis, insanity, melancholy, idiocy, madness, epilepsy, and spasms of all kinds, softening of the bones, or rickets, scoliosis and cyphosis, caries, cancer, fungus haematodes, gout,—yellow jaundice and cyanosis, dropsy,—gastralgia, epistaxis, haemoptysis,—asthma and suppuration of the lungs,—megrim, deafness, cataract and amaurosis,—paralysis, loss of sense, pains of every kind, etc., appear in our pathology as so many peculiar, distinct, and independent diseases."

For the last three centuries, if the same authority may be trusted, under the influence of the more refined personal habits which have prevailed, and the application of various external remedies which repel the affection from the skin, Psora has revealed itself in these numerous forms of internal disease, instead of appearing, as in former periods, under the aspect of an external malady.

These are the three cardinal doctrines of Hahnemann, as laid down in those standard works of Homoeopathy, the "Organon" and the "Treatise on Chronic Diseases."

Several other principles may be added, upon all of which he insists with great force, and which are very generally received by his disciples.

1. Very little power is allowed to the curative efforts of nature. Hahnemann goes so far as to say that no one has ever seen the simple efforts of nature effect the durable recovery of a patient from a chronic disease. In general, the Homoeopathist calls every recovery which happens under his treatment a *cure*.

2. Every medicinal substance must be administered in a state of the most perfect purity, and uncombined with any other. The union of several remedies in a single prescription destroys its utility, and, according to the "Organon," frequently adds a new disease.

3. A large number of substances commonly thought to be inert develop

224 Examining Holistic Medicine

great medicinal powers when prepared in the manner already described; and a great proportion of them are ascertained to have specific antidotes in case their excessive effects require to be neutralized.

4. Diseases should be recognized, as far as possible, not by any of the common names imposed upon them, as fever or epilepsy, but as individual collections of symptoms, each of which differs from every other collection.

5. The symptoms of any complaint must be described with the most minute exactness, and so far as possible in the patient's own words. To illustrate the kind of circumstances the patient is expected to record, I will mention one or two from the 313th page of the "Treatise on Chronic Diseases,"—being the first one at which I opened accidentally.

"After dinner, disposition to sleep; the patient winks."

"After dinner, prostration and feeling of weakness (nine days after taking the remedy)."

This remedy was that same oyster-shell which is to be prescribed in fractions of the sextillionth or decillionth degree. According to Hahnemann, the action of a single dose of the size mentioned does not fully display itself in some cases until twenty-four or even thirty days after it is taken, and in such instances has not exhausted its good effects until towards the fortieth or fiftieth day,—before which time it would be absurd and injurious to administer a new remedy.

So much for the doctrines of Hahnemann, which have been stated without comment, or exaggeration of any of their features, very much as any adherent of his opinions might have stated them, if obliged to compress them into so narrow a space.

Does Hahnemann himself represent Homoeopathy as it now exists? He certainly ought to be its best representative, after having created it, and devoted his life to it for half a century. He is spoken of as the great physician of the time, in most, if not all Homoeopathic works. If he is not authority on the subject of his own doctrines, *who is?* So far as I am aware, not one tangible discovery in the so-called science has ever been ascribed to any other observer; at least, no general principle or law, of consequence enough to claim any prominence in Homoeopathic works, has ever been pretended to have originated with any of his illustrious disciples. He is one of the only two Homoeopathic writers with whom, as I shall mention, the Paris publisher will have anything to do with upon his own account. The other is Jahr, whose Manual is little more than a catalogue of symptoms and remedies. If any persons choose to reject Hahnemann as not in the main representing Homoeopathy, if they strike at his authority, if they wink out of sight his deliberate and formally announced results, it is an act of suicidal rashness; for upon his sagacity and powers of observation, and experience, as embodied in his works, and especially in his Materia Medica, repose the foundations of Homoeopathy as a practical system.

So far as I can learn from the conflicting statements made upon the subject, the following is the present condition of belief.

1. All of any note agree that the law *Similia similibus* is the only fundamental principle in medicine. Of course if any man does not agree to this the
name Homoeopathist can no longer be applied to him with propriety.

2. The belief in and employment of the infinitesimal doses is general, and
in some places universal, among the advocates of Homoeopathy; but a distinct
movement has been made in Germany to get rid of any restriction to the use
of these doses, and to employ medicines with the same license as other practitioners.

3. The doctrine of the origin of most chronic diseases in Psora, notwithstanding Hahnemann who says it cost him twelve years of study and research
to establish the fact and its practical consequences, has met with great neglect
and even opposition from very many of his own disciples.

It is true, notwithstanding, that, throughout most of their writings which
I have seen, there runs a prevailing tone of great deference to Hahnemann's
opinions, a constant reference to his authority, a general agreement with the
minor points of his belief, and a pretense of harmonious union in a common
faith.[3]

.   .   .

The three great asserted discoveries of Hahnemann are entirely unconnected
with and independent of each other. Were there any natural relation between
them it would seem probable enough that the discovery of the first would have
led to that of the others. But assuming it to be a fact that diseases are cured
by remedies capable of producing symptoms like their own, no manifest relation
exists between this fact and the next assertion, namely, the power of the infinitesimal doses. And allowing both of these to be true, neither has the remotest
affinity to the third new doctrine, that which declares seven-eighths of all chronic
diseases to be owing to Psora.

.   .   .

Let us look a moment at the first of his doctrines. Improbable though it
may seem to some, there is no essential absurdity involved in the proposition
that diseases yield to remedies capable of producing like symptoms. There are,
on the other hand, some analogies which lend a degree of plausibility to the
statement. There are well-ascertained facts, known from the earliest periods of
medicine, showing that, under certain circumstances, the very medicine which,
from its known effects, one would expect to aggravate the disease, may contribute to its relief. I may b permitted to allude, in the most general way, to
the case in which the spontaneous efforts of an overtasked stomach are quieted
by the agency of a drug which that organ refuses to entertain upon any terms.
But that *every* cure ever performed by medicine should have been founded upon
this principle, although without the knowledge of a physician; that the

Homoeopathic axiom is, as Hahnemann asserts, "the *sole* law of nature in therapeutics," a law of which nothing more than a transient glimpse ever presented itself to the innumerable host of medical observers, is a dogma of such sweeping extent, and pregnant novelty, that it demands a corresponding breadth and depth of unquestionable facts to cover its vast pretensions.

So much ridicule has been thrown upon the pretended powers of the *minute doses* that I shall only touch upon this point for the purpose of conveying, by illustrations, some shadow of ideas far transcending the powers of the imagination to realize. It must be remembered that these comparisons are not matters susceptible of dispute, being founded on simple arithmetical computations, level to the capacity of any intelligent schoolboy. A person who once wrote a very small pamphlet made some show of objecting to calculations of this kind, on the ground that the highest dilutions could easily be made with a few ounces of alcohol. But he should have remembered that at every successive dilution he lays aside or throws away ninety-nine hundredths of the fluid on which he is operating, and that, although he begins with a drop, he only prepares a millionth, billionth, trillionth, and similar fractions of it, all of which, added together, would constitute but a vastly minute portion of the drop with which he began. But now let us suppose we take one single drop of the Tincture of Camomile, and that the *whole* of this were to be carried through the common series of dilutions.

A calculation nearly like the following was made by Dr. Panvini, and may be readily followed in its essential particulars by any one who chooses.

For the first dilution it would take 100 drops of alcohol.

For the second dilution it would take 10,000 drops, or about a pint.

For the third dilution it would take 100 pints.

For the fourth dilution it would take 10,000 pints, or more than 1,000 gallons, and so on to the ninth dilution, which would take ten billion gallons, which he computed would fill the basin of Lake Agnano, a body of water two miles in circumference. The twelfth dilution would of course fill a million such lakes. By the time the seventeenth degree of dilution should be reached, the alcohol required would equal in quantity the waters of ten thousand Adriatic seas. Trifling errors must be expected, but they are as likely to be on one side as the other, and any little matter like Lake Superior or the Caspian would be but a drop in the bucket.

Swallowers of globules, one of your little pellets, moistened in the mingled waves of one million lakes of alcohol, each two miles in circumference, with which had been blended that one drop of Tincture of Camomile, would be of precisely the strength recommended for that medicine in your favorite Jahr's Manual, against the most sudden, frightful, and fatal diseases![4]

And proceeding on the common data, I have just made a calculation which shows that this single drop of Tincture of Camomile, given in the quantity ordered by Jahr's Manual, would have supplied every individual of the whole human family, past and present, with more than five billion doses each, the action of each dose lasting about four days.

Yet this is given only at the quadrillionth, or fourth degree of potency, and various substances are frequently administered at the decillionth or tenth degree, and occasionally at still higher attenuations with professed medicinal results. Is there not in this as great an exception to all the hitherto received laws of nature as in the miracle of the loaves and fishes? Ask this question of a Homoeopathist, and he will answer by referring to the effects produced by a very minute portion of vaccine matter, or the extraordinary diffusion of odors. But the vaccine matter is one of those substances called *morbid poisons,* of which it is a peculiar character to multiply themselves, when introduced into the system, as a seed does in the soil. Therefore the hundredth part of a grain of the vaccine matter, if no more than this is employed, soon increases in quantity, until, in the course of about a week, it is a grain or more, and can be removed in considerable drops. And what is a very curious illustration of Homoeopathy, it does not produce its most characteristic effects until it is already in sufficient quantity not merely to be visible, but to be collected for further use. The thoughtlessness which can allow an inference to be extended from a product of disease possessing this susceptibility of multiplication when conveyed into the living body, to substances of inorganic origin, such as silex or sulphur, would be capable of arguing that a pebble may produce a mountain, because an acorn can become a forest.

As to the analogy to be found between the alleged action of the infinitely attenuated doses, and the effects of some odorous substances which possess the extraordinary power of diffusing their imponderable emanations through a very wide space, however it may be abused in argument, and rapidly as it evaporates on examination, it is not like that just mentioned, wholly without meaning. The fact of the vast diffusion of some odors, as that of musk or the rose, for instance, has long been cited as the most remarkable illustration of the divisibility of matter, and the nicety of the senses. And if this were compared with the effects of a very minute dose of morphia on the whole system, or the sudden and fatal impression of a single drop of prussic acid, or, with what comes still nearer, the poisonous influence of an atmosphere impregnated with invisible *malaria,* we should find in each of these examples an evidence of the degree to which nature, in some few instances, concentrates powerful qualities in minute or subtile forms of matter. But if a man comes to me with a pestle and mortar in his hand, and tells me that he will take a little speck of some substance which nobody ever thought to have any smell at all, as, for instance, a grain of chalk or of charcoal, and that he will, after an hour or two of rubbing and scraping, develop in a portion of it an odor which, if the whole grain were used, would be capable of pervading an apartment, a house, a village, a province, an empire, nay, the entire atmosphere of this broad planet upon which we tread; and that from each of fifty or sixty substances he can in this way develop a distinct and hitherto unknown odor; and if he tries to show that all this is rendered quite reasonable by the analogy of musk and roses, I shall certainly be justified in considering him incapable of reasoning, and beyond the reach of my argument. What if, instead of this, he professes to develop new and wonderful medicinal powers from the same speck of chalk or charcoal, in such proportions as would impregnate every pond, lake, river, sea, and ocean of our globe, and appeals to the same analogy in favor of the probability of his assertion.

All this may be true, notwithstanding these considerations. But so extraordinary would be the fact, that a single atom of substances which a child might swallow without harm by the teaspoonful could, by an easy mechanical process, be made to develop such inconceivable powers, that nothing but the strictest agreement of the most cautious experimenters, secured by every guaranty that they were honest and faithful, appealing to repeated experiments in public, with every precaution to guard against error, and with the most plain and peremptory results, should induce us to lend any credence to such pretensions.

The third doctrine, that *Psora,* the other name of which you remember, is the cause of the great majority of chronic diseases, is a startling one, to say the least. That an affection always recognized as a very unpleasant personal companion, but generally regarded as a mere temporary incommodity, readily yielding to treatment in those unfortunate enough to suffer from it, and hardly known among the better classes of society, should be all at once found out by a German physician to be the great scourge of mankind, the cause of their severest bodily and mental calamities, cancer and consumption, idiocy and madness, must excite our unqualified surprise. And when the originator of this singular truth ascribes, as in this page now open before me, the declining health of a disgraced courtier, the chronic malady of a bereaved mother, even the melancholy of the love-sick and slighted maiden, to nothing more nor less than the insignificant, unseemly, and almost unmentionable ITCH, does it not seem as if the very soil upon which we stand were dissolving into chaos, over the earthquake-heaving of discovery?

And when one man claims to have established these three independent truths, which are about as remote from each other as the discovery of the law of gravitation, the invention of printing, and that of the mariner's compass, unless the facts in their favor are overwhelming and unanimous, the question naturally arises, Is not this man deceiving himself, or trying to deceive others?

I proceed to examine the proofs of the leading ideas of Hahnemann and his school.

In order to show the axiom, *similia similibus curantur* (or like is cured by like), to be the basis of the healing art,—"the sole law of nature in therapeutics,"—it is necessary,—

1. That the symptoms produced by drugs in healthy persons should be faithfully studied and recorded.

2. That drugs should be shown to be always capable of curing those diseases most like their own symptoms.

3. That remedies should be shown *not* to cure diseases when they do not produce symptoms resembling those presented in these diseases.

1. The effects of drugs upon healthy persons have been studied by Hahnemann and his associates. Their results were made known in his Materia Medica, a work in three large volumes in the French translation, published about eight years ago. The mode of experimentation appears to have been, to take the substance on trial, either in common or minute doses, and then to set down every little sensation, every little movement of mind or body, which occurred within many succeeding hours or days, as being produced solely by the substance employed. When I have enumerated some of the symptoms attributed to the power of the drugs taken, you will be able to judge how much value is to be ascribed to the assertions of such observers.

The following list was taken literally from the Materia Medica of Hahnemann, by my friend M. Vernois, for whose accuracy I am willing to be responsible. He has given seven pages of these symptoms, not selected, but taken at hazard from the French translation of the work. I shall be very brief in my citations.

"After stooping some time, sense of painful weight about the head upon resuming the erect posture."

"An itching, tickling sensation at the outer edge of the palm of the left hand, which obliges the person to scratch." The medicine was acetate of lime, and as the action of the globule taken is said to last twenty-eight days, you may judge how many such symptoms as the last might be supposed to happen.

Among the symptoms attributed to muriatic acid are these: a catarrh, sighing, pimples; "after having written a long time with the back a little bent over, violent pain in the back and shoulder-blades, as if from a strain,"— "dreams which are not remembered,—disposition to mental dejection,—wakefulness before and after midnight."

I might extend this catalogue almost indefinitely. I have not cited these specimens with any view to exciting a sense of the ridiculous, which many others of those mentioned would not fail to do, but to show that the common accidents of sensation, the little bodily inconveniences to which all of us are subject, are seriously and systematically ascribed to whatever medicine may have been exhibited, even in the minute doses I have mentioned, whole days or weeks previously.

To these are added all the symptoms ever said by anybody, whether deserving confidence or not, as I shall hereafter illustrate, to be produced by the substance in question.

The effects of sixty-four medicinal substances, ascertained by one or both of these methods, are enumerated in the Materia Medica of Hahnemann, which may be considered as the basis of practical Homoeopathy. In the Manual of Jahr, which is the common guide, so far as I know, of those who practise Homoeopathy in these regions, two hundred remedies are enumerated, many of which, however, have never been employed in practice. In at least one edition there were no means of distinguishing those which had been tried upon the sick from the others. It is true that marks have been added in the edition employed here, which serve to distinguish them; but what are we to think of a standard *practical* author on Materia Medica, who at one time omits to designate the proper doses of his remedies, and at another to let us have any means of knowing whether a remedy has ever been tried or not, while he is recommending its employment in the most critical and threatening diseases?

I think that, from what I have shown of the character of Hahnemann's experiments, it would be a satisfaction to any candid inquirer to know whether other persons, to whose assertions he could look with confidence, confirm these pretended facts. Now there are many individuals, long and well known to the scientific world, who have tried these experiments upon healthy subjects, and utterly deny that their effects have at all corresponded to Hahnemann's assertions.

I will take, for instance, the statements of Andral (and I am not referring to his well-known public experiments in his hospital) as to the result of his own trials. This distinguished physician is Professor of Medicine in the School of Paris, and one of the most widely known and valued authors upon practical and theoretical subjects the profession can claim in any country. He is a man of great kindness of character, a most liberal eclectic by nature and habit, of unquestioned integrity, and is called, in the leading article of the first number of the "Homoeopathic Examiner," "an eminent and very enlightened allopathist." Assisted by a number of other persons in good health, he experimented on the effects of cinchona, aconite, sulphur, arnica, and the other most highly extolled remedies. His experiments lasted a year, and he stated publicly to the Academy of Medicine that they never produced the slightest appearance of the symptoms attributed to them. The results of a man like this, so extensively known as one of the most philosophical and candid, as well as brilliant of instructors, and whose admirable abilities and signal liberality are generally conceded, ought to be of great weight in deciding the question.

M. Double, a well-known medical writer and a physician of high standing in Paris, had occasion so long ago as 1801, before he had heard of Homoeopathy, to make experiments upon Cinchona, or Peruvian bark. He and several others took the drug in every kind of dose for four months, and the fever it is pretended by Hahnemann to excite never was produced.

M. Bonnet, President of the Royal Society of Medicine of Bordeaux, had occasion to observe many soldiers during the Peninsular War, who made use of Cinchona as a preservative against different diseases,—but he never found it to produce the pretended paroxysms.

If any objection were made to evidence of this kind, I would refer to the express experiments on many of the Homoeopathic substances, which were given to healthy persons with every precaution as to diet and regimen, by M. Louis Fleury, without being followed by the slightest of the pretended consequences. And let me mention as a curious fact, that the same quantity of arsenic given to one animal in the common form of the unprepared powder, and to another after having been rubbed up into six hundred globules, offered no particular difference of activity in the two cases. This is a strange contradiction to the doctrine of the development of what they call dynamic power, by means of friction and subdivision.

In 1835 a public challenge was offered to the best-known Homoeopathic physician in Paris to select any ten substances asserted to produce the most striking effects; to prepare them himself; to choose one by lot without knowing which of them he had taken, and try it upon himself or an intelligent and devoted Homoeopathist, and, waiting his own time, to come forward and tell what substance had been employed. The challenge was at first accepted, but the acceptance retracted before the time of trial arrived.

From all this I think it fair to conclude that the catalogues of symptoms attributed in Homoeopathic works to the influence of various drugs upon healthy persons are not entitled to any confidence.

2. It is necessary to show, in the next place, that medicinal substances are always capable of curing diseases most like their own symptoms. For facts relating to this question we must look to two sources; the recorded experience of the medical profession in general, and the results of trials made according to Homoeopathic principles, and capable of testing the truth of the doctrine.

No person, that I am aware of, has ever denied that in some cases there exists a resemblance between the effects of a remedy and the symptoms of diseases in which it is beneficial. This has been recognized, as Hahnemann himself has shown, from the time of Hippocrates. But according to the records of the Medical profession, as they have been hitherto interpreted, this is true of only a very small proportion of useful remedies. Nor has it ever been considered as an established truth that the efficacy of even these few remedies was in any definite ratio to their power of producing symptoms more or less like those they cured.

Such was the state of opinion when Hahnemann came forward with the proposition that all the cases of successful treatment found in the works of all preceding medical writers were to be ascribed solely to the operation of the Homoeopathic principle, which had effected the cure, although without the physician's knowledge that this was the real secret. And strange as it may seem, he was enabled to give such a degree of plausibility to this assertion, that any person not acquainted somewhat with medical literature, not quite familiar, I should rather say, with the relative value of medical evidence, according to the sources whence it is derived, would be almost frightened into the belief, at seeing the pages upon pages of Latin names he has summoned as his witnesses.

It has hitherto been customary, when examining the writings of authors of preceding ages, upon subjects as to which they were less enlightened than ourselves, and which they were very liable to misrepresent, to exercise some little discretion; to discriminate, in some measure, between writers deserving confidence and those not entitled to it. But there is not the least appearance of any such delicacy on the part of Hahnemann. A large majority of the names of old authors he cites are wholly unknown to science. With some of them I have been long acquainted, and I know that their accounts of diseases are no more to be trusted than their contemporary Ambroise Paré's stories of mermen, and similar absurdities. But if my judgment is rejected, as being a prejudiced one, I can refer to Cullen, who mentioned three of Hahnemann's authors in one sentence, as being "not necessarily bad authorities; but certainly such when they delivered very improbable events;" and as this was said more than half a century ago, it could not have had any reference to Hahnemann. But although not the slightest sign of discrimination is visible in his quotations,—although for him a handful of chaff from Schenck is all the same thing as a measure of wheat from Morgagni,—there is a formidable display of authorities, and an abundant proof of ingenious researches to be found in each of the great works of Hahnemann with which I am familiar.

It is stated by Dr. Leo-Wolf, that Professor Joerg, of Leipsic, has proved many of Hahnemann's quotations from old authors to be adulterate and false. What particular instances he has pointed out I have no means of learning. And it is probably wholly impossible on this side of the Atlantic, and even in most of the public libraries of Europe, to find anything more than a small fraction of the innumerable obscure publications which the neglect of grocers and trunk-makers has spared to be ransacked by the all-devouring genius of Homoeo-pathy. I have endeavored to verify such passages as my own library afforded me the means of doing. For some I have looked in vain, for want, as I am willing to believe, of more exact references. But this I am able to affirm, that, out of the very small number which I have been able to trace back to their original authors, I have found two to be wrongly quoted, one of them being a gross misrepresentation.

The first is from the ancient Roman author, Caelius Aurelianus; the second from the venerable folio of Forestus. Hahnemann uses the following expres-sions,—if he is not misrepresented in the English Translation of the "Organon": "Asclepiades on one occasion cured an inflammation of the brain by adminis-tering a small quantity of wine." After correcting the erroneous reference of the Translator, I can find no such case alluded to in the chapter. But Caelius Aurelianus mentions two modes of treatment employed by Asclepiades, into both of which the use of wine entered, as being in the highest degree irrational and dangerous.[5]

In speaking of the oil of anise-seed, Hahnemann says that Forestus observed violent colic caused by its administration. But, as the author tells the story, a young man took, by the counsel of a surgeon, an acrid and virulent medicine, the name of which is not given, which brought on a most cruel fit of the gripes and colic. After this another surgeon was called, who gave him oil of anise-seed and wine, which increased his suffering.[6] Now if this was the Homoeopathic remedy, as Hahnemann pretends, it might be a fair question why the young man was not cured by it. But it is a much graver question why a man who has shrewdness and learning enough to go so far after his facts, should think it right to treat them with such astonishing negligence or such artful unfairness.

Even if every word he had pretended to take from his old authorities were to be found in them, even if the authority of every one of these authors were beyond question, the looseness with which they are used to prove whatever Hahnemann chooses is beyond the bounds of credibility. Let me give one instance to illustrate the character of this man's mind. Hahnemann asserts, in a note annexed to the 110th paragraph of the "Organon," that the smell of the rose will cause certain persons to faint. And he says in the text that substances which produce peculiar effects of this nature on particular constitutions cure the same symptoms in people in general. Then in another note to the same paragraph he quotes the following fact from one of the last sources one would have looked to for medical information, the Byzantine Historians.

"It was by these means" (*i.e.* Homoeopathically) "that the Princess Eudosia with rose-water restored a person who had fainted!"

Is it possible that a man who is guilty of such pedantic folly as this,—a man who can see a confirmation of his doctrine in such a recovery as this,—a recovery which is happening every day, from a breath of air, a drop or two of water, untying a bonnet-string, loosening a stay-lace, and which can hardly help happening, whatever is done,—is it possible that a man, of whose pages, not here and there one, but hundreds upon hundreds are loaded with such trivialities, is the Newton, the Columbus, the Harvey of the nineteenth century!

The whole process of demonstration he employs is this. An experiment is instituted with some drug upon one or more healthy persons. Everything that happens for a number of days or weeks is, as we have seen, set down as an effect of the medicine. Old volumes are then ransacked promiscuously, and every morbid sensation or change that anybody ever said was produced by the drug in question is added to the list of symptoms. By one or both of these methods, each of the sixty-four substances enumerated by Hahnemann is shown to produce a very large number of symptoms, the lowest in his scale being ninety-seven, and the highest fourteen hundred and ninety-one. And having made out this list respecting any drug, a catalogue which, as you may observe in any Homoeopathic manual, contains various symptoms belonging to every organ of the body, what can be easier than to find alleged cures in every medical author which can at once be attributed to the Homoeopathic principle; still more if the grave of extinguished credulity is called upon to give up its dead bones as living witnesses; and worst of all, if the monuments of the past are to be mutilated in favor of "the sole law of Nature in therapeutics"?

There are a few familiar facts of which great use has been made as an entering wedge for the Homoeopathic doctrine. They have been suffered to pass current so long that it is time they should be nailed to the counter, a little operation which I undertake, with perfect cheerfulness, to perform for them.

The first is a supposed illustration of the Homoeopathic law found in the precept given for the treatment of parts which have been frozen, by friction with snow or similar means. But we deceive ourselves by names, if we suppose the frozen part to be treated by cold, and not by heat. The snow may even be actually *warmer* than the part to which it is applied. But even if it were at the same temperature when applied, it never did and never could do the least good to a frozen part, except as a mode of regulating the application of what? of *heat.* But the heat must be applied *gradually,* just as food must be given a little at a time to those perishing with hunger. If the patient were brought into a warm room, heat would be applied *very rapidly,* were not something interposed to prevent this, and allow its gradual admission. Snow or iced water is exactly what is wanted; it is not cold to the part; it is very possibly warm, on the contrary, for these terms are relative, and if it does not melt and let the heat in, or is not taken away, the part will remain frozen up until doomsday. Now the treatment of a frozen limb by heat, in large or small quantities, is not Homoeopathy.

The next supposed illustration of the Homoeopathic law is the alleged successful management of burns, by holding them to the fire. This is a popular mode of treating those burns which are of too little consequence to require any more efficacious remedy, and would inevitably get well of themselves, without any trouble being bestowed upon them. It produces a most acute pain in the part, which is followed by some loss of sensibility, as happens with the eye after exposure to strong light, and the ear after being subjected to very intense sounds. This is all it is capable of doing, and all further notions of its efficacy must be attributed merely to the vulgar love of paradox. If this example affords any comfort to the Homoeopathist, it seems as cruel to deprive him of it as it would be to convince the mistress of the smoke-jack or the flat-iron that the fire does not literally "draw the fire out," which is her hypothesis.

But if it were true that frost-bites were cured by cold and burns by heat, it would be subversive, so far as it went, of the great principle of Homoeopathy. For you will remember that this principle is that *Like* cures *Like,* and not that *Same* cures *Same;* that there is *resemblance* and not *identity* between the symptoms of the disease and those produced by the drug which cures it, and none have been readier to insist upon this distinction than the Homoeopathists themselves. For if *Same* cures *Same,* then every poison must be its own antidote,—which is neither a part of their theory nor their so-called experience. They have been asked often enough, why it was that arsenic could not cure the mischief which arsenic had caused, and why the infectious cause of small-pox did not remedy the disease it had produced, and then they were ready enough to see the distinction I have pointed out. O no! it was not the hair of the same dog, but only of one very much like him!

A third instance in proof of the Homoeopathic law is sought for in the acknowledged efficacy of vaccination. And how does the law apply to this? It is granted by the advocates of Homoeopathy that there is a resemblance between the effects of the vaccine virus on a person in health and the symptoms of small-pox. Therefore, according to the rule, the vaccine virus will cure the small-pox, which, as everybody knows, is entirely untrue. But it prevents small-pox, say the Homoeopathists. Yes, and so does small-pox prevent itself from ever happening again, and we know just as much of the principle involved in the one case as in the other. For this is only one of a series of facts which we are wholly unable to explain. Small-pox, measles, scarlet-fever, hooping-cough, protect those who have them once from future attacks; but nettle-rash and catarrh and lung fever, each of which is just as Homoeopathic to itself as any one of the others, have no such preservative power. We are obliged to accept the fact, unexplained, and we can do no more for vaccination than for the rest.

I come now to the most directly practical point connected with the subject, namely,—

What is the state of the evidence as to the efficacy of the proper Homoeopathic treatment in the cure of diseases.

As the treatment adopted by the Homoeopathists has been almost universally by means of the infinitesimal doses, the question of their efficacy is thrown open, in common with that of the truth of their fundamental axiom, as both are tested in practice.

We must look for facts as to the actual working of Homoeopathy to three sources.

1. The statements of the unprofessional public.

2. The assertions of Homoeopathic practitioners.

3. The results of trials by competent and honest physicians, not pledged to the system.

I think, after what we have seen of medical facts, as they are represented by incompetent persons, we are disposed to attribute little value to all statements of wonderful cures, coming from those who have never been accustomed to watch the caprices of disease, and have not cooled down their young enthusiasm by the habit of tranquil observation. Those who know nothing of the natural progress of a malady, of its ordinary duration, of its various modes of terminating, of its liability to accidental complications, of the signs which mark its insignificance or severity, of what is to be expected of it when left to itself, of how much or how little is to be anticipated from remedies, those who know nothing or next to nothing of all these things, and who are in a great state of excitement from benevolence, sympathy, or zeal for a new medical discovery, can hardly be expected to be sound judges of facts which have misled so many sagacious men, who have spent their lives in the daily study and observation of them. I believe that, after having drawn the portrait of defunct Perkinism, with its five thousand printed cures, and its million and a half computed ones, its miracles blazoned about through America, Denmark, and England; after relating that forty years ago women carried the Tractors about in their pockets, and workmen could not make them fast enough for the public demand; and then showing you, as a curiosity, a single one of these instruments, an odd òne of a pair, which I obtained only by a lucky accident, so utterly lost is the memory of all their wonderful achievements; I believe, after all this, I need not waste time in showing that medical accuracy is not to be looked for in the florid reports of benevolent associations, the assertions of illustrious patrons, the lax effusions of daily journals, or the effervescent gossip of the tea-table.

Dr. Hering, whose name is somewhat familiar to the champions of Homoeopathy, has said that "the new healing art is not to be judged by its success in isolated cases only, but according to its success in general, its innate truth, and the incontrovertible nature of its innate principles."

We have seen something of "the incontrovertible nature of its innate principles," and it seems probable, on the whole, that its success in general must be made up of its success in isolated cases. Some attempts have been made, however, to finish the whole matter by sweeping statistical documents, which are intended to prove its triumphant success over the common practice.

It is well known to those who have had the good fortune to see the "Homoeopathic Examiner," that this journal led off, in its first number, with a grand display of everything the newly imported doctrine had to show for itself. It is well remarked, on the *twenty-third page* of this article, that "the comparison of bills of mortality among an equal number of sick, treated by divers methods, is a most poor and lame way to get at conclusions touching principles of the healing art." In confirmation of which, the author proceeds upon the *twenty-fifth page* to prove the superiority of the Homoeopathic treatment of cholera, by precisely these very bills of mortality. Now, every intelligent physician is aware that the poison of cholera differed so much in its activity at different times and places, that it was next to impossible to form any opinion as to the results of treatment, unless every precaution was taken to secure the most perfectly corresponding conditions in the patients treated, and hardly even then. Of course, then, a Russian Admiral, by the name of Mordvinow, backed by a number of so-called physicians practising in Russian villages, is singularly competent to the task of settling the whole question of the utility of this or that kind of treatment; to prove that, if not more than eight and a half per cent of those attacked with the disease perished, the rest owed their immunity to Hahnemann. I can remember when more than a hundred patients in a public institution were attacked with what, I doubt not, many Homoeopathic physicians (to say nothing of Homoeopathic admirals) would have called cholera, and *not one* of them died, though treated in the common way, and it is my firm belief that, if such a result had followed the administration of the omnipotent globules, it would have been in the mouth of every adept in Europe, from Quin of London to Spohr of Gandersheim. No longer ago than yesterday, in one of the most widely circulated papers of this city, there was published an assertion that the mortality in several Homoeopathic Hospitals was not quite five in a hundred, whereas, in what are called by the writer Allopathic Hospitals, it is said to be eleven in a hundred. An honest man should be ashamed of such an *argumentum ad ignorantiam*. The mortality of a hospital depends not merely on the treatment of the patients, but on the class of diseases it is in the habit of receiving, on the place where it is, on the season, and many other circumstances. For instance, there are many hospitals in the great cities of Europe that receive few diseases of a nature to endanger life, and, on the other hand, there are others where dangerous diseases are accumulated out of the common proportion. Thus, in the wards of Louis, at the Hospital of La Pitiè, a vast number of patients in the last stages of consumption were constantly entering, to swell the mortality of that hospital. It was because he was known to pay particular attention to the diseases of the chest that patients laboring under those fatal affections to an incurable extent were so constantly coming in upon him. It is always a miserable appeal to the thoughtlessness of the vulgar, to allege the naked fact of the less comparative mortality in the practice of one hospital or of one physician than another, as an evidence of the superiority of their treatment. Other things being equal, it must always be expected that those institutions and individuals enjoying to the highest degree the confidence of the community will lose the largest proportion of their patients; for the simple reason that they will naturally be looked to by those suffering from the gravest class of diseases; that many, who know that they are affected with mortal disease, will choose to die under their care or shelter, while the subjects of trifling maladies, and merely troublesome symptoms, amuse themselves to any extent among the fancy practitioners. When, therefore, Dr. Muhlenbein, as stated in the "Homoeopathic Examiner," and quoted in yesterday's "Daily Advertiser," asserts that the mortality among his patients is only one per cent since he has practised Homoeopathy, whereas it was six per cent when he employed the common mode of practice, I am convinced by this, his own statement, that the citizens of Brunswick, whenever they are *seriously* sick, take good care not to send for Dr. Muhlenbein!

It is evidently impossible that I should attempt, within the compass of a single lecture, any detailed examination of the very numerous cases reported in the Homoeopathic Treatises and Journals. Having been in the habit of receiving the French "Archives of Homoeopathic Medicine" until the premature decease of that Journal, I have had the opportunity of becoming acquainted somewhat with the style of these documents, and experiencing whatever degree of conviction they were calculated to produce. Although of course I do not wish any value to be assumed for my opinion, such as it is, I consider that you are entitled to hear it. So far, then, as I am acquainted with the general character of the cases reported by the Homoeopathic physicians, they would for the most part be considered as wholly undeserving a place in any English, French, or America periodical of high standing if, instead of favoring the doctrine they were intended to support, they were brought forward to prove the efficacy of any common remedy administered by any common practitioner. There are occasional exceptions to this remark; but the general truth of it is rendered probable by the fact that these cases are always, or almost always, written with the single object of showing the efficacy of the medicine used, or the skill of the practitioner, and it is recognized as a general rule that such cases deserve very little confidence. Yet they may sound well enough, one at a time, to those who are not fully aware of the fallacies of medical evidence. Let me state a case in illustration. Nobody doubts that *some* patients recover under every form of practice. Probably all are willing to allow that a large majority, for instance, ninety in a hundred, of such cases as a physician is called to in daily practice, would recover, sooner or later, with more or less difficulty, provided nothing were done to interfere seriously with the efforts of nature.

Suppose, then, a physician who has a hundred patients prescribes to each of them pills made of some entirely inert substance, as starch, for instance. Ninety of them get well, or if he chooses to use such language, he cures ninety of them. It is evident, according to the doctrine of chances, that there must be a considerable number of coincidences between the relief of the patient and the administration of the remedy. It is altogether probable that there will happen two or three *very striking* coincidences out of the whole ninety cases, in which it would seem evident that the medicine produced the relief, though it had, as we assumed, nothing to do with it. Now suppose that the physician publishes these cases, will they not have a plausible appearance of proving that which, as we granted at the outset, was entirely false? Suppose that instead of pills of starch he employs microscopic sugarplums, with the five million billion trillionth part of a suspicion of aconite or pulsatilla, and then publishes his successful cases, through the leaden lips of the press, or the living ones of his female acquaintances,—does that make the impression a less erroneous one? But so it is that in Homoeopathic works and journals and gossip one can never, or next to never, find anything but successful cases, which might do very well as a proof of superior skill, did it not prove as much for the swindling advertisers whose certificates disgrace so many of our newspapers. How long will it take mankind to learn that while they listen to "the speaking hundreds and units, who make the world ring" with the pretended triumphs they have witnessed, the "dumb millions" of deluded and injured victims are paying the daily forfeit of their misplaced confidence!

I am sorry to see, also, that a degree of ignorance as to the natural course of diseases is often shown in these published cases, which, although it may not be detected by the unprofessional reader, conveys an unpleasant impression to those who are acquainted with the subject. Thus a young woman affected with *jaundice* is mentioned in the German "Annals of Clinical Homoeopathy" as having been cured in twenty-nine days by pulsatilla and nux vomica. Rummel, a well-known writer of the same school, speaks of curing a case of jaundice in thirty-four days by Homoeopathic doses of pulsatilla, aconite, and cinchona. I happened to have a case in my own household, a few weeks since, which lasted about ten days, and this was longer than I have repeatedly seen it in hospital practice, so that it was nothing to boast of.

Dr. Munneche of Lichtenburg in Saxony is called to a patient with a sprained ankle who had been a fortnight under the common treatment. The patient gets well by the use of arnica in a little more than a month longer, and this extraordinary fact is published in the French "Archives of Homoeopathic Medicine."

In the same journal is recorded the case of a patient who with nothing more, so far as any proof goes, than *influenza,* gets down to her shop upon the sixth day.

And again, the cool way in which everything favorable in a case is set down by these people entirely to their treatment, may be seen in a case of croup reported in the "Homoeopathic Gazette" of Leipsic, in which leeches, blistering, inhalation of hot vapor, and powerful internal medicine had been employed, and yet the merit was all attributed to one drop of some Homoeopathic fluid.

I need not multiply these quotations, which illustrate the grounds of an opinion which the time does not allow me to justify more at length; other such cases are lying open before me; there is no end to them if more were wanted; for nothing is necessary but to look into any of the numerous broken-down Journals of Homoeopathy, the volumes of which may be found on the shelves of those curious in such matters.

A number of public trials of Homoeopathy have been made in different parts of the world. Six of these are mentioned in the Manifesto of the "Homoeopathic Examiner." Now to suppose that any trial can absolutely *silence* people, would be to forget the whole experience of the past. Dr. Haygarth and Dr. Alderson could not stop the sale of the five-guinea Tractors, although they proved that they could work the same miracles with pieces of wood and tobacco-pipe. It takes time for truth to operate as well as Homoeopathic globules. Many persons thought the results of these trials were decisive enough of the nullity of the treatment; those who wish to see the kind of special pleading and evasion by which it is attempted to cover results which, stated by the "Homoeopathic Examiner" itself, look exceedingly like a miserable failure, may consult the opening flourish of that Journal. I had not the intention to speak of these public trials at all, having abundant other evidence on the point. But I think it best, on the whole, to mention two of them in a few words,—that instituted at Naples and that of Andral.

There have been few names in the medical profession, for the last half century, so widely known throughout the world of science as that of M. Esquirol, whose life was devoted to the treatment of insanity, and who was without a rival in that department of practical medicine. It is from an analysis communicated by him to the "Gazette Médicale de Paris" that I derive my acquaintance with the account of the trial at Naples by Dr. Panvini, physician to the Hospital della Pace. This account seems to be entirely deserving of credit. Ten patients were set apart, and not allowed to take any medicine at all,—much against the wish of the Homoeopathic physician. All of them got well, and of course all of them would have been claimed as triumphs if they had been submitted to the treatment. Six other slight cases (each of which is specified) got well under the Homoeopathic treatment,—none of its asserted specific effects being manifested. All the rest were cases of grave disease; and so far as the trial, which was interrupted about the fortieth day, extended, the patients grew worse, or received no benefit. A case is reported on the page before me of a soldier affected with acute inflammation in the chest, who took successively aconite, bryonia, nux vomica, and pulsatilla, and after *thirty-eight days* of treatment remained without any important change in his disease. The Homoeopathic physician who treated these patients was M. de Horatiis, who had the previous year been announcing his wonderful cures. And M. Esquirol asserted to the Academy of Medicine in 1835, that this M. de Horatiis, who is one of the prominent personages in the "Examiner's" Manifesto published in 1840, had subsequently renounced Homoeopathy. I may remark, by the way, that this same periodical, which is so very easy in explaining away the results of these trials, makes a mistake of only six years or a little more as to the time when this at Naples was instituted.

M. Andral, the "eminent and very enlightened allopathist" of the "Homoeopathic Examiner," made the following statement in March, 1835, to the Academy of Medicine: "I have submitted this doctrine to experiment; I can reckon at this time from one hundred and thirty to one hundred and forty cases, recorded with perfect fairness, in a great hospital, under the eye of numerous witnesses; to avoid every objection I obtained my remedies of M. Guibourt, who keeps a Homoeopathic pharmacy, and whose strict exactness is well known; the regimen has been scrupulously observed, and I obtained from the sisters attached to the hospital a special regimen, such as Hahnemann orders. I was told, however, some months since, that I had not been faithful to all the rules of the doctrine. I therefore took the trouble to begin again; I have studied the practice of the Parisian Homoeopathists, as I had studied their books, and I became convinced that they treated their patients as I had treated mine, and I affirm that I have been as rigorously exact in the treatment as any other person."

And he expressly asserts the entire nullity of the influence of all the Homoeopathic remedies tried by him in modifying, so far as he could observe, the progress or termination of diseases. It deserves notice that he experimented with the most boasted substances,—cinchona, aconite, mercury, bryonia, belladonna. Aconite, for instance, he says he administered in more than forty cases of that collection of feverish symptoms in which it exerts so much power, according to Hahnemann, and in not one of them did it have the slightest influence, the pulse and heat remaining as before.

These statements look pretty honest, and would seem hard to be explained away, but it is calmly said that he "did not know enough of the method to select the remedies with any tolerable precision."[7] Who are they that practice Homoeopathy, and say this of a man with the Materia Medica of Hahnemann lying before him? Who are they that send these same globules, on which he experimented, accompanied by a little book, into families, whose members are thought competent to employ them, when they deny any such capacity to a man whose life has been passed at the bedside of patients, the most prominent teacher in the first Medical Faculty in the world, the consulting physician of the King of France, and one of the most renowned practical writers, not merely of his nation, but of his age? I leave the quibbles by which such persons would try to creep out from under the crushing weight of these conclusions to the unfortunates who suppose that a *reply* is equivalent to an *answer.*

Dr. Baillie, one of the physicians in the great Hôtel Dieu of Paris, invited two Homoeopathic practitioners to experiment in his wards. One of these was *Curie,* now of London, whose works are on the counters of some of our bookstores, and probably in the hands of some of my audience. This gentleman, whom Dr. Baillie declares to be an enlightened man, and perfectly sincere in his convictions, brought his own medicines from the pharmacy which furnished Hahnemann himself, and employed them for four or five months upon patients in his ward, and with results equally unsatisfactory, as appears from Dr. Baillie's statement at a meeting of the Academy of Medicine. And a similar experiment was permitted by the Clinical Professor of the Hôtel Dieu of Lyons, with the same complete failure.

But these are old and prejudiced practitioners. Very well, then take the statement of Dr. Fleury, a most intelligent young physician, who treated homoeopathically more than fifty patients, suffering from diseases which it was not dangerous to treat in this way, taking every kind of precaution as to regimen, removal of disturbing influences, and the state of the atmosphere, insisted upon by the most vigorous partisans of the doctrine, and found not the slightest effect produced by the medicines. And more than this, read nine of these cases, which he has published, as I have just done, and observe the absolute nullity of aconite, belladonna, and bryonia, against the symptoms over which they are pretended to exert such palpable, such obvious, such astonishing influences. In the view of these statements, it is impossible not to realize the entire futility of attempting to silence this asserted science by the flattest and most peremptory results of experiment. Were all the hospital physicians of Europe and America to devote themselves, for the requisite period, to this sole pursuit, and were their results to be unanimous as to the total worthlessness of the whole system in practice, this slippery delusion would slide through their fingers without the slightest discomposure, when, as they supposed, they had crushed every joint in its tortuous and trailing body.

3. I have said, that to show the truth of the Homoeopathic doctrine, as announced by Hahnemann, it would be necessary to show, in the third place, that remedies never cure diseases when they are not capable of producing similar symptoms. The burden of this somewhat comprehensive demonstration lying entirely upon the advocates of this doctrine, it may be left to their mature reflections.

It entered into my original plan to treat of the doctrine relating to *Psora,* or itch,—an almost insane conception, which I am glad to get rid of, for this is a subject one does not care to *handle without gloves.* I am saved this trouble, however, by finding that many of the disciples of Hahnemann, those disciples the very gospel of whose faith stands upon his word, make very light of his authority on this point, although he himself says, "It has cost me twelve years of study and research to trace out the source of this incredible number of chronic affections, to discover this great truth, which remained concealed from all my predecessors and contemporaries, to establish the basis of its demonstration, and find out, at the same time, the curative medicines that were fit to combat this hydra in all its different forms."

But, in the face of all this, the following remarks are made by Wolff, of Dresden, whose essays, according to the editor of the "Homoeopathic Examiner," "represent the opinions of a large majority of Homoeopathists in Europe."

"It cannot be unknown to any one at all familiar with Homoeopathic literature, that Hahnemann's idea of tracing the large majority of chronic diseases to actual itch has met with the greatest opposition from Homoeopathic physicians themselves." And again, "If the Psoric theory has led to no proper schism, the reason is to be found in the fact that it is almost without any influence in practice."

We are told by Jahr, that Dr. Griesselich, "Surgeon to the Grand Duke of Baden," and a "distinguished" Homoeopathist, actually asked Hahnemann for the *proof* that chronic diseases, such as dropsy, for instance, never arise from any other cause than itch; and that, according to common report, the venerable sage was highly incensed *(forct courroucé)* with Dr. Hartmann, of Leipsic, another "distinguished" Homoeopathist, for maintaining that they certainly did arise from other causes.

And Dr. Fielitz, in the "Homoeopathic Gazette" of Leipsic, after saying, in a good-natured way, that Psora is the Devil in medicine, and that physicians are divided on this point into diabolists and exorcists, declares that, according to a remark of Hahnemann, the whole civilized world is affected with Psora. I must therefore disappoint any advocate of Hahnemann who may honor me with his presence, by not attacking a doctrine on which some of the disciples of his creed would be very happy to have its adversaries waste their time and strength. I will not meddle with this excrescence, which, though often used in time of peace, would be dropped, like the limb of a shell-fish, the moment it was assailed; time is too precious, and the harvest of living extravagances nods too heavily to my sickle, that I should blunt it upon straw and stubble.

NOTES

1. Hahnemann died in 1843.
2. The degrees of DILUTION must not be confounded with those of POTENCY. Their relations may be seen by this table:—

1st dilution,—One hundredth of a drop or grain.
2d   "   One ten thousandth.
3d   "   One millionth,—marked $\overline{\text{I}}$.
4th   "   One hundred millionth.
5th   "   One ten thousand millionth.
6th   "   One millionth millionth, or one billionth,—marked $\overline{\text{II}}$.
7th   "   One hundred billionth.
8th   "   One ten thousand billionth.
9th   "   One million billionth, or one trillionth,—marked $\overline{\text{III}}$.
10th   "   One hundred trillionth.
11th   "   One ten thousand trillionth.
12th   "   One million trillionth, or one quadrillionth,—marked $\overline{\text{IV}}$.,—and so on indefinitedly.

The large figures denote the degrees of POTENCY.

3. Those who will take the trouble to look over Hull's Translation of Jahr's Manual may observe how little comparative space is given to remedies resting upon any other authority than that of Hahnemann.

4. In the French edition of 1834, the proper doses of the medicines are mentioned, and Camomile is marked IV. Why are the doses omitted in Hull's Translation, except in three instances out of the whole two hundred remedies, notwithstanding the promise in the preface that "some remarks upon the *doses used* may be found at the head of each medicine"? Possibly because it makes no difference whether they are employed in one Homoeopathic dose or another; but then it is very singular that such precise directions were formerly given in the same work, and that Hahnemann's "experience" should have led him to draw the nice distinctions we have seen in a former part of this Lecture (p. 227).

5. *Caelius Aurel. De Morb. Acut. et Chron.* lib. I. cap. xv, *not* xvi. Amsterdam. Wetstein, 1755.

6. *Observ. et Curat. Med.* lib. XXI. obs. xiii. Frankfort, 1614.

7. *Homoeopathic Examiner*, vol. i. p. 22.

"Nothing is left to the caprice of the physician. ('In a word, instead of being dependent upon blind chance, that there is an infallible law, guided by which the physician MUST select the proper remedies.')" *Ibid.,* in a notice of Menzel's paper.

Edward Erwin, Ph.D.

Holistic Psychotherapies: What Works?

I

The therapies to be discussed include: Reichian therapy, Bioenergetics, the Alexander technique, Rolfing, and dream therapy. Before discussing their theoretical foundations, two prior questions should be asked: Are these techniques forms of psychotherapy and are they holistic?

The term *psychotherapy* is sometimes used in a relatively narrow sense to apply only to those verbal or insight therapies that developed out of psychoanalysis, but in recent years the term has been used more broadly to include any kind of *psychological* therapy (including behavior therapy). In this broader sense, dream therapy, Reichian therapy, and Bioenergetics clearly qualify as psychotherapies, although the latter two also include body massage. For that reason, they are sometimes referred to as the "new body psychotherapies," [1] or more simply as "body therapies."[2] Rolfing and the Alexander technique are also included in the category of *body therapy,* but because they lack a psychological component they probably should not be classified as "psychotherapy," unless the use of the term is extended further to include any nondrug, nonsurgical treatment for psychological problems.

A second question is: Are these therapies "holistic"? Some writers use this term for therapies that treat "the whole person," i.e., those that combine psychological treatment with body massage. However, it is then unclear why dream therapy should count as a holistic therapy. Moore and Moore address this point in the following way: "While dream therapy does not provide any physical treatment per se, holistic dream therapists emphasize the interrelationshp of spirit, mind, and body."[3] This characteristic, however, does not distinguish dream therapists from those cognitive therapists or psychoanalysts who also emphasize the same interrelationship. The same authors do note some other relevant characteristics, including the following: Dream therapy "validates" the concept that individuals create disease and well-being; it is an ancient form of

245

therapy; it is similar to meditation and visualization; and its use assumes that each person is composed of multiple personalities created by his dreams and expressed in all of the characters in his dreams.[4] I think that there are problems in appealing to these additional characteristics in explaining why dream therapy and the other therapies mentioned earlier should all be grouped together, but I will not pursue the point here. I will simply note that these therapies form a heterogeneous class: It may not be useful to classify all of them as "holistic" or as "psychotherapies." In referring to them as *holistic psychotherapies,* I am following, but not endorsing, the practice of others who write about these techniques.

Reichian Therapy

Reichian therapy is the progenitor of some of the other body therapies; it is also based on an elaborate and interesting theory. For these reasons, I will discuss it first and in more detail.

The developer of Reichian therapy, Wilhelm Reich, began his career as a Freudian analyst. Although he later disagreed with Freud, and was dropped from the Vienna Psychoanalytic Society, many of his early clinical ideas were developed within a psychoanalytic framework. As Reich himself reconstructs his thought, one of the key questions he tried to answer was: Is the Freudian theory of the etiology of neurosis complete?[5] As Reich points out, Freud drew a sharp distinction between actual neuroses and psychoneuroses. The former were thought to be caused by *contemporary* disturbances in a person's sexual life. Their cure was to be found, not in psychoanalysis, but in elimination of the detrimental sexual activity. The psychoneuroses, including hysteria and compulsion neurosis, also had a sexual etiology, but the precipitating events occurred in the patient's childhood. The treatment of choice for such problems was, of course, psychoanalysis.

A second question of interest to Reich was this: Could an organic basis be found for the neuroses? Psychoanalysis provided a purely psychological explanation of neurotic symptoms and a psychological method of treatment, but Freud warned his fellow analysts, according to Reich,[6] that eventually psychoanalysis would have to be established on an organic basis.

A third question was related to the second: Is psychoanalytic theory part of the natural sciences? Karl Jaspers, in anticipating the conclusions of Jurgen Habermas, Paul Ricoeur, and some contemporary analysts, argued that the answer to this question is no. Quantitative measurement is essential to the natural sciences, but missing from psychoanalysis: Analysts do not measure; they merely provide interpretations of psychic phenomena.

As will be seen shortly, Reich found an answer to all three of the aforementioned questions in his theory of the orgasm, which he initially formulated to account for certain facts found in his practice of psychoanalysis. Of the hundreds of cases in which he either observed or treated patients, he claims there was not a single woman who did not have a vaginal orgastic disturbance.[7] In roughly sixty to seventy percent of the male patients, there were also gross genital disturbances: The patients were either incapable of having an erection or suffered from premature ejaculation.

Reich then reached two important conclusions: (1) The severity of every form of psychic illness is directly related to the severity of the genital disturbance; and (2) the prospects of cure and the success of the cure are directly dependent upon the possibility of establishing the capacity for full genital gratification.[8]

Reich also concluded that a genital disturbance constituted the *energy* source of neurotic symptoms. Neurosis has an organic basis; it is caused by inadequately disposed of—i.e., unsatisfied—sexual excitation.[9] If this is correct, however, there cannot be, Reich reasoned, even a single case of neurosis with undisturbed genitality.[10] Yet, when he read a paper discussing his new ideas to the Vienna Psychoanalytic Society, two fellow analysts replied that they knew any number of female patients (presumably neurotics) who had a completely healthy genital life. In addition, Reich had to concede that even among his own patients approximately thirty to forty percent of the males had no apparent genital disturbance. The known clinical facts did not fit the orgasm theory, at least as it was initially formulated. Reich's solution to his problem was to revise his theory by redefining the idea of "orgastic impotence." He points out that the standard criteria for impotence, lack of either erective or ejaculative potency, make no reference to what he terms "functional, economic and experiential components." To make room for these elements, Reich stipulates that "orgastic potency" be defined as follows: "Orgastic potency is the capacity to surrender to the streaming of biological energy, free of any inhibitions; the capacity to discharge completely the dammed-up sexual excitation through involuntary, pleasurable convulsions of the body."[11] When "orgastic potency" is defined in this way, the apparent counterexamples to his theory vanish: He finds not a single case of a neurotic, male or female, who is orgastically potent.

Given the technical character of his definition, how can we tell when a patient becomes orgastically potent? Reich lists ten criteria, although he adds that these criteria are incomplete.[12] Reich's description of his criteria is rather complex; it will suffice here merely to summarize most of them.[13] In the voluntary phase of an orgastically gratifying sexual act, erection is pleasurable and not painful. The female genital becomes hyperemic and moist in a specific way through the profuse secretion of the genital glands. The man and woman are tender toward each other and there are no contradictory impulses. The man's urge to penetrate deeply increases, but does not take on the sadistic form of "wanting to pierce through," as in the case of compulsion neurotic characters. In the involuntary phase, the increase of the excitation can no longer be controlled and the physical excitation becomes more and more concentrated in the genital area. Later, excitation mounts rapidly and sharply to climax. Consciousness becomes more or less clouded, and the orgastic excitation takes hold of the entire body.

The key ideas of Reich's orgasm theory are that all neuroses develop because of a genital disturbance (i.e., the absence of orgastic potency), caused in turn by dammed up sexual energy, and that the elmination of the genital disturbance is the most important goal of therapy. These ideas take Reich beyond Freudian theory, but he originally saw them as important *additions* to Freud's views. He agrees with Freud that the primary prerequisite of therapy is to make the patient conscious of his or her repressed sexual impulses, but he points out that this may or may not result in a cure. What is crucial is whether the lifting of the repression also eliminates the energy source of the neurosis, the sexual stasis, and thereby eliminates the genital disturbance. By a sexual *stasis,* Reich means the damming up of sexual energy. So, if whatever is causing the sexual stasis is not removed, the mere lifting of repressions will not produce a cure.

Reich also goes beyond Freudian theory in hypothesizing a particular organic cause of neurosis, the damming up of sexual energy. However, this idea, too, is fitted into a Freudian framework. Reich agrees with Freud that conflicts develop during the oedipal period. The central conflict is the sexual relationship between child and parent. Such a conflict causes a slight disturbance in the balance of sexual energy, which in turn intensifies the conflict. Thus, the psychic conflict and the stasis (the damming up of somatic excitation) mutually augment one another. Whether the oedipus conflict becomes pathological or not depends upon the degree to which the sexual energy is discharged.

In sum, Reich's orgasm theory provides answers to (at least) three questions of importance to him. Is the Freudian theory of the etiology of neurosis incomplete? Reich answers in the affirmative. What Freud thought of as distinct kinds of neurosis, actual neurosis and psychoneurosis, overlap: *All* neuroses are caused by a disturbance of the capacity for orgastic gratification. Can an organic basis for the neuroses be found? Yes, the damming up of physical, sexual energy is the cause of the incapacity for orgastic gratification. Is psychoanalytic theory (or, the theory that supplants it) part of the natural sciences? Again, yes. The quantitative measurement that Jaspers insisted was the *sine qua non* of the natural sciences can be found in the study of neurosis: The dammed-up sexual energy that underlies all neurosis is a physical stuff that can be measured quantitatively.

While developing the theory of the orgasm, Reich continued his work as a psychoanalyst. He found, as did other analysts, that many patients have difficulty in following the basic rule of analysis: to open themselves completely to the analyst. They exhibit what Reich terms "character resistances." The neurotic character traits as a whole, he notes, act as a compact defense mechanism against the efforts of the analyst.[14] This "armor," as Reich calls it, serves on the one hand as a defense against the analyst and stimuli from other external sources; on the other, it provides a means of gaining mastery over the libido, which is continuously pushing forward from the id.[15] This "character armor" displays itself not only in what patients say, but primarily in the *way* in which they act: the manner in which they recount their dreams, produce associations, commit slips, etc. The key, then, to analyzing the typical character resistance is to scrutinize the *manner* in which the patient speaks, walks, and gestures (how one smiles or sneers, whether one speaks coherently or incoherently, how one is polite or aggressive).[16]

Reich concluded that for a successful therapy, it was necessary to break down the character resistances that inhibited the patient from opening up to the analyst. His technique for doing this was at first very similar to the orthodox Freudian technique. He would analyze *how* the patient acted and try to trace the origin of the character resistance to the original oedipal conflict. Reich claims that by analyzing the character resistance and offering his interpretations to the patient, he produced an emotional response in the patient and not merely an intellectual understanding of the neurosis. In contrast, other analysts, who analyzed only the content of the patient's communications, often produced only intellectual insight and no satisfactory cure.

In the next stage of his theoretical development, Reich went far beyond traditional psychoanalysis. In 1933, he treated a man who offered considerable resistance to the uncovering of his passive homosexual fantasies. This resistance, Reich claims, was overtly expressed in the extremely stiff attitude of his throat and neck.[17] After a successful attack on the patient's defenses, the neck muscles relaxed, but powerful impulses then broke through: The pallor of his face changed from white to yellow to blue; he experienced violent pains in the neck and head, as well as diarrhea and other unpleasant physical symptoms. The stiff neck, Reich inferred, had served the function of inhibiting the biological energy that was released when the muscles relaxed. Later, Reich found that whenever a muscular tension was dissolved, one of the three basic biological excitations of the body broke through—anxiety, hate, or sexual excitation. He had earlier produced similar breakthroughs after dissolving character armorings by psychological means, but not in such a complete and powerful manner. He concluded that character armorings are functionally identical with muscular "attitudes" (chronic spasms). By "functionally identical," Reich means that muscular and character armorings have the same function in the psychic mechanism: They can replace one another and influence one another. He then found that if a character defense did not respond to analysis, he could modify it by directly affecting the musculature; and, conversely, if some bodily attitude (chronic muscular spasm) did not change, he could affect it by modifying its expression in the patient's character through analysis. He writes: "I was now able to eliminate a typical friendly smile which obstructed the analytic work, either by describing the expression or by directly disturbing the muscular attitude, e.g., pulling up the chin."[18]

In his later writings, Reich stresses that the essential function of the muscular armor is that of preventing the orgasm reflex and that this reflex will develop as a matter of course when the muscular rigidity is broken down, and *only* when that occurs. Consequently, Reich, in opposition to some Reichian therapists, appears to place much more emphasis on body manipulation than on dissolving character defenses through psychological means. Another difference between Reich and some Reichean clinicians is that he extended his researches beyond clinical psychology into biology and physics. He claims to have discovered a primordial cosmic energy, which he termed "orgone energy," and which exists in humans and other living organisms as a kind of biological energy. Reich claims that orgone energy could be seen under certain experimental conditions and could be measured on a Geiger-Muller counter.[19] Reich also invented an orgone accumulator, a box-like apparatus large enough for a person to sit in, and used it to treat cancer patients. This practice caused him problems with the Food and Drug Administration: They judged his cancer treatment to be worthless and obtained an injunction prohibiting the treatment. Reich was later found guilty of disobeying the injunction and was sentenced to two years in prison. An associate, Dr. Michael Silvert, was sentenced to one year and one day in prison. Part of the decree issued against Reich stipulated that many of his works be destroyed. On August 23, 1956, and again on March 17, 1960, all copies of many of Reich's most important books and scientific papers were loaded into a truck under the supervision of agents of the Food and Drug Administration; were then transported to lower Manhattan, New York; and were burned. Reich died in prison; Dr. Silvert served his term and then committed suicide.

Whatever the merits of Reich's orgone research, an understanding of this later work is not needed to grasp the rationale underlying Reichian therapy. Some Reichians do use the term "orgone therapy" to describe their treatment technique, but they are not necessarily committed to the existence of orgone energy. The following is a brief description of Reichian therapy (alternatively called "orgone therapy" or "character-analytic vegetotherapy").

The aim of Reichian therapy is to dissolve neurotic character and muscular armorings, thereby releasing repressed sexual energy and eventually establishing full orgastic potency.[20] As noted earlier, some Reichians reject his almost exclusive reliance on body work to achieve potency. Hoff claims that body work and character analysis are indispensable, complementary parts of Reichian work, and that the character analysis gives the whole therapy meaning and direction. However, not all Reichians agree. Nelson takes the position that certain patients may be worked on solely with body therapy; for patients who do not respond, character analysis should also be used.[21]

The Reichian who uses character analysis will try to identify those traits that constitute the character armoring, the patient's overall defense system. The therapist will do this by observing how a patient talks and walks, his or her facial expressions, mannerisms, posture and gestures. The next step is to make the patient emotionally aware of these characteristics, to "feel" them as opposed to merely intellectually understanding that they exist. Hoff gives the example of a patient with a habitual smile that appears even when the client is discussing something painful. The smile is seen as a block to the natural flow of feelings.

The analyst would begin by repeatedly bringing the smile to the patient's attention. He might then point out the incongruity between smiling and talking of something painful. He might also urge the client to wiggle his face, or scowl, or to make other expressions incompatible with the smile, or to exaggerate the smile. At the same time, the analyst would look for resentment or other signs of resistance that are likely to surface when a client's character defenses are dissolved. The analyst will later help the client to see the smile and other traits as neurotic symptoms, to experience the underlying feelings that the character traits defend against, and to sense the roots of his defense patterns in his past.

Besides using character analysis, the Reichian therapist will typically use body work to dissolve the muscular armoring. Reich claimed that the armoring has a segmented arrangement. There are seven major segments, or "rings": the ocular, the oral, the neck, the chest and arms, the diaphragmal, the abdominal, and the pelvic area, including the legs. Reich held that all the segmented rings have to be loosened and that the therapist should begin with the first ring and work downward in a sequential fashion. Some of the techniques for dissolving the muscle spasms of each ring are as follows: deep breathing and repeated screaming; deep massage of spastic areas; working with facial expressions (including making faces, stretching the eyes and mouth open, and wiggling the face and forehead); pushing down on the chest while the patient exhales or screams; working with the gag reflex (yawning or coughing); maintaining stress positions while breathing deeply and expressing the pain; and active "bioenergetic" movements, such as pounding, stamping or kicking.[22]

Bioenergetics

The developer of bioenergetics, Alexander Lowen, was a student of Reich and is sometimes described as a "Reichian." Although Lowen has developed his own therapy, much of the underlying theory is either borrowed from or is heavily influenced by Reichian theory. Hence, the discussion of Lowen's theoretical ideas can be relatively brief. A fuller account can be found in Lowen's work entitled *Bioenergetics*.[23]

Lowen tells how he began therapy with Reich in 1942. Lowen, wearing only a pair of bathing trunks, was instructed to lay on a bed and to bend his knees, relax, and breathe with his mouth open. Reich then told him to breathe properly; his chest was not rising and falling with each breath. Lowen complied, but nothing significant happened until Reich told him to drop his head back and to open his eyes wide. When he did this, ". . . a scream burst from my throat."[24] After Lowen repeated the procedure, the scream "happened" to him again. (Lowen uses the word "happened" to indicate that the screams were involuntary and were in some sense "distant" from him.)

In a later session, Lowen's body began rocking involuntarily. He then got off the bed and began pounding it with both fists. As Lowen was doing this, his father's face appeared on the bedsheet, and he then realized that he was striking his father in response to a spanking given to him as a young boy.

After about nine months of therapy with Reich, Lowen found out what had caused the screams in the first session.[25] He had sensed on several occasions that there was an image he was afraid to see. One day, it did appear: an image of his mother's face on the ceiling, looking down with an expression of intense anger.[26] He then relived an experience he had had when he was a nine-month-old infant. He had been lying in a carriage outside his home and had been crying persistently for his mother. His mother had been busy inside the house. When she came out in response to the crying, she was furious because of the interruption.

Despite some early breakthroughs, Lowen's therapy reached an impasse after about a year. After Reich suggested that the therapy be terminated, Lowen broke down and cried deeply. He rejected Reich's advice about quitting therapy, and from then on he made progress. After a year off (in 1944), he resumed therapy in 1945 and within a short time the orgasm reflex came through consistently. Lowen points out that this response is not the same as the orgastically satisfying sexual act that is the ultimate goal of Reichian therapy.[27] The orgasm *reflex* does not involve having an orgasm; rather, it consists of an undulating movement of the body. The pelvis moves spontaneously forward with each exhalation of breath and backward with each inhalation. Although the orgasm reflex is confined to the therapy setting, it is likely, Lowen contends, to be a prerequisite for achieving an orgastically satisfying sexual response outside of therapy.[28]

After taking time off to attend medical school, Lowen renewed therapy, first with a Reichian therapist, and then with an associate no longer connected with the organization of Reichian doctors, Dr. John Pierrakos. While working with Pierrakos and on himself, Lowen developed the basic ideas of bioenergetics.[29] He retained some of Reich's fundamental concepts, but rejected others. For example, Lowen accepts the Reichian concepts of character and bodily "armoring" (defenses). He argues, as did Reich, that mere insight into the cause of one's problem is not sufficient for lasting therapeutic improvement. There is another important factor, the energetic factor, that must be considered.[30] This factor, the pent up energy in the body, is dealt with by body massage and other body work. However, Lowen argues (against the later Reich) that body work (vegetotherapy) is not therapeutic by itself. Character analysis is also needed to give the patient insight into etiology. A change in personality, Lowen notes, can be sustained only if there is sufficient insight as a result of a working through of the patient's problems.[31]

Lowen also rejects the Reichian idea that *the* goal of therapy should be a healthy orgastic response. Sexuality, Lowen contends, is the key issue in all neurotic problems, but disturbances in sexual functioning can be understood only within the framework of the total personality.[32] Consequently, he accepts several therapeutic goals including: the elimination of the patient's presenting symptom or complaint, getting the patient more in touch with his body (e.g., by making him aware of the muscular tensions that may contribute to his problem), and making the patient more realistic about his life.

On Lowen's theory, there are four layers of personality.[33] The first, the ego layer, contains the psychic defenses (e.g., denial, distrust, blaming, projection, rationalization, and intellectualization). The second outermost layer, the muscular, contains the chronic muscular tensions that support and justify the ego defenses, while protecting against the underlying layer of suppressed feelings that the patient dare not express. The third layer, the emotional layer, includes suppressed feelings of rage, panic or terror, despair, sadness, and pain. The innermost layer, the core (or heart), is that from which the desire to love and be loved derives.

The first layer is treated by making the patient aware of his or her ego defenses (denial, distrust, and so on), but modifying this layer rarely affects layers two or three. Layer three is worked on by getting the patient to open and vent his or her feelings: to scream and cry; to express rage, sadness, and fear. However, working with the third layer alone, Lowen notes, will also not suffice. When the person leaves the therapy setting, he will reinstate his defenses. If one works directly with layer two, the muscular, one can move into layers one or three whenever necessary. By working with muscular tensions, one can help the patient understand how his psychological defenses are conditioned by his body rigidity, and open up suppressed feelings by mobilizing the contracted muscles that block expression. However, as noted earlier, Lowen insists that body work is not itself therapeutic. All three outermost layers must be worked on with the goal of reaching through to layer four, the core or heart. The four layers would still exist if this were accomplished, but they would be coordinating and expressive layers rather than defensive ones. The person who reached this ideal state would love whatever he does, whether it be work, play, or sex; he would respond emotionally in all situations (being angry, sad, frightened, or joyful depending on the situation); his feelings would be free from contamination by suppressed emotions stemming from childhood experiences; and because his muscular layer would be free from chronic tensions, his actions and movements would be graceful and effective. Lowen notes that no one achieves this ideal state, but we all can approach it.

In working on the three outer personality layers, the Lowenian therapist makes use of some of the same strategies used by many Reichian therapists. For example, he will often begin with breathing exercises.[34] Attempts are made to make the patient aware of his character armoring, or, in Lowenian terms, ego defenses. The subject is also encouraged to scream and kick, and to express rage, fear, and other emotions. Lowenians also make use of body massage. However, they are not committed to the Reichian idea that there are seven rings of muscular armoring and that each ring must be dissolved in sequence, beginning with the head and working downwards. Lowenians also make less use of body massage; they substitute do-it-yourself exercises and stress positions.[35] In one of the standard stress positions, the patient spreads his legs, with his toes turned inward, bends his knees and arches his back. The position is held for several minutes. In another, the patient bends forward and touches the floor lightly with his fingertips, keeping the knees bent slightly.[36] The purpose of these exercises is to achieve "grounding." A person who is grounded is not "hung up"; he is not operating under any illusions.[37]

In addition to using stress positions and exercises as part of the body work, Lowenian therapists also use a "breathing stool." The patient lies with his back on the stool (originally, a small step ladder with a blanket strapped on it) in order to stimulate his breathing.

Dream Therapy

Dream interpretation is common to psychoanalysis, Jungian analysis, and other kinds of psychotherapy. For that reason, it can be misleading to classify it as a separate kind of psychotherapy. However, it may be used as the sole or primary method of treatment by some therapists and by individuals who belong to dream groups and who treat themselves. In any event, whether considered as a therapy in its own right or as a component of a therapeutic package, we can still ask about the benefits of interpreting dreams. Some advocates make no therapeutic claims, but others do. For example, Moore and Moore give the following list of disorders that can be treated by dream therapy: psychosomatia, skin disorders, tumors, neuritis, bursitis, emotional disorders, melancholia, fear, repression, depression, anxiety, alcoholism, tobacco dependency, obesity, and ulcers.[38]

Just as there are different kinds of dream therapists, there are different theories of dream interpretation, but some general assumptions are shared by many therapists. One example is that dreams are symbolic pictures that represent how one views oneself, one's relationship with others, and the world at a particular time. Dreams then provide insights into feelings, beliefs, and actions; this is one reason that dream interpretation has been employed by holistic practitioners.[39]

In addition to being seen as symbolic pictures, dreams are also believed by many to reflect elements in the unconscious. In his book *Dreams and Healing,* Sanford points out that the healing in our dreams is especially evident if we are in danger of being overwhelmed by the unconscious.[40] When the forces of the unconscious are rising up into consciousness, great anxiety results as long as we do not understand our psychological situation; this presents the threat of a psychosis or a crippling neurosis. In such circumstances, the images of our dreams give us invaluable aid in presenting us with a picture of what it is that is pressing upon us. Working with our dreams, absorbing their meaning, Sanford contends, strengthens and enlightens us and makes possible a connection between our states of consciousness and our turbulent inner forces. He also notes that the unconscious affects us negatively when we do not have a picture of what is acting on us, but when we do have such an image, the power of the unconscious is healing and transformative.[41] This suggests a third assumption shared by Sanford and many other dream therapists: that the insight afforded by understanding our dreams is therapeutic, at least in certain circumstances.

Just as therapists may disagree about certain therapeutic details, they may also disagree about how to proceed in interpreting dreams and about how to use dream interpretation in therapy. There is, then, no single technique that may be termed "dream therapy"; different techniques are used by therapists employing different theories, although, again, there are some elements common to many therapeutic practices. Sanford holds, and many dream therapists would agree, that the first step in using dreams in therapy is to encourage the client to record his dream.[42] It is also helpful, he notes, for the client to read his dream aloud in a therapy session, and, sometimes, for the therapist to repeat the dream to the client.

The next step is to encourage the client to think of associations to the dream.[43] This step, on Sanford's view, is essential for discovering the meaning of the dream. If the therapist were to leap in too quickly with an interpretation, vital pieces of information might be missed. However, sometimes the client cannot think of any associations. When this occurs, Sanford sometimes tries to stimulate the dreamer's imagination by asking him to explain one of the dream elements as if one were talking to a visitor from Mars. For example, if the client has had a dream about ships, he is asked to explain what a ship is, pretending that his listener knows nothing at all about ships. This encourages the client to think of new associations to the elements of the dream.

At other times, Sanford claims, no meaningful association occurs because the symbolism comes from the realm of the collective unconscious.[44] In this sort of case, the knowledge of the therapist is extremely important in providing the correct interpretation. Therapists who do not share Sanford's Jungian orientation may disagree about his explanation of the lack of associations, but may agree that the therapist should suggest an interpretation *provided* that care is taken to avoid imposing a theory upon the dream if it does not fit.

If a dream interpretation does emerge, we can be most confident of its correctness when it satisfactorily explains all of the elements of the dream. However, Sanford apparently does not believe that finding an interpretation that fits is sufficient to establish the correctness of the interpretation. The crucial test is the reaction of the dreamer. When a dream has been understood correctly, there may be an "aha! so that's it" reaction, a kind of gut level "yes." If we must force ourselves to accept an intepretation by an intellectual effort or trick, then we can be sure that the interpretation is wrong. The unconscious, which has produced the dream in the first place, "knows" when it is correctly understood.[45]

The Alexander Technique and Rolfing

As explained earlier, it is doubtful that either Rolfing or the Alexander technique is a form of psychotherapy. It is not even clear that the latter is a kind of therapy. As pointed out by one defender of the technique, Dr. Wilfred Barlow, people went to Alexander "for education and not cure."[46] However, some proponents do see it as a rival to either Bioenergetics or Reichian therapy,[47] and some writers on holistic medicine do refer to it and to Rolfing as examples of "holistic psychotherapy." For these reasons, both techniques will be discussed here, but only very briefly.

One problem in giving even a brief description of the Alexander technique is that Alexander and his followers fail to describe it very extensively. Richard Hodge claimed that the technique was "uncommunicable on paper" and, more recently, Jones concludes: "The problem of how to use words to convey sensory experiences to someone who has not had the experience before continued to plague Alexander and all who have written about the technique since, and it has not yet been solved."[48] Despite these disclaimers, some Alexanderians do attempt to describe the technique and its origins.[49]

Frederick Mathias Alexander discovered his technique in the early 1890s, during a period in which he worked as an actor in Australia. One night, he lost his voice and was forced to leave the stage. Using mirrors, he later discovered the cause of the problem: While speaking, every movement he made was accompanied by a slight tendency to pull his head backward and down. This, he discovered, was part of a whole body pattern that also included lifting his chest and hollowing his back.[50] This pattern, furthermore, was present in everything he did. What initiated the pattern of movement, he found, was a small but perceptible contraction of the muscles at the back of the neck. This contraction pulls the head slightly backward and down, and then causes a suppression of the spine, which, when repeated hundreds of times a day, interferes with the smooth operation of the muscular and nervous systems and all the vital organs.[51] The Alexander technique is a procedure for preventing the neck muscles from contracting unnecessarily prior to any movement; one learns to do this by moving the head upward and away from the body. Barker describes the technique as follows:

> The road to the recuperation of our diminished faculties which we will learn in this book, and which is the essence of the Alexander technique, may be enunciated as follows: As you begin any movement or act, move your whole head upward and away from your whole body, and let your whole body lengthen by following that upward direction.[52]

The technique can apparently be self-taught by means of "the Basic Movement."[53] Sit in a chair and turn your head from side to side, and look at the floor and ceiling. Take notice of any tenseness in the muscles of the neck or any crackling sounds in the spine. Next, while turning your head slowly from side to side, perform the Basic Movement: move your head up and away from your torso and let your body follow. Continue to allow your whole head to move up and away from the body while you perform the turning movement, so that your neck lengthens above your shoulders.[54]

Many who learn the Alexander technique report experiencing a "kinesthetic lightness" in their actions. Some advocates of the technique also suggest more profound and lasting benefits. Barker quotes Frank Pierce Jones as finding "an almost immediate increase in mental and emotional control" after learning the technique.[55] Nikolas Tinbergen is said to have affirmed, in his 1973 acceptance speech for the Nobel Prize in medicine, the possibility that the following problems might be favorably affected by the technique: rheumatism, certain forms of arthritis, asthma, circulation defects, sexual failures, migraines, and depressive states.[56] Barker suggests that the technique may be of use in warding off other serious ailments. She refers to a survey by Dr. Wilfred Barlow of people who had long used the Alexander technique: These people had no coronaries, cancers, strokes, rheumatoid arthritis, discs, ulcers, neurological or severe mental disorders. Barlow called the statistic "almost unbelievable" and concluded that ninety-nine percent of the population need the technique.

Some proponents of the technique would not want to claim for it all of the profound physical and psychological benefits listed above. Jones, for example, disavows. the claim that the technique cures disease.[57] Whatever benefits are produced, he suggests the following three hypotheses to explain how the technique works:

1. The reflex response of the organism to gravity is a fundamental feedback mechanism that integrates other reflex systems.

2. Under civilized conditions this mechanism is commonly interfered with by habitual, learned responses that disturb the tonic relation between head, neck, and trunk.

3. When this interference is perceived kinesthetically, it can be inhibited. By this means the antigravity response is facilitated and its integrative effect on the organism is restored.[58]

Rolfing, or Structural Integration, is a technique developed by Ida Rolf. The underlying theory holds that the force of gravity and poor posture combine to throw the body out of proper alignment. The result is that the muscles of certain areas are thrown into unnatural contraction. As muscle builds up, connective tissues called "fascia" develop in the body.[59] Other effects follow. Tightness spreads throughout the fascial network, the joints lose their freedom, and circulation is restricted. Pain, anger, and other emotional states are repressed and held in the tense musculature.[60]

Rolfing is essentially a kind of massage that lasts for exactly ten sessions of one hour each. In the first session, the therapist observes the undressed client and looks for postural abnormalities. The client is photographed on all sides, both in the first session and in the last.

The client is made to lie on a table while the therapist begins massages using considerable force and pushing deeply into the body. The idea is to release the thickened fascia by applying pressure with the therapist's hands, elbows, and knuckles. The last three sessions are devoted to attempts to "re-integrate" the body after the first seven have been used to loosen it up.

Stanway notes that many clients report a feeling of deep pressure and some-times excruciating pain, while others report a feeling of increased lightness and awareness, and a fresh outlook on life.[61] There are also reports of more specific psychological effects, such as a reduction in anxiety.[62] The evidence for these and other therapeutic claims will be examined in the next section.

II

Experimental Evidence

The experimental literature on the holistic psychotherapies is not extensive. In fact, a computer search of *Psychological Abstracts* failed to turn up a single controlled outcome study dealing with real patients for any of these therapies. One study, perhaps the only controlled outcome study in the literature, dealt with twenty-four male and twenty-four female student volunteers who received Rolfing (Structural Integration). The authors, Weinberg and Hunt, randomly assigned twelve members of each sex to either an experimental (Rolfing) group or a control group. Those in the experimental group were Rolfed twice a week for five weeks, each session lasting approximately one hour. Those in the con-trol group were not Rolfed but were brought into the laboratory twice a week for five weeks and given a series of exercises that (allegedly) would increase their general physical well-being. This was done to insure that each group received equal attention.

Before treatment, all subjects were given state anxiety and trait anxiety questionnaires, each of which is a twenty-item survey. The state questionnaire asks a subject to indicate how he feels at a particular time by checking one of four responses for each of twenty statements, such as "I feel upset." The trait questionnaire asks a subject to indicate his general anxiety level by checking one of four responses for each of twenty statements, such as "I lack self-confidence." The lowest possible score on each questionnaire is 20, the highest possible score is 80, and the average score on the state questionnaire is approximately 35. There was no significant difference on either measure between the two groups, but there was a signficant difference in the average state anxiety scores before and after Rolfing. Subjects were given the state anxiety questionnaire a total of four times, twice before treatment in a pre-instrumentation phase of the study and twice after treatment in a post-instrumentation phase. The study incorpo-rated these phases in order to gather information about the effects of Rolfing on neuromuscular patterning of energy as well as its effects on anxiety. This additional information was gathered by asking subjects, both before and after treatment, to engage in five daily activities (such as lifting a stool) while being measured with an electromyographic instrument. Subjects were given the state anxiety survey both before and after the use of this instrument. Those in the Rolfing group showed a decrease from 38.5 to 28.7 in the pre-instrumentation phase and a decrease from 30.8 to 26.1 in the post-instrumentation phases before and after Rolfing. The subjects in the control group did not show similar decreases; their mean state anxiety scores increased slightly from 34.5 (pre-instrumentation) after five weeks of placebo treatment, and in the post-instrumentation phases decreased only slightly (from 34.9 to 33.4). The authors take the greater reduction in average state anxiety scores in the experimental group as evidence that the Rolfing did reduce state anxiety in that group. They point out, however, that additional research would be needed to determine the exact causal link between anxiety reduction and any specific aspect of Rolfing.

Although Weinberg and Hunt's results are interesting, a good deal more research will be needed before we have firm evidence showing that Rolfing is useful in treating anxiety in typical patients. First, the subjects in the Weinberg and Hunt study were not known to be suffering from clinically significant anxiety. Second, no evidence was provided that the placebo treatment was equal in credibility to the Rolfing. (The fact that the controls in the pre-instrumentation phase showed a slight *increase* in anxiety after completion of the placebo treatment, but showed a decrease from 34.5 to 30.8 after being subjected to electromyographic readings before receiving the placebo, suggests that the placebo was not very believable.) Thus, the hypothesis that the difference in outcomes between the control and the experimental groups was due to different expectations was not ruled out. Finally, the study makes no attempt to answer the important question: Does Rolfing have any beneficial effect on anxiety, or any other clinical problem, that would not be produced by massage? To answer this question, it would be helpful to include massage plus a believable clinical rationale as a placebo control in future studies of Rolfing.

In addition to Rolfing, the Alexander technique has also been the subject of experimental study. Jones studied changes in body movements that take place after using the technique, but he did not do any controlled outcome studies of the *clinical* effects of the technique.[63]

The above studies are virtually the only controlled studies of the holistic psychotherapies. Although a computer search may fail to identify all existing studies, it is quite unlikely that there is a body of favorable controlled outcome studies supporting the efficacy of even one of these therapies. In the absence of such evidence, most reviewers of psychotherapy outcome literature would conclude that claims of effectiveness for these therapies are unwarranted. It is likely, however, that advocates of these therapies would rest their therapeutic claims on other types of evidence. I turn next to the clinical evidence.

Clinical Evidence

Evidence from uncontrolled clinical case studies is generally regarded by *reviewers* of outcome literature as too weak to be confirmatory, but not everyone agrees; and therapists often place a higher value on clinical than on experimental evidence. Luborsky and Spence, in writing of psychoanalysts, point out that it is rare that a therapist knows of even two quantitative studies of the therapy— and rarer still that a therapist's practice will change as a result of such knowledge. They comment: "A common and *probably justified* response to quantitative research is 'Does this finding agree with clinical knowledge?'"[64] Paul Meehl also points out that most psychologists (including himself) who think psychoanalytic theory has much to commend it have become convinced, not because of their knowledge of experimental studies, but because of their experience as patients and therapists.[65] Although Meehl is very much aware of the epistemological problems in using clinical data, he does argue that *sometimes* such data can be confirmatory.

If this favorable attitude toward clinical data is shared by methodologists as sophisticated as Luborsky, Spence, and Meehl, it cannot be dismissed as the obvious consequence of methodological naivete. Some argument is needed to demonstrate that controlled study is necessary. Before presenting such an argument, I will comment briefly on Meehl's views.

Meehl argues that some clinical phenomena are so dramatic, they involve such a *sudden* and *marked* change in the patient, that they are likely to be persuasive even to a skeptic.[66] As one of his main examples, he cites the case of a woman he treated for a full-blown physician phobia, which prevented her from having a needed physical examination for several years. The woman realized that her reaction was "silly"; she attributed it to the psychic trauma she suffered after having a hysterectomy. After seventy-five or eighty sessions, Meehl inferred that when the patient was a child, an examining physician had discovered that she had masturbated. In a later session, in which the patient had a fairly profound memory of the doctor's examining table, and intense anxiety as well as a feeling of nausea, she recalled, with only minimal assistance on Meehl's part, the physician's question about masturbation and her answer. The morning after her discovery, she made an appointment with a doctor (and apparently kept it). Meehl concludes: "I think most fair-minded persons would agree that it takes an unusual skeptical resistance for us to say that this step-function in clinical status was 'purely a suggestive effect,' or a reassurance effect, or due to some other transference leverage or whatever (75th hour!) rather than that the remote memory was truly repressed and the lifting of repression efficacious."[67]

I think that many fair-minded persons would find Meehl's account of this case persuasive. It is probably because of cases of this kind, the dramatic cases, that therapists become convinced that their treatment sometimes works and that their clinical theory is correct. Nevertheless, I doubt that anyone *should* be convinced by Meehl's example. Let us assume that Meehl's memory has not failed him at all and that his account of the case has omitted no crucial detail. Still, how do we know that the alleged cause of the phobia, the doctor's discovery of the child's masturbation, did occur? It was Meehl who first concluded that it did. How does he know that he did not subtly suggest to the patient that an event of this kind, or even the specific event, was at the root of her phobia? Even on the day she *seemed* to recall the doctor's questioning her about her masturbation, she did so with at least some assistance from Meehl. The patient herself, according to Meehl's account, believed that *he* had implanted the memory; it was only later that she concluded that the "remembered" event did occur.[68] Second, and more importantly, even if the event did occur, what evidence is there that it played any causal role at all in her phobia? How do we rule out the possibility that the psychic trauma of the hysterectomy, which we know did occur, was sufficient to produce the phobia, and would have done so even in the absence of the childhood event? (The hysterectomy explanation may even be more plausible. If the childhood event caused the phobia, did the phobia exist before the hysterectomy? If it did, some explanation is needed as to how the patient managed to have the operation. Did she do so without having a prior examination?) Third, suppose it were true that an upsetting childhood experience with a doctor was the cause of the phobia. There is still an unwarranted inferential leap in concluding that the experience was repressed and not simply forgotten. If one already assumes that repression is common in the etiology of phobias, as Meehl presumably does, then the inference may seem plausible; however, if the evidence for the causal role of, and even the very existence of, repression is very weak, then the inference is not warranted.[69]

If Meehl's account of his case is not accepted, how can we explain the sudden and dramatic change in the patient? One plausible possibility is that a placebo-induced change occurred. Meehl points out that the patient came to believe that the early traumatic experience did lead to her phobia.[70] After undergoing psychoanalysis for at least seventy-five sessions, she also presumably believed that discovering the root cause was likely to dissolve the phobia. It is not implausible to think that the patient became convinced, as the result of her seeming discovery, that she could now call her doctor and would not suffer great anxiety. This explanation fits with experimental data concerning the use of placebos in treating phobias, even if the phobias in such studies are generally of a milder sort, and it does not require the several unwarranted assumptions crucial to Meehl's explanation.[71]

Consider another case of dramatic change. As noted in section I, in one of his therapy sessions with Reich, Lowen experienced an involuntary rocking of his body. He then began pounding with his fists the bed he had been lying on, and saw his father's face on the bedsheet. He concluded that he had been striking his father in response to a spanking given to him in childhood. One thing that is difficult to accept in this account is that Lowen literally *saw* his father's face on the bedsheet. Lowen is presumably not claiming that there literally was a face on the bedsheet, something that could have been seen by Reich or some other bystander. Is he claiming to have suffered an hallucination? If he is, then it needs to be explained how either Reich's massage or Lowen's pounding on the bed could have triggered an hallucination in someone not psychotic. I do not say that it is impossible that he was hallucinating, but it is more plausible to think that it was *as if* he was seeing his father's face. Perhaps he wanted to see it. Lowen, after all, was by this time thoroughly steeped in and sympathetic to at least parts of Freudian theory. It is not surprising that he would seem to see his father or that he would infer that his pounding of the bed was a response to his father's spanking. What very well may have been crucial in his therapeutic experience was not his therapy but his commitment to Freudianism and the expectations, beliefs, and desires generated by that commitment.

I have discussed the cases described by Meehl and Lowen to illustrate a point: that even in very dramatic cases, without experimental control, it is generally difficult to rule out alternative explanations of client improvement. I am not going to argue, however, that clinical confirmation is *logically* impossible, or even that it is always impossible in practice. I have elsewhere cited a plausible case of clinical confirmation: Lovaas's use of electric shock in modifying the self-injurious behavior of an autistic child.[72] The conclusion I want to argue for is that it is *generally* not possible (in practice) to confirm an outcome hypothesis without doing a controlled study; the reasons for this conclusion create a strong presumption that uncontrolled clinical case studies will generally not suffice.

Suppose we do have a case where the patient's change is so sudden and dramatic that there is no plausible explanation except that the therapy caused the change. We would still have to rule out the possibility that the therapy was effective only because some unusual circumstances coalesced in a manner not likely to be repeated. Kazdin discusses an extraordinary case in which placebo factors apparently reversed the effects of a serious cancer.[73] We would not be entitled to infer from this one case that placebo treatment of the same kind is a generally effective treatment for the same kind of cancer. However, it is just this sort of conclusion that we seek to establish in assessing the value of psychological therapies. We want to know, not if it worked once, but if it is *generally* effective, at least for a certain kind of problem and patient. The history of outcome research provides evidence, however, that no simple study, not even a well-controlled one, is likely to warrant the hypothesis that a therapy is generally effective. Consider the history of systematic desensitization research. Its originator, Joseph Wolpe, provided suggestive, encouraging case studies, but these were not sufficient to settle the outcome issue. In 1969, Paul reviewed a number of studies, found that at least eight were well controlled, and concluded that for the first time in the history of psychological research, a causal connection had been established between a psychological therapy and a beneficial outcome. However, more than half a dozen years later, after many more controlled studies were done, there remained reasonable doubts as to whether systematic desensitization was more effective than a credible placebo.[74] This case is not unique. For almost any psychological therapy, a series of studies is needed to provide firm evidence that a therapy is generally effective. Once that is conceded, then a problem arises immediately in trusting uncontrolled studies, the problem of "therapy integrity."[75] If we look at a series of studies, we need to know that the same (alleged) cause was present in each. For some therapies, it is relatively easy to gain such assurance. For instance, that is true of a therapeutic package, such as systematic desensitization, which is composed of a few ingredients that can be specified in operational terms. The problem is more acute with, for example, the Alexander technique, which, according to many of its practitioners, is difficult even to describe. With some of the other holistic therapies, a problem may arise because many therapists combine the therapy, or parts of it, with other therapies. That sometimes occurs, for example, with Bioenergetics, Reichian therapy, and dream therapy. A second basic problem is to establish that a particular therapeutic benefit was produced and to what extent. Kazdin points out some of the difficulties in using any single outcome measure, such as therapist's ratings, self-report inventories, projective tests, behavioral measures or psychophysiological tests.[76] The standard recommendation for resolving these difficulties is to use multiple outcome measures,[77] but problems will remain if none of the measures has been validated (which is common in clinical case studies) or if the measures do not agree. Even after it has been established that a certain effect did occur, questions might remain about the value of that effect. This is not likely to pose a deep problem if the client's alcoholic behavior, anxiety, or depression has been diminished, but there can be disagreement about the value of vaguely described outcomes, such as "an increase in personal growth" or "an enhancement of autonomy."

Assuming that a holistic therapy has been used and a therapeutic benefit produced in a series of cases, there remains the problem of establishing a causal connection between the therapy and the benefit. This requires ruling out what are often termed a "spontaneous remission" and a "placebo" hypothesis. The first explains the beneficial change in the client in terms of events, occurring outside the therapy sessions, that are likely to have occurred even if formal therapeutic help had not been received; the second explains improvement in terms of factors present in therapy sessions that are not part of the therapy, such as the client's expectation of being helped. Although there may be exceptional cases, it is generally not possible to rule out either of these competing hypotheses on the basis of clinical case studies. The therapist may be able to judge that therapy X was employed and that a beneficial effect, Y, followed, but it still remains to be shown that the effect would not have occurred in the absence of treatment. In the dramatic cases, such as the one cited by Meehl, it may sometimes be possible to do that; the spontaneous remission hypothesis may be too implausible. However, even in these cases, as again illustrated by Meehl's example, there will remain the difficulty of eliminating the placebo hypothesis.

In sum, there are serious conceptual and epistemological problems, well-known to most reviewers of outcome literature, that arise even when controlled studies are used. Because uncontrolled case studies almost never have suitable devices for resolving these problems, there is good reason for concluding that clinical evidence alone is not likely to establish the general effectiveness of any holistic psychotherapy.

Theoretical Support

A therapeutic theory might be roughly correct and yet the therapy inefficacious, or, conversely, the theory might be incorrect and yet the therapy efficacious. Nevertheless, if a theory explains why a particular therapy is remedial for a certain problem, the evidence for the theory might lend at least some weak support for the therapeutic claim. This reasoning is presumably accepted by some advocates of holistic therapy: They accept the underlying clinical theory for a certain therapy, and use the theory as support for the prediction that a proper use of the therapy is likely to produce certain benefits. The cogency of this line of reasoning will depend, in part, on the evidence for the clinical theory. How firm is the evidence for holistic clinical theories? I will begin with Reichian theory.

Reichian theory is an amalgam of mini-theories that Reich developed over a period of years, combined with parts of Freudian theory. As noted earlier, one of Reich's first theoretical contributions was his orgasm theory: that every psychic disorder is due to a genital disturbance and that the prospects for cure are dependent upon establishing the capacity for full genital satisfaction. This theory has continued to provide the theoretical rationale for making orgastic satisfaction the main goal of Reichian therapy. It also holds that all neurosis has an organic source, the damming up of sexual energy, and this could bolster the idea that psychological therapy needs to be supplemented by body therapy (although the argument would have to be fleshed out somewhat, and it need not provide the only reason for using body therapy). Reich's original support for the orgasm theory was based on his finding that all of his female neurotic patients and sixty to seventy percent of his male patients had gross genital disturbances. However, his theory holds that given the etiology of neurosis, there cannot be even one case of neurosis with undisturbed genitality.[78] Yet, his fellow analysts reported that they had had any number of female patients who were exceptions to Reich's thesis; and some of Reich's own male patients were also counter-instances. As noted earlier, Reich reacted by revising his theory: he redefined the idea of "orgastic impotence." Given his new definition, a neurotic male could be capable of full erection or a female capable of orgasm, and yet be "orgastically impotent." To be orgastically potent, someone must meet the ten complex criteria that Reich lays down, and even the satisfaction of these criteria, he implies, may not be sufficient.[79] Given the difficulty of meeting all of these criteria, it would not be surprising if Reich was correct: *All* of his neurotic patients lacked "orgastic potency" (in his sense). However, what reason does he have for believing that all or most *non-neurotic* patients are orgastically potent? How many non-neurotics has he or anyone else examined to see if they meet all of the complex conditions stipulated? He does not mention any such cases. What reason, then, do we have for thinking that neurotics *generally* differ from non-neurotics in the capacity for "orgastic impotence" (in Reich's technical sense)? In the absence of such reason, what evidence is there that all neurosis is caused by a genital disturbance?

A second key theoretical idea of Reich, that of "character armor," is linked to Freudian theory. For example, Reich holds that this armor provides the neurotic with a means of gaining mastery of the libido, which is continually pushing forward from the id.[80] This view presupposes that there is an id and a Freudian unconscious. If this presupposition has not yet been confirmed, then Reich's view about character armoring is also dubious.[81] Even if the concept of armoring is divorced entirely from Freudian theory (which I doubt can be done), there remain difficulties posed by the success of rival therapies. Some of the behavioral and cognitive therapies have proved useful in the treatment of various kinds of neurotic problems such as phobias, obsessive-compulsive disorders, and depression.[82] Furthermore, the therapeutic gains have often been enduring and have often been achieved without bringing about symptom substitution. In using the therapies in question, such as systematic desensitization, no attempt is made to eliminate character armorings. Thus, the success of these therapies casts doubt on the hypothesis that the elimination of neurosis requires the breaking down of the patient's character armoring.

The success of rival therapies also presents a problem for the Reichian claim that neurotics have a muscular armoring arranged in seven segments (or rings), and that therapeutic success requires the use of body work to loosen each ring, beginning with the first. If this contention were true, it would be difficult to explain how the behavioral and cognitive therapies are successful without the use of body work to attack the muscular armoring.

Those who practice Bioenergetics often reject the Reichian claim that a therapist must attack in sequence each of the seven rings of muscular armoring, but they are committed to Reich's view that neurotics have both a character and muscular armoring.[83] Thus, justified doubts about the existence (or at least the clinical significance) of these armorings weakens the credibility of the underlying theory of Bioenergetics. In addition, the success of the behavior therapies raises doubts about Lowen's claim that character analysis is needed to give the patient insight into the etiology of his problems[84]; the behavior therapies generally do not require insight into etiology in order to achieve therapeutic gains. Finally, Lowen postulates four layers of personality (the ego, the muscular, the emotional, and the core) and claims that therapeutic success requires working on all three outermost layers in order to reach the "core." However, he presents no evidence that any of these layers exist, and his therapeutic claim is also undermined by the success of therapies that make no attempt to deal with any of these layers.

As noted earlier, there is more than one theory of dream interpretation. Some accounts presuppose Freud's theory that all dreams are wish-fullfillments.

During sleep, repressed wishes express themselves in a disguised form, the manifest or apparent content of the dream. Through dream analysis, we can discover the underlying content (the latent meaning) and thereby gain important insights into our repressed wishes. At least this much of Freudian theory is apparently presupposed, for example, by Sanford[85] and other therapists who hold that dream analysis gives us insight into the forces in our unconscious that cause anxiety (and even crippling neuroses and psychoses) when they are not understood. Insofar as the rationale for dream analysis presupposes Freud's dream theory, it runs into evidential difficulties posed by recent criticisms of the arguments for that theory.[86]

Even a dream therapist who rejects the theory that all dreams are wish-fulfillments may accept other assumptions agreeable to Freudians. Moore and Moore for example, hold that dreams are symbolic of pictures that represent how we (unconsciously) view ourselves and our relationships with others. A second assumption that they and most other dream therapists hold is that dreams *generally* have a *correct* interpretation, so that when we decode them properly we gain useful insights into ourselves. The warrant for these two assumptions, however, is challenged by recent neurological theories of dreaming that appear to provide better explanations of all the known facts about dreaming than do purely psychological theories.[87] It is not that the two assumptions just mentioned are inconsistent with these neurological accounts; rather, the neurological theories render the two assumptions otiose (we no longer need them to explain known facts about dreaming).

The bearing that neurological accounts have on psychological theories of dreaming is still controversial.[88] Nevertheless, a modest point can be made. If the plausibility of these neurological theories is conceded, one cannot just assume without argument that dreams *generally* are symbolic pictures that represent how we view ourselves or that dreams generally have a correct interpretation. Even if these two assumptions can be established, at least two additional assumptions are needed, given the standard arguments for doing dream analysis. First, we need to assume that there is some way to establish that a certain interpretation is correct; otherwise, neither patient nor therapist will be able to distinguish between dream insights and pseudoinsights. Therapists holding different theories—Freudians, Alderians, Jungians, and others—will often disagree about how to interpret the same sort of dream. How are we to tell which theorist is correct? Sanford suggests that the patient should be encouraged to think of associations to the dream; when none are forthcoming, the therapist should try to stimulate the patient's imagination.[89] A dream interpretation is most likely to be correct when it gives a satisfactory explanation of all the relevant data, including the elements of the dream and the patient's associations. The key difficulty with Sanford's suggestion is that the patient's so-called "free associations" are often influenced by covert or overt suggestions of the therapist.[90] Sanford also points out that the reaction of the dreamer is crucial.[91] If the client must force himself to accept an interpretation, we can be sure that it is wrong.

Sanford's reason for saying this is that the unconscious, which has produced the dream in the first place, knows when it is correctly understood.[92] However, he gives no evidence that this theory about the unconscious is correct. If we do not assume Sanford's theory about what the unconscious "knows," then why believe that the reaction of the client is crucial? The client may accept or reject an interpretation because of promptings of the therapist, or because of certain theories he or she holds, or for any one of many reasons having little to do with the correctness of the interpretation.

Another assumption shared by many dream therapists is that the insights afforded by dream analysis have therapeutic value. That could be true, but the role of insight in producing favorable therapeutic change is still a matter of considerable controversy. The fact that the behavior therapies are effective with certain clinical problems without relying on client insight is reason for thinking that insight is not necessary for improvement[93]; the weakness of the evidence for the various insight therapies being able to produce greater changes than a credible placebo is reason to doubt that insight is sufficient.[94] It is still open to the dream therapist to argue that for certain kinds of clinical problems and clients, the *kind* of insight produced by dream analysis has therapeutic value. However, the relevant kinds must be specified and some evidence for the claim must be provided. It is no longer plausible to assume without evidence that if only genuine insights were produced, then therapeutic improvement would generally result.

Finally, it might turn out that dream analysis is not only of little clinical value, but is actually harmful, although at present this is speculative. What I have in mind is the fate of the Crick and Mitchison theory that postulates a reverse learning mechanism in which dreaming modifies certain undesirable modes of interaction of network cells in the cerebral cortex. In effect, we dream in order to forget, and forgetting is necessary to prevent an overloading of stored associations. Crick and Mitchison point out that on their model, remembering one's dreams should perhaps not be encouraged, because such remembering helps to retain patterns of thought best forgotten.[95]

In sum, for some therapists, the cogency of their rationale for doing dream analysis is dependent on the arguments for Freud's dream theory and these arguments have recently been severely criticized.[96] Even those therapists who do not rely on Freudian theory often use a rationale that includes the following assumptions: (1) dreams are generally symbolic pictures that represent how we view ourselves and others; (2) dreams generally have a correct interpretation; (3) there is a reliable procedure for determining the correct interpretation; and (4) the insights gained by dream analysis have therapeutic value. Unless some other argument is offered, all four of these assumptions need to be justified; subject to caveats already expressed, there is some reason to question the evidence for (1) and (2), and even more reason to reject the warrant for (3) and (4).

The theory underlying the Alexander technique and Rolfing is rather slight. The main rationale for using either technique appears to be that, in the view of its advocates, it works. Jones explains the working of the Alexander technique in terms of three hypotheses about the effects of gravity, the learning of responses interfering with the relations between the head, neck and trunk, and an anti-gravity effect produced by the technique (see section I of this paper).[97] Jones does not provide any evidence, however, that either gravity or learning produces the effects he mentions, or that the Alexander technique produces an "antigrav-ity" effect. Furthermore, even if all three hypotheses were rendered plausible, they would not provide reason for thinking that the technique is useful in treating psychological problems.

The underlying theory of Rolfing (Structural Integration) also talks about the effects of gravity, as well as poor posture: the combined result of the two is that the body is thrown out of proper alignment. So far, the theory says nothing surprising. That people suffer from poor posture and that they might benefit in some way from a vigorous massage (such as that provided in Rolfing) has a certain antecedent plausibility. The remainder of the theory—that poor posture throws certain muscles into unnatural contraction; that, in consequence, there develops connective tissues called "fascia"; that, as a further consequence, pain, anger, and other emotional states are repressed and held in the tense muscula-ture; and that Rolfing, by breaking down the fascia, releases the repressed emotional states and brings about beneficial psychological changes—is not so obviously correct. Without some independent support for this part of the theory, the theoretical rationale by itself does not give much plausibility to the prediction that Rolfing will generally produce useful psychological changes over and above those produced by a vigorous massage.

CONCLUSION

What holistic psychotherapies work and for which types of problems and patients? My conclusion is that for *none* of the therapies considered is there firm evidence that the therapy is generally more effective than a credible placebo in relieving any sort of clinical problem or in producing any kind of therapeutic benefit. I have not, however, considered the question of whether any of these therapies is ineffective, or whether any produces harmful effects.

My skeptical conclusion is based upon an examination of the relevant experimental, clinical, and theoretical arguments supporting the holistic therapies. There is a kind of indirect evidence, however, that I have not considered and should comment on. Frank[98] argues that the relative superiority of psycho-therapy of whatever form over no treatment has been conclusively demonstrated by massive meta-analyses of controlled studies of psychotherapy by Smith, Glass, and Miller[99] and Shapiro and Shapiro.[100] I have two comments. First, recent criticisms of meta-analyses have shown that they have *not* demonstrated what Frank claims.[101] Second, I question the use of the "no treatment" criterion as a standard for evaluating psychotherapies. If that standard is used, then we do not need meta-analysis or individual controlled studies to show that any particular therapy is effective for *some* problems. All we need do is establish that the therapy is credible to certain patients, and then argue on the basis of the evidence of the effectiveness of credible placebos that the therapy is likely to be effective with those patients. However, if a therapy is no more effective than a credible placebo, then certain untoward consequences follow.[102] The kinds of credible placebos used in psychotherapy research are often inexpensive, simple procedures, such as the use of a sugar pill.[103] If the holistic psychotherapies are no more effective than these, then it is preferable in most cases to use a less expensive alternative. An exception might arise when a client believes that, say, Bioenergetics alone will help his problem. In these unusual cases, however, it is probably simpler and more honest to dissuade the client of his false belief. Second, if a particular form of psychotherapy is effective only because of the client's faith in it, then the standard underlying clinical theory of why it works is false. Third, if any credible placebo will do just as well as any holistic psychotherapy, then there is little justification in spending time or money in training people how to use these techniques. It is not sufficient, then, to show that the holistic psychotherapies are better than nothing. *If* they are worth no more than less expensive, credible placebos, then their underlying theories are false; there is little justification for providing training in the holistic therapies; and there is little, if any, warrant for their continued use.

NOTES

1. M. Brown, "The New Body Psychotherapies," *Psychotherapy: Theory, Research and Practice* 10 (1973):98-116.
2. M. Moore and L. Moore, *The Complete Handbook of Holistic Health* (Englewood Cliffs, N.J.: Prentice-Hall, 1983).
3. Ibid., 212.
4. Ibid.
5. W. Reich, *Selected Writings: An Introduction to Orgonomy* (New York: Farrar, Straus and Giroux, 1951), 16.
6. Ibid., 40.
7. Ibid., 24.
8. Ibid.
9. Ibid., 21.
10. Ibid., 26.
11. Ibid., 29.
12. Ibid.
13. Ibid., 29-37.
14. Ibid., 49.
15. Ibid.
16. Ibid., 53.
17. Ibid., 108.

18. Ibid., 110.
19. D. Broadella, *William Reich: The Evolution of His Work* (London: Vision Press, 1973).
20. R. Hoff, "Overview of Reichian Therapy," in E. Bauman et al. (eds.), *Holistic Health Handbook* (Berkeley, Calif.: And/Or Press, 1978), 205.
21. A. Nelson, "Orgone (Reichian) Therapy in Tension Headache," *American Journal of Psychiatry* 30 (1976):103-11.
22. Hoff, op. cit.
23. A. Lowen, *Bioenergetics* (New York: Penguin Books, 1976).
24. Ibid., 17.
25. Ibid., 20.
26. Ibid.
27. Ibid., 28.
28. Ibid.
29. Ibid., 38.
30. Ibid., 327.
31. Ibid.
32. Ibid., 29.
33. Ibid., 117-24.
34. Brown, op. cit.
35. Ibid.
36. Lowen, op. cit., 39-40.
37. Ibid., 185.
38. Moore and Moore, op. cit., 209.
39. Ibid., 201.
40. J. Sanford, *Dreams and Healing* (New York: Paulist Press, 1978), 33.
41. Ibid., 34.
42. Ibid., 53.
43. Ibid., 51.
44. Ibid., 52.
45. Ibid., 54.
46. F. P. Jones, *Body Awareness in Action* (New York: Schocken Books, 1976), 89.
47. Ibid., 1.
48. Ibid., 33.
49. S. Barker, *The Alexander Technique* (New York: Bantam Books, 1978).
50. Ibid.
51. Ibid., 15.
52. Ibid., 24.
53. Ibid., 27.
54. Ibid., 25-36.
55. Ibid., 5.
56. Ibid., 7.
57. F. P. Jones, op. cit., 83.
58. Ibid., 151.
59. A. Stanway, *Alternative Medicine* (New York: Penguin Books, 1979).
60. R. Pierce, "Rolfing," in E. Bauman et al. (eds.), *The Holistic Health Handbook* (Berkeley, Calif.: And/Or Press, 1978). See also, R. Weinberg and V. Hunt, "Effects of Structural Integration on State-trait Anxiety," *Journal of Clinical Psychology* 35 (1979):319-322.
61. A. Stanway, op. cit.
62. R. Weinberg and V. Hunt, "Effects of Structural Integration on State-trait Anxiety," *Journal of Clinical Psychology* 35 (1979):319-22.
63. F. P. Jones, op. cit.
64. L. Luborsky and D. Spence, "Quantitative Research on Psychoanalytic Therapy," in A. Bergin and S. Garfield (eds.), *Psychotherapy and Behavior Change: An Empirical Analysis* (New

York: John Wiley and Sons, 1971), 408, my italics.

65. P. Meehl, "Subjectivity in Psychoanalytic Inference: The Nagging Persistence of Wilhelm Fleiss's Achensee Question," in J. Earman (ed.), *Testing Scientific Theories: Minnesota Studies in the Philosophy of Science, Vol. X* (Minneapolis, Minn.: University of Minnesota Press, 1983).

66. Ibid., 355.

67. Ibid., 358.

68. Ibid.

69. A. Grünbaum, *The Foundations of Psychoanalysis: A Philosophical Critique* (Berkeley Calif.: University of California Press, 1984). See also, E. Erwin. "Psychotherapy and Freudian Psychology," in S. Modgil and C. Modgil (eds.), *Han Eysenck: A Psychologist Searching for a Scientific Basis for Human Behavior* (London: Falmer Press, 1984).

70. P. Meehl, op. cit., 358.

71. J. Lick, "Expectancy, False Galvanic Skin Response, Feedback and Systematic Desensitization in the Modification of Phobic Behavior," *Journal of Consulting & Clinical Psychology* 43 (1975): 557-67. See also, T. Rosenthal, "Social Cueing Processes," in M. Hersen, R. Eisler, and P. M. Miller (eds.), *Progress in Behavior Modification, Vol. 10* (New York: Academic Press, 1980).

72. E. Erwin, *Behavior Therapy: Scientific, Philosophical and Moral Foundations* (New York: Cambridge University Press, 1978).

73. A. Kazdin, *Research Design in Clinical Psychology* (New York: Harper & Row, 1980).

74. A Kazdin and L. Wilcoxin, "Systematic Desensitization and Nonspecific Treatment Effects: A Methodological Evaluation," *Psychological Bulletin* 83 (1976): 729-58. See also, E. Erwin, *Behavior Therapy: Scientific, Philosophical and Moral Foundations.*

75. A. Kazdin, "General Discussion," in J. Williams and R. Spitzer (eds.), *Psychotherapy Research: Where Are We and Where Should We Go?* (New York: Guilford Press, 1984), 113.

76. A. Kazdin, *Research Design in Clinical Psychology* (New York: Harper & Row, 1980).

77. P. Kendall and J. Norton-Ford, "Therapy Outcome Research Methods," in P. Kendall and J. Butcher (eds.), *Handbook of Research Methods in Clinical Psychology* (New York: John Wiley & Sons, 1982).

78. W. Reich, op. cit., 21.

79. Ibid., 29.

80. Ibid., 49.

81. See A. Grünbaum, *The Foundations of Psychoanalysis: A Philosophical Critique* and E. Erwin, "Psychotherapy and Freudian Psychology," for doubt about the evidence.

82. E. Erwin, *Behavior Therapy: Scientific, Philosophical and Moral Foundations;* see also S. Rachman and G. T. Wilson, *The Effects of Psychological Therapy* (New York: Pergamon, 1980) and A. Kazdin and G. T. Wilson, *Evaluation of Behavior Therapy: Issues, Evidence and Research Strategies* (Cambridge, Mass.: Ballinger, 1978).

83. A. Lowen, op. cit.

84. Ibid., 327.

85. J. Sanford, op. cit., 333.

86. C. Glymour, "The Theory of Your Dreams," in R. Cohen and L. Laudan (eds.), *Physics, Philosophy and Psychoanalysis: Essays in Honor of Adolf Grünbaum* (Boston: D. Reidel, 1983); see also A. Grünbaum, op. cit.

87. See J. Hobson and R. McCarley, "The Brain as a Dream State Generator: An Activation-synthesis Hypothesis of the Dream Process," *American Journal of Psychiatry* 134 (1977): 1335-48; see also F. Crick and G. Mitchison, "The Function of Dream Sleep," *Nature* 304 (1983): 111-14.

88 .See G. Vogel, "An Alternative View of the Neurobiology of Dreaming," *American Journal of Psychiatry* 135 (1978): 1531-1535, for a reply to Hobson and McCarley.

89. J. Sanford, op. cit., 51.

90. A. Grünbaum, op. cit.

91. J. Sanford, op. cit., 54.

92. Ibid.

93. S. Rachman and G. T. Wilson, op. cit.

94. L. Prioleau, M. Murdock, and N. Brody, "An Analysis of Psychotherapy versus Placebo Studies," *Behavioral & Brain Sciences* 6 (1983): 275-85.

95. F. Crick and G. Mitchison, op. cit., 114.

96. C. Glymour, op. cit.; A. Grünbaum, op. cit.

97. F. P. Jones, op. cit., 151.

98. J. Frank, "Therapeutic Components of All Psychotherapies," in J. Myers (ed.), *Cures by Psychotherapy: What Effects Change?* (New York, Praeger, 1984).

99. M. Smith, G. Glass, and T. Miller, *The Benefits of Psychotherapy* (Baltimore, Md.: The Johns Hopkins University Press, 1980).

100. D. A. Shapiro and D. Shapiro, "Meta-analysis of Comparative Therapy Outcome Research: A Critical Appraisal," *Behavioral Psychotherapy* 10 (1982):4-25.

101. See S. Rachman and G. T. Wilson, *The Effects of Psychological Therapy*, op. cit.; H. J. Eysenck, "Special Review: The Benefits of Psychotherapy, A Battlefield Revisited," *Behavioral Research & Therapy* 21 (1983):315-20; E. Erwin, "Establishing Causal Connections: Meta-analysis and Psychotherapy," *Midwest Studies in Philosophy, Vol. IX* (1984), 421-36; and G. T. Wilson, "Limitations of Meta-Analysis in the Evaluation of the Effects of Psychological Therapy," unpublished manuscript.

102. Discussed more fully in E. Erwin, "Is Psychotherapy More Effective Than a Placebo?" in J. Hariman (ed.), *Does Psychotherapy Really Help People?* (Springfield, Ill.: Charles C. Thomas, 1984).

103. N. Q. Brill, R. R. Koegler, L. J. Epstein, and E. W. Forgy, "Controlled Study of Psychiatric Outpatient Treatment," *Archives of General Psychiatry* 10 (1964):581-95.

Edward R. Friedlander, M.D.

Dream Your Cancer Away: The Simontons

THE SIMONTON APPROACH

Oscar Carl Simonton, M.D., a board-certified radiation oncologist, and his former wife, Stephanie Matthews-Simonton, have earned widespread respect for their work with cancer patients. They are joint authors of *Getting Well Again* (24), a popular book outlining their program, which patients may carry out by themselves. The Simontons counsel cancer patients to cultivate attitudes that they claim are both optimistic and realistic. Specifically, they recommend mental imagery—the patient visualizes the cancer being destroyed by the treatment and by the immune system.

As a resident in radiation oncology during the early 1970s, Dr. Simonton was very curious about why people with cancer responded differently to treatment. Lawrence LeShan's studies had already suggested that physical illness often follows disruptive life events, and there was much talk about "stress" generally. The then-popular immune surveillance theory held that cancer cells are continually being produced in the body, but are destroyed by the immune system. Dr. Simonton was also interested in the quasimagical Silva Mind Control and related systems using relaxation and imagery.

So Dr. Simonton suggested to one of his patients, a man with "a form of throat cancer that carried a grave prognosis" (24), that his radiation therapy might work better if he would visualize the rays and "his body's white blood cells" demolishing his tumor cells. The radiation therapy resulted in a complete remission, and the patient did not die of his cancer for nine more years. He also had used imagery to improve his arthritis and his sex life.

Making pictures in the mind is an old self-help technique. For example, St. Ignatius Loyola, founder of the Jesuits, wrote a book of *Spiritual Exercises,* which urges the faithful to imagine events in the life of Christ in detail. Aleister Crowley, the famous satanist, conjured up potent mental pictures while working black magic. Contemporary occultists use guided imagery techniques extensively.

The Simontons introduced these methods to oncology.

Dr. Simonton taught other patients his picturing technique and felt the results were encouraging. He continued his research as chief of radiation oncology at Travis Air Force Base. His first study alleged a strong correlation between patients' "attitudes" following radiation therapy and treatment success (22). After this, he and Stephanie Matthews established the Cancer Counseling and Rehabilitation Center, now the Simonton Cancer Center, a nonprofit organization in Fort Worth, Texas. They promised additional data from a prospective study:

> We instigated a control with another radiation therapist in Fort Worth five months ago. Between his office and ours, we treat approximately three-fourths of the patients given radiation therapy in the city. Both offices administer standard doses of radiation therapy, and our patients are treated on the same equipment, by the same technicians. The difference between the two is the psychotherapy administered to our patients. This study should show some interesting statistics, as to whether we can change both the quality and quantity of the patient's survival time by influencing his attitude (22).

The results of this study have not appeared, nor do the Simontons mention it again.

The team also published a summary of selected articles from the scientific literature that suggested relationships among stress, the immune system, and cancer (2). Next came the popular *Getting Well Again*, which described their methods in detail. The book includes several anecdotes of clients who had done well, a summary of the status of 159 "medically incurable" patients, and a promise of additional data: "A matched control population is being developed and preliminary results indicate survival comparable with national norms and less than half the survival time of our patients" (24). These controls were apparently historical ones from *Cancer Treatment Reports,* to which the Simontons compared 225 of their own clients. For patients with widespread metastases from each of three primary sites, the Simonton clients survived several months longer. The Simontons then concluded:

> Regardless of which clusters of variables one wishes to focus on, there is sufficient literature to mandate a systematic approach to counseling cancer patients and, in a broader way, educating the public regarding the importance of the connection between mental health and physical health (25).

They also promised further studies that would be even more convincing:

> We are currently attempting to develop a group of matched controls with similar diagnoses and treatments who are not involved in a structured counseling or self-help program. A comparison of their median survival with that of those in the psychological intervention group will then serve as the basis for evaluating our future results (25).

But the Simontons' next paper was a slightly-expanded continuation of the same series. Results were similar to the previous study (26).

The Simontons have published no further data. A review of their work by the American Cancer Society quoted a letter from Ms. Matthews-Simonton, received in September, 1980: "We are in the process of preparing a five-year research plan to better research the outcomes of our work" (3). The American Cancer Society adds that "no confirmation of this plan has been obtained to date."

Stephanie Matthews-Simonton is described only as a "psychotherapist." She has recently authored a second popular book, *The Healing Family* (13), which emphasizes realistic planning, communicating, cultivating relationships, showing affection, and allowing the cancer victim to maintain autonomy as long as possible. She states that "thousands" of cancer victims have been seen by her and her former husband, but no new statistics are presented.

The cost of an intensive five-day psychotherapy program at the Simonton Cancer Center's southern-California retreat is now $1800; meals and lodging cost an additional $200 per person. However, the Simontons do not stress the need to attend their programs, but invite cancer patients everywhere to learn the techniques from their books.

The Simontons' distinguishing technique is the three-times-daily mental imagery routine. Patients choose the way they will see their recovery. They should picture themselves and their friends as already possessing whatever they wish to obtain. Especially, they visualize their conventional treatment, and their immune systems, destroying their cancers. The white cells, which represent the whole immune system, must appear strong and active. The cancer cells should look weak and nonthreatening.

The reader of *Getting Well Again* is instructed to "think of the white cell as having those characteristics that you consider most admirable and strong in yourself" (24). White dogs (eating hamburger) and white sharks (eating gray blobs) are both recommended. In a picture, a white knight with heraldry of segmented neutrophiles destroys little dragons (22). Usefully, the patient's choice of images, and the way in which the images themselves behave, reveal the patient's current problems and prognosis.

The Simontons emphasize that their cancer patients must continue with the conventional therapy prescribed by their physicians. Further, they have distinguished themselves from other holistic healers by their eagerness to prove the value of their techniques using their statistics.

The Simontons have many emulators, especially among psychologists interested in hypnosis (18, 19, 21). So far, these authors have not joined the Simontons in presenting any statistics, though they are very impressed with the new methods. An entirely different form of mental exercise has been developed by the Australian physician, Ainslie Meares, M.D., D.P.M. He opposes imagery, and instead advocates "Mental Ataraxis," an effortless stilling of the mind. This, combined with the laying-on of Meares's hands, has reportedly been associated with disappearances of some cancers, notably the melanomas (malignant moles) that are such a problem in Australia. Meares's three recent reviews cite only his own papers, and his evidence remains anecdotal (17-19).

The Simontons' popular books have many praiseworthy features. They emphasize attitudes, activities, and support systems that will be most wholesome to cancer victims. Thus, they have been lauded in the prestigious *New England Journal of Medicine* by Robert M. Mack, M.D., a surgeon and cancer victim (8). As a result of meeting with a Simonton-trained counselor and practicing imagery techniques, Dr. Mack became more hopeful, felt in control, and was more satisfied with daily life than ever before. He gained new sensitivity to human relationships and interest in spiritual matters.

To doctors caring for cancer patients, these sound like platitudes. The last two decades have been remarkable for the emergence of oncology as a specialty that cares for all the needs of the cancer patient. Yet apart from physicians, guides for people coping with cancer are difficult to find. "Reach for Recovery" is an underutilized self-help program for cancer victims; there are some other helpful books (1, 7-8, 27-28). It is especially good that *Getting Well Again* and *The Healing Family* focus on feelings, and support the treatments that practicing physicians know to be effective against cancer. Thus, I am almost sorry to disagree with the Simontons' most controversial claim—that their treatment eases or slows the natural progression of cancers.

A HOLISTIC CANCER THERAPY

Because of its emphasis on "treating the whole person," the personal and social context of illness, and its applicability to many different diseases, the Simonton approach to cancer is "holistic." But it differs from most such campaigns. Patients are required to continue with indicated radiation therapy and chemotherapy. The practices are never presented as "alternative medicine," and there are no independent theories of physiology or cosmology. There is no attempt to diagnose disease by exploring one organ of the "whole person," and no new discovery to explain the "whole" of disease (although "stress" contributes to most ills). There are no gadgets, weird diets, or bizarre physical therapies. While the Simontons profess to care greatly about each client, there is no obvious sentimentality or love-bombing to recruit new believers. They write instead like concerned clinicians. There is no talk about "wholeness" or "integration"; by contrast, the Simontons strongly endorse community, charitable, and religious activities. Best of all, unless a cancer victim elects special counseling, the cost is almost nothing.

Most holistic practitioners scorn honest research, complaining that they have no money, that such practices are degrading to individual "whole persons," or even that observation itself is unreliable (e.g., Heisenberg Uncertainty Principle). Having nothing to gain by truthful discussion, they urge their clients to "keep open minds," "think for themselves," "exercise freedom of choice." The Simontons repudiate these sophistries. Like advocates of biofeedback and hypnosis, which are recognized as having legitimate uses, they point with pride to their attempts at controlled studies.

However, the Simontons might be criticized for certain features of their work that are similar to other holistic practitioners. Like a traditional homeopath, chiropractor, or naturopath, the Simontons claim that illness indicates that the "whole person" is in need of remediation. The person is "responsible," though not culpable. The Simontons have been criticized for this, more so than holists with less claim to legitimacy (3). As one of their emulators puts it:

> Confronting the patient with the idea that he has brought on his own disease is counterproductive. It is not enough for us to try to make the distinction between blame and responsibility. The patient all too frequently does not interpret the words in the same way as we do. The patient often feels guilty and becomes much more tense when this is to be avoided at all costs. In addition, it is our experience that it is unnecessary to have the patient confront this issue in order to succeed in getting him to accept the idea that he has the potential to help himself in some very crucial and basic ways (18).

In other words, patients get upset when they hear they caused their own cancers because they have faulty attitudes. (Even cigarette smokers with lung cancer do not like to hear how they "caused" it.) The Simontons were also disturbed by the effect their promises had on their dying patients:

> Some of our early patients felt we had given them the key to certain recovery and thought, "Yes! I can do it!"—and then, as we discovered later, felt guilty if they failed to recover. These patients would come to Fort Worth approximately three to four times a year for one-week sessions and then return home. . . . Suddenly all communication would cease for several weeks, and later their families would inform us that they had died. . . . Eventually, their families brought us these last words: "Tell Carl and Stephanie that the method still works," or "Tell them it isn't their fault" (24).

Like many other systems of alternative medicine, the Simontons' imagery has its origins in magic. Two pseudoscience writers have been impressed by the metaphysical implications of meditating tumors away (5, 10). The Simontons themselves do not seem to know how their magic works. Perhaps getting the patient to relax is basic, or maybe the content of the images is critical, or maybe the change in attitudes that comes from using the imagery is the secret. Dr. Simonton has even suggested "it might be a spiritual process, God healing them, up and down the whole spectrum" (22).

Sometimes the Simontons suggest that their approach works in part by the "placebo effect," which they describe as a valuable therapeutic modality. This leads them to apologize for laetrile, the notorious cancer fraud. Another contemporary advocate of "holistic cancer therapy" praises the quacks Joseph Issels ("elimination of toxic foci"), Max Gerson (raw liver, coffee enemas, raw vegetables prepared in a miraculous chopper), and Ernesto Contreras (laetrile), as charismatic healers offering valuable placebos (9). The Simontons ignore the ethical problem—valuable placebo or no, patients pay money for treatments that are expected to be truly active.

All the Simontons' writings use certain words ambiguously, a common technique in holistic rhetoric. Such catch-words as "control," "healing," "inexplicable," "positive," "recover," "responsible," and "well" are used in contexts where their meanings are not clear. At the beginning of *Getting Well Again,* we read: "We all participate in our own health through our beliefs, our feelings, and our attitudes toward life, as well as in more direct ways, such as through exercise and diet" (24). This seems to be just a clumsy restatement of the truism that certain beliefs, feelings, and attitudes are "healthy." However, the Simontons are preparing the reader for the idea that healthy attitudes actually shrink tumors. Even the book titles are ambiguous. Does *Getting Well Again* tell a patient how to achieve a cure, effect a temporary remission, or develop a more wholesome outlook on life? Does *The Healing Family* assist the patient in obtaining a conventional cure or remission, or do the families and friends of cancer victims use the recommended imagery to cure them magically?

There are also logical fallacies. In a chapter of *Getting Well Again* concerning causes of cancer, the Simontons explain that neither carcinogenic substances, genetic predisposition, radiation, or diet alone can account for all cancer. (Viruses are not discussed, perhaps because the Simontons do not want their clients worrying about the disease being catching.) They say: "In reality, not one of these elements alone is a sufficient explanation for who gets cancer and who doesn't" (24). The authors immediately conclude that all these factors taken together cannot explain the prevalence of malignant disease. Therefore, immunosuppression due to stress must be another major factor. Similarly, in *The Healing Family,* Ms. Matthews-Simonton relates the increase in degenerative diseases to the breakup of the extended family, merely because they both occurred during our century.

Like most holists, the Simontons admire pre-industrial cultures. Without any support, they assert in *Getting Well Again* that life in the third world is less stressful than in the United States. (Apparently life in industrial Japan is also less emotionally demanding, and they cite the lower incidence of breast cancer there. The Simontons do not mention the extremely high incidence of stomach cancer in Japan.)

Though he emphasizes gathering data, Dr. Simonton asks not to be expected to "prove" his theories:

Before I began this study and had only the ideas, most of my colleagues told me that I would never be able to prove anything because there were too many variables involved. As I have accumulated more and more results, I still find that the question of scientific proof is a very difficult one (23).

Dr. Simonton follows this with an unreferenced quotation from Albert Einstein about the difficulty of "proof" in science. Whatever Dr. Einstein was really talking about, "proof" is rarely discussed today in medicine or any other branch of empirical science. Clinical decisions are made on the basis of acceptable evidence, preferably from properly-controlled studies. The rest of this essay will show that the Simontons have failed to provide such evidence.

STATISTICAL STUDIES

The study from Travis Air Force Base patients has already been cited (22). In this series, 152 patients who had just completed radiation therapy were evaluated by each of five "staff members" for their "attitudes" and "response to treatment." A very strong correlation was found between having obtained a good result from treatment and having a good attitude. None of a wide array of psychological tests were used to assess "attitude." Dr. Simonton never tells exactly what "attitudes" were being measured, though the patients with bad attitudes "said they didn't like the positivity." He fails to explain how the five raters' responses were aggregated into a single number, and he does not describe any blinds. As reported, the experiment fails to eliminate observer bias, and actually makes the staff's subjective ratings the basis of the correlation. (The "correlation coefficient" he uses seems to be merely eyeballing the table of results.)

Actually, the result does not seem very surprising. Who wouldn't be pleased if his tumor has responded to radiation? Who wouldn't be angry and bitter if, after being smugly told he could "influence" his cancer, the radiation treatment failed and death was imminent? The evidence suggests that the poor responses caused the bad attitudes instead of the converse. The logical next step would have been to repeat the study, this time judging the patients' attitudes *before* receiving radiation. The Simontons have reported no such study.

In *Getting Well Again,* Dr. Simonton presents additional data. This is a single table showing his early results at the center, on "medically incurable" patients. Among the patients listed, 22.2 percent had "no evidence of disease," 19.1 percent had "tumor regressing," and 17.1 percent had "disease stable." Buried in the text of the preceding paragraph, Dr. Simonton acknowledges that these figures include only patients currently living (63 out of 159). All the dead clients had presumably been told they could "control" their cancers.

The Simontons are nonetheless sanguine about their results, and tell the reader: "Keep in mind that 100 percent of these patients were considered medically incurable" (24). They obviously want their readers to think that their treatment has caused better results than could be expected from conventional treatment. This is blatantly misleading. "Medically incurable" cancers often regress completely as a result of conventional therapy, only to recur later. (No similar suggestions appear in Simonton publications directed to cancer physicians. Indeed, these statistics are probably no better than those for any group of patients getting good cancer care.)

Reports that the Simontons' clients survived longer than controls seem more impressive. The inside cover of the Bantam edition of *Getting Well Again* announces "the Simontons' patients have a survival rate twice the national norm." Sadly, this refers only to the length of survival, not to numbers of cures. At the time of writing, the average survival time of the 63 living Simonton clients was 24.4 months; the average survival time for the 96 dead Simonton clients was 20.3 months; and the historical controls lived 12 months. This is as close as they come to saying that they have saved lives. Similar results in Dr. Simonton's later publications have already been cited. (It is not even clear from these papers whether all cancer patients coming to the center are included in these studies.)

There are at least five plausible explanations for the survival statistics, which are not mutually exclusive.

1. The Simonton treatment, or some aspect of it, actually prolongs life.

2. Patients with more indolent tumors, or tumors that have responded well to conventional therapy, feel better and are better able to seek unconventional cures.

3. Patients with more indolent tumors, or tumors that have responded well to conventional therapy, have had more time in which to hear about the Simontons.

4. Patients who have already received better medical care are more likely to apply for additional alternative care. (Perhaps they are more intelligent, better motivated, more wealthy.)

5. Some other conscious or unconscious bias in patient selection exists.

The Simontons provide no information that would help us choose among these alternatives. This is very disappointing. They surely have some statistics on duration of illness, tumor type and grade, previous treatment and response, and performance scale, and these could easily have been incorporated into their reports.

The Simontons are aware of the problem of patient selection:

The survival times of these patients are longer than those reported in the literature. The survival times reported in the literature [from cancer treatment centers] are longer than national norms. What are some of the possible explanations? Certainly one of the obvious explanations is better treatment, coupled with a selected patient population (26).

The use of such controls is always worrisome. Recently, a group from the Mayo Clinic has been unable to verify, using a prospective, double-blind technique, the results of some of Dr. Linus Pauling's "holistic" research that relied on historic controls. They concluded that case-selection bias, rather than treatment effectiveness, must have been operating in Dr. Pauling's study, the results of which were more striking than those of the Simontons (17).

LIFE EXPERIENCE, STRESS, AND CANCER

Like most holistic practitioners, the Simontons tell clients that their lives, lifestyles, and attitudes caused the disease. Is this true?

Older studies suggested that people were more likely to get sick from diseases such as cancer during the weeks or months following a major change in their living habits. This has been called into question by more recent "life-experience research." Prospective studies since the Simontons began their work have largely failed to show the supposed association between stressful life events and the onset of various illnesses (4, 20). The whole subject of psychological influence on cancer development and progress has been reviewed by Bernard Fox (7). He concludes that the field is enormously interesting and complex, that stress often seems to suppress rather than promote cancer in experimental systems, and that most past and present research is of poor quality.

Since *Getting Well Again,* the immune surveillance theory of the origin of cancer cells has been discredited. One important observation is that patients who receive immunosuppressive treatment for various illnesses do not suffer a significant increase in the common cancers, though individual agents are associated with certain less common malignancies. (Lymphoid malignancies in these patients probably arise from cells of those portions of the immune system that are not suppressed and thus are forced to work too hard. And some of the drugs are carcinogens with various organ specificities.)

But if the Simontons ever really believed in the immune surveillance theory, they could easily have measured their clients' immune status parameters (immunoglobulin levels, counts and activities of lymphocyte types, response to various antigen challenges, and others) and checked their stress hormone levels. No such data has been published. Fox recognizes this fact when he says:

> The number of acceptable studies in humans in this field is very small, and the field cries out for good work. But merely carrying out therapy or measuring attitude, together with a look at relapse or survival time, will yield only partial answers. We should also have measures of immune function and hormonal levels to make any kind of progress in the theory (7).

CASE PRESENTATIONS

The actual cases from *Getting Well Again* that are supposed to document the effectivness of the program are unimpressive. A few pages after the reference to "matched control populations," the Simontons describe Bill and Jerry (fictitious names) on pages 14 and 15. Both have "a lung cancer, which had also spread to the brain." Both receive conventional treatment; Jerry fails to respond and soon dies while Bill responds and survives "approximately a year and a half." Neither clinical course is at all unusual in any common type of lung cancer, even with brain metastases. (If these are supposed to be matched cases, the Simontons might have mentioned whether the tumors were of the same histologic type; they sometimes include, and sometimes omit, the actual pathologic diagnosis.)

The most interesting case (pages 15–18) is that of Bob Gilley (real name), who is described as having "undifferentiated carcinoma" in the groin and abdomen. Chemotherapy was discontinued after ten months because the masses were still present. The patient sought help from the Simontons, after which he rapidly regained his strength. He remains well to this day, and has established an organization to promote the Simonton method in Charlotte, North Carolina.

Is there a better explanation for Bob Gilley's recovery? "Undifferentiated carcinoma," first appearing here, often proves to be malignant melanoma or a germ cell neoplasm. Of all common cancers, malignant melanomas are the best known for disappearing spontaneously. Germ cell tumors and other cancers may be truly cured by chemotherapy, only to be replaced by tumor-shaped masses of scar tissue, so that the good result is not recognized. Mr. Gilley describes "a residual scar nodule" where his tumor had been. But *Getting Well Again* omits all the essential details that might tell what really happened.

Dr. Simonton's original patient, James, whose throat cancer remitted completely with radiation, is not unusual (see pages 6–8). A complete, temporary remission is common in such tumors, which are most often a variety of squamous (scale-like) cell carcinoma. A nine-year survival is very good, but not extraordinary. When the patient went on to experience relief of arthritis and impotence after using imagery, it is not much of a surprise. Both problems, unlike cancer, are known to vary with a person's experiences and attitudes.

Glenn, another Simonton client, has a kidney cancer with a pulmonary metastasis that has been stable for four years; it remains stable (see pages 142–144). Such behavior is fairly common, and the finding of a single, stable metastasis will make any pathologist think immediately of renal cell carcinoma.

Charles, a patient with multiple myeloma (widespread disease of the bone marrow), discovered on routine laboratory screening, remains asymptomatic for three years without therapy, and shows a "decrease" in the amount of the serum marker (presumably a monoclonal immunoglobulin peak on serum electrophoresis). This situation (see pages 144–146) is becoming common, as more patients are screened for such abnormalities and found to have indolent lesions. Why cancer, rather than "monoclonal gammopathy of uncertain significance" (formerly "benign monoclonal gammopathy"), was diagnosed in the absence of symptoms remains unexplained.

Edith, who has breast cancer, experiences a "dramatic remission of her widespread metastases" (see pages 153–154). While the Simontons usually mention what therapies the patient has received, no such information is provided here. It is very common for disseminated breast cancer to melt away after treatment, especially after hormonal manipulation. Ellen is another woman whose breast cancer, metastatic to bone, remits so that she has "no evidence of disease." Again, the Simontons are completely silent about medical treatment.

Some other patients have malignant lymphomas ("lymphosarcomas"). These tumors, with or without treatment, are notoriously unpredictable and often are indolent even when widespread.

All of these stories are written to make it appear to ordinary readers that the Simonton method actually works against tumors. Of course, no such "case histories" appear in the articles intended for physicians.

PATIENT SATISFACTION

How do patients who choose the Simonton approach, as all or part of an "unconventional" cancer regimen, feel about it? In a recent study of 660 cancer patients, 325 were receiving both conventional and unorthodox therapy. Of these, 24 were using imagery. An additional 55 were receiving unorthodox therapy only, and of these, 21 were using imagery. Among all users of unorthodox therapies, those selecting imagery tended to be somewhat better educated, and 79 percent had some college.

Patients were evenly divided as to whether they thought the imagery had had any beneficial effect on their illness; no patient felt it was harmful. Only 22 percent of patients on imagery believed it had been effective in bringing about cure or remission, augmenting other treatments, or preventing the spread of their disease. Thus, imagery ranked far behind "metabolic therapy," "immune therapy," and "megavitamins" in terms of perceived effectiveness by its users (6).

CONCLUSIONS

1. The Simonton cancer treatment outlined in *Getting Well Again* combines commonplaces of good self-care with a bizarre technique involving visualizations.

2. Unlike other unorthodox cancer programs, the patient is expected to comply fully with treatments by conventional physicians.

3. The Simontons' have published only crude statistics on remissions and survival times for their patients, who they admit are a selected group. No report is made of data that they would be expected to possess. It seems

284 Examining Holistic Medicine

reasonable to conclude that the Simontons have been disappointed with their unpublished data.

4. The immune surveillance theory, so central to the imaging technique, is no longer widely accepted. In any case, the Simontons never described testing their patients' immune systems, which would be easy enough to do.

5. As presented in *Getting Well Again,* the Simontons' case histories are very poor evidence that their treatment controls tumors.

6. The Simontons use their key words ambiguously. They withhold critical information from the medically unsophisticated readers in order to make their evidence appear stronger. They sometimes resort to fallacious reasoning.

7. Cancer victims who have used imagery are relatively unlikely to consider it effective.

8. Some cancer victims have found the Simonton emphasis on hopefulness, autonomy, communication, and satisfaction with daily living most helpful. The popularity of their books points to the continuing need for good patient education by oncologists.

9. A physician recommending the Simontons' books to cancer victims should warn them that there is no reason to believe cancer is caused by "faulty attitudes," or that using imagery will prolong life. However, the Simonton approach makes some patients who use it feel much better.

REFERENCES

1. R. D. Abrans, *Not Alone With Cancer* (Springfield, Ill.: Thomas, 1974).

2. Jeanne Achterberg, O. Carl Simonton, and Stephanie Matthews-Simonton, *Stress, Psychological Factors, and Cancer* (Fort Worth, Texas: New Medicine Press, 1976).

3. American Cancer Society, "Unproven Methods of Cancer Mnagement: O. Carl Simonton, M. D." *CA* 32 (1982):58–61.

4. G. W. Brown, "Life Events, Psychiatric Disorder and Physical Illness," *Journal of Psychosomatic Medicine* 25 (1981): 461–73.

5. F. Capra, *The Tao of Physics* (London: Fontana, 1978).

6. B. R. Cassileth, E. J. Lusk, T. B. Strouse, and B. A. Bodenheimer, "Contemporary Unorthodox Treatments in Cancer Medicine," *Annals of Internal Medicine* 101 (1984): 105–12.

7. B. H. Fox, "Current Theory of Psychogenic Effects on Cancer Incidence and Prognosis," *Journal of Psychosocial Oncology* 1 (1983): 17–31.

8. T. A. Gonda, and J. C. Ruark, *Dying Dignified* (Menlo Park, Calif.: Addison-Wesley, 1984).

9. H. M. Howe, *Do Not Go Gentle* (New York: Norton, 1981).

10. R. S. Jones, *Physics as Metaphor* (Minneapolis: University of Minnesota Press, 1982).

11. R. M. Mack, "Lessons from Living with Cancer," *New England Journal of Medicine:* 311 (1984): 1640–44.

12. C. Magarey, "Holistic Cancer Therapy," *Journal of Psychosomatic Research* 27 (1983): 181–84.

13. S. Matthews-Simonton, *The Healing Family* (New York: Bantam, 1984).

14. A. Meares, "Stress, Meditation and the Regression of Cancer," *Practitioner* 226 (1982): 1607–9.

15. A. Meares, "A Form of Intensive Meditation Associated with the Regression of Cancer," *American Journal of Clinical Hypnosis* 25 (1982–3): 114-21.

16. A. Meares, "Psychological Mechanisms in the Regression of Cancer," *Medical Journal of Australia* 1 (1983): 583–84.

17. C. G. Moertel, T. R. Fleming, E. T. Creagan, J. Rubin, M. J. O'Connell, and M. M. Ames, "High-Dose Vitamin C Versus Placebo in the Treatment of Patients with Advanced Cancer Who have had No Prior Chemotherapy," *New England Journal of Medicine* 312 (1985): 137-41.

18. B. W. Newton, "The Use of Hypnosis in the Treatment of Cancer Patients," *American Journal of Clinical Hypnosis* 25 (1982–3): 104-13.

19. G. W. Oliver, "A Cancer Patient and Her Family: A Case Study," *American Journal of Clinical Hypnosis* 25 (1982–83): 156-60.

20. J. Schonfield, "Psychological and Life-Experience Differences between Israeli Women with Benign and Cancerous Breast Lesions," *Journal of Psychosomatic Research* 19 (1975): 229-34.

21. A. Shapiro, "Psychotherapy as Adjunct Treatment for Cancer Patients," *American Journal of Clinical Hypnosis* 25 (1982–83): 150-55.

22. O. C. Simonton, and S. Matthews-Simonton, "Belief Systems and Management of the Emotional Aspects of Malignancy," *Journal of Transpersonal Psychology* 7 (1975): 29–47; reprinted in Berkeley Holistic Health Center, *The Holistic Health Handbook* (Berkeley: And/Or Press, 1978).

23. O. C. Simonton, "What Constitutes Scientific Proof?" in Berkeley Holistic Health Center, *The Holistic Health Handbook* (Berkeley: And/Or Press, 1978).

24. O. C. Simonton, S. Matthews-Simonton, and J. L. Creighton, *Getting Well Again* (New York: Bantam, 1980).

25. O. C. Simonton, S. Matthews-Simonton, and T. F. Sparks, "Psychological Intervention in the Treatment of Cancer," *Psychosomatics,* 21 (1980): 226-33.

26. O. C. Simonton, and S. Matthews-Simonton, "Cancer and Stress: Counselling the Cancer Patient," *Medical Journal of Australia* 1 (1981): 679–83.

27. U.S. Department of Health and Human Services, *Coping with Cancer: An Annotated Bibliography of Public, Patient, and Professional Information and Education Materials* (Bethesda: NIH Publication 80–2129, 1980).

28. U.S. Department of Health and Human Services, *Coping with Cancer: A Resource for the Health Professional* (Bethesda: NIH Publication 80–2080, 1980).

Philip E. Clark, R.N., and Mary Jo Clark, P.N.P.

Therapeutic Touch:
Is There a Scientific Basis for the Practice?

Therapeutic touch, the art of interpersonal energy transfer for the purpose of healing (Krieger, Peper, & Ancoli, 1979), is an intervention that is believed by some to have potential for nursing. Workshops are being held across the country and there is at least one graduate course in the art of therapeutic touch (Krieger, 1979). Indeed, there are nurses who use the practice as a therapeutic modality (Sandroff, 1980). What empirical support exists for such practice?

Nursing literature covers several apsects of therapeutic touch. Selected articles relate the history of the laying-on-of-hands (Zefron, 1975), describe a theoretical framework in which to interpret the phenomenon of therapeutic touch (Miller, 1979), and map the human field (Boguslawski, 1979). The literature also suggests ailments that therapeutic touch may ameliorate (Boguslawski, 1979), and even describes a format for charting the effects of the intervention (Krieger, 1979). Sandroff (1980) presents an overview by three prominent nurse researchers on the subject of therapeutic touch.

Although such contributions to the literature are interesting, they do not provide empirical support for practice. To determine the validity of therapeutic touch as a treatment modality, reports of research investigating its effects must be examined. Such an examination is the intent of this article.

One of the earlier examples of research on therapeutic touch (Grad, Cadoret, & Paul, 1961) examined wound healing in mice. After wounding and wound measurement, each of 300 mice were randomly assigned to one experimental or one of two control groups. The experimental group was treated by a healer. One control group was treated by medical students who claimed no paranormal healing abilities; the other received no treatment.

Prior to wounding, the mice were observed and weighed periodically for one to two weeks to eliminate unhealthy mice. During this time, the mice were also subjected to frequent handling similar to that they would experience during treatment. The mice were anesthetized and hair was removed from a 0.8 × 1.6 inch area on the back. Oval wounds of about 0.4 × 0.8 inches were cut with scissors in such a way that the wound lay with its long axis along the spine and with the wound center 1.2 inches from the base of the tail. Wound size was measured immediately after wounding and the mice rank-ordered according to the precise wound size. The three mice with the largest wounds were randomly assigned, one to each of the three treatment groups. Random assignment continued with each of the succeeding groups of three mice. This procedure assured an equal distribution of wound sizes to the three treatment groups.

Treatment occurred in two conditions: open and closed bag (Grad et al., 1961). The open bag condition permitted the healer or medical student to place his hands in a paper bag that contained a mouse in a cage. Handling of the cage only was permitted; the mice were not handled directly. The closed bag condition permitted handling of the paper bag only. The control group receiving no treatment was also exposed to both bag conditions.

The mice were housed in 10 rooms with 30 mice per room. Of the 30 mice in a particular room, 10 mice were treated by the healer, 10 by medical students, and 10 received no treatment. All of the mice in any one room were treated under the same condition. Mice in five of the rooms were treated in the open bag condition; mice in the other rooms were treated in the closed bag condition.

Differences in wound size were assessed by a two-way analysis of variance. The investigators reported adjusting wound measurements due to moderate skewing of distribution. It was tested using the adjusted data. Homogeneity of variance was established only within each bag condition. Separate factorial analyses were applied to the means of wound measurements of mice in the open bag condition and closed bag condition.

On the 15th and 16th days of the study, the investigators found significantly smaller wound sizes for the mice treated by the healer in the open bag condition. On subsequent days, the difference in wound size was not significant. Nor was there ever a significant difference between mice treated by the healer in the closed bag condition and the mice in the control groups.

This investigation of one healer's ability by Grad et al. (1961) appears to have been well controlled. The findings, though statistically significant in the open bag condition, were transient. One must question, then, the utility of the healer, since the other groups of mice achieved a similar degree of healing by the end of the study.

A second investigation by Grad (1963) dealt with a healer's influence on the growth of barley seeds. Twenty-four peat pots, each containing 20 barley seeds, were randomly assigned to two groups of equal size. The experimental group of seeds was watered initially with a 1 percent saline solution from an open beaker held for 15 minutes by the healer with his hand extended over the beaker.

The rationale for using a 1 percent saline solution in the manner described, rather than having the healer touch the plants or their pots directly, derived from a number of previous exploratory experiments conducted by Grad. He stated that "best results were obtained under conditons of an inhibition of the normal growth of seeds" (1963, p. 118). Salt was considered an inhibiting factor and a 1 percent saline solution was considered optimal for the purpose of inhibiting growth without killing the plants.

With respect to the treatment of the watering solution as opposed to direct treatment of the plants, Grad stated: "Experiments soon demonstrated that significant differences could readily be obtained without the need for Mr. E. to treat the plants with his hands, but it was enough simply to add water, water which he had previously treated" (1963, p. 121). Speculation that heat from the healer's hands influenced the growth of experimental plants is eliminated by the use of a treated watering solution. The maintenance of double-blind conditions was simplified as the healer was not aware of which group of plants had been treated at the time he measured them.

The dependent variables were the number of plants per pot, the average height of plants per pot, and plant yield per pot. Yield was defined as "the total of all the heights of each plant in a given pot" (Grad, 1963, p. 125). Plants were counted and measured by the healer on the 8th through 13th days after treatment.

Grad reported specific measurements of the three dependent variables. Data analysis by means of a t test indicated that on one day only, the experimental group contained a significantly greater number of plants. In addition, the experimental plants were reported as significantly taller and to have had a significantly greater yield for a period of five days (Grad, 1963).

The use of the healer to prepare all pots and seeds and to measure all plants might have contributed to some bias in the study. Grad (1963) explained that the double-blind aspects of the study prevented the healer from becoming aware of which were the treated plants. Also, any additional influence due to healer contact with the pots, seeds, or plants should have been reflected in both groups and would not have contributed to the significant differences found. Grad's rationale for the use of the healer in this capacity was simply the lack of other personnel to carry out the task. Employment of another person would have eliminated this threat to internal validity. The reported results of this study seem more stable over time and, therefore, may be considered somewhat more convincing than those of the previous study.

A similar study examined the effects of two healers on rye grass seeds (MacDonald, Hickman, & Dakin, 1977). For one healer, the plant heights in the experimental group were significantly smaller than those of the control group. For the other healer, the plant heights in the experimental group were significantly greater. Although the investigators viewed the results as supporting those of Grad, such an equivocal report must be questioned.

Grad replicated his previous work with barley seeds in a series of four experiments. In the original work with barley seeds, the saline solution treated by the healer was contained in an open beaker. In this series of four experiments, the saline solution treated by the healer was contained in a stoppered bottle or in a stoppered bottle in a stapled paper bag.

The use of the paper bag was introduced as an additional measure to assure double-blind conditions. The stoppered container was used to prevent contamination of the solution by the healer's perspiration or respiration, which would have been possible in the previous experiment. Significant results in the stoppered condition would support the conclusion that something, perhaps a healing energy, had passed from the healer's hands, through the glass, to the solution.

The previous measures of mean number, height, and yield of plants were also used in these four experiments. The results were essentially mixed. The measures of plant number, height, and yield reported were only occasionally significant. At other times, no differences between groups were noted. None of the results in this series of experiments was as stable over time as those of the original work with barley seeds. For an excellent review of these studies with mice and plants, see Grad (1965).

Smith (1972) examined the potential effects of a healer and a magnetic field on the enzyme trypsin. The rationale for enzyme activity as a measure of the effects of a healer's performance is derived from biochemical evidence that cellular metabolism involves specific enzyme activity and from the supposition that illness is a result of absence of or dysfunction in enzyme activity. As stated by Smith: ". . . if enzyme failure is the ultimate physical cause of disease, any therapeutic effect should be detectable at the same level, that is, with enzyme activity" (1972, p. 15).

The investigator used four solutions of the enzyme trypsin—a control solution, a solution exposed to ultraviolet light and treated by the healer, a solution held by the healer, and a solution exposed to a magnetic field. Using a series of graphs, Smith (1972) reported means and standard deviations of the activity levels of the various solutions. No statistical tests for the signficance of the findings were reported. Smith concluded that the healer and magnetic field exerted similar effects, as those two solutions displayed increased enzyme activity.

Smith (1972) also reported two replications of this study, one using the same healer and one using three other self-proclaimed healers. The results of the initial experiment were not reproduced. Smith reported a third replication with three healers and claimed an increase in enzyme activity. Very few details with respect to any of the replications are discussed.

There was no report of statistical testing for significance of differences between activity levels of the treated and control groups. It is unknown whether the reported increases in enzyme activity demonstrated in the initial study were statistically significant or due to chance. The absence of increased enzyme activity during two of the three replication studies suggests that the initial results may have been due to chance.

The efforts of Dr. Delores Krieger merit consideration as some of the first attempts by nurses at scientific inquiry into this treatment modality. Krieger (1976) reported a significant increase in hemoglobin levels in response to the efforts of a healer. However, there are a number of questions raised by the rationale for hemoglobin as the dependent variable and by the methods used in the study.

Krieger (1976) postulated that the healer facilitates the flow of a healing energy and that this energy is bound to oxygen. Hemoglobin was chosen as a measure of this energy flow because "hemoglobin . . . is one of the body's most sensitive indicators of oxygen uptake" (Krieger, 1976, p. 123). Hemoglobin is not, however, a measure of oxygen uptake, but a measure of oxygen capacity (Selkurt, 1975). An appropriate measure of oxygen uptake is oxygen saturation of the blood.

Krieger also stated that another reason for the selection of hemoglobin was the similarity of hemoglobin to chlorophyll. She reported that "Grad found that the treated seeds . . . had a greater net weight and significantly more chlorophyll content than the control group" (Krieger, 1976, p. 122). Based on reports of Grad's studies, it is difficult to determine how this conclusion was reached. The dependent measures in Grad's research (1963, 1964, 1967) were mean number, height, and yield of plants. There are no reports of measurement of chlorophyll content. Greater chlorophyll levels could be assumed to coincide with greater yield, but without specific measurement and comparison, it is not known if significant differences in chlorophyll levels between groups were present.

Krieger's final rationale for the selection of hemoglobin as the dependent variable was that the production of hemoglobin was dependent upon the functioning of several enzymes and that "Smith's study indicated that enzyme systems responded to the laying-on-of-hands . . ." (1976, p. 124). While Smith (1972) did report an increase in trypsin activity, she did not report testing for statistical significance between pre- and posttreatment measures of enzyme activity or between the four solutions tested; nor was the increased activity reproduced in two of three replications. Therefore, Krieger's assumptions based on Smith's study are questionable.

Several methodological considerations also weakened Krieger's (1976) study. Krieger does not report the manner in which subjects for the experimental and control groups were selected. She does report using a *t* test on the variable of hemoglobin to establish the comparability of both groups. The *t* test, a test for differences in means, does not convey any information with regard to the distribution of a particular trait within groups (Huck, Cormier, & Bounds, 1974). A stronger method for assuring homogeneity of the experimental and control groups, in terms of age, sex, and hemoglobin values, would have been random assignment.

Another methodological problem was the use of meditation by some subjects, allowing for meditation as a rival hypothesis. When a healing ability or energy force, which cannot be objectively defined, demonstrated, or controlled, is an independent variable in a field study, any possible threat to internal validity should be eliminated. Control for extraneous variables is much better research methodology than the use of a chi-square to rule out any possible effects of meditation on hemoglobin.

The final methodological problem concerns the inappropriate use of multiple t tests. A more suitable method of analysis would have been an analysis of covariance, which would have adjusted posttest means to account for differences in pretest means. This test would be used provided the underlying assumptions could be met (Huck et al., 1974). The appropriate statistical analysis is critical to a correct interpretation of the data, since Hurt (1976) reported in a critique of Krieger's study (1976) that hemoglobin values of the control group also increased. This increase was significant at a probability of less than .05. The statistical tests as employed by Krieger do not account for the simultaneous gain in hemoglobin levels by both experimental and control groups, thus resulting in possibly erroneous conclusions.

This study conducted in 1976 is a replication of previous work by the same investigator (Krieger, 1973). It purported to correct several criticisms of the original study (Schlotfeldt, 1973). Similar significant increases in hemoglobin levels were reported for the experimental subjects in the previous study (Krieger, 1973).

Further work by Krieger et al. (1979) reported the objective verification of clients' relaxation during therapeutic touch. Measured physiologic variables, presumed from the text to be galvanic skin resistance, pulse, temperature, and others, indicated that the patients were relaxed. The status of these measures pretreatment, during treatment, and posttreatment were not reported. It is unknown what changes occurred in these variables during the therapeutic touch or if these changes were significant. It is unfortunate that the actual measures were not reported, because the work seems to serve as a bridge between the relaxation response and therapeutic touch for at least one subsequent investigator (Heidt, 1981).

Heidt (1981) attempted to examine the possible effects of therapeutic touch on anxiety. Pre- and posttreatment anxiety levels were assessed by questionnaire for three groups—a therapeutic touch group, a casual touch group, and a no-touch group. The investigator reported that the therapeutic touch group had significantly lower levels of anxiety than either of the other two groups. However, due to problems in research design, one must question whether or not therapeutic touch was the major factor in the anxiety reduction.

It is difficult to substantiate the validity of a questionnaire as the sole measure of an emotional response. A corroborating physiologic variable such as pulse rate, respiratory rate, or galvanic skin resistance would have provided a more explicit measure of anxiety. That the investigator did not include such a measure is surprising, in light of her review of the literature that discusses the relaxation response, a phenomenon manifested by changes in respiratory rate, pulse rate, blood pressure, etc. (Wallace, Benson, & Wilson, 1971; Beary, Benson, & Klemchuk, 1974; Benson, Beary, & Carol, 1974).

The comparison of two types of touch—therapeutic touch and casual touch—with no-touch does not answer the question of whether or not therapeutic touch itself can affect anxiety. To test for the hypothesized energy transfer between client and healer, one must control for the unusual nature of the therapy and for client expectations, in short for the placebo effect.

Heidt's (1981) experimental design compared two distinct treatments. The casual-touch group in Heidt's study did not control for the possible placebo effect because this group did not receive the behavioral stimulation of the therapeutic-touch routine. Therefore, it is impossible to determine if the anxiety reduction reported was due to an hypothesized transfer of energy or to placebo effect.

A more appropriate control group would be one that received a sham therapeutic touch procedure (i.e., the passing of the hands over the body with no energy transfer). This should be possible since therapeutic touch is defined as a purposeful act (Heidt, 1981; Krieger, 1973). Such a control group would allow the possibility of a double-blind procedure, therefore controlling more effectively for the placebo effect. Should both the actual and sham therapeutic touch procedures produce similar effects on subjects, one could conclude that some form of placebo effect was in operation. However, if only the therapeutic touch group showed significant effects, the possibility of a placebo effect would be eliminated.

A second study examining the possible effects of therapeutic touch on anxiety (Randolph, 1980) used muscle tension, galvanic skin resistance, and temperature as measures of anxiety. The experimental and control groups were exposed to a stressful movie while receiving therapeutic touch or casual touch, respectively. The observable treatment in both groups was the placement of the practitioner's hands on the subject's abdomen and back. The investigator reported no significant differences in the posttreatment measures employed to assess anxiety.

Randolph's study (1980) is the first published nursing investigation of therapeutic touch that is double-blind. It is also the first to expose two groups to what appeared to be the same procedure except, of course, that the experimental group was presumed to have received the hypothesized energy transfer involved in therapeutic touch. Finally, the research design and statistical analysis were appropriate to the question of whether or not therapeutic touch can affect anxiety.

Randolph (1980) suggested at least two possible mitigating factors that could have produced the nonsignificant results. The therapeutic touch practitioners were not allowed to apply their art in the usual way (i.e., they were not allowed to perform an assessment prior to treatment). It may be that something in the assessment phase is essential to the effects of therapeutic touch (Randolph, 1980).

Another possible mitigating effect may have been the level of health of the subjects (Randolph, 1980). Randolph dealt with healthy subjects, while previous research employed subjects, human, animal, or plant, with a natural or induced illness. Randolph's conjecture is supported by Grad (1963), who also suggested that statistically significant results were more easily obtained if the subjects were to some degree unhealthy.

The advantage with animal or plant subjects is that "illness" of relatively short course can be induced. The short duration of such induced illness would strengthen the internal validity of a study by eliminating the threat of history. Two interesting studies in psychic healing (Graham & Watkins, 1971; Wells & Klein, 1972) illustrated this methodology. The subjects were ether-anesthetized pairs of mice and the dependent variable was arousal time. Anesthesia was considered a state of "illness" and the interventions of the healers were designed to speed arousal time of the mice treated.

If the subjects are human, it is necessary to control for the placebo effect. Future studies should be double-blind. Also, exposure of control and experimental groups to the behavioral stimulation of therapeutic touch may help to control for this effect.

Since there has been at least one replicative failure with a report of mood change in the healer (Smith, 1972), and since research results have been reported consistent with the mood of the healer (Grad, 1967), some control of the healer may be necessary. To protect against mood change, the healer should live a fairly regulated life during the experimental period. Consistent meal, sleep, recreational, and exercise patterns may enhance the results of the original study and increase the chances of a replicative success, if the healer maintains a similar lifestyle for the subsequent studies.

In the final analysis, the current research base supporting continued nursing practice of therapeutic touch is, at best, weak. Well-designed, double-blind studies have thus far shown transient results (Grad, 1961), no significant results (Randolph, 1980), or are in need of independent replication (Grad, 1963). Therapeutic touch as a modality does excite interest. However, without a broader research base, it may be presumptuous to teach the art or seriously discuss the use of this practice in the treatment of illness. The practice of therapeutic touch by nurses will never gain professional credibility without clear, objective evidence to support it. Without this evidence, the nurse practitioners of therapeutic touch will be relegated to the practice of "placebo mumbo jumbo."

REFERENCES

Beary, J., Benson, H., and Klemchuk, H. "A Simple Psychophysiologic Technique which Elicits the Hypometabolic Changes of the Relaxation Response," *Psychosomatic Medicine,* 36 (1974): 115-20.

Benson, H., Beary, J., and Carol, M. "The Relaxation Response," *Psychiatry* 37 (1974):37-46.

Boguslawski, M. "The Use of Therapeutic Touch in Nursing," *Jounral of Continuing Education in Nursing* 10 (1979):9-15.

Grad, B. "A Telekinetic Effect on Plant Growth," *International Journal of Parapsychology,* 5 (1963):117-33.

———. "A Telekinetic Effect on Plant Growth. Part 2. Experiments Involving Treatment of Saline in Stoppered Bottles," *International Journal of Parapsychology* 6 (1964):473-98.

———. "Some Biological Effects of the 'Laying-on-of-hands': A Review of Experiments with Animals and Plants," *Journal of the American Society for Psychical Research,* 59 (1965):95-127.

———. "The 'Laying-on-of-hands': Implications for Psychotherapy, Gentling, and the Placebo Effect," *Journal of the American Society for Psychical Research,* 61 (1967):286-305.

Grad, B., Cadoret, R., and Paul, G. "An Unorthodox Method of Treatment of Wound Healing in Mice," *International Journal of Parapsychology,* 3 (1961):5-24.

Graham, K., and Watkins, A. "Possible Pk Influence on the Resuscitation of Anesthetized Mice," *The Journal of Parapsychology,* 35 (1971):257-72.

Heidt, P. "Effect of Therapeutic Touch on Anxiety Level of Hospitalized Patients," *Nursing Research,* 30 (1980):32-37.

Huck, S., Cormier, W., and Bounds, W. *Reading Statistics and Research* (New York: Harper & Row, 1974.

Hurt, S. "A Comment," *Psychoenergetic Systems* 1 (1976):129-30.

Krieger, D. "The Relationship of Touch with Intent to Help or Heal to Subjects' In-vivo Hemoglobin Values: A Study in Personalized Interaction," paper presented at the American Nurses' Association, Ninth Nursing Research Conference, San Antonio, Texas, March 21-23, 1973.

———. "Healing by the 'Laying-on' of Hands as a Facilitator of Bioenergetic Change: The Response of In-vivo Human Hemoglobin," *Psychoenergetic Systems,* 1 (1976):121-29.

———. *The Therapeutic Touch: How to Use Your Hands to Help or Heal* (Englewood Cliffs, N.J.: Prentice-Hall, 1979).

Krieger, D., Peper, E., and Ancoli, S. "Therapeutic Touch, Searching for Evidence of Physiological Change," *American Nurses' Association* 79 (1979):660-62.

MacDonald, R. G., Hickman, J. L., and Dakin, H. S. "Preliminary Physical Measurements of Psychophysical Effects Associated with Three Alleged Psychic Healers," in J. D. Morris, W. G. Roll, and R. L. Morris (eds.), *Research in Parapsychology* (Metuchen, N.J.: Scarecrow Press, 1977).

Miller, L. "An Explanation of Therapeutic Touch Using the Science of Unitary Man," *Nursing Forum* 18 (1979):278-87.

Randolph, G. "The Difference in Physiologic Response of Female College Students Exposed to Stressful Stimulus, When Simultaneously Treated by either Therapeutic or Casual Touch," (Doctoral dissertation, New York University, 1980). *Dissertation Abstracts International,* 41 (1980):523B, (University Microfilms No. 8017522).

Sandroff, R. "A Skeptic's Guide to Therapeutic Touch," *RN,* 43 (1980):25-30, 82ff.

Schlotfeldt, R. "Critique of the Relationship of Touch with Intent to Help or Heal to Subjects' In-vivo Hemoglobin Values: A Study in Personalized Internation," paper presented at the American Nurses' Association, Ninth Nursing Research Conference, San Antonio, Texas, March 21-23, 1973.

Selkurt, E. "Respiratory Gas Exchange and Its Transport," in E. Selkurt (ed.), *Basic Physiology for the Health Sciences* (Boston: Little, Brown & Co., 1975).

Smith, J. "Paranormal Effects on Enzyme Activity," *Human Dimensions,* 1 (1972):15-19.

Wallace, R., Benson, H., and Wilson, A. "A Wakeful Hypometabolic State," *American Journal of Physiology,* 221 (1971):795-99.

Wells, R. and Klein, J. "A Replication of a Psychic Healing Paradigm," *Journal of Parapsychology,* 36 (1972):144-49.

Zefron, L. "The History of the Laying-on of Hands in Nursing," *Nursing Forum* 15 (1975):350-63.

Edward T. Creagan, M.D., et al.

Failure of High-Dose Vitamin C (Ascorbic Acid) Therapy to Benefit Patients with Advanced Cancer

A Controlled Trial

The possible role of vitamin C in both the pathogenesis and therapy of malignant disease has been suggested by a variety of laboratory and clinical data. A deficiency of ascorbate has been reported in association with dissolution of the intercellular matrix, which might facilitate local infiltration and dissemination of neoplastic cells (1). Studies in laboratory animals have shown that ascorbate seems to concentrate in malignant tissue and thus depletes systemic reserves (2–4). Moreover, in patients with skin carcinoma, concentrations of vitamin C are higher in the tumor than in surrounding normal tissue (5). Lymphocytes, mediators of cellular immunity, contain relatively high amounts of ascorbate, and immune responsiveness has been enhanced by ascorbate administration in mice (6). Moreover, there have been some apparent regressions of adenomas after administration of ascorbate by mouth in persons with familial polyposis coli, a known premalignant condition (7).

Several nonrandomized studies have suggested that high-dose Vitamin C (10 g per day by mouth) might enhance survival and improve symptoms of patients with advanced cancer. Cameron and Campbell studied 50 such patients who had not received chemotherapy and reported five tumor regressions (10 percent) (8). These authors also reported that most patients experienced some

Reprinted by permission of the *New England Journal of Medicine*, 301 (1979):687-690. Coauthors of this article include: Charles G. Moertel, M.D.; Judith R. O'Fallon, Ph.D.; Allan J. Schutt, M.D.; Michael J. O'Connell, M.D.; Joseph Rubin, M.D.; and Stephen Frytak, M.D.

subjective benefit (8). In a later report, 50 patients who had previously received irradiation and chemotherapy were combined with the first group, and the survival of all 100 patients was compared with that of 1000 historical control cases in the records at the Vale of Leven Hospital, Loch Lomondside, Scotland (9). For each ascorbate-treated patient, 10 controls were matched on the basis of age, sex, site and histologic features of the primary tumor. The mean survival of patients given ascorbate was 210 days, as compared with 50 for the selected controls. Since this was not a randomized study, doubt has been raised concerning the comparability of ascorbate-treated patients and the control population (10). Cameron and Pauling therefore revised the original study group to exclude 10 ascorbate-treated patients with unusual cancers; they substituted 10 other patients randomly selected from the records of ascorbate-treated patients at the Vale of Leven Hospital (11). In addition, a new group of 1000 controls was selected because data on some of the initial control patients were considered unreliable and incomplete. Most of the new controls, however, were drawn from the original control population. This revised and updated analysis showed that the mean survival of patients given vitamin C was greater than 293 days, as compared with 38 for the controls.

Since bias is possible in nonrandomized studies including selected controls, we conducted a randomized, controlled double-blind trial to evaluate the effect of vitamin C on symptoms and survival in patients with advanced and preterminal cancer.

PATIENTS AND METHODS

All patients had histologically documented advanced cancer, and all were able to take medications by mouth. All were unsuitable for treatment with systemic chemotherapy, either because of progression of disease after previous efforts or because their general condition precluded cytotoxic regimens.

Relatively few pediatric patients met the eligibility criteria. No patients had leukemia. Patients were stratified on the basis of a performance score of 2 versus 3 or 4 on the Eastern Cooperative Oncology Group scale (in which a score of 0 indicates a fully active patient, whereas 4 indicates bedridden); patients with a score of 3 or 4 were grouped as one stratum. The patients were also classified on the basis of site of primary tumor (colon, stomach, lung, pancreas, breast and other) and then randomized to one of two groups: those given vitamin C (10 g per day by mouth in four divided doses, or a total of twenty 0.5-g capsules daily) and those given the same number of capsules containing a comparably flavored lactose placebo. Both drugs were given as identical capsules, dispensed in bottles of 1000, which were identified only by code number. The drug supply was renewed at six-week intervals as needed. Neither patient nor investigator knew which drug was being administered. Treatment was continued until death or until the patient was no longer able to take medications by mouth. At two-week intervals, patients reported the amount and frequency of the drug taken, the status of their symptoms and body weight.

A total of 150 patients were entered into the clinical trial. Patient and tumor characteristics for the 123 patients who took the study medication are listed in Tables 1 and 2. Twenty-seven patients elected not to participate after randomization, but before taking the first dose of vitamin C or placebo. These patients (12

Table 1. Patient Characteristics

CHARACTERISTIC	VITAMIN C GROUP	PLACEBO GROUP
No. of patients	60	63
Age, yr		
<45	2	4
46-65	26	27
>65	32	32
Sex		
Male	37	39
Female	23	24
Performance score*		
2	12	13
3	39	43
4	9	7

*Eastern Cooperative Oncology score: 0 (fully active) to 4 (totally disabled).

assigned randomly to the placebo group and 15 to the vitamin C group) were considered unevaluable for comparative drug effects but were analyzed separately for survival. Their characteristics are shown in Table 3.

Chi-square tests of homogeneity were performed to compare the distributions of the following five pretreatment clinical characteristics between the two treatment groups: age, sex, site of primary tumor, initial performance score and previous treatment. Kaplan-Meier survival curves were plotted separately for the two treatment groups and tested for inequality by use of the Gehan-Wilcoxon and log-rank tests. A Cox covariate analysis was performed, using the survival data from the 123 treated patients (12).

RESULTS

Survival

The survival curves for the 123 patients treated with vitamin C and with placebo are shown on page 302 in Figure 1. There was no significant difference in survival between the two groups (log-rank test; $P = 0.61$). We were unable to show any survival benefit according to tumor site. Note that the two treatment groups

Table 2. Tumor Characteristics and Previous Treatment.

CHARACTERISTIC	VITAMIN C GROUP	PLACEBO GROUP
No. of patients	60	63
Site		
Colorectal	24	26
Pancreas	12	12
Lung	6	6
Stomach	5	3
Other	13	16
Grade of anaplasia (Broder's)		
1, 2	29	27
3, 4	17	23
Not stated	14	13
Previous treatment		
None	5	4
Radiation therapy	17	18
Chemotherapy	52	56

are evenly balanced in age, sex, site of primary tumor, initial performance status and previous treatment (Tables 1 and 2).

Cox covariate analysis showed that none of the six potentially prognostic factors was significantly associated with survival in the 123 treated patients. Only performance score was even marginally associated ($P = 0.08$) after taking into account the effects of the remaining factors.

The one long-term survivor in this study is a patient with metastatic islet-cell carcinoma, massive hepatomegaly and jaundice who had shown no response

Table 3. Characteristics of 27 Patients Who Took No Study Drug.

CHARACTERISTIC	NO. OF PATIENTS
Age, yr	
<45	1
46-65	13
>65	13
Sex	
Male	19
Female	8
Performance score*	
2	3
3	19
4	5
Previous treatment	
None	7
Radiation therapy	9
Chemotherapy	17
Site of primary tumor	
Colorectal	4
Pancreas	4
Lung	4
Stomach	4
Other	11
Grade of anaplasia (Broder's)	
1, 2	6
3, 4	16
Not stated	5

*Eastern Cooperative Oncology Group score: 0 (fully active) to 4 (totally disabled).

to many previous attempts at chemotherapy. After entering the study, he showed improvement in symptoms and some reduction in serum bilirubin. He was still alive 63 weeks after entering the study. This patient received the lactose placebo.

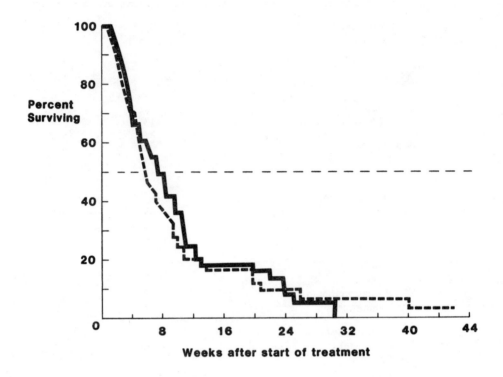

FIGURE 1. High-Dose Vitamin C versus Placebo and Survival Results in Patients with Advanced Cancer. The solid line shows survival in 60 patients given Vitamin C. The dashed line shows survival in 63 patients given the lactose placebo.

Symptom Reduction and Side Effects

Fifty-eight percent of the patients given the placebo and 63 percent of those given vitamin C claimed some improvement in symptoms during treatment. There were no statistically significant differences in symptoms between the two treatment groups (Table 4).

Mild nausea and vomiting were the most frequent toxic reactions, affecting about 40 percent of patients, but there were no statistically significant differences in the number of episodes between the two groups (Table 4). There was no noteworthy excess of heartburn or other upper-gastrointestinal-tract symptoms in patients given vitamin C, nor was there any documented occurrence of renal calculi.

Analysis of Untreated Patients

An interesting group of patients in this study are those who accepted randomization but subsequently elected not to participate. These patients, in a nonrandomized study, would be presumed to be included only in the nontreated historical controls (Table 3). These patients were excluded from the above analysis because they would not show evidence of the effect of vitamin C or placebo.

The 27 patients who did not receive treatment had a significantly worse (log-rank test; $P = 0.017$) survival than the 123 patients who did take the medication. The median survival in the untreated patients was 25 days, as compared with 51 for treated patients.

DISCUSSION

We were unable to demonstrate any statistically significant benefit of high-dose vitamin C in selected patients with advanced cancer. It should be noted, however,

Table 4. Symptomatic Results and Side Effects.

	VITAMIN C GROUP		PLACEBO GROUP	
	NO.	%	NO.	%
Improvement				
Appetite	14/53	26	12/52	23
Strength	14/53	26	7/53	13
Activity Level	22/53	42	22/53	42
Pain Control	12/49	24	7/48	15
Toxicity				
Nausea	27/60	45	27/63	43
Vomiting	22/60	37	22/63	35
Heartburn	16/60	27	15/63	24
Diarrhea	20/60	33	20/63	32
Leg swelling	34/60	57	28/63	44
Other	30/60	50	26/63	41

that only nine of our 123 patients had not previously received chemotherapy or radiation therapy. It is therefore impossible to draw any conclusions about the possible effectiveness of vitamin C in previously untreated patients. In Cameron and Campbell's report of a 10 percent regression rate in 50 patients with widely disseminated cancer, none had received definitive prior treatment and presumably were more immunocompetent than our patients. Since vitamin C may have an impact on host resistance to cancer (13), we recognize that earlier immunosuppressive treatment might have obscured any benefit provided by this agent. Nevertheless, the nonrandomized study (9) that showed a fourfold enhancement of survival with vitamin C included patients who had received conventional cancer treatment (i.e., cytotoxic agents and radiation therapy). This improvement could not be substantiated by our study.

There is evidence that vitamin C maintains immunocompetence. Although patients with advanced cancer who have previously been treated with irradiation or chemotherapy are indeed immunosuppressed, they are not totally incapable of mounting an immune response. In two previous studies of patients with advanced cancer who were selected on the basis of essentially the same criteria used in this study, we found that 80 percent were capable of responding to recall skin tests (O'Connell, M. J., O'Fallon, J. R., Ritts, R. E., et al: unpublished data), and 56 percent responded to dinitrochlorobenzene (14). One might expect, therefore, that vitamin C would exert some restorative influence in patients whose immune apparatus has been compromised by earlier treatment efforts. If such an effect did occur in our patients, it was not seen in their clinical improvement.

We cannot recommend the use of high-dose vitamin C in patients with advanced cancer who have previously received irradiation or chemotherapy.

REFERENCES

1. E. Cameron, L. Pauling, and B. Leibovitz, "Ascorbic Acid and Cancer: A Review," *Cancer Research* 39 (1979):663-81.

2. E. Boyland, "The Selective Absorption of Ascorbic Acid by Guinea-pig Tumor Tissue," *Biochemical Journal* 30 (1936):1221-24.

3. B. Sure, R. M. Theis, and R. T. Harrelson, "Influence of Walker Carcinosarcoma on Concentration of Ascorbic Acid in Various Endocrines and Organs," *American Journal of Cancer* 36 (1939):252-56.

4. A. F. Watson, "The Chemical Reducing Capacity and Vitamin C Content of Transplantable Tumors of the Rat and Guinea-pig," *British Journal of Experimental Pathology* 17 (1936):124-34.

5. M. J. Moriarty, S. Mulgrew, J. R. Malone, et al., "Results and Analysis of Tumor Levels of Ascorbic Acid," *Irish Journal of Medical Science* 146 (1977):74-78.

6. B. V. Siegel and J. I. Morton, "Vitamin C and the Immune Response," *Experientia* 33 (1977):393-95.

7. J. J. DeCosse, M. B. Adams, J. F. Kuzma, et al., "Effect of Ascorbic Acid on Rectal Polyps of Patients with Familial Polyposis," *Surgery* 78 (1975):608-12.

8. E. Cameron and A. Campbell, "The Orthomolecular Treatment of Cancer. II. Clinical Trial of High-Dose Ascorbic Acid Supplements in Advanced Human Cancer," *Chemico-Biological*

Interactions 9 (1974):285-315.

9. E. Cameron and L. Pauling, "Supplemental Ascorbate in the Supportive Treatment of Cancer: Prolongation of Survival Times in Terminal Human Cancer," *Proceedings of the National Academy of Sciences (USA)* 73 (1976):3685-89.

10. J. H. Comroe, Jr., "Experimental Studies Designed to Evaluate the Management of Patients with Curable Cancer," *Proceedings of the National Academy of Sciences (USA)* 75 (1978): 4543.

11. E. Cameron and L. Pauling, "Supplemental Ascorbate in the Supportive Treatment of Cancer: Reevaluation of Prolongation of Survival Times in Terminal Human Cancer," *Proceedings of the National Academy of Sciences (USA)* 75 (1978):4538-42.

12. D. R. Cox, "Regression Models and Life Tables," *Journal of the Royal Statistical Society (B)* 34 (1972):187-220.

13. E. Cameron and L. Pauling, "The Orthomolecular Treatment of Cancer. I. The Role of Ascorbic Acid in Host Resistance," *Chemico-Biological Interactions* 9 (1974): 273-83.

14. C. G. Moertel, R. E. Ritts, Jr., A. J. Schutt, et. al., "Clinical Studies of Methanol Extraction Residue Fraction of *Bacillus Calmette-Guérin* as an Immunostimulant in Patients with Advanced Cancer," *Cancer Research* 35 (1975):3075-83.

Correspondence on
Vitamin C Therapy of Advanced Cancer

To the Editor:

This letter is written out of courtesy to Dr. Linus Pauling, who has requested that we clarify an introductory statement in our article pertaining to vitamin C therapy for advanced cancer (1).

In the 1976 report covering their nonrandomized observations of 100 terminal cancer patients treated with high-dose vitamin C, Cameron and Pauling stated "All of the patients are treated initially in a perfectly conventional way, by operation, use of radiotherapy, and administration of hormones and cytotoxic substances" (2). On the basis of this statement, we stated that their patients had received radiation and chemotherapy. Drs. Pauling and Cameron have subsequently informed us that because of the prevailing standards of cancer treatment in Scotland at that time, only four of their 100 patients had actually received chemotherapy, and only 20 had received irradiation. Therefore, our study differs from that of Cameron and Pauling, not only because our study was randomized, double-blind and placebo controlled, but also because our study included a greater proportion of patients previously given chemotherapy. Dr. Pauling believes that prior chemotherapy may have negated the benefits of vitamin C.

We must of course stand by our conclusion that high-dose vitamin C is of

Reprinted by permission of the *New England Journal of Medicine*, 301 (1979):1399.

no value in patients who have been treated in a conventional manner according to accepted standards of cancer management in the United States today. Any contention that previous chemotherapy prevented our patients from achieving the extraordinary survival increase claimed by Drs. Cameron and Pauling must be considered highly speculative at best. Our patients were entered into the study only when they were well beyond any acute immunosuppressive effects of previous therapy. Our earlier studies in patients similarly selected indicated that the great majority are capable of mounting a definite immune response to both recall antigens and de novo sensitization (3). Nevertheless, as we stated in our manuscript, the results of our investigation can be applied directly only to the population we studied.

On the basis of available evidence, we do not consider it conscionable to withhold oncologic therapy of known value to give the cancer patient large amounts of vitamin C. Any claims for benefit from high-dose vitamin C at any stage of malignant disease remain to be established by properly designed prospective, randomized, and concurrently controlled studies. We hope that Drs. Pauling and Cameron will agree that such scientifically acceptable evidence should be obtained before this treatment is publicly advocated for clinical use.

Edward T. Creagan, M.D.
Charles Moertel, M.D.
Mayo Clinic

Rochester, MN 55455

REFERENCES

1. E. T. Creagan, C. G. Moertel, J. R. O'Fallon, et al., "Failure of High-Dose Vitamin C (Ascorbic Acid) Therapy to Benefit Patients with Advanced Cancer: A Controlled Trial," *New England Journal of Medicine* 301 (1979):687-90.

2. E. Cameron and L. Pauling, "Supplemental Ascorbate in the Supportive Treatment of Cancer: Prolongation of Survival Times in Terminal Human Cancer," *Proceedings of the National Academy of Sciences (USA)* 73 (1976):3685-89.

3. C. G. Moertel; R. E. Ritts, Jr.; A. J. Schutt; et al., "Clinical Studies of Methanol Extraction Residue Fraction of *Bacillus Calmette-Guérin* as an Immunostimulant in Patients with Advanced Cancer," *Cancer Research* 35 (1975):3075-83.

To the Editor:

This letter is a comment on the paper by Creagan et al. (1) entitled, "Failure of High-Dose Vitamin C (Ascorbic Acid) Therapy to Benefit Patients with Advanced Cancer: A Controlled Trial," and the letter by Creagan and Moertel (2).

The paper by Creagan et al. misrepresents the Vale of Leven study (3-6) in stating that 50 of the 100 ascorbate-treated patients, rather than only four, had received prior chemotherapy.

Answering a letter from me, Dr. Moertel wrote on May 6, 1977, "I feel it is essential in our first evaluation of ascorbic acid that we make every effort to duplicate the conditions which existed in the clinical trial conducted by Cameron but to use a randomized prospective study design rather than the historical controls employed by Cameron," and on August 8, 1978, I sent to Dr. Moertel a letter containing the following sentences: "In my last letter to you I pointed out to you that the patients studied by Dr. Cameron had not received chemotherapy. The cytotoxic drugs damage the body's protective mechanisms, and vitamin C probably functions largely by potentiating these mechanisms. Accordingly, if you hope, as you stated in your letter, to repeat the work of Cameron as closely as possible, you should be careful to use only patients who have not received chemotherapy. . . . Otherwise the trial cannot be described as repeating the work of Cameron." Dr. Moertel in his reply wrote, "Certainly in any presentation of this data I can assure you we will call attention to the fact that the majority of our patients had had prior chemotherapy, whereas in the study conducted by you and Dr. Cameron it was clearly stated that none of the patients had had prior chemotherapy."

Despite this assurance and despite the transmission of information outlined above, Creagan et al. published a misleading report. The title of their paper should have been, "Failure of High-Dose Vitamin C (Ascorbic Acid) Therapy to Benefit Patients with Advanced Cancer Who Have Received Prior Chemotherapy: A Controlled Trial," and the article should not have misrepresented Dr. Cameron's work.

Dr. Cameron and I have concluded our recent analysis of the evidence with the following words (6): "With the possible exception of during intensive chemotherapy, we strongly advocate the use of supplemental ascorbate in the management of all cancer patients from as early in the illness as possible. We believe that this simple measure would improve the overall results of cancer treatment quite dramatically, not only by making the patients more resistant to their illness but also by protecting them against some of the serious and occasionally fatal complications of the cancer treatment itself. We are quite convinced that in

Reprinted by permission of the *New England Journal of Medicine,* 302 (1980): 694.

the not too distant future supplemental ascorbate will have an established place in all cancer-treatment regimes."

Linus Pauling
Linus Pauling Institute of Science
and Medicine

Menlo Park, CA 94025

REFERENCES

1. E. T. Creagan, C. G. Moertel, J. R. O'Fallon, et al., "Failure of High-Dose Vitamin C (Ascorbic Acid) Therapy to Benefit Patients with Advanced Cancer: A Controlled Trial," *New England Journal of Medicine* 301 (1979): 687-90.

2. E. T. Creagan and C. G. Moertel, "Vitamin C Therapy of Advanced Cancer," *New England Journal of Medicine* 301 (1979): 1399.

3. E. Cameron and A. Campbell, "The Orthomolecular Treatment of Cancer. II. Clinical Trial of High-Dose Ascorbic Acid Supplements in Advanced Human Cancer," *Chemico-Biological Interactions* 9 (1974): 285-315.

4. E. Cameron and L. Pauling, "Supplemental Ascorbate in the Supportive Treatment of Cancer: Prolongation of Survival Times in Terminal Human Cancer," *Proceedings of the National Academy of Sciences (USA)* 73 (1976): 3685-89.

5. *Idem.* "Supplemental Ascorbate in the Supportive Treatment of Cancer: Reevaluation of Prolongation of Survival Times in Terminal Human Cancer," *Proceedings of the National Academy of Sciences (USA)* 75 (1978): 4538-42.

6. *Idem. Cancer and Vitamin C: A Discussion of the Nature, Causes, Prevention, and Treatment of Cancer, with Special Reference to the Value of Vitamin C* (Menlo Park, Calif.: Linus Pauling Institute of Science and Medicine, 1979).

The above letter was referred to Drs. Moertel and Creagan, who offer the following reply:

To the Editor:

Dr. Pauling, in quoting from personal letters, makes the point that we had assured him that we would make every effort to reproduce the conditions of his study. He fails, however, to quote from other portions of our correspondence in which we carefully detailed the limitations of such effort— specifically, that our population of patients would consist of those in whom previous standard therapy, including radiation and chemotherapy, had failed.

Reprinted by permission of the *New England Journal of Medicine,* 302 (1980): 694-95.

In addition, Dr. Pauling was given a full copy of our protocol, which documented these criteria for the selection of patients. As Dr. Pauling's last quotation indicates, he was fully aware of the criteria; and the implication, made above and in press releases, that we had promised Dr. Pauling that we would study only patients previously unexposed to chemotherapy, is not true.

In considering a series of statements made by Drs. Pauling and Cameron it was difficult to be certain whether all, none, or some of their patients had received radiation or chemotherapy at the Vale of Leven Hospital. In addition, Dr. Cameron informed us that patients from this hospital were referred to other centers if they required such treatment. In our introduction we relied directly on Cameron and Pauling's published and uncorrected words, "All of the patients are treated initially in a perfectly conventional way, by operation, use of radiotherapy, and administration of hormones and cytotoxic substances" (1). As we had assured Dr. Pauling, we stated unequivocally in our discussion section that the great majority of their patients had not received radiation or chemotherapy and that this constituted a distinct difference in the two study populations. Before publication we forwarded a full copy of our manuscript to Dr. Pauling. When he informed us that he did not think that we had amplified this point sufficiently, we volunteered a statement of clarification to the *Journal* that only 17 of their patients had received prior radiation, and only four prior chemotherapy (numbers supplied by Dr. Cameron). Although we consider the scientific point trivial, we think that we have adequately discharged our voluntarily assumed obligation to Dr. Pauling.

Overshadowing such minor quibbling is the major obligation that both we and Dr. Pauling must assume to cancer patients and the general public. On the basis of claims derived from speculation and nonrandomized studies endorsed by the Pauling name, megadoses of vitamin C are being used by thousands of patients with cancer, and such treatment has been embraced by the metabolic-therapy cults (2). Our randomized double-blind study indicates that for at least one segment of the population of cancer patients, such treatment is of no value.

The name of Dr. Linus Pauling is one of the most revered in American science, and rightly so. We hope very much that Dr. Pauling will join us in discouraging patients with cancer from using high-dose vitamin C or any other cancer treatment unless it has been proved to be of value by properly designed scientific study.

Charles G. Moertel, M.D.
Edward T. Creagan, M.D.
Mayo Clinic

Rochester, MN 55901

REFERENCES

1. E. Cameron and L. Pauling, "Supplemental Ascorbate in the Supportive Treatment of Cancer: Prolongation of Survival Times in Terminal Human Cancer," *Proceedings of the National Academy of Sciences (USA)* 73 (1976): 3685-89.

2. L. Pauling and E. Cameron, "Vitamin C and Cancer," in R. W. Bradford and M. L. Culbert (eds.), *The Metabolic Management of Cancer* (Los Altos, Calif.: Robert W. Bradford Foundation, 1979), 141-44.

Charles G. Moertel, M.D., et al.

High-Dose Vitamin C Versus Placebo in the Treatment of Patients with Advanced Cancer Who Have Had No Prior Chemotherapy

A Randomized Double-Blind Comparison

In 1974 a report by Cameron and Campbell raised the possibility that high-dose vitamin C might be of value in the treatment of advanced cancer.[1] It stated that among 50 patients who were treated with vitamin C at a daily dose of 10 g, 5 had objective tumor regressions. Later, Pauling joined Cameron in reporting an expansion of this series to 100 patients.[2] They compared their treated patient group with 1000 historical control patients drawn from a review of records at the Vale of Leven Hospital, Loch Lomondside, Scotland. They claimed a striking survival advantage for their patients treated with vitamin C, who had a mean survival of 210 days as compared with 50 days for the selected control patients. In a later report they revised their study by replacing 10 of their initial treated patients with 10 new ones and replacing approximately 50 percent of their 1000 historical controls.[3] In this revised version, the survival of patients taking vitamin C, from the date when their disease became untreatable, was increased to a mean of 293 days or more, and that of the controls was decreased to 38 days. This extraordinary survival gain with simple and relatively nontoxic therapy, particularly when reported by a Nobel laureate (Pauling), quite naturally attracted considerable attention as well as causing widespread use of this treatment by patients with advanced cancer. The validity of this therapeutic claim, however, could be subject to question because historically controlled stud-

Reprinted by permission of the *New England Journal of Medicine*, 312 (1985):137-141. Co-authors of this article include: Thomas R. Fleming, Ph.D.; Edward T. Creagan, M.D.; Joseph Rubin, M.D.; Michael J. O'Connell, M.D.; and Matthew M. Ames, Ph.D.

ies in the treatment of both malignant and nonmalignant diseases have frequently produced results that could not be confirmed by more scientifically rigorous prospective and randomized studies.

We had previously attempted to validate the results of Cameron and Pauling in a prospective randomized trial that was double blinded to prevent any inadvertent bias.[4] We selected patients for study according to the published criteria of Cameron and Pauling: i.e., all the patients had proved terminal cancer and "all were treated initially in a perfectly conventional manner by operation, use of radiation therapy, and administration of hormones and cytotoxic substances."[2] The survival curves of our vitamin C–treated and our placebo-treated patients were essentially identical.

In the randomized double-blind study mentioned above, patients were chosen to match the published description of the patients chosen by Cameron and Pauling—i.e., all the patients had previously been treated by conventional means, including the use of cytotoxic drugs. The majority of patients in that randomized study had received prior chemotherapy. In discussions of our initial study, Dr. Pauling stated that, in fact, only 4 of their 100 patients had been treated with cytotoxic drugs, since chemotherapy was not frequently employed at the Vale of Leven Hospital.[5] He speculated that our study did not duplicate the strongly positive results he had reported because "the cytotoxic drugs damage the body's protective mechanisms, and vitamin C probably functions largely by potentiating these mechanisms." Although the scientific basis for this conclusion seemed to us obscure, we could not disprove Dr. Pauling's contention with the evidence produced by our study. Because the issue of the possible effectiveness of vitamin C for advanced cancer remains one of public concern, we thought an additional study was warranted.

The present study was undertaken to test the thesis put forth by Cameron and Pauling that high-dose vitamin C is effective therapy for advanced cancer in patients who have had no previous exposure to chemotherapy. For this trial we elected to study patients with advanced cancer of the large bowel because this was the most frequent tumor type in the study of Cameron and Pauling and one for which they claimed a striking improvement in survival with vitamin C therapy. We felt ethically justified in studying this group of patients without first offering cytotoxic drugs because in our opinion there is no known form of chemotherapy for colorectal cancer that has been demonstrated to produce substantive palliative benefit or extension of survival.

METHODS

All the patients selected for study had histologic proof of advanced adenocarcinoma established as having originated in the colon or rectum. All were beyond any reasonable hope of potentially curative surgery or radiation therapy. All were ambulatory and capable of taking oral medication. None had received any chemotherapy.

Before study each patient had a physical examination with appropriate laboratory studies and chest radiography. Measurements were made of any accessible tumor masses or enlarged liver as well as of any pulmonary metastases seen on chest films. The nature and purpose of the study was fully discussed with each patient, with specific emphasis on the fact that they would receive either vitamin C or an inert placebo on the basis of random assignment. A signed informed-consent form was obtained.

Patients were stratified according to the interval from the time unresectable disease was diagnosed, the sites of metastasis (lungs, liver, or other sites), and whether there were measurable areas of malignant disease. Patients were randomly assigned to receive either 10 g of vitamin C daily or placebo (lactose). Both were prepared in identical opaque gelatin capsules and dispensed in coded bottles. The patient, physician, and everyone else involved in the patient's care were unaware of the actual drug assignment. The code for the drug assignments of individual patients was not broken until the study was closed. Patients were asked to take five capsules by mouth four times daily. Each capsule contained either 500 mg of vitamin C or placebo. Patients were further asked to record their actual drug intake each day on a form provided for that purpose. Patients were reevaluated at four weeks and every eight weeks thereafter. This reevaluation included a medical history, physical examination, pertinent laboratory studies, chest radiography, assessment of weight and performance status, and measurement of accessible tumor areas. Therapy was continued as long as the patient was able to take oral medications or until there was evidence of marked progression of the malignant disease. Progression was declared if there was an increase of more than 50 percent in the product of the perpendicular diameters of any area of known malignant disease, if new areas of malignant disease appeared, if there was substantial worsening of symptoms or performance status, or if there was a loss of body weight of 10 percent or more.

Statistical Analysis

The vitamin C and placebo regimens were compared with respect to the duration of survival after randomization, the time to disease progression, the probability of objective regression among patients in whom this could be measured, toxicity, and effects on pretreatment symptoms.

Survival curves were constructed by the Kaplan-Meier method.[6] The log-rank[7] statistic was employed to assess the consistency of the data with the equality of survival curves, and the Cox partial-likelihood-score statistic[8] was used to assess the consistency of the data with the hypothesis that vitamin C will yield at least a 25 percent improvement in survival over that with placebo. In addition, stratified and unstratified Cox proportional-hazards models[8] were employed to inspect the association of treatment with survival when covariates were adjusted. P values were one-sided or two-sided as indicated.

RESULTS

A total of 101 patients were entered into this study and randomly assigned to treatment. A single patient, without knowledge of treatment assignment, withdrew consent after randomization but before taking the first drug dose. This patient's data were canceled and not included in our analysis. All the remaining 100 patients were found to be eligible, were appropriately started on therapy, and were therefore included in our analysis.

Patient Characteristics

The characteristics of our patients and their disease are listed according to treatment arm in Table I. This table also shows the influence of each factor on survival, providing one-year survival probabilities and log-rank P values. Overall, there was a good balance between the treatment groups, particularly with regard to factors that were found to influence prognosis—i.e., the location of metastasis, the interval between the diagnosis of unresectable disease and study entry, and the histologic grade. It is noteworthy that the overwhelming majority of patients were in excellent general condition. All were capable of working full- or part-time (their scores on the Eastern Cooperative Oncology Group's performance test were either 0 or 1; scores on that test range from 0, fully active, to 4, totally disabled). Seventy-two percent were asymptomatic. Only four patients had had any prior radiation therapy.

Somewhat more than half the patients who have discontinued participation in this study (58 of 98) have received subsequent chemotherapy. Most of these have been treated with fluorouracil either alone or in combination with other agents. The proportion of patients receiving subsequent chemotherapy is comparable between the treatment arms (57.1 and 58.8 percent).

Patient Compliance

Compliance was assessed through patients' recordings of their daily drug intake, which were accurately maintained by 96 of our 100 patients. In the main, patient compliance was excellent. The total doses were known to be at least 75 percent of the expected amount in all but 8 patients. One of these stopped treatment because he found the symptoms he associated with therapy intolerable. He was receiving placebo. Two other patients reduced the daily dose because of intolerable gastrointestinal symptoms, and both were taking vitamin C. Two patients (one taking vitamin C, the other placebo) stopped their drug intake without evidence of disease progression because they wished to leave the study and receive chemotherapy. One patient stopped treatment (placebo) on the recommendation of her physician, one stopped for an unknown reason (vitamin C), and one temporarily interrupted therapy (vitamin C) because of a myocardial infarction. The remaining patients reported regular drug intake ac-

Table 1. Characteristics of 100 Patients with Advanced Colorectal
Cancer According to Treatment Arm.

CHARACTERISTIC	PLACEBO REGIMEN	VITAMIN C REGIMEN	TOTAL	1-YEAR SURVIVAL	P VALUE*
No. of patients	49	51	100	46.9	—
Interval from diagnosis to randomization					
< 3 weeks	7	8	15	7.6	0.003
3-8 weeks	29	29	58	46.8	
> 8 weeks	13	14	27	66.7	
Site of metastases					
Lung	9	8	17	69.3	0.005
Liver	27	31	58	37.1	
Other	13	12	25	53.5	
Presence of measurable disease					
Yes	19	19	38	41.1	0.50
No	30	32	62	50.1	
ECOG† performance score					
0	29	26	55	49.5	0.63
1	20	25	45	43.8	
Age (yr)					
< 50	2	6	8	25.0	0.17
50-69	27	28	55	51.1	
> 70	20	17	37	45.6	
Sex					
Male	31	26	57	51.2	0.86
Female	18	25	43	41.3	
Prior radiation treatment					
Yes	3	1	4	50.0	0.35
No	46	50	96	46.8	
Histologic grade ‡					
1-2	37	34	71	56.5	0.005
3-4	9	14	23	25.4	

*Two-sided P values were determined by the log-rank statistic.
†ECOG denotes Eastern Cooperative Oncology Group.
‡Broder's grade: 1, well differentiated, to 4, highly undifferentiated. The grade was unknown in three patients on each treatment arm.

cording to instructions, usually stopping treatment only when symptoms of disease progression developed. The median duration of drug intake was 2.5 months with vitamin C (range, 1 day to 15.6 months) and 3.6 months with placebo (range, 7 days to 25.5 months). These differences reflect differences in the intervals to disease progression (see below).

To further ensure compliance, 11 consecutive patients were selected during the course of our study for urinary assays of ascorbate that employed the a, a'-dipyridyl ultraviolet absorption method of Sullivan and Clarke.[9] Patient selection was made at an arbitrarily chosen time in our study and without knowledge of the drug assignment of individual patients. The laboratory was also blinded as to drug assignment. Patients were not told the purpose of the urine collection; they were simply asked to submit a 24-hour specimen. Five patients who were later determined to have been assigned vitamin C all had high urine levels of ascorbate ($\geq$ 2 g per 24 hours). Of the 6 assigned to placebo, 5 had negligible levels that were within the range of normal controls for our assay method ($\leq$ 0.55 g per 24 hours). A single patient had an intermediate value between these two ranges. This patient had poorly controlled diabetes and was taking several drugs for the control of pain and depression. Since our assay method was not completely specific for ascorbate it is possible that this patient had interfering substances in the urine that were associated with the same ultraviolet absorbance as ascorbic acid.

Toleration of Therapy

Most patients tolerated therapy very well. As we found in our previous study, the overall incidence of side effects ascribed by patients to treatment was low, without any clear evidence of a specific toxicity of vitamin C. Only for pyrosis was there an increase with vitamin C over placebo (18 percent as compared with 6 percent), but this difference was not statistically significant.

Objective Response to Therapy

A total of 38 patients had clearly measurable areas of malignant disease at the time of study entry (19 assigned to vitamin C, 19 to placebo). The predominant measurable metastatic sites were the liver (17 patients), the lungs (16), or both (3). No patient had any evidence of tumor regression.

Symptomatic Response

Because of the relatively early stage of metastatic disease in our patients, most were asymptomatic; when symptoms were present they were usually mild. Among 11 vitamin C-treated patients with pretreatment symptoms, 7 (64 percent) claimed some degree of symptomatic relief. Among 17 placebo-treated patients, 11 (65 percent) claimed relief.

Interval to Progression

As of this writing, 96 of our 100 patients have had disease progression as defined above. The distributions of time intervals from the beginning of therapy to the start of progression are shown in Figure 1. For patients taking vitamin C the median survival was 2.9 months, and for placebo-treated patients it was 4.1 months. It is unlikely that vitamin C produces even a 25 percent increase over placebo in the interval between initiation of therapy and progression of disease ($P \approx 0.01$). This is a one-sided P value obtained from a multivariate Cox analysis assessing the consistency of the data with a hazard ratio of 1.25.

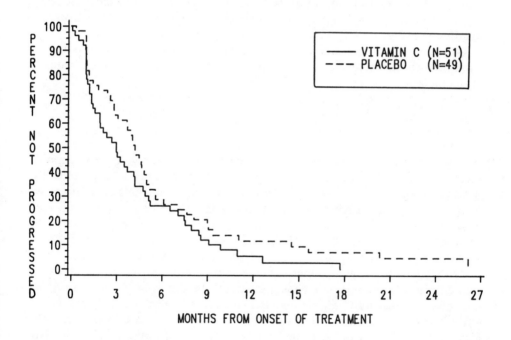

Figure 1. Time from the Beginning of Therapy to Disease Progression, According to Treatment Assignment in 100 Patients with Advanced Cancer.

Survival

As of this writing 85 of our 100 patients have died. The distributions of survival times are shown in Figure 2. The curves are similar through the first year of follow-up, with 49 and 47 percent surviving for one year on vitamin C and placebo, respectively. There is, however, a substantially larger proportion of long-term survivors in the placebo group. There is no reasonable likelihood that vitamin C produces even a 25 percent increase in survival times over placebo ($P = 0.017$) This is a one-sided P value derived by employing the stratified Cox proportional-hazards model to test for the consistency of the data with a hazard ratio of 1.25. The P value is adjusted for the influence of the histologic grade in a model stratified according to the site of the metastases and the interval from diagnosis to randomization. Incidentally, the one-sided P values were 0.006 from the unstratified analysis adjusting for the three factors above and 0.001 from the unadjusted analysis that used the Cox partial-likelihood-score statistic.

The absence of any survival improvement from vitamin C was also apparent when we inspected the subset of patients who did not receive subsequent chemotherapy.

DISCUSSION

It is very clear that this study fails to show a benefit for high-dose vitamin C therapy of advanced cancer. Certainly, these were patients who presumably would have had their protective mechanisms as intact as possible in the presence of incurable cancer. They were ambulatory, had only minimal symptoms, and were maintaining a good nutritional status, and the great majority were capable of working full- or part-time. All were at least one month past any surgical stress, none had received prior chemotherapy, and only 4 percent had received prior radiation therapy (a proportion substantially smaller than in the study of Cameron and Pauling[2]). We chose for study the tumor type that was most commonly treated by Cameron and Pauling and that in their study showed a striking survival advantage for vitamin C therapy. In spite of this seemingly ideal setting, vitamin C performed no better than a dummy medication. No patient had measurable tumor shrinkage, the malignant disease in patients taking vitamin C progressed just as rapidly as in those taking placebo, and patients lived just as long on sugar pills as on high-dose vitamin C. Surprisingly, and perhaps by chance, there were more long-term survivors receiving placebo than vitamin C.

It would appear that the most substantive difference between our study and that of Cameron and Pauling was that theirs was a retrospective comparison between selected study patients and historical control patients, whereas ours was prospective, randomized, and double blinded. Randomization and double

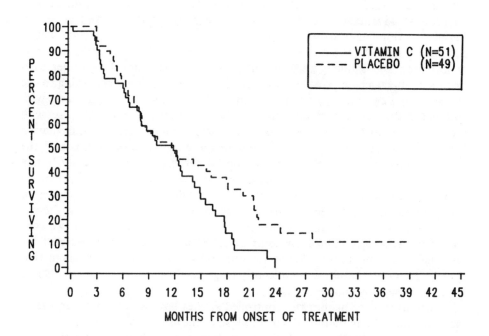

Figure 2. Survival Time from the Beginning of Therapy,
According to Treatment Assignment.

blinding served to protect against any possible conscious or unconscious bias on the part of the investigators as patients were selected for treatment assignment and as their therapeutic results were evaluated. There was no such protection against bias for Cameron and Pauling as they selected and then reselected the patients they decided to evaluate for their first and second reports.

Prospective randomization ensured that all patients who were eligible for the study and who agreed to participate were chosen from the same patient population during the same period and would therefore be at comparable risk for favorable or unfavorable prognostic conditions. With such a study design, two consecutive trials involving well over 200 patients have failed to demonstrate any perceptible antineoplastic effect of high-dose vitamin C for advanced cancer.

In the face of this evidence it would seem appropriate to ask why the 100 patients with cancer who were selected by Cameron and Pauling for high-dose vitamin C lived many times longer than their selected historical control patients, whereas our patients who were randomly assigned to vitamin C treatment had no survival advantage whatsoever over those assigned to the control group. Certainly, prior chemotherapy can no longer be considered an important factor, and we are left with the inevitable conclusion that the apparent positive results of Cameron and Pauling were the product of case-selection bias rather than treatment effectiveness. We selected cases for our earlier study according to the characteristics described by Cameron and Pauling; i.e., we selected patients with terminal disease in whom all conventional treatments, including those with cytotoxic substances, had failed. For both our placebo-treated and our vitamin C-treated patients, the survival times were quite comparable to those of the untreated historical control patients of the Cameron and Pauling study. When in the present study we selected patients with a much more favorable prognosis who had had no prior chemotherapy, however, the median survival times of both treated and untreated groups were quite comparable to those of the patients Cameron and Pauling selected for treatment with vitamin C. If we conducted a historically controlled comparison between the patients selected for our first study and those selected for our second study, we could claim that either placebo or vitamin C significantly lengthened patient survival. Neither of these conclusions would be valid.

Uncontrolled or historically controlled studies have a necessary purpose in the evaluation of any therapeutic method, since they serve to develop a hypothesis of therapeutic effectiveness. Such studies, however, rarely prove such effectiveness, which in most circumstances should be established by prospective randomized study. Whether one is dealing with the treatment of the common cold or of cancer, and whether one is dealing with a benign vitamin or a highly toxic chemotherapy program, it would seem to serve the interest of the patient best for public advocacy of a proposed treatment to be withheld until that treatment had been proved effective by definitive studies of sound scientific design.

REFERENCES

1. E. Cameron and A. Campbell, "The Orthomolecular Treatment of Cancer. II. Clinical Trial of High-Dose Ascorbic Acid Supplements in Advanced Human Cancer," *Chemico-Biological Interactions* 9 (1974): 285-315.

2. E. Cameron and L. Pauling, "Supplemental Ascorbate in the Supportive Treatment of Cancer: Prolongation of Survival Times in Terminal Human Cancer," *Proceedings of the National Academy of Sciences (USA)* 73 (1976): 3685-89.

3. *Idem.*, "Supplemental Ascorbate in the Supportive Treatment of Cancer: Reevaluation of

Prolongation of Survival Times in Terminal Human Cancer," *Proceedings of the National Academy of Sciences (USA)* 75 (1978): 4538-42.

4. E. T. Creagan, C. G. Moertel, J. R. O'Fallon, et al., "Failure of High-Dose Vitamin C (Ascorbic Acid) Therapy to Benefit Patients with Advanced Cancer: A Controlled Trial," *New England Journal of Medicine* 301 (1979): 687-90.

5. L. Pauling, "Vitamin C Therapy of Advanced Cancer," *New England Journal of Medicine* 302 (1980): 694.

6. E. Kaplan and P. Meier, "Nonparametric Estimation from Incomplete Observations," *Journal of the American Statistical Association* 53 (1958): 457-81.

7. N. Mantel, "Evaluation of Survival Data and Two New Rank Order Statistics Arising in Its Consideration," *Cancer Chemotherapy Reports* 50 (1966): 163-70.

8. D. R. Cox, "Regression Models and Life-tables," *Journal of the Royal Statistical Society (B)* 34 (1972): 187-220.

9. M. X. Sullivan and H. C. N. Clarke, "A Highly Specific Procedure for Ascorbic Acid," *Journal of the Association of Official Agricultural Chemists* 38 (1955): 514-18.

Varro E. Tyler, Ph.D.

Hazards of Herbal Medicine

INTRODUCTION

A very wide chasm now exists between the scientific study of plant drugs—a part of the discipline known as pharmacognosy—and the field of popular herbal medicine. The former is an exact science, requiring considerable knowledge of biology, chemistry, and pharmacology for a mastery of its subject matter. The latter is, at best, a commercial enterprise and, at worst, a fraud, composed of varying parts of outdated information, folklore, superstition, wishful thinking, hokum, and even hoax. Due to the commercial attraction of popular herbal medicine and the fact that anyone who is able to read a newspaper or grow parsley in a garden can become an "expert" in the field overnight (at least in his or her own mind), it is not surprising that the writings on popular herbal medicine now outnumber those in scientific pharmacognosy in the range of thousands to one (see Figure 1). Their availability is also much greater. Such literature advocating the use of particular herbs for specific conditions and diseases is available in every health food store and shopping-mall bookstore in the United States, whereas the sale of books on pharmacognosy, medical botany, and the like are usually restricted to dealers supplying the needs of professional students.

Still, the only way to gain a real understanding of any facet of herbs or their use is through the application of scientific method. All other methods lead to delusion. In writing about science, it becomes necessary to use the terminology of science, particularly, in this case, the nomenclature of botany, chemistry, and pharmacology. It is hoped that this will not deter the reader from pursuing an interest in the field, because this is the only feasible method of presentation if fact is to be clearly differentiated from fiction and truth from falsehood.

In the context of their late twentieth-century use, herbs have acquired a new specialized definition. The term now refers to crude drugs of vegetable origin selected and utilized, primarily by laypersons, for the treatment of disease

Figure 1. Typical recent books advocating the use of some potentially hazardous herbal remedies.

states (often of a chronic nature) or to attain or to maintain a state of improved health. Several features of this new definition require elaboration.

Although in some societies herbs may be prescribed by recognized medical practitioners, this is occurring with decreasing frequency as safe and effective medicines in fabricated dosage forms become more universally available. Thus their selection and use is primarily a function of nonprofessionals. They are employed not only to cure diseases but also to improve resistance to illness. This latter usage coupled with a relatively low level of activity, even in those conditions where they are effective, combine to promote their use over relatively long periods of time. Such chronic utilization may cause special problems in the use of plant materials possessing low levels of toxicity. Thus it becomes very important to recognize the potential hazards, especially in long-term use, of various herbal medications (see Figure 2). Such hazards may conveniently be divided into general and specific types.

  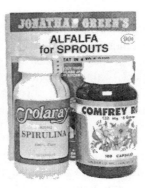

Figure 2. Commercial packages of selected, potentially hazardous herbal remedies: *left* to *right*—sassafras (carcinogen), devil's claw (frequent bacterial contamination), chamomile (allergen), ginseng (hormone-like effects), spirulina (frequent insect contamination), alfalfa seeds (promote autoimmune disorder), and comfrey root (carcinogen).

GENERAL HAZARDS

The first of the general hazards involved in the employment of herbal remedies is implied by the definition itself: the herbs are "selected and employed, primarily by laypersons." A review of the literature available to such individuals in the United States and in Western Europe reveals an appreciable information gap between what professionals actually know about the safety and efficacy of herbal remedies and what is being told to the public about them. Literature for the uninitiated essentially focuses on advocacy; it is developed to promote the use of the product. In many cases, it is merely copied, sometimes with an unintentional change in meaning, from such compilers of herbal lore as the sixteenth-century German monk Otto Brunfels, the seventeenth-century English astrologer-apothecary Nicholas Culpeper, or more recent sources of a similar nature.

Some of the modern misstatements are interesting if not enlightening. Lucas (1), for example, reports that American Indians had long, straight hair because they washed it with sarsaparilla, a vegetable drug found to contain the male hormone testosterone. Bethel (2) notes that herb tea is a far more effective healing agent than isolated principles. Leyel (3) writes that lily-of-the-valley is not poisonous and does not produce harmful results even if taken over an extended period. Griffin (4) postulates that diabetes is caused when parasites invade the pancreas and that these may be driven out by pumpkin seeds or black walnuts. Leek (5) considers poke root a valuable remedy for scabies, ulcers, ringworm, chronic rheumatism, dysmenorrhea, and dyspepsia. Heinerman (6) attributes the sharp taste of echinacea to its content of a caffein glycoside. The Wrens (7) repeat Parkinson's advice that burdock root will "wonderfully help" the bites of snakes and mad dogs. Bankhofer and Kurth (8) quote Kneipp's statement to the effect that herbs can never harm, only help. Mességué (9) believes that celandine applied externally will not only cure rheumatism, gout, and kidney trouble, but is also effective in the treatment of jaundice, insomnia, asthma, bronchitis, atherosclerosis, and angina. This list of herbal fantasies could be expanded almost indefinitely, but enough examples have been cited to illustrate the relative unreliability of modern herbal literature.

Another general hazard of herbal remedies relates to their acquisition either by purchase or by self-collection. In most countries, laws and regulations governing the sale of herbs are inadequate to protect the consumer from adulterated, contaminated, or even substituted products. For example, a study published in Germany in 1978 (10) revealed that almost all packages of devil's claw (secondary storage roots of *Harpagophytum procumbens* DC.)* examined were heavily contaminated with coliform bacteria, especially *E. coli*. As such, they were definitely hazardous to health and should not have entered into commerce.

Spirulina is a dried blue-green alga obtained from at least two species of the genus *Spirulina* Turpin. Recommended for its postulated, but unproven, appetite depressant effect, it is frequently infested with insects (11). Examination of shipments to the United States from Mexico revealed unacceptable levels of ephedra fly fragments in many of them. Since this insect is often associated with the alga, extreme care in production and processing is required if this problem is to be eliminated.

German or Hungarian chamomile should consist of flowerheads of *Matri-*

---

*By convention, the name of the person or persons who first conferred a particular scientific name on a plant appears in abbreviated form following the species epithet. Thus, DC. stands for Augustin de Candolle, L. for Carl von Linné, Raf. for Constantine Rafinesque, etc. Comprehensive lists of appropriate abbreviations of these botanists' names appear in standard reference works, such as *Hortus Third*.

caria chamomilla L., but in many cases, the entire overground portion of the flowering plant is harvested mechanically and sold for the preparation of herbal tea bags (12). The resultant product with its decreased volatile oil content is definitely an inferior one. When grown in certain areas of Egypt, chamomile must be sprayed with an insecticide as frequently as ten to twelve times per year (13). Depending upon the identity of the pesticide employed, toxic residues may pose a definite health hazard to consumers, yet tests for them are neither required nor routinely conducted.

Lack of adequate quality-control procedures for herbs may extend even to identification of the vegetable material. A woman in Colorado purchased a package labeled burdock root (*Arctium lappa* L.) from a so-called health food store and drank a tea prepared from it (14). She was subsequently admitted to the hospital and diagnosed as suffering from atropine poisoning; the tea was analyzed and found to contain large amounts of that alkaloid. Since burdock root does not contain atropine, it must be concluded that belladonna root, or some similar product, was erroneously substituted in its place.

Self-collection and self-identification of herbs is likewise a hazardous practice for most consumers. As the world population tends to become more urbanized, fewer and fewer individuals have even a practical knowledge of systematic botany. Thus, for most persons, this does not present a safe alternative for the acquisition of herbal remedies.

It is necessary to mention one further hazard of a general nature that may be associated with the use of herbal remedies. Since many have no demonstrated efficacy, yet are ardently recommended in the popular literature, their use might conceivably delay or even prevent a disease sufferer from seeking more appropriate medical treatment. Many conditions ranging from arthritis to cancer will yield to prompt, effective therapy, but neglect can result in a much diminished quality of life or a life-threatening situation.

SPECIFIC HAZARDS

Carcinogens

Because the specific hazards associated with herbal medications are quite numerous, it is appropriate in a general survey of this sort to group them according to the types of physiologic risk involved. Carcinogens are today of foremost concern to many individuals. At least four basic types exist among the herbs: pyrrolizidine alkaloids, phenylpropanoid compounds, aristolochic acid, and tannins. In addition, tumor promoters—chemicals that do not themselves cause tumors but increase the incidence of tumors caused by exposure to a carcinogen— will be considered in this category. The classic examples of such tumor promoters are the phorbol esters of *Croton tiglium* L., but diterpene esters with tumor-promoting activity occur throughout the plant families Euphorbiaceae (spurge) and Thymelaeaceae (mezereon).

The hepatotoxic pyrrolizidine alkaloids occur in a number of plant species, but most of the commonly used herbs containing them are found in the Boraginaceae (borage family) and Compositae (daisy family). In the liver, the alkaloids are metabolized to pyrroles that are chemically active, serving as biological alkylating agents (15). Alkylaton is a widespread mechanism of toxicity, and many mutagens and carcinogens function by this mechanism. Toxic pyrrolizidine alkaloids have been definitely identified in a number of popular herbs. These include echimidine and symphytine in comfrey (*Symphytum officinale* L.); these same two alkaloids plus six others in Russian comfrey (*S.* x *uplandicum* Nym.); senkirkine in coltsfoot (*Tussilago farfara* L.); senecionine in life root (*Senecio aureus* L.); senecionine, retrorsine, and four others in dusty miller (*S. cineraria* DC.); retrorsine, senecionine, senkirkine, and six others in ragwort (*S. jacobaea* L.); fuchsisenecionine and senecionine in *Fuchskreuzkraut* [*S. nemorensis* L. ssp. *fuchsii* (Gmel.) Čelak]; and senecionine plus three others in common groundsel (*S. vulgaris* L.) (16). Even borage (*Borago officinalis* L.), long believed to be an innocuous if not a particularly useful herb, has recently been found to contain lycopsamine and supinidine viridiflorate, two suspected poisons. The low concentration of these alkaloids in the plant probably accounts for the lack of any acute toxicity reports associated with the use of borage (17).

Traces of two pyrrolizidine alkaloids, tussilagine and isotussilagine, have also been detected in echinacea. Both *Echinacea augustifolia* DC. and *E. purpurea* (L.) Moench were found to contain 0.006 percent of tussilagine in the dried plant materials (18). Fortunately, these alkaloids are not carcinogenic, but the finding does serve to emphasize the widespread distribution of pyrrolizidine derivatives in both the above-mentioned plant families. It also points out the importance of precise identification of the alkaloids in these two families before arriving at conclusions regarding their carcinogenicity.

Safrole, a phenylpropane derivative, comprises about 80 percent of the volatile oil obtained from the root bark of sassafras [*Sassafras albidum* (Nutt.) Nees]. The bark was once widely employed as an herbal remedy and flavoring agent in the United States, but its use was banned more than twenty years ago when safrole was shown to induce hepatic tumors in rats and both hepatic tumors and subcutaneous angiosarcomas in mice (19).

There is still some controversy about the applicability of these results to humans. A proximate carcinogen of safrole is 1'-hydroxysafrole, and investigations using very small amounts of isotopically labeled safrole were unable to detect the presence of this metabolite in man (20). Further studies are required to determine the degree of risk incurred by users of sassafras; however, based upon present data, restrictions on the use of this product are certainly desirable.

Another phenylpropanoid compound, ß-asarone, has been shown to induce the formation of malignant tumors in the duodenal region of rats. It is a prominent constituent in the volatile oil obtained from the rhizome (subterranean stem) of certain chromosomal races of calamus (*Acorus calamus* L.), an herb long used for its carminative and stomachic properties (21). Calamus oil obtained from triploid and, especially, tetraploid plants has been shown to contain up to about 90 percent of ß-asarone, and concentrations of that compound in the rhizomes themselves may exceed 8 percent.

However, recent studies have demonstrated that the oil of the diploid plant, *A. calamus* L. var. *americanus* (Raf.) Wulff, corresponds in other respects to the oil from the triploid plant but is essentially free of the carcinogenic ß-asarone. Employment of this variety thus provides an accepable alternative to the complete cessation of use of this ancient herbal remedy (22).

Various species of *Aristolochia* (birthwort), but particularly *A. clematitis* L., have been used since antiquity for their wound-healing properties. In modern times, extracts of the plants were thought to increase bodily resistance to infection by activating the phagocytotic activity of the leukocytes. Consequently, they were extensively used in Europe for this purpose (23). The active principles are several nitrophenanthrene carboxylic acid derivatives known as the aristolochic acids. Studies in rats have now shown that some animals treated daily with 1 mg./kg. of aristolochic acid for periods of three months subsequently developed malignant tumors of the stomach and other vital organs. All rats treated with doses of 10 mg./kg. for the same period developed cancer (24). As a result of these studies, all pharmaceutical products containing aristolochic acid have been withdrawn from the market in Germany.

Considerable evidence of an epidemiological nature now exists to support the hypothesis that continued long-term consumption of plant material with a high concentration of condensed catechin tannin leads to an increased incidence of esophageal cancer (25). A number of herbal materials ranging from betel nut (*Areca catechu* L.) to common tea [*Camellia sinensis* (L.) O. Kuntze] fall into this category. Interestingly, when the tannins in a beverage such as tea are bound by the addition of milk, the hazard is eliminated or, at least, greatly reduced (26).

Fortunately, such ancient plant remedies as the purgative croton seeds derived from *Croton tiglium* L. in the family Euphorbiaceae and the vesicant mezereon bark obtained from *Daphne mezereum* L. in the Thymelaeaceae have largely fallen into disuse, even as herbal remedies. However, some widely consulted references (27, 28) continue to describe them as valued medicinal agents, and several other plants belonging to these two families continue to be used as drugs in various countries.

During the last decade, it has been demonstrated that many species of both families contain irritant, and usually toxic, diterpene ester derivatives of either tigliane, daphnane, or ingenane. These compounds exhibit tumor-promoting properties in mouse skin, and included among them are the most potent such promoters so far discovered (29). The promoters, while not causing cancer in and of themselves, may be viewed as a subclass of cocarcinogens that interact with other factors to induce carcinoma.

Obviously, the effects of compounds that produce them in such a subtle and indirect manner are somewhat difficult to verify, especially in humans. But there is now evidence of their relevance to the etiology of human cancer in Curaçao where *Croton flavens* L. is a widely used cure-all, and the incidence of esophageal cancer is high. This substantiation of the small-animal data should prompt extreme caution in the use of any herbal materials originating from the families Euphorbiaceae or Thymelaeaceae.

Photosensitizers

The herbs to be discussed next are actually somewhat related to the carcinogens. However, because ultraviolet radiation is required to activate their toxicity and because not all of them cause malignancies, they are more properly classified as photosensitizers. Furocoumarins of the so-called psoralen type, particularly bergapten and xanthotoxin, have been shown to act as potent phototoxic and photomutagenic or even carcinogenic agents when materials containing them are contacted or ingested (30). Psoralens are particularly abundant in members of the Umbelliferae (parsley or carrot family) and Rutaceae (rue family). Common psoralen-containing herbs include angelica (*Angelica archangelica* L.), dong quai (*Angelica polymorpha* Maxim. var. *sinensis* Oliv.), and lovage (*Levisticum officinale* W. D. J. Koch) in the former, as well as rue (*Ruta graveolens* L.) in the latter family.

A recent case in the state of Indiana demonstrates the potential hazards of such herbs. A woman who had read in a popular magazine that rue was a useful insect repellent rubbed some of the leaves on her arms and on those of her two young children. The resulting first- and second-degree burns with associated blisters required weeks of treatment by a medical specialist. In addition to paying the physician's fees, the family subsequently spent more than $150 during this period on prescription drugs, including antihistamines, steroids, and antibiotics (31).

Another inducer of photosensitivity is hypericin, a naphthodianthrone derivative found in St. John's wort (*Hypericum perforatum* L.). While the resulting dermatitis and inflammation of the mucous membranes are ordinarily not as severe as the symptoms resulting from the psoralens, they are sufficient to require a warning to individuals to cease using this herb should they appear (32).

Allergens

Most plant materials can act as allergens, at least in sensitive individuals, but those herbs consisting of flowers or flowering tops with their associated pollen grains are particularly likely to function in this way. Included in this category is the widely used chamomile tea, which may be prepared from the flower heads of either *Matricaria chamomilla* L. (German or Hungarian chamomile) or *An-*

themis nobilis L. (Roman or English chamomile). Teas made from these and from the flowers of other members of the family Compositae, including yarrow (*Anthemis nobilis* L.), marigold (*Calendula officinalis* L.), and goldenrod (*Solidago* spp.), may also cause contact dermatitis, anaphylaxis, and related hypersensitivity reactions in allergic individuals (33).

Another member of the Compositae known to produce allergic reactions on local application is arnica, the flower heads of *Arnica montana* L. and several related species. In the form of a tincture, the drug is commonly used to treat bruises, aches, and sprains. It is also a constituent of various cosmetic preparations ranging from soaps to bath oils. Repeated application of arnica to the skin often results in a kind of contact dermatitis characterized by localized reddening, swelling, and blister formation. This is attributed to its content of several sesquiterpene lactones (e.g., arnifolin, helenalin, xanthalongin), which are capable of reacting with cell proteins to produce adducts that then act as allergens (23).

Allergenic reactions may be quite idiosyncratic in character. One such case is the reported development of severe asthma in a patient following repeated exposure to garlic dust (34). It is presumed that such allergies could develop in sensitive individuals following repeated exposure to any herbal material; consequently, they do not require any particular emphasis here.

Herbs Producing Hormone-like Effects

Glycyrrhizin, a triterpenoid saponin glycoside, is found in the rhizome and roots of *Glycyrrhiza glabra* L. (Spanish licorice), its variety *glandulifera* Waldst. et Kit. (Russian licorice), and other varieties that yield a yellow, sweet wood. When ingested in quantity over a period of time, the compound induces pseudoaldosteronism, a condition characterized by sodium and water retention and potassium depletion. Hypertension followed by heart failure and cardiac arrest may ensue (35).

Quantities of licorice containing 0.7 g. to 1.4 g. of glycyrrhizin consumed daily for periods of one to four weeks induced serious symptoms in a group of volunteers (36). Licorice often contains 7 percent to 8 percent of glycyrrhizin, and recipes calling for daily consumption of a concentrated decoction in quantities equivalent to at least 7 g. or 8 g. of the crude drug (ca. 0.5 g. to 0.6 g. of glycyrrhizin) are commonly found in the literature (37). It is therefore easy to understand how the product might produce toxic effects, especially in those persons already suffering from cardiac problems and hypertension.

Plants of the ginseng group, including Oriental ginseng (*Panax pseudoginseng* Wall.), American ginseng (*P. quinquefolius* L.), and Tienchi-ginseng [*P. notoginseng* (Burk.) F. H. Chen] all contain very complex mixtures of triterpenoid saponins that possess hormonal activity. These compounds account for the plants being used since remote times as cure-alls or panaceas, aphrodisiacs, and, more recently, as adaptogens—products that produce a state of increased resistance of the body to stress and overcome disease by increasing the general vitality and strengthening normal body functions. The same is true to a lesser extent for a related plant, Siberian ginseng or eleuthro [*Acanthopanax senticosus* (Rupr. et Maxim. ex Maxim.) Harms], which belongs to the same plant family, Araliaceae, as the other ginsengs and contains some similar saponin glycosides in addition to other constituents (38).

Scientific evidence supporting the beneficial effects of ginseng is scanty, although abundant favorable testimony of an anecdotal nature does exist. Many persons have also reported subjective stimulation or "jitteriness" following consumption of higher doses of ginseng (39).

A clinical study of 133 long-term ginseng users seemed to point to a definite ginseng-abuse syndrome in about 10 percent of the patients, who suffered from hypertension together with nervousness, sleeplessness, skin eruptions, and morning diarrhea (40, 41). But other subjects experienced just the opposite symptoms, including hypotension and a tranquilizing effect. This is not surprising since the study included anything labeled "ginseng," and many such products are misbranded or adulterated; further, no control group was included. However, taken as a whole, the effects observed mimicked those of corticosteroid poisoning and strongly suggested a steroid mechanism of action operating through the adrenal cortex or the pituitary gland.

Other hormone-like effects have been reported to result from ingestion of ginseng. A seventy-year-old woman developed swollen, tender breasts with diffuse nodularity after taking the herb for three weeks (42). These symptoms subsided when ginseng administration was discontinued but reappeared twice following repeated termination and resumption of use. Post-menopausal bleeding has also been noted in older patients following ingestion of ginseng (23).

There is now sufficient evidence to conclude that drugs of the ginseng group can produce toxic effects in humans, particularly when consumed in large amounts over extended periods of time. Caution in their use is certainly advisable for persons suffering from hypertension or nervous disorders.

Teratogens

The teratogenic constituents of herbs fall into several different chemical classes, but many of them are alkaloids, at least one group of which has been discussed previously in connection with its carcinogenic activity. The pyrrolizidine alkaloid heliotrine administered to pregnant rats caused their offspring to be deformed and their development to be generally retarded (43). Such effects may be attributed to the alkylating properties of dehydroheliotrine, a metabolite of heliotrine. The toxic alkaloid occurs in the common heliotrope (*Heliotropium europaeum* L.), long used as a folk remedy in Europe, and in other species of the genus as well (16). Incidentally, in some of the species, heliotrine is accompanied by the active carcinogen lasiocarpine.

Nicotine, found in a number of species of tobacco, especially *Nicotiana tabacum* L., is a pyridine alkaloid shown to act as a teratogen in mice and chicks (43). Although experiments for teratogenesis with lobeline and related pyridine alkaloids in Indian tobacco (*Lobelia inflata* L.) have apparently not been carried out, their structural similarities with nicotine cause them to be somewhat suspect. Coniine, the major piperdine alkaloid in poison hemlock (*Conium maculatum* L.), produced birth defects in calves born to cows fed the compound during the fifty-fifth to seventy-fifth days of gestation.

Veratrum californicum Dur., western hellebore, figured prominently as a remedy among various Indian tribes of Nevada who used it as a contraceptive, a treatment for venereal disease and snakebite, and even to promote wound healing (44). Three steroidal alkaloids, cyclopamine, cycloposine, and jervine, each characterized by a fused furanopiperidine ring E/F arrangement, have been demonstrated to produce birth defects in sheep, cattle, goats, chick embryos, rats, hamsters, and rabbits (43). Only veratrum alkaloids containing the described ring arrangement were found to be teratogens.

Cellular Respiratory Inhibitors

Vegetable materials derived from the subfamily Prunoideae of the Rosaceae often contain cyanogenic glycosides, that is, compounds which on hydrolysis yield extremely toxic hydrocyanic acid (45). The most prominent such product currently used in herbal medicine is the kernel of various varieties of *Prunus armeniaca* L., commonly referred to as apricot pits. These contain up to about 8 percent amygdalin, which has erroneously but nevertheless ubiquitously become identified as laetrile. Although laetrile has been proven ineffective in the treatment of cancer (46, 47), it is still widely employed as a folk remedy.

Apricot pits contain, in addition to amygdalin, an enzyme mixture known as emulsin, which, on contact, effects hydrolysis of the amygdalin, thereby producing glucose, benzaldelyde, and hydrocyanic acid. This reaction takes place quite slowly under the acidic conditions prevailing in the stomach but, following passage of the materials into the alkaline medium of the duodenum, occurs with great rapidity. Absorption of the hydrocyanic acid from that site and the resultant production of histotoxic anoxia is then so rapid that intervention becomes difficult or impossible.

Amygdalin (laetrile) has also been reported to cause skeletel defects in the offspring of pregnant hamsters to which it had been administered orally (48). Consequently, its toxic effects may be much broader than previously supposed.

The concentration of amygdalin in apricot pits from different varieties of the plant varies greatly. Seeds of the wild apricot yielded more than twenty times as much hydrocyanic acid (217.0 mg. per 100 g. of moist seed) as those from a cultivated variety (8.9 mg. per 100 g.) (49).

Essentially the same comments apply to drugs such as the seeds of bitter almonds [*Prunus amygdalus* Batsch var. *amara* (DC.) Focke] and the bark of wild cherry (*Prunus serotina* Erh.). Although the latter contains prunasin

(D-mandelonitrile glucoside) instead of amygdalin, the hydrolytic end products are the same. Fortunately, these two products are not ordinarily ingested in sufficient quantities to produce serious health problems.

Cathartics

Many herbs contain glycosides of various anthraquinones, anthranols, and anthranones, which function as cathartics based on their ability to stimulate peristalsis by increasing the tone of the smooth muscle in the wall of the large intestine. Included in this category are aloe (dried latex of various *Aloe* spp.), buckthorn berries (ripe fruits of *Rhamnus catharticus* L.), cascara sagrada (bark of *Rhamnus frangula* L.), rhubarb (rhizome and root of Asian *Rheum* spp.), and senna (leaflets of *Cassia acutifolia* Del. and *C. angustifolia* Vahl.) (50).

Occasional use of these drugs in proper dosage is ordinarily without hazard, except possibly in the case of aloe and senna preparations, which should be avoided by pregnant women since their constituents may stimulate the uterine musculature as well as that of the large intestine (23). However, long-term use leads to habituation and development of a so-called laxative habit, in which ever-increasing doses are required to obtain the desired effect. Such chronic misuse can also result in electrolyte imbalances, including hypokalemia, hypocalcemia, and hyponatremia with ultimately serious consequences for the health of the consumer.

Many authoritative references on herbal medicine continue to list a number of plant materials containing cathartic resins. These are strong local irritants and, as such, act on the lining of the intestine to induce profuse watery stools. For this reason, they are called hydragogue cathartics or drastic purgatives. Examples of such products include colocynth [fruit pulp of *Citrullus colocynthis* (L.) Schrad.], ipomea (root of *Ipomoea orizabensis* Ledenois), jalap [root of *Exogonium purga* (Wender.) Benth.], and podophyllum (rhizome and roots of *Podophyllum peltatum* L.) (51).

The seeds of plants containing irritant fatty oils also continue to be discussed in such references. Aside from castor oil, which is used extensively as a pure, cold-pressed product and not as an herbal remedy, the only one of note is croton seeds. The carcinogenic properties of its oil have already been discussed.

Even occasional internal use of such violent irritants, especially on the basis of a self-determined need, is difficult to justify. These products were basically discarded from the physician's list of useful medicines years ago and should likewise be deleted from the listings of beneficial herbal remedies.

Abortifacients and Irritants

Several volatile oils and the plants containing them have long been utilized in folk medicine as emmenagogues or, somewhat less euphemistically, abortifacients. Included in the group are parsley [fruit of *Petroselinum crispum* (Mill.)

Nym. ex A. W. Hill], savin (tops of *Juniperus sabina* L.), American pennyroyal [leaves and tops of *Hedeoma pulegioides* (L.) Pers.], European pennyroyal (leaves and tops of *Mentha pulegium* L.), tansy [leaves and tops of *Chrysanthemum vulgare* (L.)], rue (leaves of *Ruta graveolens* L.), turpentine (oleoresin of *Pinus palustris* Mill.), and juniper (fruit of *Juniperus communis* L.).

Volatile oils cause intense irritation of various tissues. All of those listed tend to produce pelvic congestion through intestinal irritation, but safe doses are not effective, and only toxic doses induce abortion (52). Such toxic doses are more readily achieved with the respective volatile oils than with the plant materials themselves, although pregnant women should certainly be cautious in using internally any quantity of these natural drugs.

Many of the volatile oils contain constituents that produce deleterious reactions other than abortion. For example, pulegone in pennyroyal oil is both hepatotoxic and pulmonary toxic in mice, as are two other constituent terpenes, isopulegone and menthofuran (53). Since peppermint oil obtained from plants of *Mentha piperita* L. possessing a high percentage of young tissue may contain up to 30 percent of menthofuran (54), this finding would seem to question the advisability of chronic use of that oil, at least in large amounts. Fortunately, peppermint oils with a high menthofuran content are considered inferior because of their disagreeable cloying odor, and those containing much smaller amounts (3 to 12 percent) are normally marketed.

Apiol, a stearoptene from parsley oil used as an emmenagogue, produces degenerative lesions in both the liver and the kidneys (52). Thujone is an ingredient in many volatile oils used as abortifacients; it makes up as much as 95 percent of certain tansy oils (55). However, it is also an important constituent in volatile-oil-containing plants not used to induce abortion. Thujone occurs in concentrations ranging from 3 percent to 12 percent in wormwood oil obtained from *Artemesia absinthium* L. Long employed as an anthelmintic and flavoring agent in alcoholic beverages, wormwood is now known to be neurotoxic because of its contained thujone (56), and its use is proscribed in most countries (57).

The allegation that devil's claw, the secondary storage roots of *Harpagophytum procumbens* DC., induces abortion requires verification (33). It may be based on the misinterpretation of a statement by Watt and Breyer-Brandwijk that the drug is used by African natives to alleviate pain in pregnant women and especially in those anticipating a difficult delivery (58).

Miscellaneous Toxic Effects

ALFALFA—Reports that alfalfa seeds lowered plasma cholesterol levels in human subjects (59) prompted increased ingestion of both the seeds and the sprouts of *Medicago sativa* L. by health-oriented individuals. However, further studies in monkeys revealed that long-term use resulted in a condition resembling systemic lupus erythematosus (SLE), an autoimmune disorder that affects connective tissue (60). Since the SLE-like syndrome was also induced by feeding of a diet containing 1 percent L-canavanine, that nonprotein amino acid, which occurs in alfalfa seeds in concentrations up to nearly 1.5 percent (61), was identified as the causative agent.

A direct toxic effect of L-canavanine has not been entirely ruled out, but it is more likely that the unusual amino acid replaces arginine in a vital metabolic process such as the formation of histones. This would disturb the interaction of the histones with nucleic acid, due to a reduction in pH. Alternatively, L-canavanine may be cleaved to form urea and L-canaline; the latter compound is an antimetabolite that acts as a growth inhibitor in both plants and animals.

MISTLETOE—This is a widely used but extremely imprecise name applied to a number of species and subspecies of parasitic shrubs of the family Loranthaceae. American mistletoe refers to *Phoradendron tomentosum* (DC.) Engelm., and European mistletoe designates *Viscum album* L., of which three subspecies are generally recognized. The former species is believed to stimulate smooth muscle and increase blood pressure, the latter to relax smooth muscle and lower blood pressure.

Although the berries of both types of mistletoe have long been considered poisonous, the leaves, used in the form of a tea, constitute a widely used herbal remedy. Both plants contain similar toxic proteins designated phoratoxin and viscotoxins, respectively. On injection into mammals, these compounds induce hypotension, bradycardia, negative inotropic effect on the heart muscle, and vasoconstriction of vessels in skin and skeletal muscle (62). Their effects following oral ingestion in humans have not been carefully studied, although gastro-enteritis has been reported (63).

POKEWEED—The poisonous principles of *Phytolacca americana* L. have not been specifically identified although a saponin mixture designated phytolacca-toxin and a proteinaceous mitogen called PWM are usually said to be responsible. Whatever its specific identity, most of the toxicity occurs in the root, less in the leaves and stems, and still less in the mature berries (64). The roots are most commonly employed in herbal medicine for their alterative, cathartic, and emetic effects.

Ingestion of pokeweed produces severe stomach cramps, persistent vomiting, followed by slowed, difficult breathing, weakness, convulsions and even death. One cup of tea prepared from about 2 g. of pokeroot caused a forty-three-year-old woman to be hospitalized and to require twenty-four hours of intensive medical treatment before her condition stabilized (65).

CONCLUSIONS

The preceding comprehensive, but by no means exhaustive, survey of some potential hazards associated with the uninformed use of herbal medications has revealed that, contrary to popular belief, many such remedies suffer from the same kinds of disadvantages associated with conventional drugs. Some are inherently toxic, many have associated, unpleasant, even serious, side effects, and all must be used with intelligence and understanding if they are to be at all effective. Unfortunately, because of the paucity of careful scientific and clinical studies in the field, this is difficult for the professional; for the layman with access only to advocacy literature, it is almost impossible.

This brings us to the final hazard associated with this interesting but—from the scientific viewpoint—woefully neglected field. Lack of definitive knowledge regarding the constituents, the pharmacology, and the therapeutic effects of herbs renders their use imprecise at best, dangerous at worst. Fortunately, by the continued efforts of many dedicated scientists and clinicians, this is one hazard that can eventually be overcome. Let us look forward to that time.

REFERENCES

1. R. Lucas, *The Magic of Herbs in Daily Living* (West Nyack, N.Y.: Parker Publishing Co., 1972), 98.

2. M. Bethel, *The Healing Power of Herbs* (North Hollywood, Calif.: Wilshire Book Co., 1972), 12.

3. C. F. Leyel, *Culpeper's English Physician & Complete Herbal* (North Hollywood, Calif.: Wilshire Book Co., 1972), 72.

4. L. Griffin, *Insulin-versus-Herbs and the Diabetic* (Salt Lake City, Utah: Hawkes Publishing Inc., 1977), 20.

5. S. Leek, *Herbs: Medicine & Mysticism* (Chicago, Ill.: Henry Regnery Co., 1975), 198–199.

6. J. Heinerman, *The Science of Herbal Medicine* (Orem, Utah: Bi-World Publishers, 1979), 56.

7. R. C. Wren and R. W. Wren, *Potter's New Cyclopaedia of Botanical Drugs and Preparations*, new ed. (Hengiscote, England: Health Science Press, 1975), 54–55.

8. H. Bankhofer and H. Kurth, *Das praktische Handbuch der Naturheilkunde* (Bayreuth: Gondrom Verlag, 1982), 198.

9. M. Mességué, *Health Secrets of Plants and Herbs* (New York: William Morrow and Co., Inc., 1979), 84–88.

10. S. Schmidt, "'Teufelskralle' vielfach bakteriell bedenklich," *Deutsche Apotheker Zeitung,* 118 (1978): 1808–09.

11. Anon., "Tiny Fly Halts Spirulina Shipments," *Health Foods Business* vol. 28, no. 5 (1982): 38.

12. C. Franz, "Arzneidrogen: Qualitatssicherung durch Anbau und Züchtung," *Deutsche Apotheker Zeitung* 122 (1982): 1413–17.

13. A. Walther, W. Hübel, and A. Nahrstedt, "Herz- und kreislaufwirksame Drogen und Reinheitsanforderungen an Drogen im Mittelpunkt," *Deutsche Apotheker Zeitung,* 122 (1982): 1547–1555.

14. P. D. Bryson, A. S. Watanabe, B. H. Rumack, and R. C. Murphy, "Burdock Root Tea Poisoning," *Journal of the American Medical Association* 239: (1978): 2157.

15. R. J. Huxtable, "Herbal Teas and Toxins: Novel Aspects of Pyrrolizidine Poisoning in the United States," *Perspectives in Biology and Medicine* 24 (1980): 1–14.

16. L. W. Smith and C. C. J. Culvenor, "Plant Sources of Pyrrolizidine Alkaloids," *Journal of Natural Products* 44 (1981): 129–52.

17. K. M. Larson, M. R. Roby, and F. R. Stermitz, "Unsaturated Pyrrolizidines from Borage *(Borago officinalis)*, A Common Garden Herb," *Journal of Natural Products* 47 (1984): 747–48.

18. E. Röder, H. Wiedenfeld, T. Hille, and R. Britz-Kirstgen, "Pyrrolizidine in *Echinacea angustifolia* DC. und *Echinacea purpurea* M.," *Deutsche Apotheker Zeitung* 124 (1984): 2316–18.

19. International Agency for Research on Cancer Working Group, "Safrole, Isosafrole and Dihydrosafrole," *IARC Monographs on the Evaluation of the Carcinogenic Risk of Chemicals to Man* 1 (1972): 169–74.

20. M. S. Benedetti, A. Malnoë, and A. L. Broillet, "Absorption, Metabolism and Excretion of Safrole in the Rat and Man," *Toxicology* 7 (1977): 69–83.

21. J. M. Taylor, W. I. Jones, E. C. Hagan, M. A. Gross, D. A. Davis, and E. L. Cook, "Toxicity of Oil of Calamus (Jammu Variety)," *Toxicology and Applied Pharmacology* 10 (1967): 405.

22. K. Keller and E. Stahl, "Kalamus: Inhaltstoffe und ß-Asarongehalt bei verschiedenen Herkunften," *Deutsche Apotheker Zeitung* 122 (1982): 2463–66.

23. E. Röder, "Nebenwirkungen von Heilpflanzen," *Deutsche Apotheker Zeitung* 122 (1982): 2081–92.

24. Anon., "Arzneimittelrisiko Aristolochiasaure," *Deutsche Apotheker Zeitung* 121 (1981): 1170.

25. J. F. Morton, "Economic Botany in Epidemiology," *Economic Botany* 32 (1978): 111–16.

26. J. F. Morton, "Tea with Milk," *Science*, 204 (1979): 909.

27. R. C. Wren and R. W. Wren, op. cit., 102, 205.

28. M. Grieve, *A Modern Herbal*, vols. 1 and 2 (New York: Dover Publications, Inc., 1971), 234, 531–32.

29. E. Hecker, "Structure Activity Relationship in Diterpene Esters Irritant and Carcinogenic to Mouse Skin," in *Carcinogenesis*, vol. 2, *Mechanisms of Tumor Promotion and Carcinogenesis*, T. J. Slaga, A. Sivak, and R. K. Boutwell, eds. (New York: Raven Press, 1978), 11–48.

30. A. Kornhauser, W. G. Warner, A. L. Giles, Jr., "Psoralen Phototoxicity: Correlation with Serum and Epidermal 8-methoxypsoralen and 5-methoxypsoralen in the Guinea Pig," *Science* 217 (1982): 733–35.

31. J. Gengler, "'Natural' Repellent Turns into a Nightmare for Family," *Gary Post-Tribune* (July 31, 1982), A1, A3.

32. V. E. Tyler, *The Honest Herbal* (Philadelphia, Pa.: George F. Stickley Co., 1982), 197–98.

33. M. Abramowicz, ed., "Toxic Reactions to Plant Products Sold in Health Food Stores," *Medical Letter on Drugs and Therapeutics* 21 (1979): 29–31.

34. J. A. Lybarger, J. S. Gallagher, D. W. Pulver, A. Litwin, S. Brooks, and I. L. Bernstein, "Occupational Asthma Induced by Inhalation and Ingestion of Garlic," *Journal of Allergy and Clinical Immunology* 69 (1982): 448–54.

35. V. E. Tyler, L. R. Brady, and J. E. Robbers, *Pharmacognosy*, 8th ed. (Philadelphia, Pa.: Lea & Febiger, 1981), 69.

36. M. T. Epstein, E. A. Espiner, R. A. Donald, and H. Hughes, "Effect of Eating Liquorice on the Renin-angiotensin Aldosterone Axis in Normal Subjects," *British Medical Journal* 1 (1977): 488–90.

37. R. C. Wren and R. W. Wren, op. cit., 187.

38. V. E. Tyler, op. cit., 106–10.

39. Anon., "Ginseng," *Lawrence Review of Natural Products* 2 (1981): 45–48.

40. R. K. Siegel, "Ginseng Abuse Syndrome," *Journal of the American Medical Association* 241 (1979): 1614–15.

41. R. K. Siegel, "Ginseng and High Blood Pressure," *Journal of the American Medical Association* 243 (1980): 32.

42. B. V. Palmer, A. C. V. Montgomery, and J. C. M. P. Monteiro, "Gin Seng and Mastalgia," *British Medical Journal* 1 (1978): 1284.

43. R. F. Keeler, "Toxins and Teratogens of Higher Plants," *Lloydia* 38: (1975): 56–86.

44. P. Train, J. R. Heinrichs, and W. A. Archer, *Medicinal Uses of Plants by Indian Tribes of Nevada: Contributions toward a Flora of Nevada, No. 45* (Beltsville, Md.: U.S.D.A., Plant Industry Station, 1957), 98–99.

45. V. E. Tyler, L. R. Brady, and J. E. Robbers, op. cit., 70–72.

46. C. G. Moertel, et al., "A Clinical Trial of Amygdalin (Laetrile) in the Treatment of Human Cancer," *New England Journal of Medicine* 306 (1982): 201–206.

47. A. S. Relman, "Closing the Books on Laetrile," *New England Journal of Medicine* 306 (1982): 236.

48. C. C. Willhite, "Congenital Malformations Induced by Laetrile," *Science* 215 (1982): 1513–15.

49. J. S. Sayre and S. Kaymakcalan, "Cyanide Poisoning from Apricot Seeds Among Children in Central Turkey," *New England Journal of Medicine* 270 (1964): 1113–15.

50. V. E. Tyler, L. R. Brady, and J. E. Robbers, op. cit., 57–67.

51. M. Pahlow, *Das grosse Buch der Heilpflanzen* (Munich: Gräfe und Unzer GmbH, 1979), 499.

52. T. Sollmann, *A Manual of Pharmacology*, 7th ed. (Philadelphia and London: W. B. Saunders, Co., 1948), 148.

53. W. P. Gordon, A. J. Forte, R. J. McMurtry, J. Gal, and S. D. Nelson, "Hepatotoxicity and Pulmonary Toxicity in Pennyroyal Oil and Its Constituent Terpenes in the Mouse," *Toxicology and Applied Pharmacology* 65 (1982): 413–24.

54. E. Guenther, "The Peppermint Oil Industry in Oregon and Washington States," *Perfumery and Essential Oil Record* 52 (1961): 632–42.

55. E. Stahl and G. Schmitt, "Chemische Rassen bei Arzneipflanzen, II Mitt.: Über die verschiedenartig zusammengesetzten ätherischen Öle des Rainfarns," *Archiv der Pharmazie und Berichte der Deutschen Pharmazeutischen Gesellschaft* 197 (1964): 385–91.

56. Y. Millet, J. Jouglard, M. D. Steinmetz, P. Tognetti, P.: Joanny, and J. Arditti, "Toxicity of Some Essential Plant Oils: Clinical and Experimental Study," *Clinical Toxicology* 18: (1981): 1485–98.

57. V. E. Tyler, "Wormwood's Green Alchemy," *Garden* vol. 5, no. 5 (1981): 14–15, 31.

58. J. M. Watt and M. G. Breyer-Brandwijk, *The Medical and Poisonous Plants of Southern and Eastern Africa*, 2nd ed. (Edinburgh: E. & S. Livingstone Ltd., 1962), 830.

59. M. R. Malinow, P. McLaughlin, and C. Stafford, "Alfalfa Seeds: Effects on Cholesterol Metabolism," *Experientia* 36 (1980): 562–64.

60. M. R. Malinow, E. J. Bardana, Jr., B. Pirofsky, S. Craig, and P. McLaughlin, "Systemic Lupus Erythematosus-like Syndrome in Monkeys Fed Alfalfa Sprouts: Role of a Nonprotein Amino Acid," *Science* 216 (1982): 415–17.

61. E. A. Bell, "Canavanine in the Leguminosae," *Biochemical Journal* 75 (1960): 618–20.

62. V. E. Tyler, L. R. Brady, and J. E. Robbers, op. cit., 489–90.

63. W. H. Lewis, "Plants for Man: Their Potential in Human Health," *Canadian Journal of Botany* 60 (1982): 310–15.

64. Anon., "Pokeweed," *Lawrence Review of Natural Products* 2 (1981): 17–18.

65. W. H. Lewis and P. R. Smith, "Poke Root Herbal Tea Poisoning," *Journal of the American Medical Association* 242 (1979): 2759–60.

Larry D. Young, Ph.D.

Holistic Medicine's Use of Biofeedback

A casual perusal of many of the available treatises on holistic medicine yields a remarkable number of references to biofeedback. Appreciation of the almost iconic role accorded biofeedback by many holistic writers requires, as background, an operational understanding of both biofeedback and the tenets of holistic medicine.

BIOFEEDBACK

According to Blanchard and Epstein, "biofeedback is a process in which a person learns to reliably influence physiological responses of two kinds: either responses which are not ordinarily under voluntary control or responses which ordinarily are easily regulated but for which regulation has broken down due to trauma or disease."[1] The process subsumed under the generic label "biofeedback" consists of three basic operations. First, a particular physiological response (e.g., heart rate or peripheral skin temperature) is detected and amplified (usually electronically). Secondly, this biological signal is converted into an easily comprehended form. Finally, this transformed biological signal is fed back to the individual on a relatively immediate basis. With this information many individuals can learn to produce reliable changes in the particular physiological response. Implicit within both the definition and the operations listed is the idea that the individual is attempting to control or change his or her physiological response for a particular purpose. That is, biofeedback refers to purposeful, goal-directed activity and not simply to exposure to a feedback display.

Almost from the initial demonstration of physiological self-regulation and the coining of the term *biofeedback* in the late 1960s, interest and speculation have been directed toward potential clinical applications of the procedures. Biofeedback has been the subject of controversy within the realms of scientific experimentation and theorizing as well as in the arena of clinical application, although the term *furor,* employed by some holistic writers to describe this debate, is overly dramatic. Over the course of the past fifteen years, biofeedback has developed a degree of scientific respectability that permits investigators to publish research in respected journals representing a wide range of disciplinary specialties.

HOLISTIC MEDICINE

Most discussions of holistic medicine emphasize several themes with the following representing an overview of the most commonly expressed beliefs. It is commonly asserted that psychological and physiological parameters are interdependent, although this assertion is frequently elaborated in a manner that gives predominance to mental factors. This prominence of psychology occurs in considerations of pathogenesis as well as of treatment (e.g., "all states of health/illness are psychosomatic"). In accordance with the belief that a person's state of health is influenced by all the forces that impinge on him or her, holists assert that treatment must be concerned with the whole person (body, mind, and spirit) in order for complete healing to occur. The goal of this healing, frequently expressed as the restoration of balance or harmony within the patient's life, is a state of health characterized as extending beyond the absence of disease to a condition, often referred to as "wellness," endowed with special powers of resilience. It is axiomatic within the holistic framework that the patient must assume a more active role with greater responsibility in his or her own health care. While in the preceding general description of its tenets holistic medicine does not appear to violate the tradition of current clinical practice, its proponents frequently position themselves in opposition to traditional scientific medicine. Advocates of holistic medicine commonly defend their controversial and antiscientific philosophy and practices by referring to their position as a new and alternative scientific medical paradigm.[2]

From a holistic perspective, then, biofeedback demonstrates the importance of psychological processes inasmuch as it represents mental control over physiological responses, permits clinical intervention to be directed to both mental and physical spheres of a person's life as they influence one another (i.e., the whole person), and involves the patient in his or her own treatment. Furthermore, biofeedback is accorded a prominent role in both the restoration of intrapersonal harmony and the prevention of future disease or disharmony. Consequently, biofeedback has been accorded the honor of ushering in, or even of coercing recognition of, a revolutionary new (holistic) paradigm in medicine. This superficial convergence of biofeedback and holistic medicine allows holists to borrow the scientific respectability of biofeedback and use it to "prove" the validity of several basic holistic tenets and thereby to support the entire structure of holistic medicine. A more extensive critical examination of the general principles underlying holistic philosophy has been reported elsewhere.[3]

This essay will describe the manner in which biofeedback is presented by holistic writers. Specific emphasis will be placed on the perspective of biofeedback found in the holistic literature regarding the implicit definition employed, the purpose or goal of clinical application, the principles guiding application and evaluation, and other claims regarding biofeedback. It is my intention to evaluate holistic medicine's use of biofeedback rather than to provide a critical evaluation of clinical biofeedback itself. Interested readers can obtain the latter information from several other sources.[4]

STYLE OR MANNER OF PRESENTATION

Inasmuch as other commentators have described holistic medicine as unscientific or even antiscientific, it is reasonable to expect the same attitudes to characterize holistic presentations of biofeedback. Several interrelated manifestations of these attitudes are expressed with consistency. Most presentations are written in a literary style that emphasizes the intuitive and appears to address either a lay audience or an audience who endorses most holistic presuppositions. In many of these presentations biofeedback is mentioned in conjunction with other holistic health practices as if all were accepted equally. Few of the holistic descriptions of biofeedback are typified by the caution, precision, and clarity of thought characteristic of most rigorous scientific writing. Although there do exist rigorous theoretical and empirical presentations of biofeedback, these typically are not made by holists. Although writing for both of these nonprofessional audiences can be a legitimate enterprise, it becomes susceptible to criticism when it comprises all the supporting evidence that exists for a particular position (in this case, holistic biofeedback). Biofeedback and its application are frequently discussed in what are labeled "overviews." Even if this strategy is not deliberate, it does provide a convenient justification for oversimplification.

Many of the articles espousing a holistic approach employ a great deal of "reasoning" by analogy or illustration. This phenomenon occurs regularly in attempts to convince the reader that feedback principles operate universally. Unfortunately, the argument is never taken past the point of superficial similarity to explore whether the processes or mechanisms that govern biofeedback applications are identical in substance or only in appearance with those in the illustration.

In much of the holistic literature, the clinical experience of the authors functions as both the source and the interpreter of evidence. The practical manifestation of this point is that anecdotal reports and uncontrolled case studies abound as substantiation of particular claims. It is also not uncommon for these case presentations to focus on dramatic or sensational effects that may be emotionally compelling but are of minimal scientific value. Similarly, there is a tendency for some authors to describe biofeedback in terms of the behavior and particularly the experience of an undefined "average patient," a technique that communicates less in substance than in appearance.

When published research pertaining to biofeedback and its application is discussed, the data are often overinterpreted in such a way that the "implications" of a particular study not uncommonly occupy a position of greater prominence than do the results themselves. This is especially troublesome when these speculations are not clearly differentiated from evidence and when they fail to take into consideration established physiological mechanisms or other potentially mitigating factors. Equally disturbing is the occasional occurrence of claims that are patently wrong, such as the statement that biofeedback was theoretically legitimized by Neal Miller's conclusive proof that "only one kind of learning" existed,[5] or the implication that extraocular muscular tension contributes to glaucoma.[6] The presence of these obviously false claims serves to detract from biofeedback's credibility, especially to a professional audience.

Finally, it is not uncommon to find misrepresentation in the discussion of biofeedback research. Although these are usually trivial distortions, they occasionally, and more seriously, appear to be extrapolations of holistic dogma. For example, Pelletier, in discussing a particular research project by Shapiro, Tursky, and Schwartz claims that "a connection was made between mind and body as a critical step in helping carry over the learning from the clinic to daily life."[7] However, this study was not conducted with patients, so the clinical issue of carry-over into daily life is irrelevant; secondly, inasmuch as no attempt was made to assess these carry-over effects, there existed no data to evaluate; and thirdly, the Shapiro, et al. study was not designed to address in systematic fashion the experience of psychological-physiological covariation. In fact, an anecdotal comment constitutes the only "evidence" for a mind-body connection found in the original report. Thus, there is absolutely no basis *in the evidence* for concluding that experiencing this mind-body connection is a "critical step" for anything. Pelletier next focuses on the investigation's report that heart rate and blood pressure responses were minimally correlated during periods when feedback was provided for only one response. Based only on this single observation, Pelletier expounds upon the implication that an individual could "fragment the functions of his neurophysiological system and create a disruptive pattern" and continues with the discussion of "discontinuities between psychological and physiological processes," which "constitute the essence of psychosomatic disorders." The presentation just described constitutes a gross misrepresentation of the Shapiro, et al. investigation in which holistic dogma takes precedence over the original report.

In summary, the preceding section illustrates several specific ways in which the unscientific and antiscientific attitudes of holistic medicine are expressed in the context of discussing biofeedback. In the next sections the focus will shift from contextual and stylistic points to factors specifically pertaining to biofeedback.

A HOLISTIC PERSPECTIVE ON BIOFEEDBACK

Definition

Although most holistic writers do not go through the exercise of deliberately spelling out in operational terms what they include under the label of "biofeedback," it is usually possible to ascertain their implicit definition from careful reading. Unfortunately, not all holistic writers employ the same meaning when they discuss biofeedback and, occasionally, the same writer will fail to use the term consistently. The definition suggested by Blanchard and Epstein accurately reflects one way the word is used in the holistic literature. This definition includes the idea that an individual is attempting to control a specific aspect of his or his own physiology and that this change is in a particular direction and for a clearly identified purpose. Additionally, this use of the term is frequently accompanied by the idea that a medically pathological response is being corrected.

In contrast to this, one frequently encounters in the holistic literature instances in which biofeedback apparently refers to little more than simple psychophysiological monitoring. The use of the label "biofeedback" seems to derive from the use of commercial biofeedback equipment for on-line physiological assessment rather than from the deliberate attempt to control a physiological response with the assistance of electronic equipment for a specific therapeutic purpose. Pelletier, for example, stresses the need for accurate, ongoing information in order for both patient and therapist to assess progress, and he identifies biofeedback as a means of obtaining this objective information. In his illustration of a patient who discovers that he is masking his sadness and anger with laughter, Pelletier identifies biofeedback as the crucial component in this therapeutic breakthrough, yet there is no indication that the patient was trying to self-regulate a physiological response for therapeutic purposes. These and other references identifying clinical biofeedback as "a powerful tool yielding an unprecedented, highly accurate method of monitoring physiological states"[8] correspond minimally with the Blanchard and Epstein definition.

Other holistic writers use biofeedback to refer to an even broader, more vague, and more poorly defined phenomenon. These uses range from discussions of "noninstrumental biofeedback" and a "biofeedback model of pain" to the claim that yogic regulation of basal metabolic rate was probably the earliest use of biofeedback.[9] In these various discussions several different concepts emerge. First, there is a notion of biofeedback, apparently derived from communications theory, which signifies information about an act. When used in this manner, the term biofeedback does not necessarily imply a deliberate attempt to control the physiological response. Secondly, biofeedback sometimes is alleged to be comparable to biological feedback. This use of the term is very similar to an engineering concept and often is illustrated with examples from neural circuits or endocrine system mechanisms. This presumed parallel is very misleading in that there is no evidence to support the idea that the processes, principles, or mechanisms governing biofeedback are comparable to those underlying biological or engineering feedback, as is claimed. Therefore, when various holistic writers discuss biofeedback they may be employing quite dissimilar concepts. At times, it is difficult to determine precisely which meaning of "biofeedback" is being used. This definitional "fuzziness" allows holists to claim that they are utilizing biofeedback in the treatment of a particular problem and to appropriate biofeedback's legitimacy when the actual procedures do not constitute biofeedback. Such practices are deceptive whether or not they are intentionally so.

Purposes or Goals for Biofeedback

Holistic advocates of biofeedback not infrequently allude to its demonstrated efficacy as a therapeutic procedure. It is important to recognize that, *without elaboration,* any such claim is incomplete. That is, inasmuch as biofeedback is a generic term—as is surgery—it is important to specify more precisely the combination of various parameters for which this efficacy is claimed. First, information should be provided regarding the type of biofeedback that is alleged to be effective. For example, there is no compelling a priori reason to believe that biofeedback of heart rate should be comparable to biofeedback of electromyographic (EMG) activity (electrical impulses associated with muscle fiber contraction) or of peripheral skin temperature or of electroencephalographic (EEG) activity (brainwaves) in the treatment of any particular disorder. In fact, some of these types of biofeedback may never have been tried in the treatment of a particular disorder. Secondly, claims for biofeedback's efficacy are incomplete without a thorough specification of the presenting problem of the patient. Whitehead and Schuster have reported that fecal incontinence due to rectal noncompliance cannot be treated with biofeedback but that fecal incontinence due to sphinceter sensory or motor impairment does respond positively to biofeedback.[10] Finally, a statement regarding the purpose and/or goal of employing biofeedback is a necessary portion of any claim of biofeedback's efficacy, a point that will be elaborated later. To summarize, it is logically inappropriate to conclude that a positive clinical outcome for one type of biofeedback designed for one purpose and in relation to one clinical problem necessarily justifies the wholesale endorsement of any type of biofeedback for almost any purpose and for other clinical problems. Even though some of these parallel claims may be plausible, they nonetheless must be established by empirical evidence.

Historically, clinical biofeedback has been applied to two types of circumstances. The first of these pertains to situations in which the target physiological response that the patient is attempting to control and the presenting clinical problem are directly and intimately related. An example of this type of application would be the attempt of hypertensive patients to control a feedback signal that reflects the level of either their systolic or diastolic blood pressure.[11] By way of contrast, the second broad type of application is more indirect. Here, the patient's presenting clinical complaint is regarded as the consequence of "stress" and the target physiological response that the patient is attempting to control with biofeedback is presumed to be an index of this "stress." Biofeedback, in this case, is the means for assisting the patient in learning to reduce the physiological manifestation of the underlying stress, which, in turn, is the presumed cause of his or her physical complaint. An illustration of this indirect approach might be teaching hypertensive patients to decrease frontalis muscle tension levels with EMG biofeedback in order to reduce stress and thereby decrease their elevated blood pressure.[12] It should be noted that it is more difficult within this indirect paradigm to demonstrate that the biofeedback procedures are directly responsible for the clinical improvement than is the case with more "direct" applications. Holistic applications of clinical biofeedback typically have eschewed the narrower, direct use of biofeedback in favor of broader, more indirect goals for its application.

One of the more frequent uses of biofeedback by holists is in teaching general relaxation as an intervention for stress-related disorders. However, holistic application often has required that patients achieve an altered state of consciousness as a necessary intermediate step in achieving the ultimate therapeutic goal of "healing." Pelletier's view is that, "such a state is a prerequisite for self-understanding and is the basis for constructive alterations in behavior."[13] Such an emphasis is consistent with holistic doctrines that reify phenomenological constructs and assert the preeminence of mental over physical factors. However, there is no evidence that such a prerequisite is necessary or that such a subjective, phenomenological focus is superior to a more scientifically acceptable formulation. A primary impediment to empirical evaluation of this alleged essentiality is the lack of acceptable criteria defining such states as "relaxed internal awareness" or "harmony of mind and body."

Advocates of a holistic position have preferred these broad, indirect purposes for biofeedback but have expanded the scope of its application even further. Among the broader goals toward which "biofeedback" (or psychophysiological monitoring that is labeled biofeedback) has been directed within a holistic framework is the provision of objective information to both patient and therapist regarding the patient's physiological reactions to various psychological stimuli or the evaluation (in an unspecified, but "objective," fashion) of the patient's progress in therapy. Biofeedback is also employed in order to have the patient demonstrably involved in his or her own treatment as well as to increase the patient's motivation to persist with whatever treatment regimen has been selected. A related purpose for which biofeedback is used by some holistic practitioners is to demonstrate to patients that they are capable either of exercising control over their bodily responses to stress or over *something* in problematic circumstances (and, therefore, presumably are capable of influencing other factors in the same situation). Another stated holistic goal or purpose for employing biofeedback is to assist individuals in self-exploration or self-understanding. The rationale supporting this particular application is usually enunciated in a vague and spiritualized manner. It is in this vein that Pelletier claims that patients can use the concomitant meditative state to "interrogate their unconscious" and correct potential problems before they result in anxiety or physical symptoms.[14] Similarly, Shealy claims that "each day you will tune in, more and more to the universal life force—you may want to call it God. . . ."[15] An additional purpose for employing clinical biofeedback is often stated by holistic proponents in terms of moving away from the correction of some (unspecified) pathology toward global preventive medicine, health maintenance, and personal growth. Sobel has even suggested that biofeedback be included as part of the basic public school curriculum.[16] These extremely speculative goals are accompanied by neither empirical evidence nor a plausible justification other than the banal rationale that increasing people's competence to cope with stress should have prophylactic effects.

Several of the purposes just mentioned constitute legitimate concerns within a treatment setting. For example, convincing a patient that he or she does respond physiologically to certain thoughts or environmental circumstances may be a prerequisite (although this is not to be guaranteed) for obtaining a commitment to change his or her behavior, circumstances, and so on. Likewise, a patient's motivation to adhere to a treatment regimen may increase the likelihood of a successful outcome. Nonetheless, it is critical to understand that these goals, although important, are limited and are incidental to the central purpose or goal of the therapy itself. Enhanced compliance with an ineffective treatment would not be expected to produce a positive treatment outcome. Furthermore, it is desirable that successful treatment outcomes be attributed to the treatment itself rather than simply to incidental effects such as motivational changes. If increased motivation results in behavioral change then there is an alternative explanation for at least a portion of the therapeutic outcomes. Furthermore, if these motivational changes *alone* lead to clinical improvement comparable to that produced by the treatment itself, then the only rational basis for prescribing this particular treatment for the condition in question is for the placebo value. It is important to realize that many of these incidental treatment goals can be achieved by means other than biofeedback. Biofeedback may be effective, convenient, and currently stylish; however, it is by no means the only technique by which these incidental treatment goals can be achieved. In fact, there is little, if any, evidence that biofeedback has even been compared with, much less found superior to, other procedures for achieving the incidental purposes discussed above. This means that biofeedback, in these circumstances, is used primarily as a gimmick and that its selection is based upon plausibility or personal preference rather than adequate empirical evidence.

Holistic writers fail to make the appropriate discrimination between the art and the science of therapy. Many, if not most, of the purposes noted above can be subsumed legitimately under the art of good clinical practice. When biofeedback is used in the limited manner described above there can be no legitimate claim that it constitutes the active treatment component, or that there is a logical basis for attributing therapeutic outcomes to biofeedback itself. Holistic writers are indiscriminate in their claims about biofeedback's efficacy, for they generally fail to specify whether the goal or purpose of a particular biofeedback application is direct, indirect, or incidental. Consequently, they appropriate evidence of clinical efficacy for one purpose and use it as evidence to justify virtually any other application in which they are interested.

As a corollary to the observation that the holistic literature is vague regarding the purpose and goal for biofeedback, it should be noted that this literature either ignores or obscures the degree and appropriateness of the relationship of these goals to the presenting problem. It is not apparent that holistic authors perceive that the legitimacy or appropriateness of a particular goal or purpose for biofeedback may vary fundamentally and significantly depending upon the population in question. To illustrate, Gladman and Estrada allege that in the context of an illness experience biofeedback, in particular, provides an opportunity for patients to share their illness with their physicians and to improve the quality of their life inasmuch as biofeedback is a tool for treating both the patient and the illness.[17] Self-understanding and personal growth might be desirable goals for some individuals (ignoring for the moment the issue of whether biofeedback can contribute to the achievement of these goals) and may occur in some medical patients as a result of their medical condition, its treatment, and/or its outcome. Nevertheless, these observations do not warrant redefining these (possibly desirable) changes as *clinical* goals and imposing them on physicians and therapists with regard to every patient. For example, biofeedback can assist many patients to reduce or eliminate their headache activity; it is not capable of giving their life new meaning as some have implied. Such claims are misrepresentative inasmuch as transcendent meaning derives from a value-laden philosophy rather than from a scientific technique. Reducing headache activity is a legitimate clinical goal; giving life new meaning is a legitimate religious goal. The critical point is that the two goals are fundamentally different even if they are both legitimate and occasionally occur simultaneously. Inasmuch as biofeedback has a historical tradition of use with medical patients, the failure of holists to acknowledge the gross inappropriateness of their quasi-religious goals for biofeedback in such a context has a damaging effect on the medical community's perception of biofeedback's appropriateness for other goals.

In contrast to the preceding discussion of the lack of appropriateness of clinical biofeedback for achieving personal growth and self-understanding among medical patients, one might argue that the use of biofeedback in conjunction with some spiritual philosophy in nonpatients is a matter of personal choice. At one level, the practice differs little from the use of the "E-meter" in L. Ron Hubbard's "Dianetics" to measure electrical currents, except that the latter generally is recognized as a religious cult practice rather than a third-party reimbursable therapy. At another level, however, these fringe or questionable holistic purposes for biofeedback have broader negative effects on individuals who would not otherwise be involved. Specifically, the use of biofeedback for frivolous, clinically irrelevant purposes (this does not refer to nonclinical scientific research) taints the perception of the procedure by both the medical community and the general public. Legitimate practitioners of biofeedback may experience a type of prejudicial "guilt by association" with a resultant negative impact on their professional status and clinical practice. An additional group that suffers the indirect detrimental impact of a tainted perception of biofeedback is comprised of those patients who would have benefited from biofeedback but who were deterred, either personally or by their physician, from seeking biofeedback services. Thus, the inappropriate and illegitimate claims for biofeedback, even with nonpatients, are not neutral but rather are detrimental to the well-being of a large number of individuals who are otherwise separate from the issue.

Just as holistic writers fail to indicate clearly and consistently what they mean when they use the term biofeedback, so too they often fail to indicate the specific purpose for which they are employing biofeedback in therapy. Consequently, holists impede the education of other health care professionals regarding appropriate uses, and limitations, of biofeedback.

While holists may not actively strive to obscure several of the above distinctions regarding the legitimacy and appropriateness of the different purposes and goals for clinical biofeedback, it nonetheless is undeniable that they benefit when these issues are not raised and these distinctions are not made. This vagueness allows holists to usurp the scientific legitimacy from certain goals in particular contexts and to apply it to other purposes in other contexts for which such claims are not justified.

Claims and Principles Guiding Biofeedback Application

Turning from issues of definition and purpose in the use of biofeedback, let us next consider those principles (and underlying assumptions) enunciated by holists which presumably guide the operation of biofeedback. As we have noted previously, biofeedback finds general application within holistic medicine in the area of stress management where it is employed primarily in general relaxation training. The general paradigm outlined earlier is that patients are taught to control a physiological manifestation of stress, thereby achieving relaxation and stress reduction with an accompanying decline in their initial symptoms and an increase in their well-being.

The concept of "stress" toward which these interventions are directed is predominantly an intuitive idea that is frequently discussed as a modern Western phenomenon (e.g., a variant of "hurry sickness"). Flynn, for example, argues that health and well-being require the harmonious integration of our "self-system" and "world order."[18] At one point Pelletier comments that the "negative interplay of mind and body leads to disease while their positive interaction results in health and well-being," but he provides little of substance beyond this banality.[19] It is seldom clear whether or not holists exclude anything from the scope of "stress-related disorders" inasmuch as they often assert categorically that all disorders are "psychosomatic." Holists' simplistic notions of "stress" fail to take into account Weiner's observation that stress can function to either predispose an organism to disease, initiate the pathophysiological changes, or exacerbate a condition that already exists.[20] Also ignored is Weiner's point that these three functions may be accompanied by different psychophysiological mechanisms. Likewise, holistic notions of the manner in which psychological or behavioral factors influence bodily changes are relatively naive. To illustrate, the finding that psychologically "well-adjusted" cancer patients have relatively higher mortality rates runs counter to prevailing holistic doctrine.[21] Similarly, the report that relatively "acute" and "chronic" exposure to stressors differentially effects the responding of the immune system is not readily incorporated into the holistic framework.[22] What holists have done in this context, however, is to borrow terms from other areas (such as regulation/disregulation or integration), leave them poorly defined, and use them to discuss the negative relationship of "stress" to health.

This same simplistic dogma frequently dominates holistic discussions of physiology or psychophysiology. One dramatic example is the often-cited three "basic principles" that underlie clinical biofeedback.[23] These are: (1) *any* biological function that can be monitored and amplified by electronic instrumentation and fed back to a person through *any* one of his five senses *can be* regulated by that individual; (2) "*every* change in the physiological state is accompanied by *an appropriate* change in the mental emotional state, conscious or unconscious, and conversely, *every* change in the mental emotional state, conscious or unconscious, is accompanied by *an appropriate* change in the physiological state"; and (3) a meditative state of deep relaxation is conducive to the establishment of voluntary control by allowing the individual to become aware of sublimal imagery, fantasies, and sensations (emphasis added). These "underlying principles" are more properly regarded as unsubstantiated beliefs or perhaps even as fantasies themselves. Additionally, they are structured in such a manner that they are practically impervious to experimental falsification. However, several brief comments are also in order.

It should be noted in relation to the first of these three dogmatic assertions that self-regulation strategies have not been investigated with all biological functions and thus, this claim may be supported by fantasy as much as by evidence. Secondly, inasmuch as feedback typically is delivered within visual or auditory, and occasionally tactile, modalities there is little evidence that feedback delivered within olfactory or gustatory modalities is comparably efficacious. Thirdly, given that individuals differ in the degree to which they are capable of effecting physiological change in a particular direction on command (a reasonable requirement considering the fact that "self-regulation" implies more than simply physiological change), the implied claim that *all* individuals are capable of learning to regulate any or all responses is unrealistic. Finally, even if this first assertion were largely accurate and individuals were able to control any biological response, it does not follow that the degree of control would be sufficient for a clinically significant result. It is this first principle that allows holists to confidently assert the efficacy of biofeedback in the treatment of virtually any medical problem without being restricted by current knowledge or physiological mechanisms or by lack of evidence. Holists are thereby freed from the constraining effects that data exert on normal science. Dossey even goes so far as to claim that "a new view of the body begins to emerge. Far from being comprised of dumb organs, body parts can be said to unconsciously think. . . ."[24]

The second of the three "principles" is essentially a statement without meaning. That is, not only are there no standards for determining what constitutes "appropriate" change in either psychological or physiological states, but also the inclusion of unconscious states into the assertion permits any imaginable data to be interpreted as consistent with the principle. Pelletier himself acknowledges that, "many subtle shifts in the mental processing of thoughts, images, and emotions do not appear to have any neurophysiological correlates"; and he admits this in a chapter that begins with an assertion of the "basic principles."[25] However, no comment is addressed to these contradictory claims, a fact that may contribute to understandable confusion.

Although the third basic holistic belief alleged to form the foundation of the practice of biofeedback identifies the state of deep relaxation as conducive to the development of voluntary control, there is no evidence that such a state is either necessary or sufficient for establishing all voluntary control. In fact, for self-regulation of certain responses (such as training quadriplegic patients to increase their blood pressure to prevent fainting due to orthostatic hypotension) such a deeply relaxed state may even be counterproductive. Furthermore, the implication that imagery, fantasies, and so on are *necessary* in the establishment of all types of voluntary control is an expression of dogma rather than data.

One of the claims holists make for the operation of biofeedback is that the procedure serves to regulate a poorly controlled physiological system. Shealy construes this as "stabiliz[ing] the autonomic nervous system. Once you achieve such control, emotional stress is regularly canceled, and no longer harmful to the body."[26] Although Schwartz refers to this function as "augmenting inherent homeostatic mechanisms,"[27] Pelletier sees the process in broader terms, "the self-regulatory capacity of the psychosomatic system is not produced by instrumentation but is permitted to reemerge."[28] These romanticized descriptions of biofeedback come very close to equating autonomic nervous system liability with "stress." They also conclude, again with no logical justification, that an undesirable physiological response necessarily implies the presence of a particular type of defect, a defect in the body's self-regulatory capacity.

Holistic writing often creates the mistaken impression that the body normally reacts as an undifferentiated whole. For example, Pelletier claims that it is "possible for an individual to fragment the function of his neurophysiological system and create a disruptive pattern."[29] This "interconnectedness" presumably allows the clinician to select any physiological response for biofeedback based on the premise that the act of self-regulating one response will alter the entire neurophysiological system and thereby alleviate the psychosomatic disorder. He clearly enunciates this perspective in his claim that "any neurophysiological function which the individual self-regulates through biofeedback increases the probability of his attaining this highest state of unstressed relaxation."[30] Several problems with this holistic position—that the body normally responds in a global, undifferentiated fashion—remain after the rhetoric of "integration," "disruption," or "fragmentation" is eliminated. The first problem pertains to data; evidence from throughout the field of psychophysiology fails to support the position. It has long been known that different physiological responses do not always change in the same direction or to a comparable degree in response to a particular environmental demand. Not only are various physiological responses not always highly correlated with one another, these physiological responses are not always highly correlated with subjective experience. Additionally, the same physiological response may change in different directions depending upon the precise demands that the environmental task places on the individual. In response to the possible holistic counter-argument that these data somehow fail to address the real holistic position (perhaps because this evidence is not what is meant by "fragmentation" or a "disruptive pattern"), it must be noted that holists fail to provide any a priori criteria to indicate when the lack of correlation meets holistic qualifications for fragmentation and when it does not. Even Schwartz, who normally is a proponent of holistic doctrine, commented that the holistic practice of using biofeedback of alpha EEG without regard for cerebral localization is widely recognized as being psychophysiologically "simplistic."[31] He extended his criticism with the observation that, since altered states of consciousness can be achieved in a variety of ways, EEG biofeedback may be "irrelevant for this goal."

A second, and closely related, implication of this holistic belief in "neurophysiological fragmentation" is that various physiological responses can be employed interchangeably. Phrased in a slightly different manner, the holistic position suggests that it is irrelevant which specific physiological response is selected as an index of stress or as the response on which the biofeedback signal is based. Thus, Pelletier can refer to a patient who "monitors his own anxiety level by means of EMG biofeedback" and yet ignore the facts that (1) the electromyographic level (rather than "biofeedback") is not isomorphic with the subjective state of anxiety and (2) some patients respond to stress with physiological change in systems other than the skeletal muscle system.[32] To illustrate briefly the contrasting point that various physiological responses are not interchangeable with one another, a recent report demonstrated that patients suffering from one of four medical disorders traditionally regarded as psychosomatic (essential hypertension, migraine headache, tension headache, and rheumatoid arthritis) respond to stress with differing profiles or patterns of psychophysiological change.[33] This investigation is a typical rather than an isolated example of "individual response stereotopy," a phenomenon that refers to reliable between-group differences in patterns of psychophysiological responding. These data, which strongly suggest that different physiological responses are not necessarily equivalent or inter-changeable, are consistent with most traditional explanations of the theoretical mechanisms of biofeedback. That is, most nonholistic theories of biofeedback strongly imply that it does matter which physiological response is selected as the basis for the feedback signal used in treating different disorders.

Although we have just discussed holistic medicine's promotion of biofeed-back as a tool in teaching relaxation, it should be noted that this issue has generated considerable controversy in traditional circles.[34] The debate is most sharply focused on the question of whether the physiological control learned by means of biofeedback is general in nature (i.e., a comprehensive shift in multiple physiological systems in the direction of relaxation and decreased arousal) or whether these biofeedback effects are specific (i.e., restricted to the particular physiological response on which the feedback signal is based). Holistic writers have added a measure of confusion to this controversy. For example, Pelletier first claims that biofeedback is an important part of treatment in which patients learn "a generalized state of meditative relaxation," and then later, in the same chapter, he enunciates the contradictory statement that "any single system of biofeedback training is more likely to emphasize specificity than to induce an overall pattern."[35] Unfortunately, he fails either to retract his prior assertions or to provide a revised rationale for using biofeedback in general relaxation training.

A further point governing the application of biofeedback, which has received considerable emphasis within holistic medicine, concerns the importance of indi-vidual differences. Aside from using this tenet as a platform for criticizing supposedly "rigid" perspectives of treatment, there is little evidence that holists utilize this principle in their own clinical work in a more appropriate fashion than do other clinicians. Furthermore, such phrases as "uniquely integrated" and "the learning process is unique with each individual"[36] have the potential for being used to absolve holists of the responsibility for providing a rational basis for their interventions.

In relation to several of the points in this section (e.g., interchangeability of various physiological responses versus emphasis of a particular response; gen-eralized relaxation versus specificity of change), holists have demonstrated a remarkable proclivity for constructing plausible intuitive arguments in support of opposing points of view and seldom have attempted to reconcile or "integrate" their own contradictory positions. This dexterity has considerable intuitive appeal and may even promote the appearance of increased sensitivity to individual differences. Unfortunately, on closer examination these contradictory assertions have the impact of eroding the public perception that there is a rational basis for using biofeedback in treatment. The potential harm of such a negative public perception and diminished public confidence in biofeedback is not restricted to the ideas or practices specifically identified with "holistic medicine."

Principles Guiding Evaluation of Clinical Biofeedback

In previous reviews of the clinical biofeedback literature it has been suggested that published evidence be evaluated along several dimensions in order to determine the therapeutic potential for an intervention.[37] These dimensions are:

(1) the degree of clinical meaningfulness of the changes obtained;
(2) the quality of the experimental design used in gathering or reporting the data;
(3) the extent of follow-up obtained or reported;
(4) the proportion of the treated patient sample which improved significantly;
(5) the degree of replicability of the results;
(6) the degree to which changes obtained in the clinic/laboratory transferred to the patient's natural environment;
(7) the degree of change in the biological response for which feedback training was supplied.

Of the preceding seven dimensions, the first five can be applied to the evaluation of *any* medical treatment and are not restricted to the evaluation of biofeedback. Elaboration of these seven dimensions, or of experimental design in general, would be largely tangential to the focus of the present discussion; however, interested readers are referred to the previously cited articles for a more thorough analysis. The important point to remember is that the majority of nonholistic ˙nvestigators and clinicians believe that biofeedback should be evaluated by the same empirical standards as other therapeutic procedures. The perspective of holistic medicine toward the evaluation of clinical biofeedback is somewhat different.

It should be noted at the outset that the evaluation question of whether or not biofeedback produces clinically significant effects presupposes that the procedure is neither confounded with other treatments nor employed in a manner that would preclude an unambiguous assessment of its effects. It is at these points that much of holistic medicine's use of biofeedback is deficient. The use of biofeedback for incidental purposes or as a gimmick does not qualify as clinical biofeedback (except perhaps in the opinion of holists) and should not be evaluated as such. However, inasmuch as one purpose of clinical investigation is to permit results to be logically and unambiguously attributed to specific interventions, then the broad definition of biofeedback preferred by holists has often functioned as an obstacle to this goal. In particular, biofeedback is often included as one component of a larger holistic intervention "package," which may consist of several other procedures of varying reliability. In these instances, even when the purpose for adding biofeedback to a multi-technique treatment is not incidental or "gimmicky," unless the experimental design compares the effects on the appropriate dependent variables of deliberately including or excluding biofeedback from the treatment package, it is logically impossible to evaluate the relative contribution of biofeedback to the treatment outcome, much less to attribute therapeutic success to the procedure.

A more fundamental barrier is encountered in the underlying philosophy and attitude that many holistic practitioners and writers hold toward the concept of rigorous empirical research. Holists display a superficial veneer of acceptance toward research and frequently cite basic research when the latter coincides with holistic beliefs. Beneath this superficial acceptance, however, several themes in holistic medicine converge in such a fashion that the legitimacy of the entire process of scientific research in clinical biofeedback is disavowed. Specifically, the elevation of clinical experience as the supreme standard devalues the concept of rational objective measurement. Secondly, the importance of individual differences has been taken to such an extreme (e.g., each person is "uniquely integrated") that the traditional concept of the generality of lawful, regular effects is made to appear ridiculous. This holistic exaggeration of the importance of the individual results in a reliance upon anecdotal case studies, which are often dramatic, to "prove" various points about biofeedback. Furthermore, this extreme individualistic focus occasionally is combined with a humanistic clinical concern to produce results that are clearly antiscientific. Derner expresses this position well: "Did the successful therapeutic result come about because of biofeedback, through the psychodynamic psychotherapy, or the combination of both? I do not know. I do know she had symptoms . . . before treatment. . . . I know that after treatment the symptoms did not return, even though the drugs were eliminated."[38] An attitude that regards as irrelevant the knowledge of those factors responsible for improvement opens the door for superstition and speculation; indeed, it opens the door for *any* practice that is labelled "therapy." Furthermore, it makes no contribution to rational planning of treatment for other patients with similar complaints, thereby abandoning scientific medicine for the crapshoot of intuition. A final facet of holistic philosophy that is antagonistic to any type of traditional research is an essentially irrational and antiscientific world view, a perspective that regards traditional science as a "prejudice in constructing our world along the lines of cause and effect."[39]

It is inevitable that biofeedback will be combined with other treatment procedures in clinical practice. However, if it is to be used rationally then effective parameters of application must be elucidated. These may or may not vary for different medical problems and they can encompass a broad spectrum of variables, including those related to both patient and therapist personality and the nature of the patient-therapist interaction during biofeedback training. Holists mistakenly criticize a scientific perspective of biofeedback for ignoring these latter factors. Yet, in place of the scientific position that these factors and their interactions must be empirically evaluated in order to make *informed* decisions, holists simply substitute the dogmatic assertion of their own ideology. Thus, the holistic position leads away from, rather than toward, improved understanding of the circumstances and mechanisms of effective clinical biofeedback.

SUMMARY

Many of the specific criticisms of holistic medicine that have been expressed elsewhere are also applicable to holistic presentations of biofeedback. In fact, the position of prominence that many holists accord biofeedback virtually assures that it will be particularly susceptible to these distorting practices. We have seen that the holistic promotion and elaboration of biofeedback has been characterized by ambiguity of definition, failure to specify the goals or purposes for which biofeedback is utilized, distortion and oversimplification of the psychophysiological principles underlying the operation and application of biofeedback, and unwarranted claims and practices in evaluating biofeedback. Additionally, during this brief review of the holistic literature pertaining to biofeedback and its uses, one ironic factor was repeatedly encountered. After the nebulous smoke screen of jargon had been penetrated and holistic attacks on traditional medicine and traditional psychology were deflected, the holistic claims for biofeedback frequently stood under greater (self-)indictment than did the claims of their traditional counterparts. One example is the contrast between the holistic criticism that traditional medicine is insensitive to the complexity of clinical problems and holistic practices that ignore or trivialize psychophysiological mechanisms or psychosocial realities.

However, in marked contrast with the majority of holistic therapies, biofeedback is accorded respectability within the scientific community. This is the result of empirical data obtained from scientifically acceptable investigation that support the efficacy of biofeedback for the treatment of particular disorders.

The scientific respectability of biofeedback, in conjunction with its superficial convergence with many holistic tenets, is likely to maintain biofeedback's position of prominence within holistic medicine. It is understandable and desirable that the traditional scientific and clinical communities reject both the spurious philosophy and the unfounded practices of holistic medicine. However, this action should not be undertaken uncritically or as a mere reflex reaction. It should be emphasized that there is no empirical basis for the wholesale rejection of biofeedback, as there may be for other therapies promoted by holists. Although biofeedback is not a panacea for all ailments, it has demonstrated its positive contribution to the treatment of a variety of disorders. Any uncritical rejection of biofeedback, or a rejection that demands a higher standard of proof than is demanded for other types of interventions, robs patients of a potentially beneficial treatment, impugns the professional integrity of a number of clinicians and is as illegitimate and irrational as is the uncritical promotion of biofeedback by holists. The appeal that is being made in this chapter is to the same empirical standards applicable to other interventions. Biofeedback can tolerate this scrutiny and evaluation; holistic medicine cannot.

NOTES

1. E. B. Blanchard and L. H. Epstein, *A Biofeedback Primer* (Reading, Mass.: Addison-Wesley, 1978).

2. T. S. Kuhn, *The Structure of Scientific Revolutions,* 2nd ed. (Chicago: University of Chicago Press, 1970).

3. C. Glymour and D. Stalker, "Engineers, Cranks, Physicians, Magicians," *New England Jounral of Medicine* 308 (1983):960–64.

4. See, for example, L. White and B. Tursky (eds.), *Clinical Biofeedback: Efficacy and Mechanisms* (New York: The Guilford Press, 1982).

5. P. A. R. Flynn, *Holistic Health: The Art and Science of Care* (Bowie, Md.: Robert Brady Company, 1980).

6. K. Pelletier, *Mind as Healer, Mind as Slayer: A Holistic Approach to Preventing Stress Disorders* (New York: Dell, 1977).

7. Ibid.; see also D. Shapiro, B. Tursky, and G. E. Schwartz, "Control of Blood Pressure in Man by Operant Conditioning," *Circulation Research* 26, Supplement 1 (1970):27–32.

8. K. Pelletier, *Holistic Medicine: From Stress to Optimum Health* (New York: Dell, 1979).

9. Flynn, op. cit.

10. W. E. Whitehead and M. M. Schuster, "Biofeedback in the Treatment of Gastrointestinal Disorders," in J. P. Hatch, J. G. Fisher, and J. D. Rugh (eds.), *Biofeedback: Studies in Clinical Efficacy* (New York: Plenum, in press).

11. H. Benson, D. Shapiro, B. Tursky, and G. Schwartz, "Decreased Systolic Blood Pressure Through Operant Conditioning Techniques in Patients with Essential Hypertension," *Science* 173 (1971):740–42.

12. T. A. Moeller and W. A. Love, "A Method to Reduce Arterial Hypertension Through Muscular Relaxation," unpublished manuscript, Nova University, Fort Lauderdale, Florida, 1974.

13. Pelletier, *Mind as Healer, Mind as Slayer,* op. cit.

14. Ibid.

15. C. N. Shealy, *90 Days to Self-health* (New York: Bantam, 1978).

16. D. S. Sobel (ed.), *Ways of Health* (New York: Harcourt, Brace, Jovanovich, 1979).

17. A. Gladman and N. Estrada, "Biofeedback: Uses in Healing," in H. Otto and J. Knight (eds.), *Dimensions in Holistic Healing: New Frontiers in the Treatment of the Whole Person* (Chicago: Nelson-Hall, 1979).

18. Flynn, op. cit.

19. Pelletier, *Holistic Medicine,* op. cit.

20. H. Weiner, *Psychobiology and Human Disease* (New York, Elsevier, 1977).

21. S. M. Levy, "The Process and Outcome of 'Adjustment' in the Cancer Patient: A Reply to Taylor" [Letter to the Editor] *American Psychologist* 39 (1984):1327.

22. R. Ader (ed.), *Psychoneuroimmunology* (New York: Academic Press, 1981).

23. E. E. Green, A. M. Green, and E. D. Walters, "Voluntary Control of Internal States: Psychological and Physiological," *Journal of Transpersonal Psychology* 2 (1970):1–26.

24. L. Dossey, *Space, Time and Medicine* (Boulder, Colo.: Sambhala Publications, 1982).

25. Pelletier, *Mind as Healer, Mind as Slayer,* op. cit.

26. Shealy, op. cit.

27. G. Schwartz, "Biofeedback and the Treatment of Disregulation Disorders," in D. S. Sobel (ed.), *Ways of Health,* op. cit.

28. Pelletier, *Mind as Healer, Mind as Slayer,* op. cit.

29. Ibid.

30. Ibid.

31. Schwartz, op. cit.

32. Pelletier, *Mind as Healer, Mind as Slayer,* op. cit.

33. C. D. Anderson, J. M. Stoyva, and L. J. Vaughn, "A Test of Delayed Recovery Following Stressful Stimulation in Four Psychosomatic Disorders," *Journal of Psychosomatic Research* 26 (1982):571–80.

34. B. V. Silver and E. B. Blanchard, "Biofeedback and Relaxation Training in the Treatment of Psychophysiological Disorders: Or Are the Machines Really Necessary?" *Journal of Behavioral Medicine* 1 (1978):217–39.

35. Pelletier, *Mind as Healer, Mind as Slayer,* op. cit.

36. Ibid.

37. E. B. Blanchard, "Biofeedback and the Modification of Cardiovascular Dysfunctions," in R. J. Gatchel and K. P. Price (eds.), *Clinical Applications of Biofeedback: Appraisal and Status* (Elmsford, N.Y.: Pergamon Press, 1979), 28–51; see also L. D. Young and E. B. Blanchard, "Medical Applications of Biofeedback Training: A Selective Review," in S. Rachman (ed.), *Contributions to Medical Psychology,* vol. 2 (Elmsford, N. Y.: Pergamon Press, 1980), 215–54.

38. G. Derner, "Biofeedback in Psychodynamic Psychotherapy," in J. Fosshage and P. Olsen (eds.), *Healing: Implications for Psychotherapy* (New York: Human Sciences Press, 1978), 260–68.

39. Dossey, op. cit.

Glossary

Abortefacients: drugs that kill the embryo or fetus and cause abortion.

Aconite: wolfsbane. Its juice has a variety of effects on the nervous and circulatory systems.

Acupressure: a variant of acupuncture in which the insertion of needles is replaced with the pressure of fingertips.

Acupuncture: a therapeutic technique of traditional Chinese medicine that involves inserting needles at specific points of the body in order, supposedly, to produce anaesthesia, analgesia, or treat various conditions, such as high blood pressure, ulcers, bronchitis, and depression. Also used as a diagnostic technique by feeling specific points of the body. See the essay entitled "Acupuncture: Past, Present, and Future" in this volume.

Acute bacillary dysentery: severe, bloody diarrhea usually caused by "Shigella" bacteria.

Acute myelogenous leukemia: a common cancer of the bone marrow and its youngest *neutrophils*. It occurs most often in young and middle-aged adults. Unlike leukemia in children, it is usually not cured.

Adducts: a chemical addition product; generally some natural substance that a chemist has altered slightly.

Adenocarcinoma: cancer arising from the functional cells of any gland.

Adenoma: a benign tumor arising from a gland. Many adenomas continue to perform the function of the parent gland, often to the body's harm. See *thyroid adenoma*.

Adjuvant: a treatment, not necessarily effective by itself, which makes another treatment much more effective. (Fruend's adjuvant is a wax which, when

361

administered with some other foreign material, greatly enhances the immune reaction against the other material. Adjuvant chemotherapy is typically given after cancer surgery when there is no evidence that the disease has not been entirely removed; in many instances it has been shown to increase the chances of apparent cure.)

Adrenal cortex: the outer portion of the adrenal glands, where *corticosteroid* hormones are made.

Aikido: Japanese martial art also claimed to be a way of bringing oneself into union with the environment by refining one's *ki* (life force) and harmonizing it with the *ki* of the universe, thereby supposedly achieving spiritual and psychological development and benefit.

Alexander technique: a system of posture training originated by F. Mathias Alexander, an Australian Shakespearian actor who thought that most daily movements were harmful and could lead to mental and physical tension. It is claimed that by relearning such movements a person can achieve optimal body function and performance.

Akaloids: nitrogen-containing small molecules found in various plants. Most plant drugs and poisons are alkaloids.

Allergens: substances to which an individual is peculiarly sensitive. See *allergy*.

Allergy: abnormal reactivity of a person's tissues to some foreign substance. This will be to a protein (or a metal or small molecule that complexes with the body's own protein, in which case the allergy is to the complex.) See *allergen*.

Allopathy: ("other-suffering") a term for mainstream scientific medicine coined by Samuel Hahnemann (1755–1843). He called his system homeopathy ("same-suffering") because he treated disease using dilute solutions of substances that elicited the same symptoms at high dose. Of course, Hahnemann meant to imply that the two disciplines are of equivalent merit.

Alpha EEG: brain waves, occurring 8–13/sec, typical of normal persons awake and resting quietly. Alpha waves occur mostly at the back of the head. See *electroencephalograph*.

Amaurosis: loss of vision with no apparent change in the outside or inside of the eye.

Analgesic: anything that reduces pain.

Analysis of covariance: statistical procedures for adjusting the results of an experiment for differences that exist among subjects prior to the start of the experiment. The procedures involve measuring subjects on relevant characteristics before the experimental treatment is administered; these measurements provide information about the covariate or concomitant variable(s). After the experimental treatment has been administered and the data collected, the covariate information is used to refine estimates of experimental error and to adjust treatment effects for any differences between the treatment and control groups that existed prior to the start of the experiment. Cox covariate analysis is one such procedure commonly used in medical experiments.

Anaphylaxis: sudden dilatation of the blood vessels with a drop in blood pressure. Usually due to allergy (notably to penicillin, insect stings, eggs, peanuts, or shellfish).

Anaplasia: a pathologist's term for how abnormal the cells of a cancer look. The more anaplastic, the faster the cancer will probably grow and spread.

Angina: pain. Today, the word almost always refers to *angina pectoris*.

Angina pectoris: chest pain due to *coronary* artery disease, usually *atherosclerosis*. During exertion or excitement, enough blood cannot flow to the heart muscle. While the heart muscle does not actually die (as in a "heart attack"), it cannot get enough oxygen and the patient experiences pain.

Antibiotic: a member of a class of substances made by various micro-organisms that inhibits growth of or kills other micro-organisms. Literally, "anti-life." Some are sufficiently nontoxic to humans to be used to treat infections.

Antihelminthic: antiworm medication.

Antiphlogistic: an archaic word for drugs or procedures that reduce fever. Phlogiston is a mythical substance which disappears as something burns.

Antiplatelet drugs: any of a wide range of drugs that interfere with the work of the tiny cell fragments (platelets) that plug little leaks in blood vessels. Aspirin is the most familiar of these.

Antipyretic: a modern word for drugs or procedures that reduce fever. The best-known antipyretics are aspirin and acetaminophen.

Arnica: a daisy-like flower that produces a drug with powerful effects on the heart.

Aromatherapy: the use of essential oils from plants to treat various conditions such as acne, poor circulation, influenza, depression, asthma, sinusitis, and dry skin. Specific oils in dilute form are massaged into the body or face, taken internally, or inhaled: e.g., basil for asthma, eucalyptus for influenza, peppermint for depression.

Assay: measurement of the concentration of a chemical by laboratory methods.

Asthma: bronchial asthma, an illness with recurrent bouts of wheezing, following exposure to cold air, exercise, or in people with an *allergy*. Most patients are children or young adults. The problem is that the small airways constrict.

Asymptomatic: no health complaints. An asymptomatic patient may still have evidence of disease, but does not feel it.

Atherosclerosis: accumulations of cholesterol and other substances on the inner walls of the larger arteries, as plaques which may rupture, cause obstruction, or weaken the wall. The most common cause of death in the Western world. See *occlusive vascular disease.* "Hardening of the arteries" and "arteriosclerosis" are more general terms for processes of which atherosclerosis is most common. The deposits sometimes, but by no means always, contain some calcium, which make them feel gritty. This creates the false impression that calcium, rather than cholesterol, is the problem.

Atlas: the first of the *cervical vertebrae* in the neck, which supports the skull as Atlas (in Greek mythology) held up the earth. It in turn pivots on the *axis.*

Atropine: a powerful drug and poison from a family of plants related to nightshade. Atropine works by suppressing the parasympathetic nervous system, and is the principal active ingredient of *belladonna.*

Augmentation mammoplasty: plastic surgery to make the breasts larger.

Autistic: self-centered. More generally, pathological preoccupation with one's own thinking and loss of interest in immediate environment. Autistic children are probably born with this condition; autism is also a characteristic of adult psychotics who have schizophrenia.

Autogenic therapy: relaxation and meditation techniques claimed to be a form of treatment for alcoholism, obesity, asthma, diabetes mellitus, arthritis, and anxiety as well as for improving one's ability to concentrate, endure, and perform. Based on six standard exercises in which a trainee repeats a specific phrase while attending to a specified body part with the aim of generating the autogenic state (self-generated state of relaxation), it is thought to facilitate self-balancing or self-healing capacity.

Autonomic nerves/nervous system: the system of nerves receiving instructions from the brain, but not normally under conscious control. They influence many processes in the skin and internal organs, and bring about most of the rapid changes in body function associated with feelings. See *sympathetic* and *parasympathetic.*

Axis: the second of the *cervical vertebrae* in the neck. It has a knob around which the *atlas* rotates.

ß-endorphin: beta endorphin, an important *endogenous opiate.*

Basal metabolic rate: how fast a person burns calories at rest. It is a very rough measurement of thyroid gland function.

Belladonna: a *decoction* of a European plant of the nightshade family. It is rich in the drug *atropine,* which suppresses the *parasympathetic* nerves. Italian ladies used to put some in their eyes to make their pupils larger. Thus the user of belladonna became a beautiful ("bella") woman ("donna").

Beta blockers: a class of drugs that prevents one part of the *sympathetic* half of the *autonomic nervous system* from functioning. The result is slow pulse, lowered *blood pressure,* constricted airways in the lungs, and so forth.

Biofeedback: a process in which a person learns reliably to influence physiological responses that are not ordinarily under voluntary control or that are ordinarily under voluntary control but this control has broken down because of trauma or disease. See the essay entitled "Holistic Medicine's Use of Biofeedback" in this volume.

Blood pressure: a combined function of the strength of the heartbeat, the ease at which blood passes through the arterial circulation, and the volume of blood. The systolic ("upper") blood pressure is the maximum pressure in the arteries when the heart pumps; the diastolic ("lower") blood pressure is the resting pressure between heartbeats. A dead person has 0/0 blood pressure and thus does not bleed when cut.

Bradycardia: a slow pulse, usually below 60 beats per minute.

Brainstem: the portion of the brain nearest the spinal cord, through which signals are transmitted and in which some basic natural functions are controlled.

Bronchial tubes: the larger airways within the lung; divisions of the trachea (windpipe) after it enters the chest.

Bryonia: a plant, the root of which is a powerful laxative.

Burdock root: the root of the plant that produces the familiar burrs that stick to clothing and fur. Used in folk medicine, it has little physiologic activity.

Bursitis: inflammation of a bursa. A bursa is a partially-collapsed sack, associated with a joint, filled with sticky fluid which provides lubrication for the moving parts.

Bypass surgery: a procedure usually performed in patients with atherosclerotic *coronary* artery disease. Sections of the veins are sewn at both ends into the diseased arteries so that blood can flow past an obstruction.

Caffeine glycosides: the naturally-occurring form of the stimulant that makes coffee, tea, and cola popular.

Calomel: mercurous chloride; a dangerous poison formerly used as a laxative.

Camomile: chamomile; chamomille; a flowering herb with a bitter taste and alleged medicinal properties.

Cancer: malignant *neoplasm.* An abnormal growth of cells capable of invading and destroying healthy tissue, and usually capable of spreading elsewhere in the body.

Cancer promoter: any substance that causes the cell division which enables genetically altered ("induced") cells to form malignant neoplasms.

Canker: 1) an archaic word for cancer, or other hard-to-treat ulcer in a human, animal, or plant; 2) a "canker sore" is a lesion of aphthous stomatitis, the familiar white ulcers in the mouth that appear briefly after stress.

Carcinogen: anything that causes cancer, not necessarily in humans.

Carcinogenic: causes or produces cancer. A rather nonspecific term, usually applied to certain chemicals, radiations, or viruses.

Carcinoma: cancer composed of cells that arise in epithelium (surface coverings or glands).

Caries: tooth decay, dental cavities.

Carminative: any medicine that prevents formation and passage of intestinal gas.

Cataract: opacification of the lens of the eye. Old age, diabetes, and galactosemia are important causes.

Catarrh: an archaic word for inflammation of a *mucous membrane* which thus drips fluid. The old quack remedy "Peruna" was supposed to be specific against "catarrh," which was supposedly the underlying cause of most disease.

Cathartic: laxative.

Cauterization: burning of tissue for therapy. Formerly boiling oil was used to prevent infection in wounds. Today surgeons use a tiny electric device to stop bleeding from individual small blood vessels.

Cecal: of a cecum ("caecum"), the first portion of the large intestine.

Celandine: either of two flowering herbs, one a poppy, the other a buttercup.

Cerebrospinal: of the brain and spinal cord. Cerebrospinal fluid is made in the brain and flows slowly around the spinal canal and inside the skull.

Chamomilla: see *camomile.*

Charismatic: 1) possessing the popular appeal of a natural leader; 2) pertaining to religious practices that emphasize immediate personal experience of supernatural aid.

Chelation: binding of a metal ion (charged metal atom) by a molecule of a specifically designed chemical. See *EDTA.*

Chemotherapy: using chemicals to treat disease. Today, this word usually means treating cancer by administering drugs that are thought to be more poisonous to cancer cells than to healthy cells. This is dangerous but often prolongs, improves, or saves lives. Chemotherapy should be administered by a physician who subspecializes in *oncology*, i.e., an *oncologist*.

Chi-Square Test: a statistical procedure used to determine whether the sample distribution of nominal scale data differs significantly from a specified population distribution, or to determine whether two or more distributions of such data differ significantly from one another.

Chlorophyll: the green pigment in plants that traps light and turns it into chemical energy for use in *cellular metabolism*. It is similar in structure to hemoglobin, but contains a magnesium atom rather than an iron atom.

Cholera: a very severe infectious diarrhea, caused by the comma-shaped bacterium "Vibrio cholerae." This killed many people in the United States during the last century, and is still a major health problem in India and elsewhere.

Chromatid: one of the two filaments joined at the centromere of a chromosome during cell division. One chromatid will go to each pole of the dividing cell and become a chromatid of one of the daughter cells.

Chromosome: a group of all-connected genes that stay together, with associated proteins, during cell division. Humans have 46 chromosomes in most cells.

Chronic: long-lasting, used to describe a problem or disease. The opposite is acute.

Chronic rheumatism: usually means *rheumatoid arthritis* or some related disorder (systemic lupus erythematosus, psoriatic arthritis, ankylosing spondylitis, etc.)

Cinchona: the dried bark of a Peruvian tree, the source of the antimalarial drug quinine and the cardiac drug quinidine.

Clinical: directly involving patient care. Usually used to contrast with laboratory or theoretical.

Clinical trial: an experimental study using patients to determine whether a therapy, intervention, or preventive measure is effective. Now usually taken to involve *random assignment* of subjects in a *prospective double-blind* study.

Clinician: any physician who cares directly for patients. Most medical doctors other than pathologists, diagnostic x-ray specialists, and full-time administrators are clinicians.

Colic: discomfort from distention of a hollow organ. "Biliary colic" is distention of the bile ducts, "renal colic" is a distention of the ureters (tubes leading from the kidneys to the urinary bladder), and other colics are due to distention of the stomach or bowels.

Coliform bacteria: Eschericia coli, a microbe found in normal feces and a favorite of molecular geneticists. Its whole family is sometimes called the *coliforms* too. Old word.

Colitis: inflammation of the large intestine. This may be due to bacterial, parasitic, or viral infection, or to diseases such as ulcerative colitis. Loosely, the word also describes "functional bowel disease" or "spastic colon," in which the chaotic behavior of the large bowel reflects mental stress.

Colonic irrigation: a holistic procedure to "cleanse the bowel." Practitioners emphasize that this is much more than just a high enema, though the distinction is not altogether clear. See *toxic bowel settlement.*

Color therapy: the use of colors supposedly to cure various conditions or benefit one's health. Specific colors are claimed to have specific powers: e.g., red stimulates the blood, orange increases energy, reddish orange inhibits malignant growths. Patients are diagnosed for the colors they need, sometimes with devices, then given foods of a certain color, bathed in colored lights, placed next to water in colored containers, massaged with solar-chrome salt bags, involved in color breathing meditation, etc.

Colorectal cancer: malignant neoplasms arising in the large intestine.

Coma: a state of unresponsiveness from which the patient cannot be aroused.

Compulsion neurosis: strong unwanted urges to perform meaningless or abhorrent acts, the result of intrapersonal conflicts.

Conjunctivitis: inflammation of the membrane covering the front of the eye and the inner eyelids. A common cause of a red, itchy eye. Most cases are due to allergy or infection.

Consumption: an old term for tuberculosis.

Contact dermatitis: inflammation (redness, itching, pain, cracking, and so forth) of the skin as a result of direct exposure to some substance. Poison ivy and dishpan hands are two familiar varieties.

Control: a standard against which to compare observations in order to determine their meaning. In a control trial, a group of patients whose responses serve as the standard of comparison for determining the effect of a therapy. See *control group.* Also used to mean a restraint, as in a controlled experiment where relevant conditions are kept constant in order to vary another condition and thereby determine its effects.

Control group: a sample of a population used for comparison with the sample being studied. The control group consists of people who have not been exposed to the variable being studied, but who are otherwise the same in relevant respects.

Conversion hysteria: a *psychoneurosis* in which the patient "converts" mental conflicts into symbolic illnesses. See *hysteria*.

Coronaries: the great vessels that form a "crown" (compare the word "coronation") around the base of the heart. The common cause of heart disease is *artherosclerosis (occlusive arterial disease)* of one or more of the coronaries.

Cortisol: the principal *corticosteroid* hormone regulating metabolism of glucose and other substances in humans. It is made in the adrenal cortex under the influence of the brain and anterior pituitary gland, and increases in the morning and during stress.

Corticosteroid: one of a class of *steroid* hormones made in the outer portion of the adrenal glands *(adrenal cortex)*. Big doses cause many health problems.

Cosmology: the scientific study of the entire universe. Once cosmology was the domain of magicians, occultists, and theologians. Today, honest cosmologists are astronomers and physicists, though occasional holists offer new theories of the "whole universe" to justify their treatments of the "whole person."

Cox covariate analysis: see *analysis of covariance*.

Cox proportional hazards model: see *log rank test*.

Cranial nerves: twelve pairs of nerves passing through various holes in the skull. Each pair serves a different function.

Creatinine level: amount of a breakdown product of muscle metabolism in the serum. In health, creatinine level parallels muscle mass but is always low; elevated levels are a reliable indicator of poor kidney function.

Cross-over frequencies: a measure of distance between two *genes* on a *chromosome,* based on the frequency at which they are exchanged by *homologous chromosomes* as a result of *crossing over.*

Crossing over: a process by which *homologous chromosomes* exchange sequences of genes.

Cupping: a folk-remedy for pneumonia and other illnesses. A vacuum is created in a cup which is applied to the skin "to suck out the disease."

Cyanosis: blue discoloration from lack of oxygen. Decreased *oxygen saturation,* from any cause.

Cyphosis: usually spelled "kyphosis" today; forward curvature of the *vertebral column* (spine). Hunchback.

Cytological: of a cell or cells.

Cytotoxic: poisonous to cells. See *chemotherapy*.

De novo sensitization: what is said to happen when the immune system learns to recognize a new foreign substance.

Decoction: the extract of a plant obtained by boiling.

Degenerative disorder: a word for any disease of uncertain cause which affects the elderly.

Delirium: a state of confusion due to illness or intoxication.

Dependent variable: in general, the outcome variable in a research study; colloquially, the effect. Its values depend on the values of another variable or variables.

Desensitization: a technique for treating *phobias* involving progressive exposure of the patient to the dreaded thing or situation by a supportive therapist.

Devil's claw: the root of a South African plant, currently popular among "natural healing" enthusiasts.

Diabetic gangrene: tissue death associated with diabetes, most often in the feet and legs. Diabetes narrows both large and small arteries, diminishes the ability of *neutrophils* to fight bacteria, and causes loss of sensation so that the patient cannot recognize and treat minor injuries easily.

Diastolic: see *blood pressure*.

Diathesis: a health problem, not symptomatic by itself, which makes the person more than usually susceptible to certain diseases or the effects of injuries. For example, a patient with hemophilia has a tendency to bleed, or "bleeding diathesis," and a patient with von Recklinghausen's neurofibromatosis has a tendency to develop neoplasms, or "tumor diathesis."

Diffuse nodularity: lumpy-bumpy all over, inside and out.

Dinitrochlorobenzene: a substance used as a sensitizer in *recall skin testing* of cellular immune function.

Disease rate: how common a disease is. Incidence is the frequency of new cases of a disease in a population, usually per hundred thousand people per year. Prevalence is the total number of cases of disease at a given time, usually per hundred thousand people. Incidence equals prevalence times average duration of the disease.

DNA nucleotide sequence: the series of bases in deoxyribonucleic acid, which contains the genetic code. For details, see any good popular presentation on the molecular basis of heredity.

Dorsal rami: branches of a spinal nerve that supply the back.

Double-blind study: a study in which neither investigators nor subjects know whether an individual has been assigned to the experimental group or to the control group.

Down's syndrome: trisomy 21, a common birth defect usually associated with moderate mental retardation. The underlying problem is an extra chromosome. Affected children have various malformations, more or less severe, depending on the case. However, the brain structure is grossly normal (except for some shortening of the temporal lobes.) Recently a leading holistic clinic published excerpts from an autopsy report on a boy with Down's syndrome. He had been subjected to Doman-Delcato motor patterning but died of heart problems. The clinic apparently thought that the holistic treatment had begun to correct the brain defect. Actually the anatomy, as partially reported, was exactly what any pathologist expects to find in Down's syndrome.

Dropsy: severe whole-body edema (swelling); in Holmes's day as now, usually due to cardiac failure or kidney disease.

Drosophilia: the fruit fly, an animal which possesses gigantic *chromosomes* in its salivary glands and is used to study *genetic* processes.

Duodenal: of the duodenum, portion of the gut directly beyond the outlet of the stomach. It is about one foot long and is often the site of stress-related *ulcers.*

Duodenal ulcer: an *ulcer* located in the duodenum. These are usually single, may be longstanding, are often painful, and can bleed profusely.

Dysmenorrhea: painful menstruation.

Dysmly impaired: the psychotic patient may hallucinate (see or hear things that are not there), have delusions (crazy fixed ideas), and exhibit bizarre behavior.

Dyspepsia: discomfort associated with digestion.

Eastern Cooperative Oncology Group: ECOG, an organization of *oncologists* that share results of the newest experimental cancer treatments. One of several such groups in this country.

Echinacea: a purple cone flower. This plant contains compounds with various biological activities, and it is popular in folk medicine.

Eczema: a process (not a disease) that causes reddening, itching, oozing, and later thickening and pigmentation of the upper skin. Usually a sign of *allergic* inflammation of the skin.

Edema: abnormal increase in tissue fluid. Swelling of otherwise normal tissue usually indicates edema.

EDTA: ethylene diamine tetra-acetic acid, a molecule that tightly *chelates* calcium and other metals. EDTA administered by vein binds instantly to free calcium in the blood and is quickly lost in the body's wastes. It is unwarranted to claim that EDTA removes calcium from the plaques of *atherosclerosis.*

Ego defenses: a conscious or unconscious internal mechanism for preserving self-esteem.

Electroencephalograph: a device for recording the changes in electrical charge caused by the brain, by using electrodes attached to the scalp. The "brain wave" machine, or EEG. See *alpha EEG.*

Electrolyte: any ion (charged atom or molecule) in solution. In clinical medicine, electrolytes are sodium, potassium, chloride, and bicarbonate.

Electromyograph: electroneuromyograph, a machine for measuring electrical potentials within muscle when the nerve supplying it is stimulated. Abnormal responses are seen in diseases of either muscle or nerve.

Electrophoresis: one laboratory procedure for separating proteins. One important use of *serum protein electrophoresis* in clinical medicine is to detect abnormalities of gamma globulins in the blood. See *gammopathy.*

Emmenagogues: drugs that promote the menstrual flow.

Emetic: any substance that causes vomiting.

Endocrine system: the ductless glands. These include the adrenal glands (cortex and medulla), islands of Langerhans (endocrine pancreas), parathyroids, pineal, pituitary (anterior and posterior), sex glands, and thyroid. Cells to these organs pass hormones directly into the bloodstream to affect distant tissues. The brain and other organs also have endocrine functions.

Endogenous opiate: any of a variety of substances made in the body which mimic the pain-relieving and other activities of alkaloids from opium (morphine, codeine).

Endorphin: a class of *endogenous opiate* substances.

Enzyme: a protein that greatly speeds the rate of a particular chemical reaction. Enzyme molecules are like little machines, each able to affect a particular small molecule.

Epidemiological: originally, relating to the study of outbreaks of transmissible disease in populations. Nowadays, epidemiology studies the occurrence of any disease in a human population.

Epilepsy: a layman's term for any form of seizure disorder.

Epistaxis: nosebleed.

Ergot: a poisonous mold that grows on rye. Mass poisonings have caused severe mental and physical illness. Ergot is the precursor substance for the drug LSD.

Essential hypertension: the most common form of longstanding high blood pressure. Popular wisdom, and most holistic practitioners, believe it is caused by emotions (anger, unhappiness). However, there is much evidence that the basic problem is a relative inability of the kidney to excrete sodium. (A person who has one elevated blood pressure reading while upset may be wrongly labelled as having "essential hypertension," and treated for years.) "Essential" comes from the root "essence," something subtle, like the real cause of essential hypertension.

Etiology: the cause of a disease. (Compare *pathogenesis,* meaning the mechanism by which the cause produces it. For example, a bacterium is the etiology of *cholera.* The fact that the bacterium produces a poison that acts like a hormone on the cells lining the wall of the gut is the pathogenesis.)

Experimental group: in an experiment, the group that receives the treatment is the experimental group, while the group that does not receive the treatment is the *control group.* The experimental group is exposed to the *independent variable* while the *control group* is not.

Ex post facto study: see *retrospective study.*

External validity: in social science research, this refers to the extent to which the results of an experiment can be generalized to other populations, settings, treatments, measurement devices, experimenters, and so on.

Extraocular muscular tension: how tightly stretched the muscles that move the eyes are.

Factorial analysis of variance: a statistical method for analyzing the separate and combined (interactive) influence of two or more *independent variables* on a *dependent variable.*

False negative: negative test result when the disease or condition is present.

False positive: positive test result when the disease or condition is absent.

Fascia: thin sheets of tough fibrous tissue that separate and attach layers of muscle and other soft parts.

Fecal incontinence: lack of effective function of the *sphincter* muscle of the anus. A problem for passive male homosexuals, and for patients with diseases of the nervous system (diabetes, multiple sclerosis, stroke, seizures, and many others).

Feldenkrais method: a system of exercise therapy developed in the 1940s by former judo instructor Mosha Feldenkrais in order to improve posture, breathing, coordination, and self-image. It is claimed to reestablish connections between the motor cortex and the muscular and nervous systems, such connections having been altered by physical trauma, chronic tension, and bad habits. Feldenkrais devotes his book *The Case of Nora: Body-Awareness as Healing Therapy* to his use of the system to treat a patient with speech and movement impairment.

Fluorouracil: one powerful drug used in cancer *chemotherapy.*

Frontalis muscle tension: how tightly stretched the muscles that raise the eyebrows are.

Galvanic skin response: changes in the electrical resistance of the skin's surface.

Gammopathy: any condition in which there are increased gamma globulins (a class of proteins that includes most antibodies) in the blood. Polyclonal gammopathies have many different types of gamma globulis increased and occur in generalized inflammatory disorders and longstanding liver disease. Monoclonal gammopathies have only a single type, and may (but do not necessarily) indicate cancer. See *myeloma.*

Gastralgia: an old word for a stomach ache.

Gastric ulcer: an *ulcer* in the stomach. Most are caused by acid. There may be many all at once, as during extreme stress, or one big one that lasts a long time.

Gehan-Wilcoxon test: a significance test for comparing the overall survival experience of two groups, one or both of which contain censored observations. Censored observations are observations whose exact value is not known, though it is known that an exact value does exist. In studies where the variable being measured is timed to a specific event, censored observations are common due to subjects being lost or subjects not experiencing the event when the data is analyzed. Gehan's test is a generalization of Wilcoxon's two-sample rank sum test. See *log rank test.*

Gene: a unit of hereditary material, specified by (and synonymous with) a sequence of nucleotides in DNA.

Genetics: the study of heredity and of *genes.*

Germ cell tumors: any of several types of tumors made of cells that resemble normal sex cells. These tumors arise in the sex glands or anywhere in the midline of the body, and the latter are often hard to identify as germ cell tumors. The majority of germ cells tumors that have spread are now cured by radiation or chemotherapy. Lumps of benign tissue often remain behind (as happened with Bob Gilley's tumor after he received chemotherapy).

Gigahertz: 10^9 hertz. A hertz is one cycle per second.

Glaucoma: any of several serious eye diseases in which fluid pressure inside the eyeball is too high.

Goitre: goiter; an enlarged thyroid gland, from any cause. Once very common, the usual cause was lack of iodine in the diet. Now goiter is rare because iodine is added to table salt. The cause of most goiters today is unknown and only some types cause problems.

Gout: a metabolic disease in which uric acid crystals are deposited in one or more cool joints, especially the big toe. The process is very painful.

Grip: "la grippe," an old name for the flu.

Haemoptysis: coughing up blood. Usually spelled "hemoptysis" today. In Holmes's era it usually indicated tuberculosis; now the underlying process is often lung cancer.

Hemoglobin: the iron-containing pigment within red blood cells. It carries oxygen to, and carbon dioxide from, the rest of the body.

Hepatic: of the liver.

Hepatomegaly: enlarged liver, from any cause.

Hepatotoxic: poisonous to the liver.

Hernia: an outpouching of some normal structure (usually bowel) through a weak spot in a muscular wall (usually in the groin).

Herniated disc: herniated nucleus pulposis. Protrusion of the gelatinous material at the center of a *ruptured disc* through the break. This may press on spinal nerves and be very painful.

Histologic: how a tissue appears under the light microscope. Pathologists classify cancers and other tumors according to histologic type, and this helps determine the best treatment and the outlook for the patient.

Histologic grade: the degree of *anaplasia* the pathologist finds in the worst-looking area of the tumor. Usually assigned a Roman numeral, with "I" being used for the least aggressive tumors and "III," "IV," or "V" for the worst.

Histones: a class of proteins that are associated with DNA in the nuclei of cells and control gene expression.

Historical controls: in the trial of a new treatment, the outcome of present patients receiving the new treatment may be compared with the outcome of past patients who did not receive this new treatment. The past patients would comprise a *control group* of historical controls.

Histotoxic anoxia: inability of a tissue to effectively use oxygen due to some poisoning, as in cyanide poisoning.

Homeopathy: a system of medicine originated by Samuel Hahnemann (1755–1843) in the eighteenth century, and based on three fundamental laws: viz., the doctrine that like cures like, that infinitesimal doses are medically efficacious, and that chronic disease results from suppression of the itch or psora. See the essay entitled "Homeopathy" in this volume.

Homeostatic process: all the activities of a living thing that maintain its internal environment. This includes eating, drinking, digestion, breathing, heartbeat, excretion, cell turnover, and just about everything else except perhaps reproduction (which maintains the species). Homeostasis is a characteristic of living things, not (as holists tell us) a cosmic, divinely-ordained law that means all illness can be cured by holistic medicine.

Homologous chromosomes: two *chromosomes* that make up a matching pair in a diploid cell. Human beings have twenty-three pairs of homologous chromosomes in most body cells, but only one chromosome of each pair in sex cells (sperms and eggs).

Hormone: a chemical substance made in one part of the body that acts, in small concentrations, on some other part. A chemical messenger. The word is also appropriate for synthetic hormones that resemble those that occur naturally.

Host resistance: ability of an organism (here, the cancer patient) to fight off invading micro-organisms or perhaps developing tumors.

Hydragogue cathartic: a laxative that draws water into the bowel. Milk of magnesium and epsom salts work by this method.

Hydrocephaly: too much fluid in the cavities of the brain. In children, it results from infection or malformation, and can produce a gigantic "water-head."

Hydropathy: also known as the water-cure, a system of therapy developed in the 1820s by Vincent Priessnitz and involving water (especially cold water) in the form of showers, soaks, irrigations, wet-packs.

Hyperemic: receiving more blood flow than usual. The most familiar instances of *hyperemia* (the noun) are blushing, erections, and reddening of injured, inflamed tissue.

Hypertension: high *blood pressure* from any cause. See also *essential hypertension*.

Hypoanalgesia: decreased perception of pain.

Hypocalcemia: too little calcium in the blood.

Hypokalemia: too little potassium in the blood.

Hyponatremia: too little sodium in the blood.

Hysterectomy: surgical removal of the uterus, for any reason.

Hysteria: a *psychoneurosis* in which intrapersonal conflicts manifest as symptoms resembling physical illness. Victims experience increased or decreased sensation, feelings of choking, convulsions, spasms, paralysis, blindness, and so forth. Many such patients have hysterical personalities, with lack of self-control, attention-seeking behavior, anxiety, and thoughtlessness.

Hysterical anaesthesia: inability to feel because of a *psychoneurotic* conflict. See *hysteria*.

Hysterical blindness: inability to see because of *psychoneurotic* conflict. See *hysteria*.

Iatrogenic illness: health problems caused by a doctor's treatment. Today approximately twenty percent of hospital days are due to complications of therapy.

Id: in traditional psychoanalysis, the term for all the instincts that preserve the individual and the species, especially the sexual drives. From the Greek word "idios," meaning "one's own" or "peculiar to oneself."

Immune system: a word for all the functions that fight off invading organisms or foreign tissues.

Immuno-suppression (elevation): the state of impaired (heightened) ability to repel invading micro-organisms and transplanted foreign tissues.

Immuno-suppressive: causing *immunosuppression.*

Immunocompetent: opposite of *immunosuppressed.*

Immunoglobulin: a type of protein that participates in defense against disease. An antibody. See *gammopathy.*

Immunosuppressed: having impaired ability to fight infection because of stress, disease, poor nutrition, or medical treatment. A patient may also be deliberately immunosuppressed using drugs to make successful transplantation of an organ possible. See *immunosuppressive.*

Independent variable: a variable hypothesized to influence another variable or variables in a research study; colloquially, the presumed cause. In experimental studies, the variable manipulated or under the control of the experimenter.

Indolent: lazy. As applied to disease, the word means slow to grow, progress, or spread.

Infection toxin: a poison, produced by micro-organisms, which causes disease.

Innervation: nerve supply to any part of the body.

Intercellular matrix: chemicals (mostly chains of various sugars) that form a jelly-like substance between cells in tissues.

Internal validity: in social science research, this refers to the extent to which an experiment rules out alternative explanations of its results, and thus whether those results can be attributed unequivocally to the *independent variable.*

Interspinous: between the spinous processes of the vertebrae.

Intervertebral foramen: a hole between adjacent vertebrae through which the nerves pass from the spinal cord to the body.

Intervertebral opening: *intervertebral foramen.*

In vivo: in the living organism. The opposite is *in vitro,* literally "in a glass test tube."

Iris: the portion of the eye surrounding the pupil, which varies in color from person to person. The iris is composed of many fibers and is beautiful to view under magnification. Practitioners of "iridology" claim to diagnose diseases of the various organs of the "whole person" by examining the iris.

Iris stroma: the soft mass of connective tissue fibers that make up the *iris.*

Jaundice: yellow discoloration of the skin, caused by increased bilirubin in the blood. This is a breakdown product of part of the hemoglobin molecule, and is ordinarily solubilized by the liver and passed in the bile into the intestine. If red blood cells are being broken down too rapidly, if the liver is not working properly, or if the bile cannot flow, jaundice will result. See *serum bilirubin.*

Kaplan-Meier Method: in many applications we are interested in estimating a survival function *S(t)* for a population, which gives the probability of an individual surviving at least *t* moments from an initial time. In many medical and engineering experiments, lifetimes are not available for some individuals in a sample. The Kaplan-Meier method estimates the survival function with such missing data.

Kelley ecology: an unproven cancer therapy developed by the dentist William Kelley and most notably given to the late actor Steve McQueen. Kelley maintains that cancer results from a deficiency of pancreatic enzymes; his cancer treatment involves taking such enzymes and other nutritional supplements, following a low-protein diet of uncooked and unprocessed foods, and "detoxifying" the body through fasting, hot showers, deep breathing, and enemas.

Kinesthetic: relating to "position sense," the ability to know the position of one's joints.

Kirlian photography: a type of high voltage photography claimed to reveal electromagnetic fields emanating from organic and inorganic material. It is also claimed to be a diagnostic method whereby there are characteristic fields or auras indicative of different states of health.

Korsakoff's syndrome: an incurable mental disorder caused by damage to the thalamus of the brain. Actually due to deficiency in vitamin B, it is usually seen in chronic alcoholics. Patients concoct elaborate, believable stories about their past.

Lacrimal glands: the tear glands of the eyes.

Lactose: milk sugar, a disaccharide. It is nontoxic and small doses are suitable placebos. Some people cannot digest it after infancy and large doses cause diarrhea.

Lesion: any abnormal discontinuity of tissue or loss of function of a part of the body.

Leukocyte: white blood cell. The five classic types of leukocytes are basophils, eosinophils, *lymphocytes,* monocytes, and *neutrophils.*

Libido: in traditional psychoanalysis, psychic energy, especially the sexual motivation.

Ligament: fibrous bands that surround, stabilize, and support joints.

Linkage group: a group of genes close together on a chromosome, which seldom *cross over.*

Lobelia: Indian tobacco, an herb that contains several potent alkaloids with a variety of physiologic effects. An old folk-remedy for *asthma* and most other diseases.

Log rank test: In clinical trials comparing treatments, the aim is to assess the relative effectiveness of treatments. For many kinds of cancer, the outcomes vary because of prognostic characteristics of patients instead of the treatments. Thus it is important to take into account the prognostic characteristics when analyzing a clinical trial of a cancer treatment. There are two approaches for taking account of such characteristics: those based on stratifying the data and those based on statistical regression models. Both log rank tests and Wilcoxon-type tests involve stratifying the data. Log rank tests are most sensitive to differences between treatments that occur late, while Wilcoxon-type tests are most sensitive to differences that occur early in the survival curves. The Cox proportional hazards model involves the use of statistical regression models to analyze survival data. Regression analysis seeks to find the best mathematical model for describing a *dependent variable* as a function of an *independent variable,* or for predicting the values of a *dependent variable* from the values of an *independent variable.* Multiple regression deals with the *dependent variable* as a function of more than one *independent variable.*

Lomi body work: a method of psychological and physical therapy dating from 1971. It is claimed that by restructuring a person's postural alignment his body energies will flow freely and in accordance with universal laws.

Lymphocytes: small, round cells of the immune system that are involved in the recognition and response to foreign substances and invading micro-organisms. B-lymphocytes when activated become *plasma cells* and make antibodies; T-lymphocytes of several subtypes regulate immune response and kill other cells.

Lymphoid: a term for tissues involved in immune responses and made of *lymphocytes.* These include the lymph nodes, spleen, thymus gland, tonsils, and certain nodules along the gut.

Lymphomas: solid cancers made up of *lymphocytes.* They are better referred to as malignant lymphomas. Around ten percent of cancers in adults fall into this category.

Lymphosarcomas: an old name for malignant *lymphoma*. The term has been considered obsolete for twenty years.

Macular degeneration: a poorly-understood *degenerative disease* of the most light-sensitive portion of the retina. A cause of blindness in the elderly.

Magnetic healing: a traditional category of quack devices based on the notion that magnetic force can heal most aliments. Magnetic copper bracelets, crosses, belts, and similar jewelry have been promoted for the relief of pain, especially from arthritis. The first device of this sort marketed in the United States was the Perkins Tractor, which was claimed to pull disease from the body by magnetic attraction. Recent devices include the Dotto Electronic Reactor to cure ailments such as cancer by passing a magnetic ring over the patient's body.

Malignant tissue: cancer cells, their supporting fibers and blood supply.

Mastectomy: removal of a breast, usually for cancer.

Megrim: old word for *migraine headache.*

Meiosis: a form of cell division in which chromosomes are lost, as when sex cells are made.

Melancholia: an old name for depression, based on the misconception that it was caused by increased black (melano-) bile (chol-). Liver disease, especially hepatitis, can make a person feel very sad, but the chemistry of most moods is surely more complicated. Some ancient physicians dogmatize about the "four humors" (black bile, yellow bile, phlegm, and blood), claiming imbalances caused the whole range of disease. This discredited system awaits rediscovery by today's holists, though their talk about "imbalances" and interest in the "five humors" of Chinese superstition are equally naive.

Melanoma: malignant mole; a common skin *cancer* made up of malignant melanocytes. The best name is "malignant melanoma." Melanocytes are the cells that produce pigment in the skin and elsewhere, and some melanomas continue to make pigment. The tumor is notorious for its capricious behavior, and this is the tumor of adults most likely to "cure itself" even when widespread.

Menses: the monthly shedding of the lining of the uterus. Menstruation.

Metabolic: pertaining to the chemistry of all the body processes. The noun is "metabolism." Some Mexican holists offer the degree of "Metabolic Doctor,." so that graduates can represent themselves as M.D.s.

Metabolite: the chemical end-products of *metabolism.*

Metastases: tumor masses resulting from spread of a primary *cancer* to a remote tissue or organ. See *metastatic.* The verb is *metastasize,* to spread as cancer.

Metastatic: cancer which has spread to a remote tissue or organ. See *metastases.*

Metastatic islet-cell carcinoma: cancer of the pancreatic islets that has spread (usually to the liver). The Islets of Langerhans in the normal pancreas make several hormones, the best-known of which is insulin. Islet-cell tumors may generate huge amounts of hormones, playing havoc with the body's metabolism.

Migraine headache: a type of headache related to emotions and the function of the *autonomic nervous system.* In migraine, blood vessels squeeze shut and open wide chaotically.

Minilaparotomy: a small incision (two inches or less), usually just above the pubic hairline, for simple gynecologic procedures.

Modality: a way of treating disease, usually applied when several are available. The three common modalities of treating cancer are surgery, radiation, and chemotherapy (alone or in combination).

Monoclonal: the type of *gammopathy* that can indicate either *cancer* of the gamma-globulin-producing cells or a benign condition. Detected by serum or urine protein *electrophoresis.*

Morbidity: how much overall pain and/or disability an illness causes.

Mucous membrane: one of several surfaces of the body, continuous with the skin but lacking hair or sweat glands. The linings of the anus, mouth, urethra, and vagina are all mucous membranes.

Muriatic acid: hydrochloric acid, HC1. One of the strongest mineral acids.

Mutagen: anything capable of altering the sequence of nucleotides in the DNA of a gene.

Myeloma: multiple myeloma; plasma cell myeloma; *cancer* of the immunoglobulin-producing cells (plasma cells). Most patients have a monoclonal *gammopathy* on serum or urine protein *electrophoresis,* but these and other lab tests are seldom sufficient to make the diagnosis. Some asymptomatic patients with benign monoclonal gammopathy are mistakenly told they have myeloma. True malignant myeloma often lies dormant for many years.

Myofascial: pertaining to the muscles and fascia.

Myopia: nearsightedness.

Naloxone: one *narcotic antagonist* drug.

Narcotic antagonist: any of a class of drugs that block cell surface receptors for opiate painkillers such as morphine and one's own endorphins.

Naturopathy: literally, nature cure. Naturopaths do not use surgery or synthetic pharmaceuticals; they typically use fasting, massage, vitamins, minerals, herbs, mud packs, special diets, *colonic irrigation,* and manipulation of joints to assist the supposed natural healing forces in returning one's body to a state of balance and wholeness.

Negative inotropic effect: weakens the force of individual heartbeats.

Neoplasm: any tumor. Tumors are abnormal proliferations of cells in the body that resemble a normal organ, but do not contribute to the body's overall function. "Malignant neoplasms," "malignant tumors," and *cancers* are all synonyms; these are neoplasms that invade and destroy tissue and usually can spread to other tissues.

Nephritis: technically, any inflammation of the kidney. Usually, however, the term refers to inflammation of its little filters (glomeruli). Patients have high blood pressure and pass relatively little urine, which is brown due to altered blood.

Nettle-rash: urticaria, "hives." An itchy, blotchy skin eruption usually caused by an *allergy*.

Neuritis: inflammation of a nerve from any cause. There is often pain, peculiar sensations, or weakness of the associated muscles.

Neurological: pertaining to the nervous system (brain, spinal cord, and peripheral nerves) and its diseases.

Neuron: a nerve cell. The basic functional unit of the brain and spinal cord.

Neurophysiological: relating to the function of the nervous system.

Neurosis: short for *psychoneurosis*. The adjective is "neurotic."

Neutrophils: the most common white blood cells *(leukocytes)* and the ones that aggressively attack, swallow, and kill bacteria. Familiarly called "polys," they are actually only one of three types of polymorphonuclear leukocytes.

Nucleus pulposus: the "pulpy" (semi-gelatinous) center of an intervertebral disk. See *herniated disc.*

Nux vomica: strychnine. This powerful poison was once widely used as a tonic and stimulant.

Obsessive-compulsive disorder: a neurosis in which the patient experiences unwanted thoughts (obsessions) or the unwanted need to do certain things (compulsions); or a neurotic personality and lifestyle preoccupied with unrealistic standards of behavior.

Occlusive arterial disease: usually caused by *atherosclerosis,* which narrows or obstructs the tubes (arteries) that carry blood from the heart. The basic lesion of atherosclerosis is a plaque made of fibrous tissue and cholesterol. It may contain some calcium salts but this is not the basic problem. Atherosclerotic plaques cause strokes, *angina,* heart attack, gangrene, and so forth.

Ocular: of the eye.

Oedipal conflict: in traditional psychoanalysis, the supposed desire of a five-year-old to marry the opposite-sex parent and kill the same-sex parent (the "oedipus complex"), and the resulting inner turmoil.

Oncologist: an internist or surgeon who subspecializes in the administration of *chemotherapy.* See *oncology.*

Oncology: "the science of swellings." Today, the word means the medical and surgical subspecialties of administering *chemotherapy.* See *oncologist.*

Optic nerve: the great fiber tracts that carry signals from the *retina* to the rest of the brain. Called the "second *cranial nerve,*" it is really part of the brain.

Orthostatic hypotension: a drop in *blood pressure* caused by sitting or standing up. The usual cause is either diminished blood volume or poor nervous regulation of blood vessel tone.

Osteoarthritis: a poorly-understood *degenerative disease* that damages joints, seen especially in the elderly, the overweight, and in joints that have been injured.

Osteomalacia: softening of the bones, poor mineralization of bone fibers (osteoid). Lack of effective vitamin D. The usual causes are *rickets,* poor nutrition (in the elderly), or kidney failure.

Osteopathy: a system of medical practice originated by Andrew T. Still in the 1800s and based on the theory that disease is primarily the result of mechanical derangement in tissues, and the proper therapy for this is manipulation of the spine, joints, and soft tissues.

Osteophytes: bony outgrowths, especially as the result of wear-and-tear on joints in the fingers and *vertebral column.*

Oxygen saturation: the percent of iron atoms within an arterial red blood cell that are actually carrying an oxygen molecule. In healthy nonsmokers, oxygen saturation is around 95 percent.

P value: a statement of the probability that observed differences or associations in a study could have occurred by chance. Various statistical significance tests are used for determining this probability, and they can result in either a one-sided (one-tailed) or two-sided (two-tailed) *p* value. A one-sided test is sensitive to significant differences in only one direction (greater or less), while a two-sided test is sensitive to differences in both directions (greater and less). A one-sided test applied in a study of a new therapy can reveal whether the new therapy is better than the control, while a two-sided test can reveal whether the new therapy is better or worse than the control. Two-sided tests are commonly used in medical applications, especially with new drugs or procedures, because treatments or interventions can be harmful as well as helpful.

Pancreas: the large gland located below and behind the stomach where digestive enzymes, insulin, and other substances are produced.

Parasympathetic: one of the two great divisions of the *autonomic nervous system*. Its components work individually, promoting digestion, excretion of body waste, leisurely sex, and many other activities. The parasympathetic nerves to the *iris* cause the pupil of the eye to narrow.

Parenteral: not via the intestine. This usually refers to some drug being given by injection.

Pathogen: as used today, a micro-organism that causes disease.

Pathogenesis: the mechanism by which disease occurs. Contrast "etiology," what does it, with "pathogenesis," how it is done. See *etiology*.

Pathologic: unhealthy, relating to suffering ("pathos"). Same as "pathological."

Pathology: the science of disease. The pathologist examines tissues, body fluids, or dead bodies to tell one health problem from another, and is responsible for the diagnosis of almost all serious disease.

Pathophysiologic: abnormal functioning of the body.

Pennyroyal: a plant of the mint family, widely believed to induce abortion.

Peptic ulcer: an *ulcer* of esophagus, stomach, or duodenum caused by the action of acid produced in the stomach.

Performance test: measurements of what a sick patient can and cannot do.

Peristalsis: the rhythmic movements by which the contents of the gut and some other organs are propelled.

Phagocytic: capable of devouring tiny particles, said of certain cells such as *neutrophils*.

Phenotype: how an organism appears, the result of the expression of many genes. Organisms with the same *phenotype* may have different *genotypes*.

Phobia: a neurotic fear of a particular thing or situation.

Photomutagenic: light that has the ability to damage and alter *genes*.

Photosensitizer: any substace that makes a person more easily affected by sunlight. Psoralens from a variety of plants are the best-known photosensitizers, and several common drugs do the same thing.

Phototoxic: the poisonous effects that certain types of light have on some people.

Physiologic studies: research that involves measuring changes in the body.

Pituitary gland: an endocrine gland located in the skull. It produces many hormones and response signals from other glands and from the brain.

Placebo: a physiologically inert drug or treatment that the patient is led to believe may work. The patient may feel the drug has been effective, and this confidence may itself have a health effect (the placebo effect). A majority of patients given placebos (often pills made of *lactose,* chalk or whatever) report side-effects. Whenever possible, scientific studies compare any proposed treatment with some placebo.

Plasma: 1) the noncellular portion of the blood; 2) plasma cells manufacture *immunoglobulins.*

Poke-root: the root of a common weed. When eaten, severe illness and death may result.

Polarity therapy: a system of health care developed by Dr. Randolph Stone and involving exercise, diet, body manipulation, and right thinking. It is claimed that there are energy channels running from the positive pole of the head to the negative pole of the feet, and that this system will increase and balance the energy flowing along these channels.

Prana: cosmic energy acquired and used by practitioners of yoga.

Presenting problem: the symptoms a patient reports to a physician as his initial medical complaint.

Prospective study: the distinction between a prospective and a retrospective study can be made in terms of the time period when observations are made and recorded. A retrospective study uses observations that have been made and recorded before the study, while a prospective study uses observations that are made and recorded after the study has begun. In a prospective study the investigators can plan and control how they make and record observations in accordance with the purpose of their study, while in a retrospective study the observations may have been made and recorded for other and unrelated purposes, and thus not be as appropriate or reliable.

Prostate: the gland below a man's urinary bladder, where some sexual fluids are made and stored. The gland tends to enlarge and obstruct urinary flow in older men.

Pseudo-aldosteronism: high blood pressure and low serum potassium, with low or normal serum levels of the *corticosteroid* hormone aldosterone. Too much licorice is the best-known cause.

Psychic healing: includes faith healing, laying-on-of-hands, shamanic practices, healing by meditation; more generally characterized by proponents as any form of healing that is not medical and cannot be explained in terms of current medical knowledge.

Psychosomatic: of both mind and body. A very hard word to define further. See the chapter entitled "Psychological Causation and the Concept of Psychosomatic Disease" in this volume.

Pulmonary lobectomy: removal of one lobe of the lung, usually for cancer. This results in a few cures.

Pulsatilla: an herb, the juice of which is a powerful irritant.

Pyrosis: literally, full of fire; usually a synonym for "fever."

Quadriplegic: paralyzed in both arms and both legs.

Radiograph: x-ray picture.

Radiotherapy: killing cancer cells by radiation. Generally, cancer cells are more radiosensitive than healthy cells. Some cancers can be cured by radiation, and others can be temporarily controlled.

Random assignment: in an experimental study, subjects are randomly assigned to experimental or *control group* when each subject has an equal chance of being allocated to either group.

Recall antigens: substances used in *recall skin testing*.

Recall skin tests: a way of testing the function of the T-lymphocytes. The skin of the patient suspected of being immunosuppressed is injected with some substance to which the immune system has been previously sensitized. Redness and lump at the site of injection within a few days indicates a good immune function. A poor response indicates disease and is called "anergy."

Reflexology: see *zone therapy*.

Regression rate: in cancer studies, the rate at which cancer cells disappear.

Renal calculi: kidney stones.

Renal function: a measure of how well the kidneys are working. Patients with moderately impaired renal function will feel well, but will dispose of drugs and poisons poorly.

Repression: in traditional psychoanalysis, an ego defense in which unacceptable desires and experiences are put beyond conscious recall. Repressed material supposedly causes the *psychoneuroses*.

Retina: the light-sensitive surface on the back of the eye.

Retinal receptors: the specialized light-sensitive nerve structures of the *retina*.

Retinitis: inflammation of the retina. Central retinitis is inflammation at the center of the retinus.

Retrospective study: See *prospective study*.

Rheumatic ache: the discomfort of arthritis.

Rheumatism: various painful inflammatory processes involving the joints.

Rheumatoid arthritis: a disease involving pain and damage to the joints by a malfunctioning immune system. This is the usual cause of crippling arthritis.

Rickets: vitamin D deficiency in a child, with failure of bones to mineralize and develop properly. See *osteomalacia*.

Rolfing: named after the originator, Ida Rolf, also known as structural integration. A form of massage claimed to lengthen, straighten, and balance the body in relation to the pull of gravity. Therapeutic effects and health benefits are supposed to result from bringing the head, shoulders, thorax, and legs into vertical alignment.

Ruptured disc: a break in the firm tissue at the edge of one of the discs between vertebral bodies. See *herniated disc*.

Sacrum: the bone at the base of the *vertebral column*, shaped like a downward-pointing triangle. Several pairs of spinal nerves pass through holes in its surface.

Saline solution: sodium chloride (common table salt) in water.

Scabies: a disease caused by a mite that burrows in the upper skin. It results in severe itching.

Scarlet fever: a reddening of the skin and mucous membranes, following infection (usually in the throat) by certain strains of streptococcus bacteria that are themselves infected with a virus. The actual scarlet rash is caused by a poison the infected bacteria produce. Rheumatic fever and severe heart damage may develop.

Scoliosis: sideways curvature of the *vertebral column*.

Serum beta endorphin: the laboratory measurement of the amount of *beta endorphin* in the blood.

Serum bilirubin: a measurement of the amount of pigment derived from broken-down red blood cells in the serum. Patients with increased serum bilirubin have *jaundice*.

Shiatsu: a Japanese form of massage in which thumbs and fingers are used to massage joints located along acupuncture meridians thereby supposedly bringing "vital energies" into balance.

Silex: a noncrystalline silica powder used in cements; in Holmes's day a homeopathic remedy.

Silva mind control: a system of meditation and autosuggestion claimed to help one enter a state of deep relaxation in order to then use "visualization statements" to bring about improvements in one's life.

Sinusitis: inflammation of one or more of the hollow spaces within the skull that drain into the nose.

Smallpox: a dreaded viral disease characterized by little blisters on the skin. Once a major killer, it is now thought to be extinct (thanks to vaccination).

Speciation: the process by which separated populations of closely-related organisms eventually change until they can no longer interbreed to produce fertile offspring and are thus said to be separate species.

Sphincter: anything that surrounds a tube and closes when it contracts. The pursed lips, the muscles of the anus, and the little muscles surrounding the openings of tiny blood vessels are all sphincters in the body.

Squamous: scaly, pertaining to a type of cell that covers body surfaces subject to rough treatment, such as the skin and mouth of normal people and the airways of cigarette smokers. Many cancers (squamous cell carcinomas) arise from these cells.

Statistical significance: when the *P value* of a result is less than 0.05, it is called a statistically significant result or difference from chance, and thus random variation in sampling is not a likely explanation of the result.

Steroids: a class of molecules with a characteristic structure of three six-member carbon rings and one five-member carbon ring. Many are hormones.

Stomachic: any medicine that improves appetite and digestion.

Stratification: division of a sample into subsamples according to specified criteria (e.g., age, sex, severity of disease). Often combined with *randomization* to produce a stratified random sample by first dividing a sample into strata and then selecting subjects randomly within each stratum.

Stroke: cerebrovascular accident; sudden death of a portion of the brain due (usually) to occlusion of its artery. The clinical signs and symptoms will depend on what portion of the brain is damaged. Little strokes (transient ischemic attacks) result from brief occlusions of an artery, without permanent damage.

Subcutaneous angiosarcoma: cancer arising in the blood vessels beneath the skin.

Subluxation: in chiropractic, the alleged condition in which one or more *vertebrae* become misaligned and impinge on a nerve, thereby interfering with transmission of nerve impulses to other parts of the body. The alleged condition is held to be either the cause or a main cause of dysfunction and disease anywhere in the body.

Suppuration: formation of pus. Suppuration of lungs refers to pneumonia, due to bacteria or perhaps tuberculosis.

Supraspinous: above a spine or spinous process.

Sympathetic: one of the two great divisions of the *autonomic nervous system*. The sympathetic system tends to fire all at once, especially in fight-or-flight situations. The sympathetic nerves to the *iris* cause the pupil of the eye to widen.

Sympatric speciation: *speciation* without geographical isolation.

Symptomatic response: occurs when the subject of the experiment feels sick.

Symptomatology: the symptoms of a disease. Symptoms are what the patient notices; signs are what the physician discovers.

Synapse: a junction where nerve cell membranes touch; one activates or inhibits the other. The basic unit of communication in the nervous system.

Systemic chemotherapy: cancer *chemotherapy* given to the whole person, usually by vein.

Systemic lupus erythematosus: a dreaded disease, usually seen in young women, in which the patient makes antibodies against her own cell nuclei and other body parts. Patients may have arthritis, facial rash, kidney damage, mental change, etc.

Systolic: see *blood pressure.*

t test: a statistical procedure often used with small samples to compare the means of two samples in order to determine whether differences between sample means warrant concluding that the two populations have different means.

T'ai Chi: ancient Chinese martial art based on Taoism, also claimed to be a system of meditation for directing ch'i (the so-called life force).

Tertatogen: something that can disrupt growth of a fetus to produce malformation.

Tertiary syphilis: the advanced stage of infection by the spirochete, Treponema pallidum. Most common is damage to the aorta, aortic valve, or brain. Syndromes of brain syphilis include general paresis (insanity, dementia), and tabes dorsalis (agonizing pains in the legs).

Testosterone: the principal sex *hormone* in men.

Therapeutic touch: a form of laying-on-of-hands developed by Dolores Krieger and popular with holistic nurses. See the essay entitled "Therapeutic Touch—Is There a Scientific Basis for the Practice?" in this volume.

Thyroid adenoma: a common, solitary, benign nodule in the thyroid. There are perhaps four million cases in this country today, and some require surgery if they cannot be distinguished from cancer.

Thyroidectomy: removal of the thyroid gland for any reason.

Tincture: an alcoholic extract of a plant.

Toxic: poisonous. The noun is *toxin,* poison.

Toxic bowel settlement: a mythical substance (variously described as "slimy" and "cement-like") that supposedly coats the inside of the large intestine in patients who eat anything except health food. It can be removed by *colonic irrigation,* the more often the better. "Toxic bowel settlement" is the subject of holistic books such as *Colon Health: The Key to a Vibrant Life* by Norman W. Walker, D.Sc., Ph.D., (Phoenix: O'Sullivan Woodside & Company, 1979). Walker, a chiropractor, presents drawings of barium-contrast x-rays of colons to show narrowing of the bowel due to "toxic waste" plastered on its walls. Actually, .x-rays are normal; the bowel is narrowed by the natural rhythmic movements that propel feces through it *(peristalsis).* Pathologists have opened and examined no end of large intestines and have never seen anything remotely resembling "toxic bowel settlement."

Transference: in traditional psychoanalysis, the way patients come to regard the psychotherapist as they did their parents. Studying the transference reveals the patient's inner conflicts, and the support of the therapist encourages recovery.

Trauma: any injury (mental or physical).

Trypsin: a potent enzyme, released from the pancreas and activated in the gut, that breaks down protein in food.

Tumor: synonym for *neoplasm.*

Tumor regression: partial disappearance of a neoplasm, spontaneously (rare) or as a result of therapy (common).

Two-way Analysis of Variance: the variation in a set of observations can be measured by the sums of squares of deviations from the mean. When the data can be classified in a two-way array, analysis of variance separates this sum into two components associated with the two sources of variation.

Ulcer: a disease-produced break in a body surface with erosion of underlying tissue. Most ulcers in the stomach and duodenum are well-known to be related to emotional stress.

Ulceration: formation of an *ulcer.*

Unilateral tinnitis: ringing in one ear.

Unresectable disease: a cancer that cannot be entirely removed surgically without damage to the underlying *vital* structures.

Vagus nerve: the tenth *cranial nerve,* primarily a *parasympathetic* autonomic nerve. "Vagus" comes from the same root as "vagabond," because the nerve wanders through the body, from the brain to the large intestine.

Variable: a property of a person, object, or event that varies and thus can have different values. Variables can be classified, quantified, and measured.

Vasoconstriction: narrowing of blood vessels.

Vertebrae: the bones that make up most of the spine or backbone. The typical *vertebra* (singular) is composed of a large cylindrical body, two pedicles, two laminae, two transverse processes, and one spinous process. There are eight cervical vertebrae in the neck, twelve dorsal or thoracic vertebrae in the upper back, and five lumbar vertebrae in the lower back. The whole stack is the *vertebral column.* The bottom of the spine is the *scarum* and coccyx.

Vertebral canal: the tube formed by the pedicles, laminae, and bodies of the vertebrae, through which the spinal cord passes.

Vertebral column: the spine (spinal column) above the sacrum. See *vertebrae.*

Vestibular: of the system of canals in the inner ear that sense rotation of the head, and their nerve connections in the brain.

Vestibulocochlear nerve: the eighth *cranial nerve,* which carries hearing, gravity sense, and rotation sense from the inner ear to the brain.

Virus: an infectious ultra-microscopic organism composed of a few genes, a protein capsule, and little or nothing else. It cannot reproduce except by hijacking the genetic machinery of a healthy cell.

Visualization: techniques that involve a patient in forming mental images in order to diagnose or treat his disorders. The Simonton appraoch to cancer treatment is based on such techniques; see the essay entitled "Dream Your Cancer Away*SexualThe Simontons*" in this volume. *Also known as guided imagery.*

Volatile oil: an oil that evaporates at low temperatures. Those from plants are also called "essential oils."

Whooping cough: a serious respiratory infection that causes epidemics among children. The vaccine is quite effective and prevents or controls epidemics, but a tiny percent of children have devastating damage from it. This raises many public health problems; because of the legal liability, manufacturers may be unwilling to make this particular vaccine.

Zone therapy: a method of massaging and applying pressure to the soles of the feet or the underside of the hands in order to treat all parts and organs of the body. It is claimed that there are connections between each part or organ of the body and specific points on the feet and hands. Also known as reflexology.

Selected Bibliography

BOOKS THAT PROMOTE HOLISTIC MEDICINE

Bauman, Edward, et al., editors. *The Holistic Health Handbook*. Berkeley, Calif.: And/Or Press, 1978.

Benson, Herbert. *Beyond the Relaxation Response*. New York: Times Books, 1984.

Blattner, Barbara. *Holistic Nursing*. Englewood Cliffs, N. J.: Prentice-Hall, 1981.

Bliss, Shepherd, et al., editors. *The New Holistic Health Handbook*. Lexington, Mass.: The Stephen Greene Press, 1985.

Capra, Fritjof. *The Turning Point*. New York: Bantam Books, 1982.

Carlson, Rick J. *The End of Medicine*. New York: John Wiley & Sons, 1975.

———, editor. *The Frontiers of Science and Medicine*. Chicago: Henry Regnery Company, 1975.

Chernin, Dennis, and Manteuffel, Gregory. *Health: A Holistic Approach*. Wheaton, Ill.: The Theosophical Publishing House, 1984.

Cousins, Norman. *Anatomy of an Illness as Perceived by the Patient*. New York: W. W. Norton, 1979.

De La Peña, Augustin M. *The Psychobiology of Cancer*. New York: Praeger Publishers, 1983.

Deliman, Tracy, and Smolowe, John S., editors. *Holistic Medicine: Harmony of Body, Mind, Spirit*. Reston, Va.: Reston Publishing Company, 1982.

Dossey, Larry. *Space, Time & Medicine*. Boulder, Colo.: Shambhala Publications, 1982.

———. *Beyond Illness*. Boulder, Colo.: Shambhala Publications, 1984.

Flynn, Patricia Anne Randolph. *Holistic Health: The Art and Science of Care*. Bowie, Md.: Robert J. Brady Company, 1980.

————, editor. *The Healing Continuum: Journeys in the Philosophy of Holistic Health*. Bowie, Md.: Robert J. Brady Company, 1980.

Gordon, James S.; Jaffe, Dennis T.; and Bresler, David E., editors. *Mind, Body and Health: Toward an Integral Medicine*. New York: Human Sciences Press, 1984.

Hafen, Brent Q., and Frandsen, Kathryn J. *From Acupuncture to Yoga*. Englewood Cliffs, N.J.: Prentice-Hall, 1983.
Hastings, Arthur C.; Fadiman, James; Gordon, James S., editors. *Health for the Whole Person: The Complete Guide to Holistic Medicine*. New York: Bantam Books, 1981.

Kaslof, Leslie J., editor. *Wholistic Dimensions in Healing*. Garden City, N.Y.: Doubleday & Company, 1978.
Krieger, Dolores. *Foundations for Holistic Health Nursing Practices*. Philadelphia: J. B. Lippincott Company, 1981.

Le Shan, Lawrence. *The Mechanic and the Gardener: Making the Most of the Holistic Revolution in Medicine*. New York: Holt, Rinehart and Winston, 1982.

McGarey, William A. *The Edgar Cayce Remedies*. New York: Bantam Books, 1983.
Moore, Michael C., and Moore, Lynda J. *The Complete Handbook of Holistic Health*. Englewood Cliffs, N.J.: Prentice-Hall, 1983.

Otto, Herbert A., and Knight, James W., editors. *Dimensions in Wholistic Healing*. Chicago: Nelson-Hall Incorporated, 1977.
Oyle, Irving. *The New American Medicine Show*. Santa Cruz, Calif.: Unity Press, 1979.

Pelletier, Kenneth R. *Mind as Healer, Mind as Slayer: A Holistic Approach to Preventing Stress Disorders*. New York: Dell Publishing Company, 1977.
————. *Toward a Science of Consciousness*. New York: Delacorte Press, 1978.
————. *Holistic Medicine: From Stress to Optimum Health*. New York: Dell Publishing Company, 1979.
————. *Longevity: Fulfilling Our Biological Potential*. New York: Dell Publishing Company, 1981.

Popenoe, Cris. *Wellness*. Washington, D.C.: Yes! Incorporated, 1977.

Rosenthal, Raymond F., and Gordon, James S. *The Healing Partnership: Essays for Health Professionals, Students, and Patients*. Washington, D.C.: Aurora Associates, 1984.

Salmon, J. Warren, editor. *Alternative Medicines: Popular and Policy Perspectives.* New York: Tavistock Publications, 1984.

Snyder, Paul. *Health & Human Nature.* Radnor, Pa.: Chilton Book Company, 1980.

Sobel, David S., editor. *Ways of Health: Holistic Approaches to Ancient and Contemporary Medicine.* New York: Harcourt Brace Jovanovich, 1979.

Weil, Andrew. *Health and Healing: Understanding Conventional and Alternative Medicine.* Boston: Houghton Mifflin Company, 1983.

BOOKS AND ARTICLES THAT EXAMINE
HOLISTIC MEDICINE OR RELEVANT TOPICS

Allander, Erik. "Holistic Medicine as a Method of Causal Explanation, Treatment, and Prevention in Clinical Work: Obstacle or Opportunity for Development?" In *Health, Disease, and Causal Explanations in Medicine,* edited by Lennart Nordenfelt and B. Ingemar B. Lindahl. Dordrecht, Holland: D. Reidel Publishing Company, 1984, 215–23.

Angell, Marcia. "Disease as a Reflection of the Psyche," *New England Journal of Medicine* 312 (1985):1570–72.

Avina, Robert L., and Schneiderman, Lawrence J. "Why Patients Choose Homeopathy," *Western Journal of Medicine* 128 (1978):366–69.

Ballantine, H. Thomas. "Medicine and Chiropractic," *Journal of the American Medical Association* 200 (1967):131–35.

———. "Will the Delivery of Health Care Be Improved by the Use of Chiropractic Services?" *New England Journal of Medicine* 286 (1972):237–42.

———. "Federal Recognition of Chiropractic: A Double Standard," *Annals of Internal Medicine* 82 (1975):712–13.

Barrett, Stephen, editor. *The Health Robbers: How To Protect Your Money and Your Life,* Second Edition. Philadelphia: George F. Stickley Company, 1980.

Bernstein, Jeremy. "A Cosmic Flow," *The American Scholar* 48 (1978/79):6–9.

———. "Quantum Reality," *The American Scholar* 54 (1984/85):7–14.

Brandon, Robert N. "Biological Teleology: Questions and Explanations," *Studies in History and Philosophy of Science* 12 (1981):91–105.

Callahan, Daniel. "The WHO Definition of 'Health'," *Hastings Center Studies* 1 (1973):77–87.

Carter, Richard B. *Descartes' Medical Philosophy: The Organic Solution to the Mind-Body Problem.* Baltimore: The Johns Hopkins University Press, 1983.

Cassileth, Barrie R., et al. "Contemporary Unorthodox Treatments in Cancer Medicine: A Study of Patients, Treatments, and Practitioners," *Annals of Internal Medicine* 101 (1984):105–12.

————, et al. "Psychosocial Correlates of Survival in Advanced Malignant Disease?" *New England Journal of Medicine* 312 (1985):1551–55.

Chalmers, Thomas C. "A Challenge to Clinical Investigators," *Gastroenterology* 57 (1969):631–635.

————. "The Clinical Trial," *Milbank Memorial Fund Quarterly* 59 (1981): 324–39.

Chalmers, Thomas C.; Block, Jerome B.; and Lee, Stephanie. "Controlled Studies in Clinical Cancer Research," *New England Journal of Medicine* 287 (1972):75–78.

————, et al. "A Method for Assessing the Quality of a Randomized Control Trial," *Controlled Clinical Trials* 2 (1981):31–49.

Chaves, John F., and Barber, Theodore Xenophen. "Acupuncture Analgesia: A Six-Factor Theory." In *Pain: New Perspectives in Therapy and Research,* edited by Matisyonu Weisenberg and Bernard Tursky. New York: Plenum Press, 1976, 43–65.

Churchland, Paul M. *Matter and Consciousness.* Cambridge, Mass.: The MIT Press, 1984.

Clark, Austen G. *Psychological Models and Neural Mechanisms: An Examination of Reductionism in Psychology.* Oxford: Oxford University Press, 1980.

————. "Functionalism and the Definition of Theoretical Terms," *Journal of Mind and Behavior* 4 (1983):339–52.

————. "The Logic of the Comparative Approach," *Behavioral and Brain Sciences* 7 (1984):437–38.

Cockburn, D. "A Study of the Validity of Iris Diagnosis," *Australian Journal of Optometry* 64 (1981):154–57.

Colton, Theodore. *Statistics in Medicine.* Boston: Little, Brown and Company, 1974.

Crawford, Robert. "You Are Dangerous to Your Health: The Ideology and Politics of Victim-Blaming," *International Journal of Health Services* 7 (1977):663–80.

Crelin, Edmund S. "A Scientific Test of the Chiropractic Theory," *American Scientist* 61 (1973):574–80.

————. "A Lethal Chiropractic Device," *Yale Scientific Magazine* 49 (1975):8–11.

Day, R. L., et al. "Evaluation of Acupuncture Anesthesia: A Psychophysical Study," *Anesthesiology* 43 (1975):507–17.

DeWys, William D. "How to Evaluate a New Treatment for Cancer," *Your Patient & Cancer* (May, 1982):31–36.

Dworkin, Gerald. "Taking Risks, Assessing Responsibility," *The Hastings Center Report* 11 (October 1981):26–31.

Editors of Consumer Reports Books. *Health Quackery: Consumers Union's Report on False Health Claims, Worthless Remedies, and Unproved Therapies.* New York: Holt, Rinehart and Winston, 1980.

Erwin, Edward. "Establishing Causal Connections: Meta-Analysis and Psychotherapy." In *Midwest Studies in Philosophy,* Volume IX, edited by Peter A. French, Theodore E. Uehling, and Howard K. Wettstein. Minneapolis: University of Minnesota Press, 1984, 421–36.

———. "Is Psychotherapy More Effective Than a Placebo?" In *Does Psychotherapy Really Help People?* edited by Jusuf Hariman. Springfield, Ill.: Charles C. Thomas Publisher, 1984, 37–51.

Feinstein, Alvan R. *Clinical Epidemiology: The Architecture of Clinical Research.* Philadelphia: W. B. Saunders Company, 1985.

Fitzgerald, Faith T. "Science and Scam: Alternative Thought Patterns in Alternative Health Care," *New England Journal of Medicine* 309 (1983):1066–67.

Fox, Bernard H. "Current Theory of Psychogenic Effects on Cancer Incidence and Prognosis," *Journal of Psychosocial Oncology* 1 (1983):17–31.

Fried, John. *Vitamin Politics.* Buffalo, N.Y.: Prometheus Books, 1984.

Gardner, Martin. *Fads & Fallacies in the Name of Science.* New York: Dover Publications, 1957.

Gillespie, Daniel T. *A Quantum Mechanics Primer.* London: International Textbook Company Limited, 1973.

Gillick, Muriel R. "Common-sense Models of Health and Disease," *New England Journal of Medicine* 313 (1985):700-703.

Glatstein, Eli, and Makuch, Robert W. "Illusion and Reality: Practical Pitfalls in Interpreting Clinical Trials," *Journal of Clinical Oncology* 2 (May, 1984):488-97.

Glymour, Clark, and Stalker, Douglas. Letter to Editor. *New England Journal of Medicine,* 309 (1983):800.

Guttmacher, Sally. "Whole in Body, Mind & Spirit: Holistic Health and the Limits of Medicine," *The Hastings Center Report* 9 (April 1979):15-21.

Herbert, Victor. *Nutrition Cultism: Facts and Fictions.* Philadelphia: George F. Stickley Company, 1980.

Herbert, Victor, and Barrett, Stephen. *Vitamins and "Health" Foods: The Great American Health Hustle.* Philadelphia: George F. Stickley Company, 1981.

Hill, A. Bradford. "The Clinical Trial," *New England Journal of Medicine* 247 (1952):113-19.

Hofstadter, Douglas R. "Heisenberg's Uncertainty Principle and the Many-Worlds Interpretation of Quantum Mechanics." In *Metamagical Themas: Questing for the Essence of Mind and Pattern* by Douglas R. Hofstadter. New York: Basic Books, 1985, 455-77.

Jukes, Thomas H. "Megavitamins and Food Fads." In *Human Nutrition—A Comprehensive Treatise,* Volume 4, edited by Robert E. Hodges. New York: Plenum Publishing Corporation, 1979, 257-92.

Kaufman, Martin. *Homeopathy in America: The Rise and Fall of a Medical Heresy.* Baltimore: The Johns Hopkins University Press, 1971.

Kopelman, Loretta, and Moskop, John. "The Holistic Health Movement: A Survey and Critique," *The Journal of Medicine and Philosophy,* 6 (May 1981):209–35.

Kroger, W. S. "Acupunctural Analgesia: Its Explanation by Conditioning Theory, Autogenic Training and Hypnosis," *American Journal of Psychiatry* 130 (1973):855–60.

Kuhn, Thomas S. *The Structure of Scientific Revolutions,* Second Edition. Chicago: University of Chicago Press, 1970.

Lange, Richard H. "Holistic Medicine: Is All Holistic Medicine Whole?" *New York State Journal of Medicine* 80 (1980):996–99.

Marshall, Charles W. *Vitamins and Minerals: Help or Harm?* Philadelphia: George F. Stickley Company, 1983.

Mayr, Ernst. *The Growth of Biological Thought.* Cambridge, Mass.: Harvard University Press, 1983.

Melzack, Ronald, and Katz, Joel. "Auriculotherapy Fails to Relieve Chronic Pain: A Controlled Crossover Study." *Journal of the American Medical Association,* 251 (1984):1041–43.

Michael, Max; Boyce, Thomas W.; and Wilcox, Allen J. *Biomedical Bestiary: An Epidemiologic Guide to Flaws and Fallacies in the Medical Literature.* Boston: Little, Brown and Company, 1984.

Moertel, Charles G., et al. "A Clinical Trial of Amygdalin (Laetrile) in the Treatment of Human Cancer," *New England Journal of Medicine* 306 (1982):201–206.

Nagel, Ernest. *The Structure of Science.* New York: Harcourt, Brace and World, 1961.

Nolen, William A. *Healing: A Doctor in Search of a Miracle.* New York: Random House, 1974.

Prioleau, Leslie; Murdock, Martha; and Brody, Nathan. "An Analysis of Psychotherapy Versus Placebo Studies," *Behavioral and Brain Sciences* 6 (1983):275–85.

Radner, Daisie, and Radner, Michael. *Science and Unreason.* Belmont, Calif.: Wadsworth Publishing Company, 1982.

Randolph, Gretchen L. "Therapeutic and Physical Touch: Physiological Response to Stressful Stimuli," *Nursing Research* 33 (1984):33–36.

Relman, Arnold S. "Holistic Medicine," *New England Journal of Medicine* 300 (1979):312–13.

————. "Chiropractic: Recognized But Unproved," *New England Journal of Medicine* 301 (1979):659–60.

Riegelman, Richard K. *Studying a Study and Testing a Test: How to Read the Medical Literature.* Boston: Little, Brown and Company, 1981.

Rohrlich, Fritz. "Facing Quantum Mechanical Reality," *Science* 221 (1983):1251–55.

Rose, Louis. *Faith Healing.* Hammondsworth, Middlesex, England: Penguin Books, 1971.

Rynearson, Edward H. "Americans Love Hogwash," *Nutrition Reviews,* Supplement, 32 (July 1974):1–14.

Sandroff, Ronni. "A Skeptic's Guide to Therapeutic Touch," *RN* 43 (1980):25–30, 82–83.

Schaller, Warren E., and Carroll, Charles R. *Health, Quackery & the Consumer.* Philadelphia: W. B. Saunders Company, 1976.

Shipley, Michael, et al. "Controlled Trial of Homeopathic Treatment of Osteoarthritis," *The Lancet,* 1 (1983):97–98.

Simkins, Lawrence. "Biofeedback: Clinically Valid or Oversold?" *Psychological Record* 32 (1982):3-17.

Simon, Allie; Worthen, David M.; and Mitas, John A. "An Evaluation of Iridology," *Journal of the American Medical Association* 242 (1979):1385–89.

Skrabanek, Petr. "Acupuncture and the Age of Unreason," *The Lancet* 1 (1984):1169–71.

Smith, Ralph Lee. *At Your Own Risk: The Case Against Chiropractic.* New York: Pocket Books, 1969.

Spitzer, Walter O.; Feinstein, Alvan R.; and Sackett, David L. "What Is a Health Care Trial?" *Journal of the American Medical Association* 233 (1975):161–63.

Sweet, W. H. "Some Current Problems in Pain Research and Therapy (Including Needle Puncture, 'Acupuncture')," *Pain* 10 (1981):297–309.

Tyler, Varro E. *The Honest Herbal: A Sensible Guide to Herbs and Related Remedies.* Philadelphia: George F. Stickley Company, 1982.

Wheeler, John Archibald. "Not Consciousness but the Distinction Between the Probe and the Probed as Central to the Elemental Quantum Act of Observation." In *The Role of Consciousness in the Physical World,* edited by Robert G. Jahn. Boulder, Colo.: Westview Press, 1981, 87–111.

White, Leonard, and Tursky, Bernard, editors. *Clinical Biofeedback: Efficacy and Mechanisms.* New York: The Guilford Press, 1982.

White, Leonard; Tursky, Bernard; and Schwartz, Gary E., editors. *Placebo: Theory, Research, and Mechanisms.* New York: The Guilford Press, 1985.

Whorton, James C. *Crusaders for Fitness: The History of American Health Reformers.* Princeton, N.J.: Princeton University Press, 1982.

Wikler, Daniel. "Persuasion and Coercion for Health: Ethical Issues in Government Efforts to Change Life-Styles." *Milbank Memorial Fund Quarterly* 56 (1978):303–38.

Wittes, Robert E. "Vitamin C and Cancer." *New England Journal of Medicine* 312 (1985):178–79.

Worrall, Russell S. "Pseudoscience—A Critical Look at Iridology," *Journal of the American Optometric Association* 55 (1984):735–39.

Yahn, George. "The Impact of Holistic Medicine, Medical Groups, and Health Concepts," *Journal of the American Medical Association* 242 (1979):2202–2205.

Young, James Harvey. *The Medical Messiahs: A Social History of Health Quackery in Twentieth-Century America.* Princeton, N.J.: Princeton University Press, 1967.

———. "The Persistence of Medical Quackery in America," *American Scientist* 60 (May-June 1972):318–26.

———. "The Foolmaster Who Fooled Them," *Yale Journal of Biology and Medicine* 53 (1980):555–66.

Young, Larry D., and Blanchard, Edward B. "Medical Applications of Biofeedback Training: A Selective Review." In *Contributions to Medical Psychology,* Volume 2, edited by Stanley Rachman. Elmsford, N.Y.: Pergamon Press, 1980, 215–54.

Contributors

ROBERT N. BRANDON, PH.D., is an associate professor in the Department of Philosophy at Duke University. He is the co-editor of *Genes, Organisms, Populations: Controversies over the Units of Selection,* the author of a chapter on adaptation explanations in *The New Biology and the New Philosophy of Science,* and his papers on topics in the philosophy of biology have appeared in such journals as *Philosophy of Science* and *Studies in History and Philosophy of Science.*

THOMAS C. CHALMERS, M.D., is Distinguished Service Professor of Medicine and Head of the Clinical Trials Unit at the Mount Sinai School of Medicine and Hospital, as well as president emeritus and dean emeritus of Mount Sinai School of Medicine. He has served on numerous federal advisory committees, clinical trial advisory boards and data monitoring committees, as well as on National Research Council committees of the National Academy of Sciences. Dr. Chalmers is a member of the National Academy of Sciences, the American Academy of Arts and Sciences, and a past president of the American Association for the Study of Liver Disease and the American Gastroenterological Association. He has won the Julius Friedenwald Medal for Outstanding Achievement in Gastroenterology and the Paul Lazarfeld Award for Research given by the Evaluation Research Society, and his more than two hundred and fifty publications have appeared in such leading medical journals as the *New England Journal of Medicine,* the *Journal of the American Medical Association,* the *American Journal of Medicine,* and the *Journal of Clinical Investigation.*

AUSTEN G. CLARK, PH.D., is an assistant professor in the Department of Philosophy at the University of Tulsa. He has been a postdoctoral fellow in the L. L. Thurstone Psychometric Lab at the University of North Carolina, and a research assistant professor in the Department of Psychiatry and the Department of Community and Family Medicine at Dartmouth Medical School. He is the author of *Psychological Models and Neural Mechanisms: An Examination of Reductionism in Psychology,* and his papers on topics in the philosophy of mind and the philosophy of psychology have appeared in such journals as the *Journal of Mind and Behavior* and *Behavioral and Brain Sciences.*

MARY JO CLARK, P.N.P., M.S., is an assistant professor in the Department of Community Nursing of the School of Nursing at the Medical College of Georgia. She is the editor and principal author of *Community Nursing: Health Care for Today and Tomorrow,* and the author of its companion volume, *Faculty Guide for Community Nursing: Health Care for Today and Tomorrow.* Her papers on topics in nursing have appeared in such journals as *Nursing Research, Topics in Clinical Nursing, Public Health Nursing,* and *Image: The Journal of Nursing Scholarship.*

PHILIP E. CLARK, R.N., is a captain in the Army Nurse Corps and serves as a team leader in psychiatric and mental health at the Dwight David Eisenhower Army Medical Center, Fort Gordon, Georgia. He is a contributor to *Community Nursing: Health Care for Today and Tomorrow.* His papers on topics in nursing have appeared in *Nursing Research* and *Image: The Journal of Nursing Scholarship.* He has worked extensively on computer applications in nursing research.

EDWARD T. CREAGAN, M.D., is an associate professor in the Division of Medical Oncology of the Department of Oncology at the Mayo Clinic and Graduate School of Medicine, where he has won awards for outstanding achievement and teaching in internal medicine. Dr. Creagan is a contributor to the volume *Cutaneous Melanoma: Clinical Management and Treatment Results Worldwide,* and has published more than one hundred and twenty papers, many of them on the clinical management of patients with advanced cancer, in such journals as *The Lancet,* the *New England Journal of Medicine, Cancer, Oncology,* the *American Journal of Clinical Oncology,* and *Annals of Internal Medicine.*

EDMUND S. CRELIN, PH.D., D.SC., is a professor in the Section of Anatomy of the Department of Surgery, and chairman of the Human Growth and Development Study Unit, at the Yale University School of Medicine. His research has been involved chiefly with the musculoskeletal system and birth defects, and he has published over one hundred and fifty research articles in scientific journals. He is also the author of *Anatomy of the Newborn; Functional Anatomy of the Newborn; The Human Vocal Tract: Anatomy, Function, Development and Evolution;* and five Ciba Clinical Symposia on human development. Dr. Crelin received the F. G. Blake Award as the most outstanding teacher at the Yale University School of Medicine in 1961, the Yale Physician's Associate Program Award as the most outstanding teacher in 1973 and again in

1980; in 1976 he received the Kappa Delta Award for outstanding research from the American Academy of Orthopedic Surgeons.

EDWARD ERWIN, PH.D., is a professor in the Department of Philosophy at the University of Miami. He is the author of *The Concept of Meaninglessness* and *Behavior Therapy: Scientific, Philosophical and Moral Foundations.* He has contributed chapters on psychotherapy to such books as *Paradigms in Behavior Therapy* and *Does Psychotherapy Really Help People?* and has published numerous papers on the topic in journals such as the *American Psychologist, The British Journal for the Philosophy of Science,* and *Nous.*

EDWARD R. FRIEDLANDER, M.D., is an assistant professor of pathology at Quillen-Dishner College of Medicine, East Tennessee State University, where he directs the sophomore courses in medical pathology and clinical lab use. He is a 1977 graduate of Northwestern Medical School, trained in pathology from Northwestern Memorial Hospital and Bowman-Gray School of Medicine, and board-certified in anatomic and clinical pathology. He has published in the *Journal of Chromatography* and has authored a two-volume laboratory manual for medical pathology.

CLARK GLYMOUR, PH.D., is head of the Department of Philosophy at Carnegie-Mellon University and an adjunct professor in the Department of History and Philosophy of Science at the University of Pittsburgh. He is the author of *Theory and Evidence,* an editor of *Foundations of Space-Time Theories,* and a contributor to such volumes as *Philosophical Essays on Freud* and *Testing Scientific Theories.* He has published more than forty articles on topics in the philosophy of science, the history of science, artificial intelligence, and social science in such journals as *The Journal of Philosophy, Archive for History of the Exact Sciences, Artificial Intelligence,* and *Behavioral Sciences.*

OLIVER WENDELL HOLMES, M.D., was for thirty-five years Parkman Professor of Anatomy and Physiology in the Harvard Medical School (1847–1882), and also served as dean of Harvard Medical School. He was awarded the Boylston Prize three times for his medical essays, which were published in 1883 as a volume entitled *Medical Essays.* His best known clinical contribution remains the essay "The Contagiousness of Puerperal Fever," which was the first application of the principle of asepsis to the prevention of this disease.

CHARLES G. MOERTEL, M.D., M.S., is professor of oncology at the Mayo Medical School, chairman of the Department of Oncology at the Mayo Clinic, and director of the Mayo Comprehensive Cancer Center. He has been a president of the American Society for Clinical Oncology, a member of the board of directors of societies such as the Society for Clinical Trials, and a member of the editorial board of such journals as *Cancer Research.* His awards include the

Walter Hubert Lectureship of the British Association for Cancer Research and the Ejnar Perman Memorial Lectureship and Gold Medal of the Swedish Surgical Association. He is the author of *Multiple Primary Malignant Neoplasms*, a coauthor of *Advanced Gastrointestinal Cancer*, and a contributor to such volumes as *Cancer Medicine*, *Cancer Therapy*, *Gastroenterology*, and *Principles of Cancer Treatment*, and he has published over two hundred and seventy articles in such journals as the *New England Journal of Medicine*, the *Journal of the American Medical Association*, and the *Journal of Clinical Oncology*.

DAISIE RADNER, PH.D., is an associate professor in the Department of Philosophy at the State University of New York at Buffalo. She is the author of *Malebranche: A Study of a Cartesian System* and the coauthor of *Science and Unreason*. Her papers on topics in the history of philosophy have appeared in such journals as the *Philosophical Review* and the *Journal of the History of Philosophy*. She serves as a scientific and technical consultant for the Committee for the Scientific Investigation of Claims of the Paranormal.

MICHAEL RADNER, PH.D., is an associate professor in the Department of Philosophy at McMaster University. He is the coauthor of *Science and Unreason* and the co-editor of *Theories and Methods of Physics and Psychology*. His papers on topics in the philosophy of science have appeared in such journals as *Synthese* and the *British Journal for Philosophy of Science*. He serves as a scientific and technical consultant for the Committee for the Scientific Investigation of Claims of the Paranormal.

PETR SKRABANEK, PH.D., is a lecturer in the Department of Community Health at Trinity College of the University of Dublin. He has authored three books on substance P, an important neuropeptide involved in nociception, and has co-edited a volume on substance P as well as one on bladder cancer. He has contributed chapters to volumes such as *Gut Hormones*, *Clinics in Endocrinology and Metabolism*, and *Neuropeptides and Neural Transmission*. He has published over seventy papers, many of them in the field of neurotransmitters of pain, in such journals as *The Lancet*, *Experientia*, and *Medical Hypotheses*.

DOUGLAS STALKER, PH.D., is an associate professor in the Department of Philosophy at the University of Delaware. He is the author of *Deep Structure*, a contributor to *Philosophy of Science and the Occult*, and the editor of a special issue of *Linguistics and Philosophy* entitled "Coherence." His papers on issues in the philosophy of language, aesthetics, and the methodology of science have appeared in such journals as *Foundations of Language*, *Philosophia*, *The Public Interest*, and the *New England Journal of Medicine*. He serves as a scientific and technical consultant for the Committee for the Scientific Investigation of Claims of the Paranormal, and is a member of the National Council Against Health Fraud.

VARRO E. TYLER, PH.D., is dean of the Schools of Pharmacy, Nursing, and Health Sciences at Purdue University. He was the first president of the American Society of Pharmacognosy, and has been president of the American Association of Colleges of Pharmacy, as well as the American Council on Pharmaceutical Education. He has been named a fellow in the Academy of Pharmaceutical Sciences, and his research on ergot alkaloids won him the Foundation Research Achievement Award of the American Pharmaceutical Association in 1966. Dr. Tyler is the author of approximately one hundred and eighty scientific and educational publications in various professional journals, and he is the author of or contributor to such books as *Pharmacognosy, Experimental Pharmacognosy, The Savory Wild Mushroom, Progress in Chemical Toxicology,* and *The Honest Herbal.*

JAMES C. WHORTON, PH.D., is a professor in the Department of Biomedical History of the School of Medicine at the University of Washington, Seattle. He is the author of *Before Silent Spring: Pesticides and Public Health in Pre-DDT America* and *Crusaders for Fitness: The History of American Health Reformers,* and a co-editor of *Chemistry and Modern Society.* He has contributed chapters to books such as *Unorthodox Medicine in American Society* and *The Education of American Physicians,* and has published on historical topics in such journals as the *Bulletin of the History of Medicine* and *Pharmacy in History.*

DANIEL WIKLER, PH.D., is a professor in the Program in Medical Ethics of the Department of the History of Medicine at the University of Wisconsin Medical School, and a professor in the Department of Philosophy at the University of Wisconsin. He has served as the staff philosopher for President Carter's Commission for the Study of Ethical Problems in Medicine and Biomedical and Behavioral Research, and has been the recipient of a Career Development Award in Medical Ethics from the Joseph P. Kennedy, Jr., Foundation. He has contributed more than fourteen chapters to such books as *Clinical Judgment: A Critical Appraisal, Contemporary Bioethics,* and *New Directions in Mental Health;* his articles on topics in medical ethics have appeared in such journals as *The Milbank Memorial Fund Quarterly, Philosophy and Public Affairs,* and the *Journal of the American Medical Association.*

SUSAN M. WILLIAMS, R.N., M.S.N., C.C.R.N., is an assistant clinical professor of adult and critical care nursing in the Department of Graduate Studies and Research of the College of Nursing at the Northwestern State University of Louisiana. She is the author of *Initial Management of the Patient with Multiple Injuries—Individualized Learning Module,* an editor and contributor to *Core Curriculum for Critical Care Nursing,* and an editor of *Core Review for Critical Care Nursing.* Her papers on topics in nursing have appeared in such journals as *Nursing Research* and *Utah Nurse.* She has served on the board of directors of the American Association of Critical-Care Nurses as well as that of the AACN Certification Corporation, where she has been chairperson of its Credentialing Committee and a member of its Core Curriculum Committee.

RUSSELL S. WORRALL, O.D., is an assistant clinical professor in the School of Optometry at the University of California, Berkeley, and also maintains a private practice in optometry. He has published on optical topics in such journals as the *Review of Optometry, Optometric Monthly,* and the *Journal of the American Optometric Association,* and has alerted health care professionals as well as the public to dubious and unorthodox optometric practices with publications in the *Newsletter of the California Council Against Health Fraud* and *The Skeptical Inquirer.*

LARRY D. YOUNG, PH.D., is an assistant professor in the Section on Medical Psychology of the Department of Psychiatry and Behavioral Medicine at Bowman Gray School of Medicine. He has coauthored chapters in such books as *Contributions to Medical Psychology* (Vol. 2), *Concise Textbook of Rheumatology,* and *Stress and Alcohol Use.* Dr. Young has published over thirty articles, many of them on biofeedback, in such journals as *Archives of General Psychiatry, Psychophysiology,* and *Psychological Bulletin.*